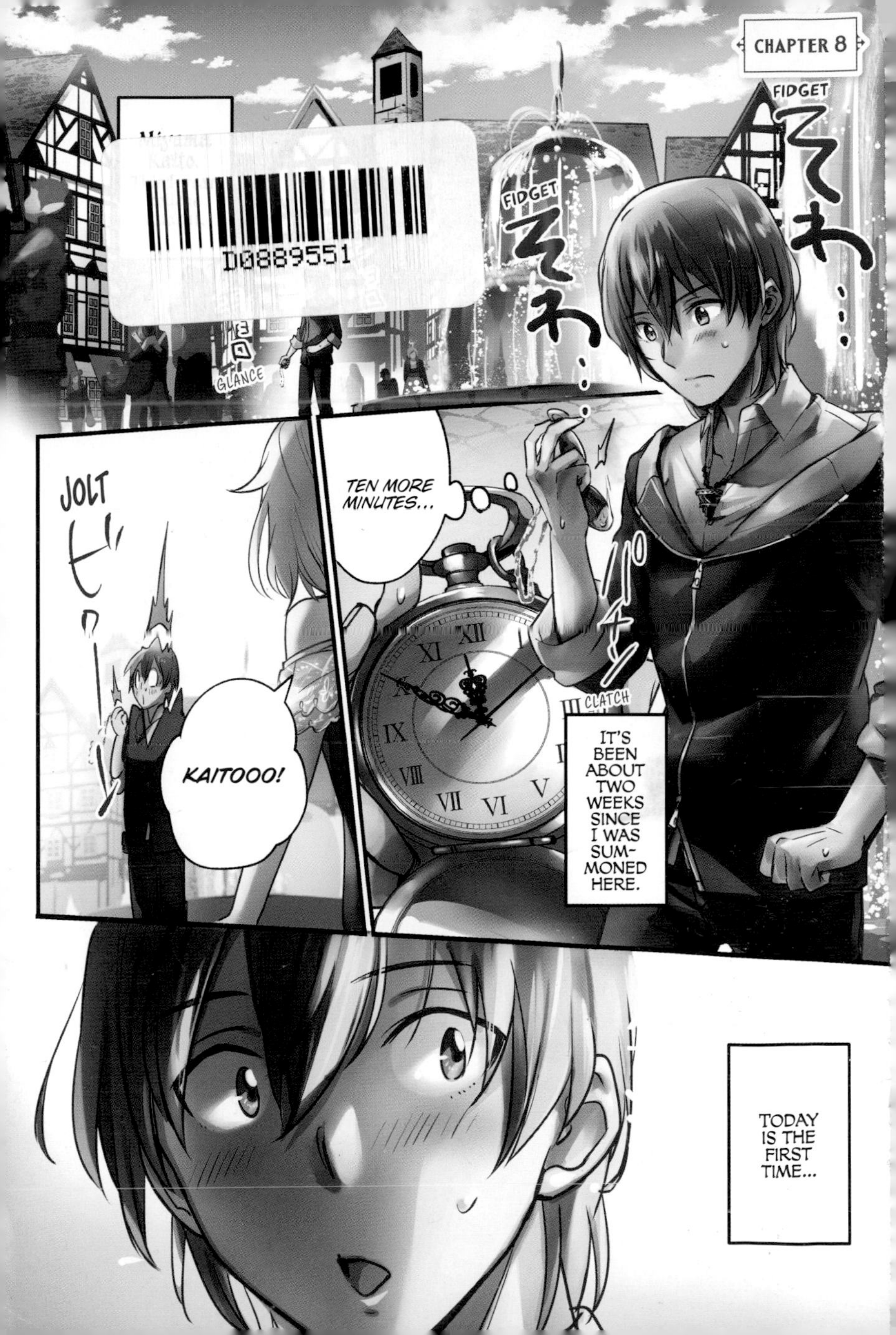

CHAPTER 8
FIDGET
FIDGET
GLANCE
TEN MORE MINUTES...
CLATCH
IT'S BEEN ABOUT TWO WEEKS SINCE I WAS SUMMONED HERE.
JOLT
KAITOOO!
TODAY IS THE FIRST TIME...

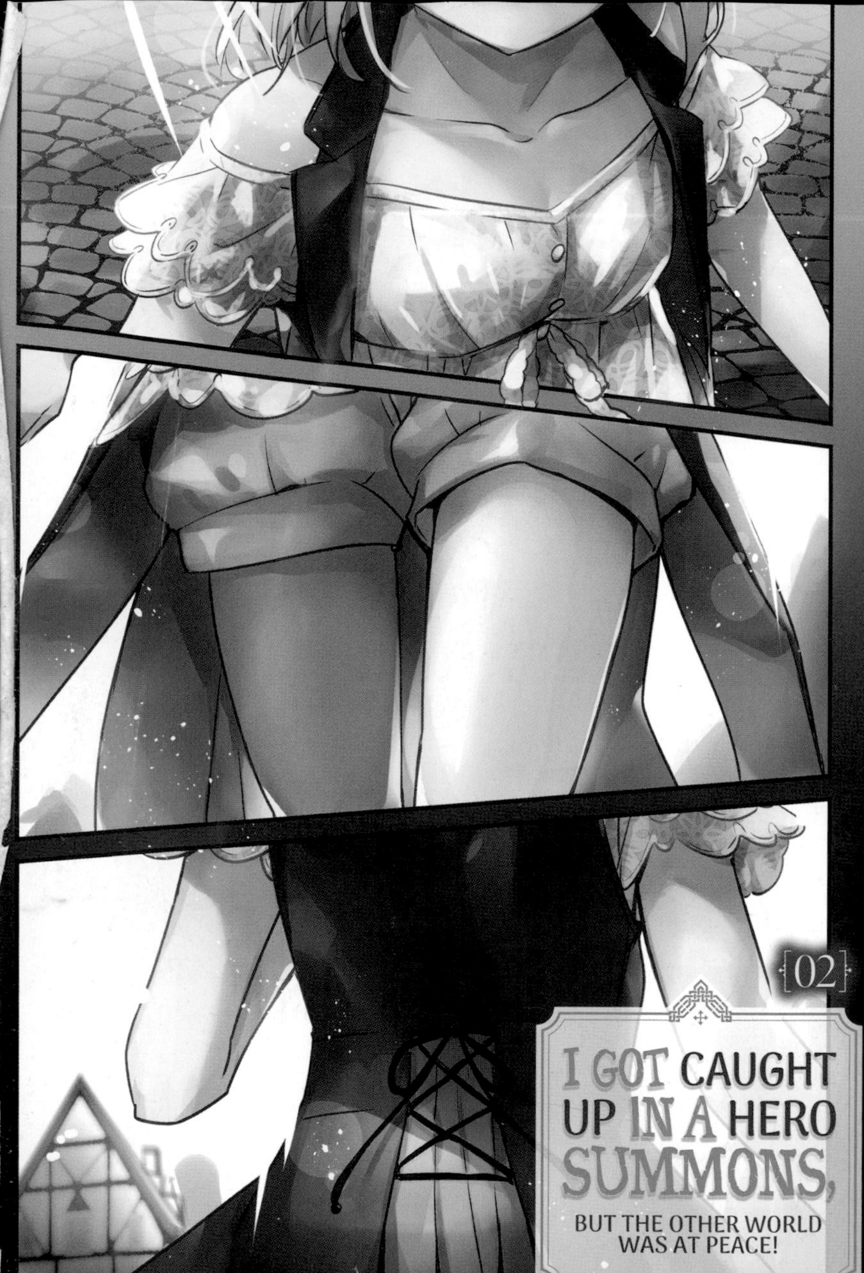
[02]
I GOT CAUGHT UP IN A HERO SUMMONS,
BUT THE OTHER WORLD WAS AT PEACE!

ART: JIRO HEIAN
STORY: TOUDAI
CHARACTER DESIGN: OCHAU

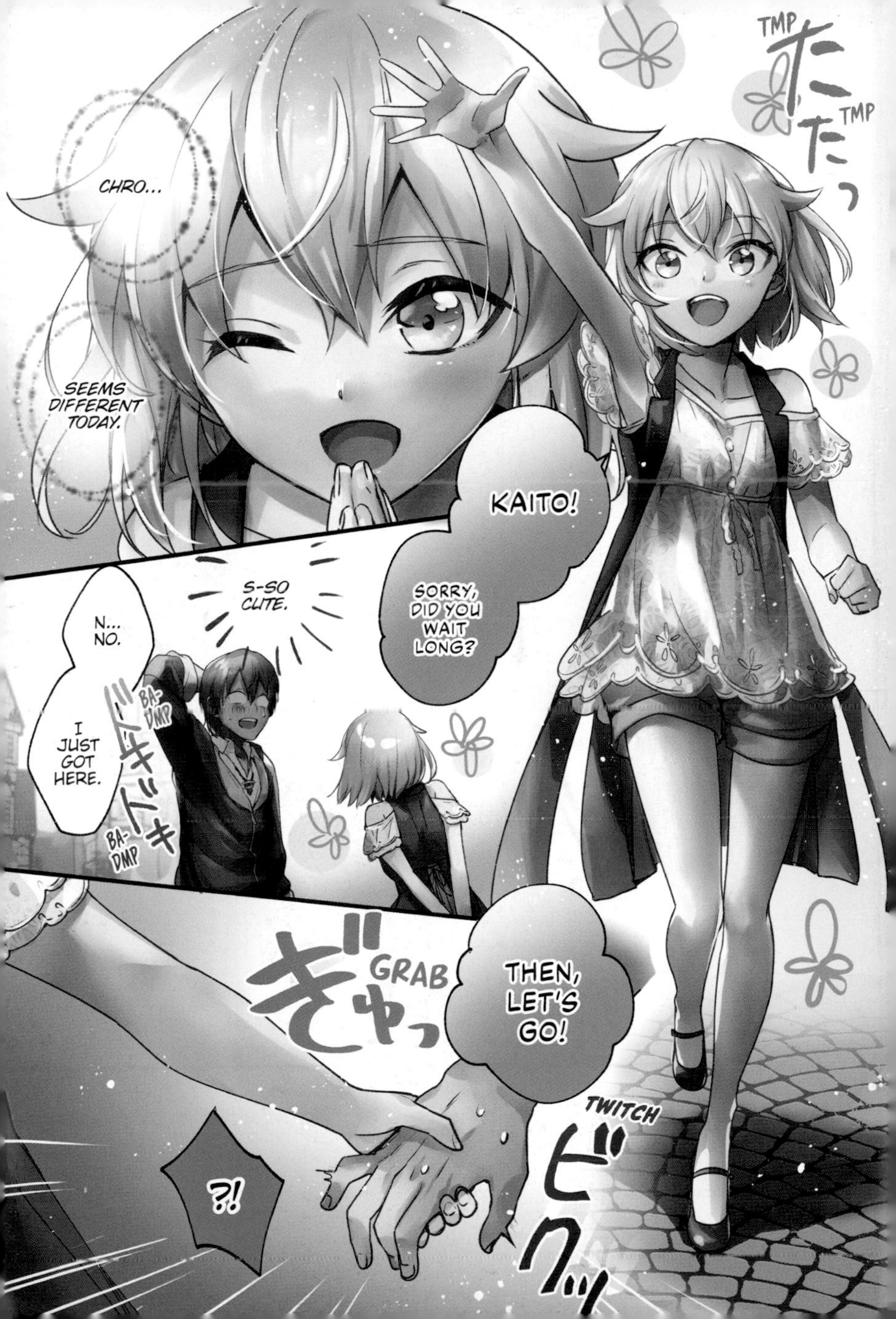
たたっ
TMP
TMP
KAITO!
SORRY, DID YOU WAIT LONG?
THEN, LET'S GO!
ビクッ
TWITCH
CHRO...
SEEMS DIFFERENT TODAY.
S-SO CUTE.
N... NO.
I JUST GOT HERE.
ドキドキ
BA-DMP
BA-DMP
ぎゅっ
GRAB
?!

[CONTENTS]

Chapter 8   [001]

Chapter 9   [029]

Chapter 10   [051]

Chapter 11   [077]

Chapter 12   [103]

Chapter 13   [129]

Side Story   [155]

PRESENTED BY
JIRO HEIAN AND TOUDAI

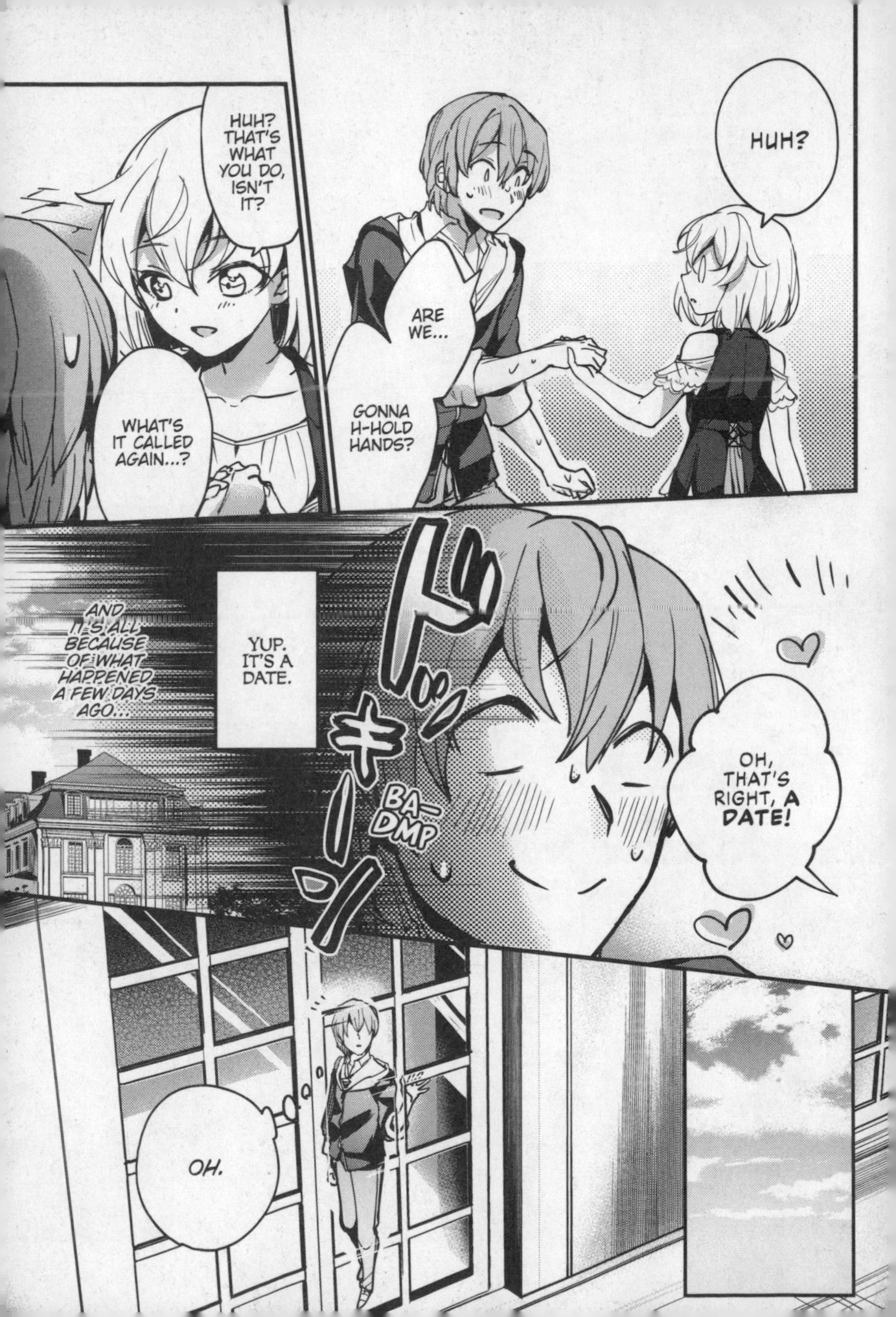
HUH?
ARE WE... GONNA H-HOLD HANDS?
HUH? THAT'S WHAT YOU DO, ISN'T IT?
WHAT'S IT CALLED AGAIN...?
OH, THAT'S RIGHT, A DATE!
BA-DMP
YUP. IT'S A DATE.
AND IT'S ALL BECAUSE OF WHAT HAPPENED A FEW DAYS AGO...
OH.

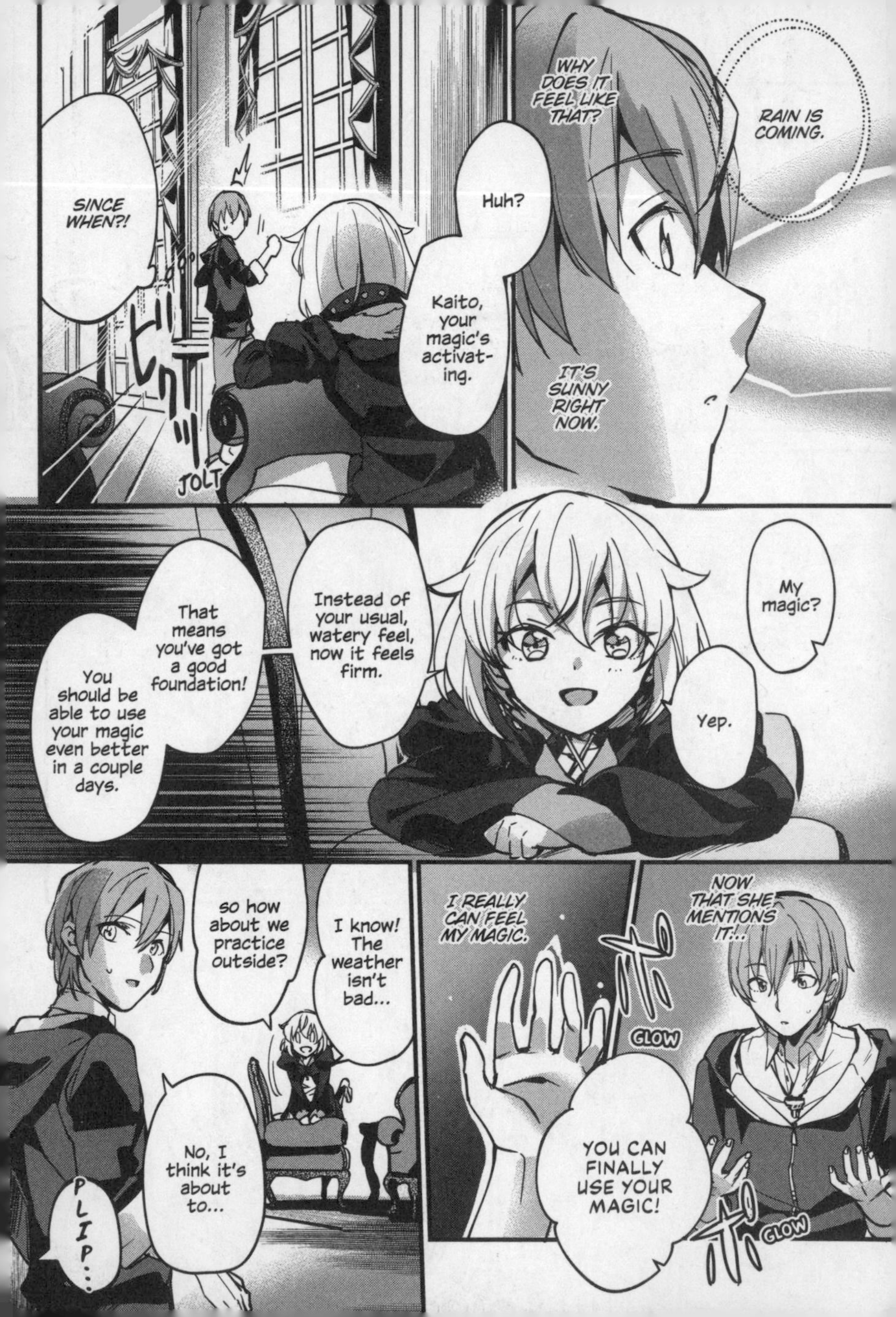
RAIN IS COMING.
IT'S SUNNY RIGHT NOW.
WHY DOES IT FEEL LIKE THAT?
Huh?
Kaito, your magic's activat-ing.
JOLT
SINCE WHEN?!
My magic?
Yep.
Instead of your usual, watery feel, now it feels firm.
That means you've got a good foundation!
You should be able to use your magic even better in a couple days.
NOW THAT SHE MENTIONS IT...
I REALLY CAN FEEL MY MAGIC.
GLOW
YOU CAN FINALLY USE YOUR MAGIC!
GLOW
I know! The weather isn't bad...
so how about we practice outside?
No, I think it's about to...
PLIP...

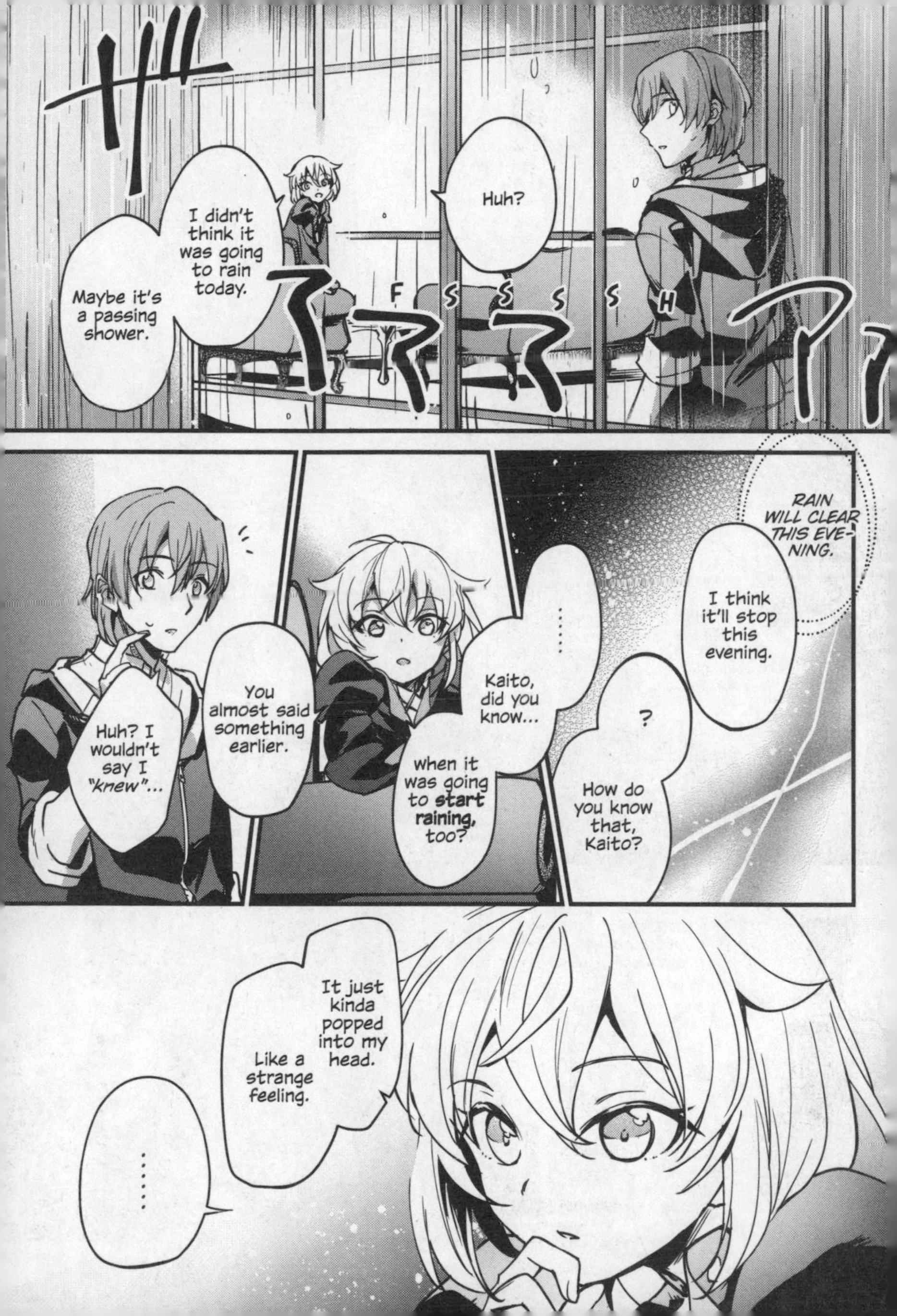
Huh?
I didn't think it was going to rain today.
Maybe it's a passing shower.
FSSSSH
RAIN WILL CLEAR THIS EVE-NING.
I think it'll stop this evening.
?
How do you know that, Kaito?
......
Kaito, did you know...
when it was going to **start raining,** too?
You almost said something earlier.
Huh? I wouldn't say I *"knew"*...
It just kinda popped into my head.
Like a strange feeling.
......

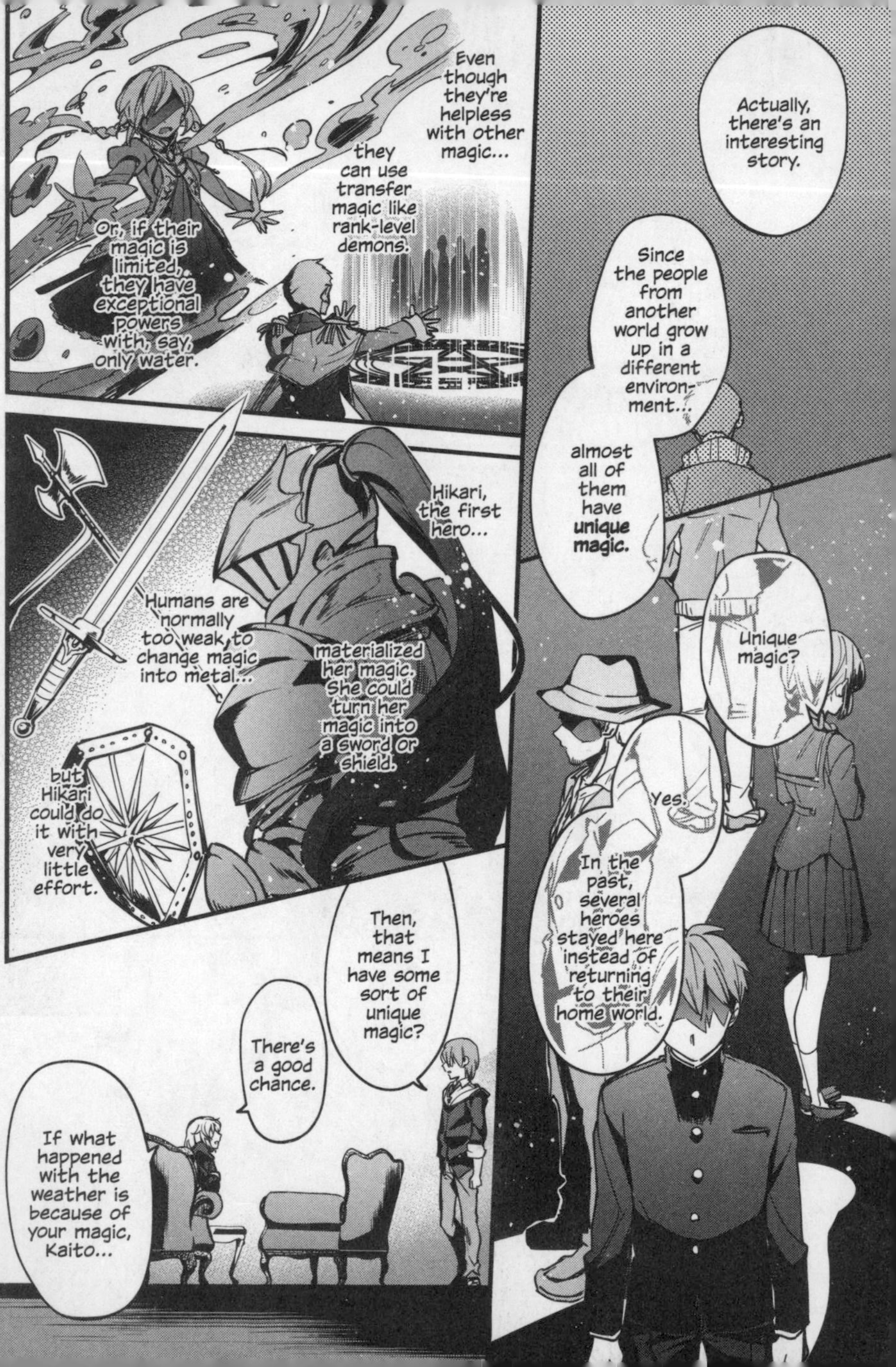
Actually, there's an interesting story.
Since the people from another world grow up in a different environ-ment...
almost all of them have **unique magic.**
Unique magic?
Yes.
In the past, several heroes stayed here instead of returning to their home world.
Even though they're helpless with other magic...
they can use transfer magic like rank-level demons.
Or, if their magic is limited, they have exceptional powers with, say, only water.
Hikari, the first hero...
materialized her magic. She could turn her magic into a sword or shield.
Humans are normally too weak to change magic into metal...
but Hikari could do it with very little effort.
Then, that means I have some sort of unique magic?
There's a good chance.
If what happened with the weather is because of your magic, Kaito...

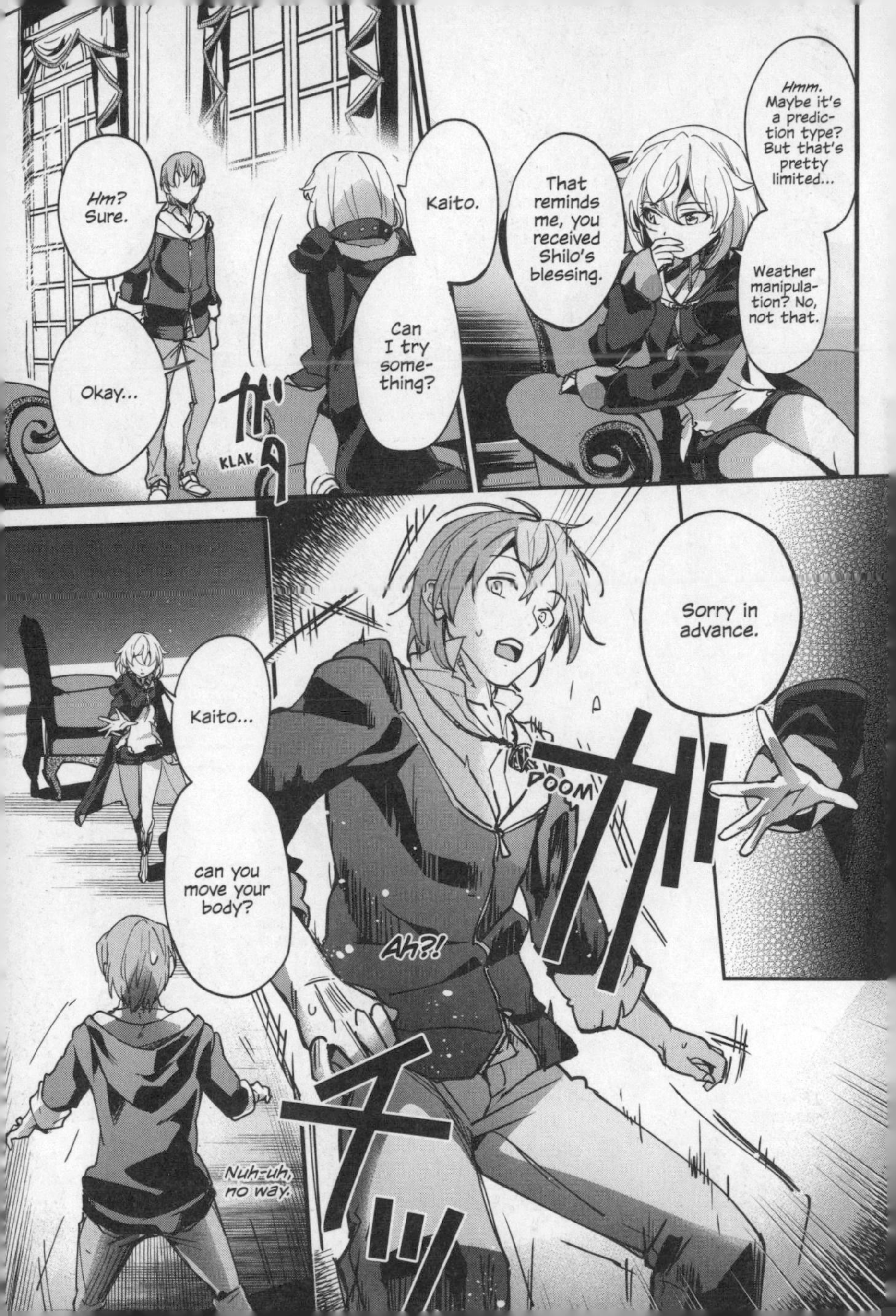

Hmm. Maybe it's a prediction type? But that's pretty limited...
Weather manipulation? No, not that.
That reminds me, you received Shilo's blessing.
Kaito.
Can I try something?
KLAK
Hm? Sure.
Okay...
Sorry in advance.
DOOM
Kaito...
can you move your body?
Ah?!
Nuh-uh, no way.

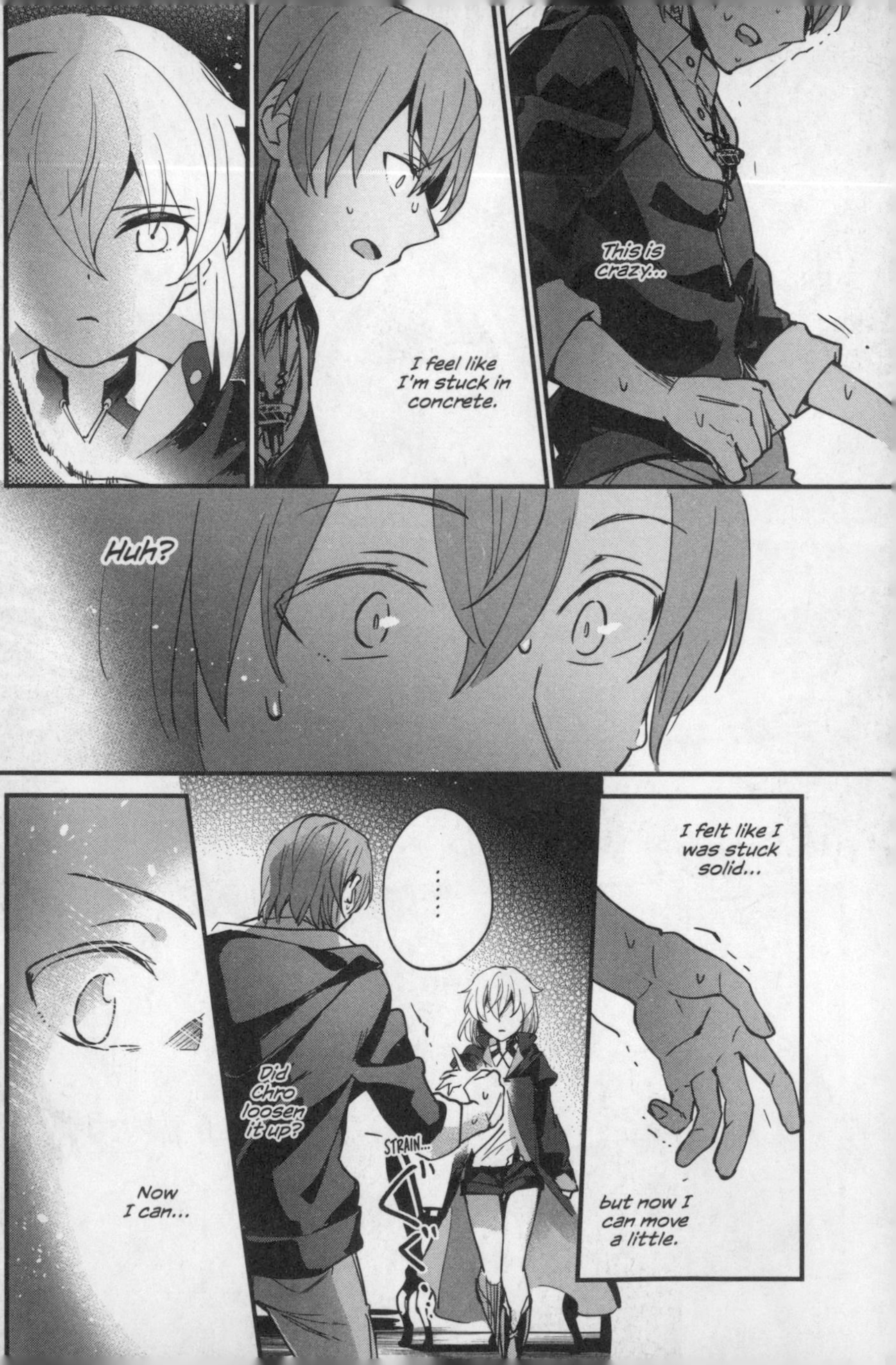
This is crazy...
I feel like I'm stuck in concrete.
Huh?
I felt like I was stuck solid...
but now I can move a little.
......
Did Chro loosen it up?
STRAIN...
Now I can...

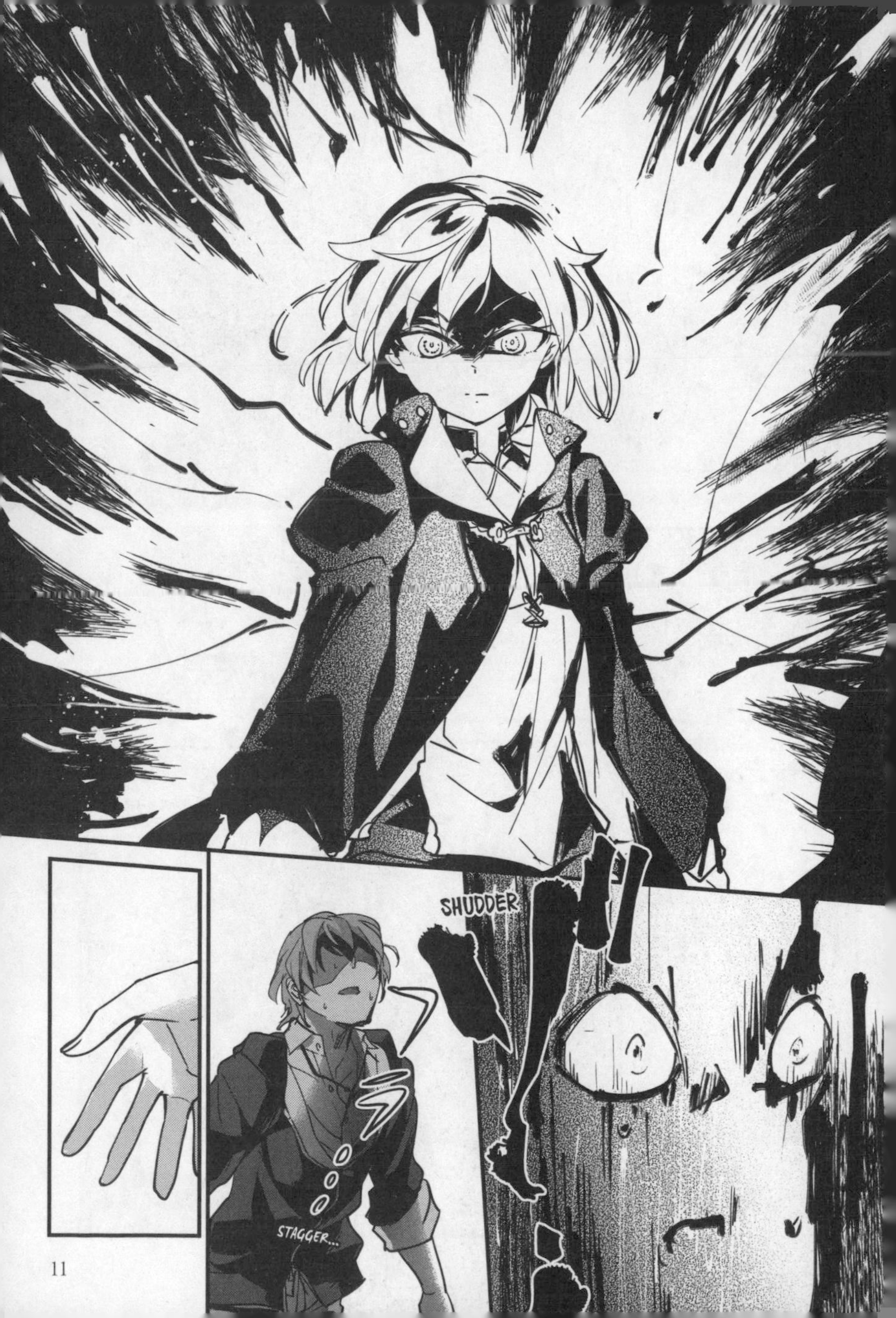
SHUDDER
STAGGER...

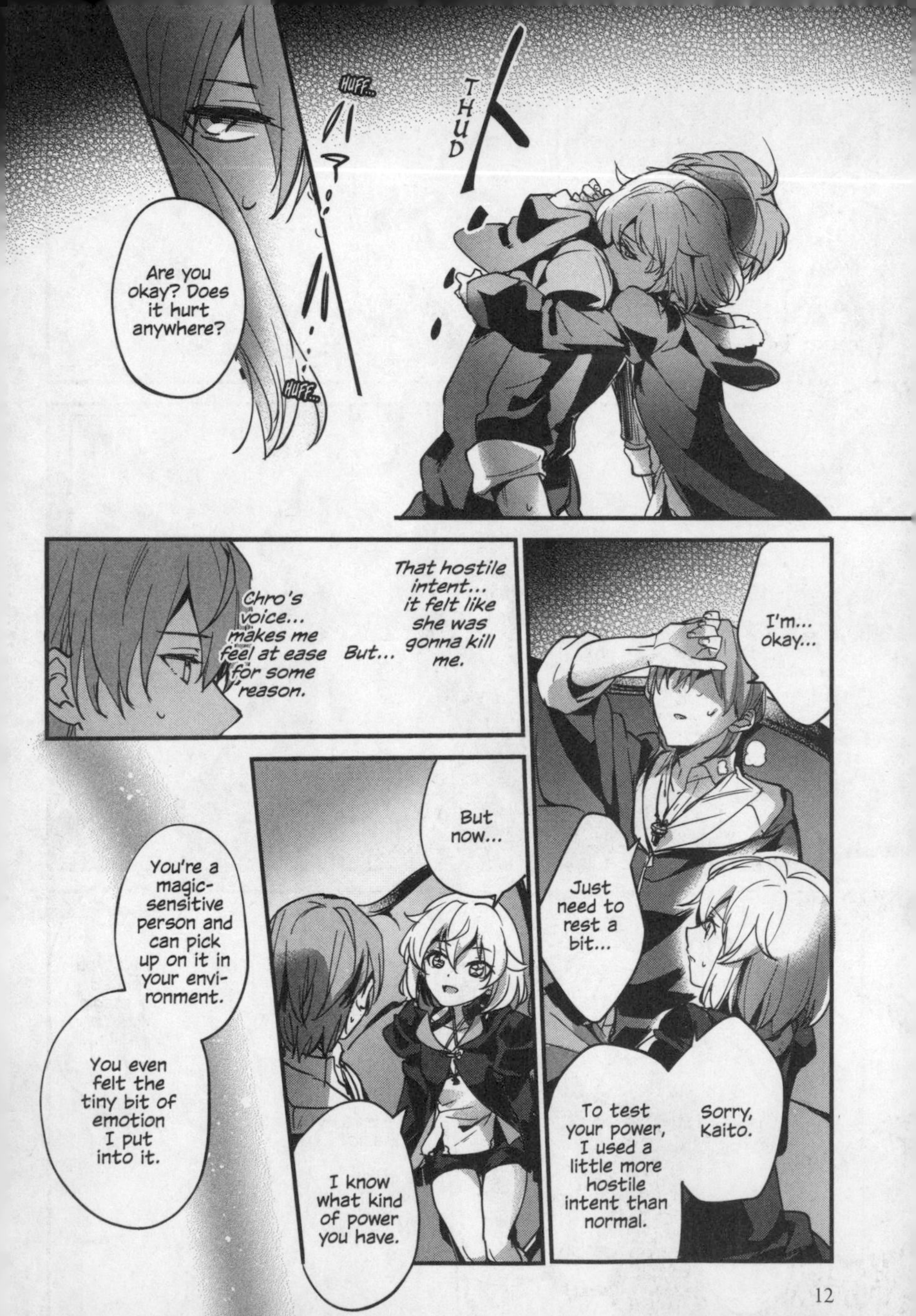
THUD
HUFF...
Are you okay? Does it hurt anywhere?
HUFF...
I'm... okay...
Just need to rest a bit...
Sorry, Kaito.
To test your power, I used a little more hostile intent than normal.
That hostile intent... it felt like she was gonna kill me.
But...
Chro's voice... makes me feel at ease for some reason.
But now...
You're a magic-sensitive person and can pick up on it in your environment.
You even felt the tiny bit of emotion I put into it.
I know what kind of power you have.

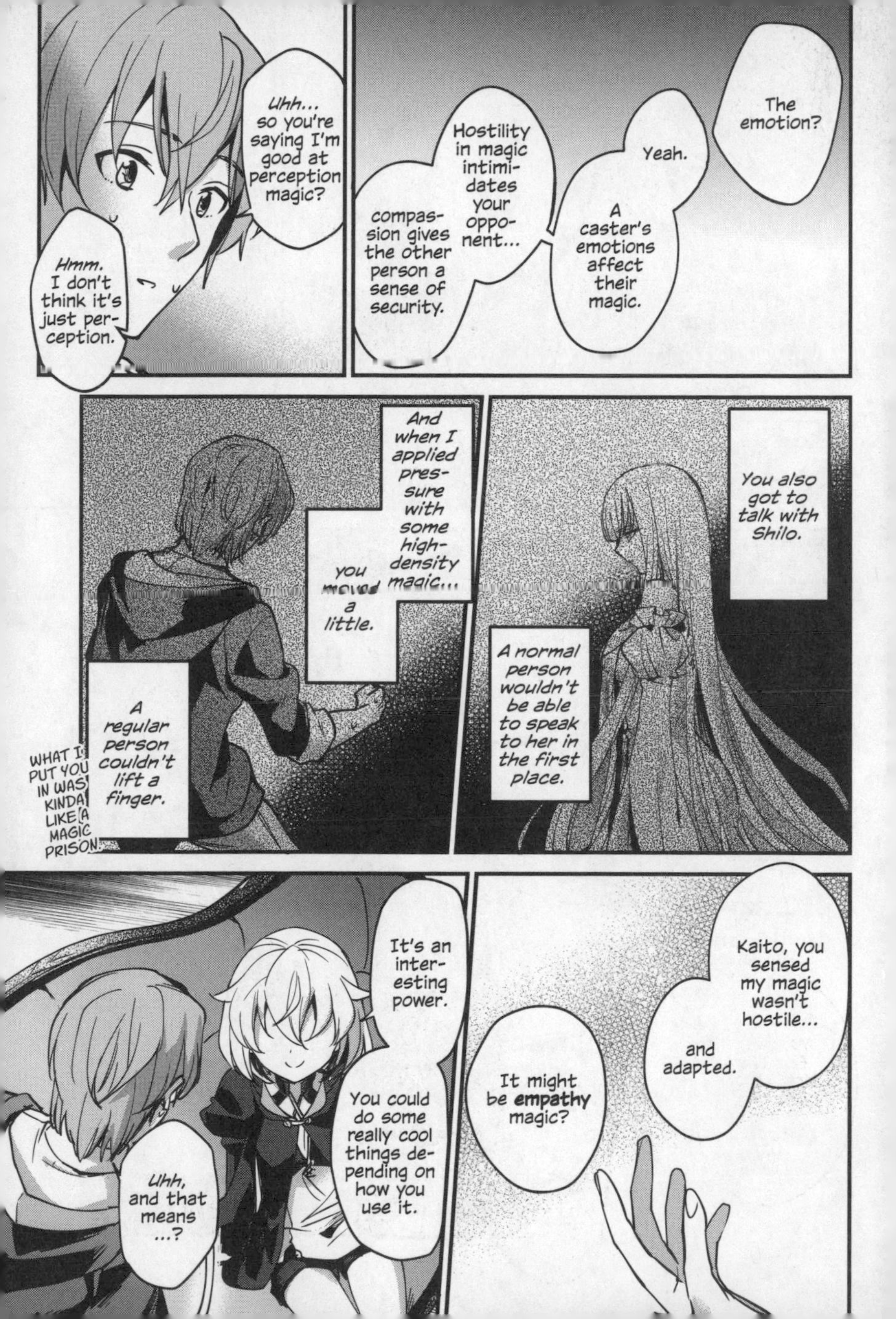
The emotion?
Yeah.
A caster's emotions affect their magic.
Hostility in magic intimidates your opponent...
compassion gives the other person a sense of security.
Uhh... so you're saying I'm good at perception magic?
Hmm. I don't think it's just perception.
You also got to talk with Shilo.
A normal person wouldn't be able to speak to her in the first place.
And when I applied pressure with some high-density magic...
you moved a little.
A regular person couldn't lift a finger.
WHAT I PUT YOU IN WAS KINDA LIKE A MAGIC PRISON.
Kaito, you sensed my magic wasn't hostile...
and adapted.
It might be **empathy** magic?
It's an interesting power.
You could do some really cool things depending on how you use it.
Uhh, and that means ...?

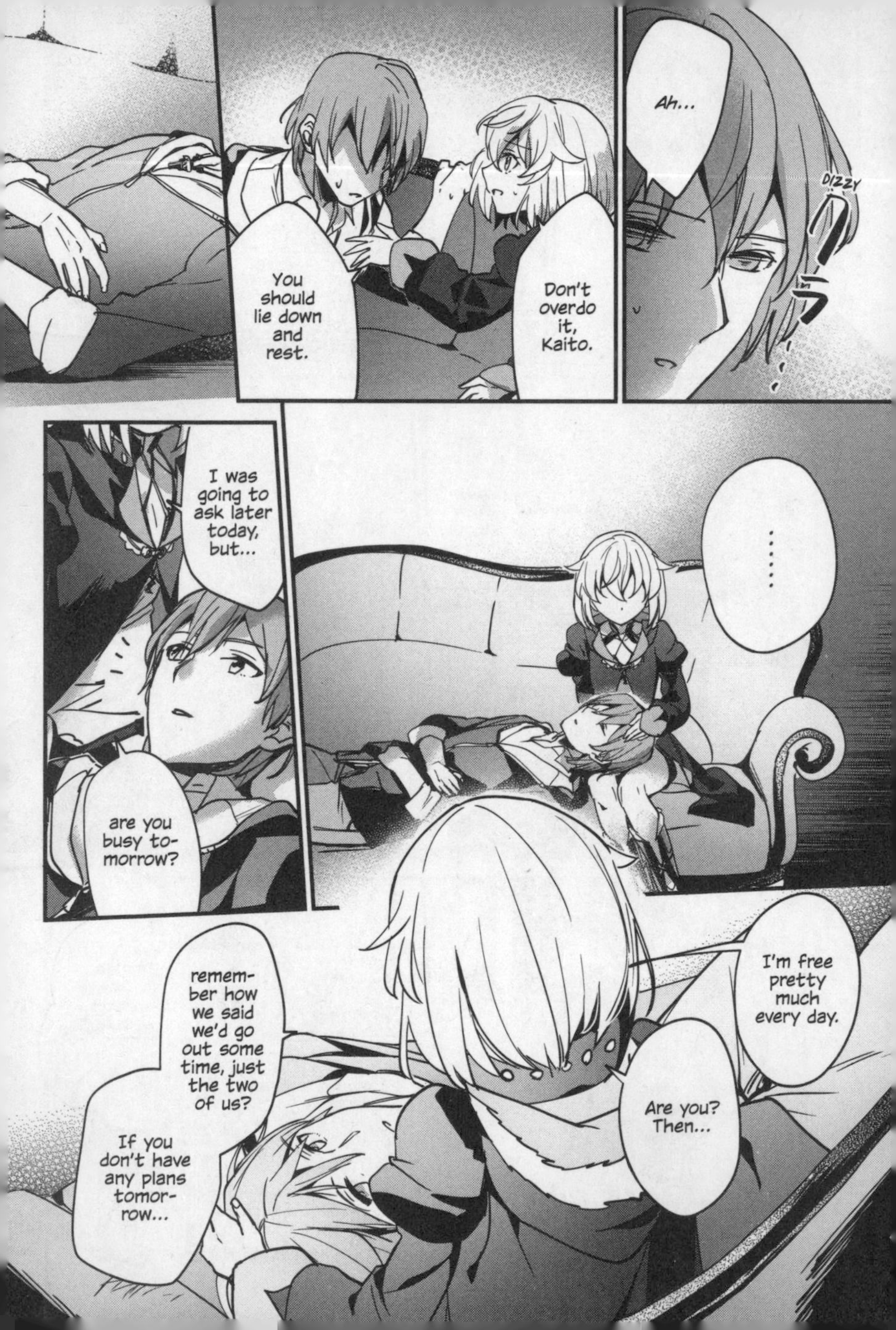
Ah...
DIZZY
Don't overdo it, Kaito.
You should lie down and rest.
......
I was going to ask later today, but...
are you busy to-morrow?
I'm free pretty much every day.
Are you? Then...
remember how we said we'd go out some time, just the two of us?
If you don't have any plans tomor-row...

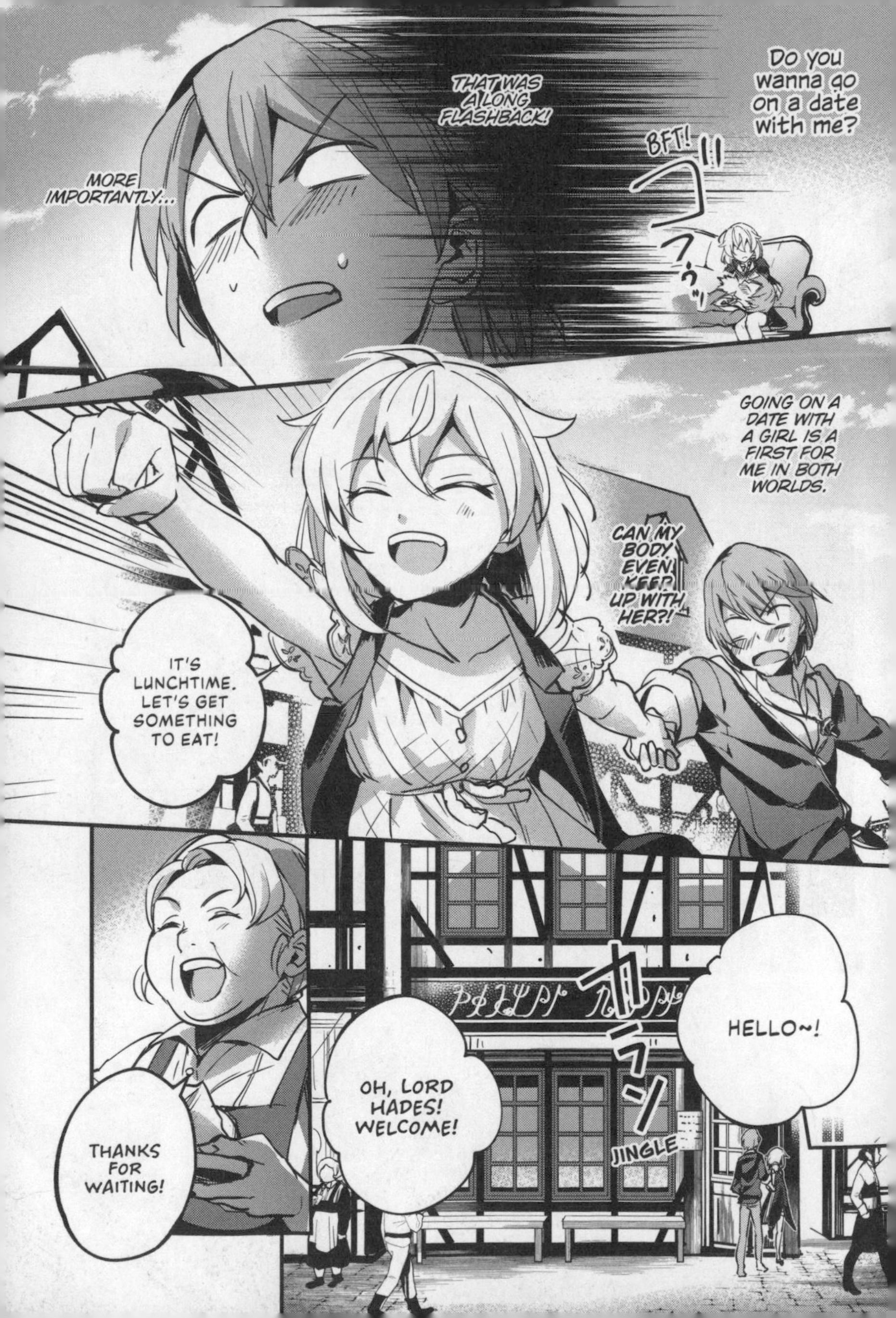
Do you wanna go on a date with me?
BFT!
THAT WAS A LONG FLASHBACK!
MORE IMPORTANTLY...
GOING ON A DATE WITH A GIRL IS A FIRST FOR ME IN BOTH WORLDS.
CAN MY BODY EVEN KEEP UP WITH HER?!
IT'S LUNCHTIME. LET'S GET SOMETHING TO EAT!
HELLO~!
JINGLE
OH, LORD HADES! WELCOME!
THANKS FOR WAITING!

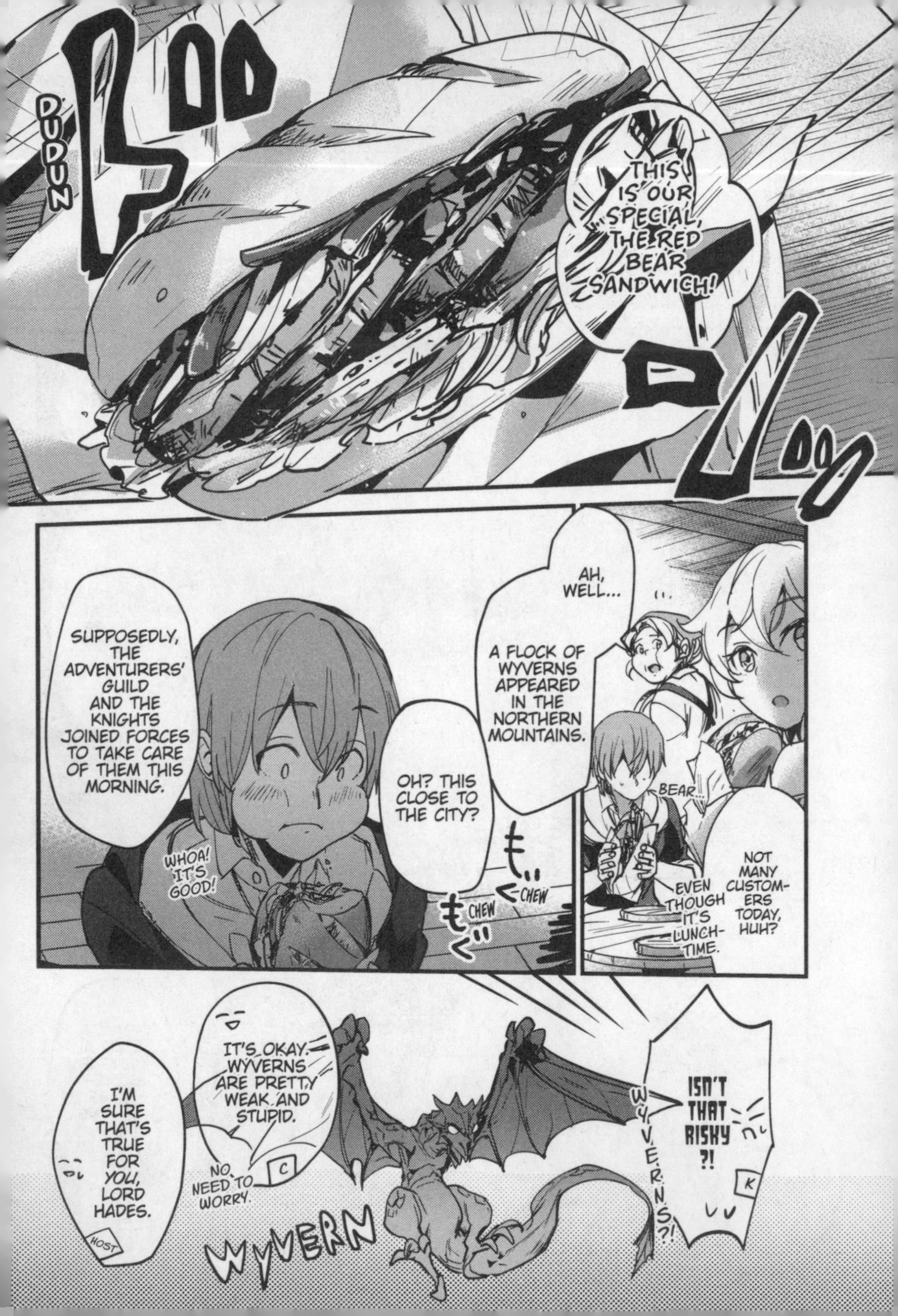
DUDUN
THIS IS OUR SPECIAL, THE RED BEAR SANDWICH!
BEAR...
NOT MANY CUSTOMERS TODAY, HUH?
EVEN THOUGH IT'S LUNCHTIME.
AH, WELL...
A FLOCK OF WYVERNS APPEARED IN THE NORTHERN MOUNTAINS.
OH? THIS CLOSE TO THE CITY?
SUPPOSEDLY, THE ADVENTURERS' GUILD AND THE KNIGHTS JOINED FORCES TO TAKE CARE OF THEM THIS MORNING.
CHEW
CHEW
WHOA! IT'S GOOD!
ISN'T THAT RISKY?!
WYVERNS?!
K
IT'S OKAY. WYVERNS ARE PRETTY WEAK AND STUPID.
NO NEED TO WORRY.
C
I'M SURE THAT'S TRUE FOR YOU, LORD HADES.
HOST
WYVERN

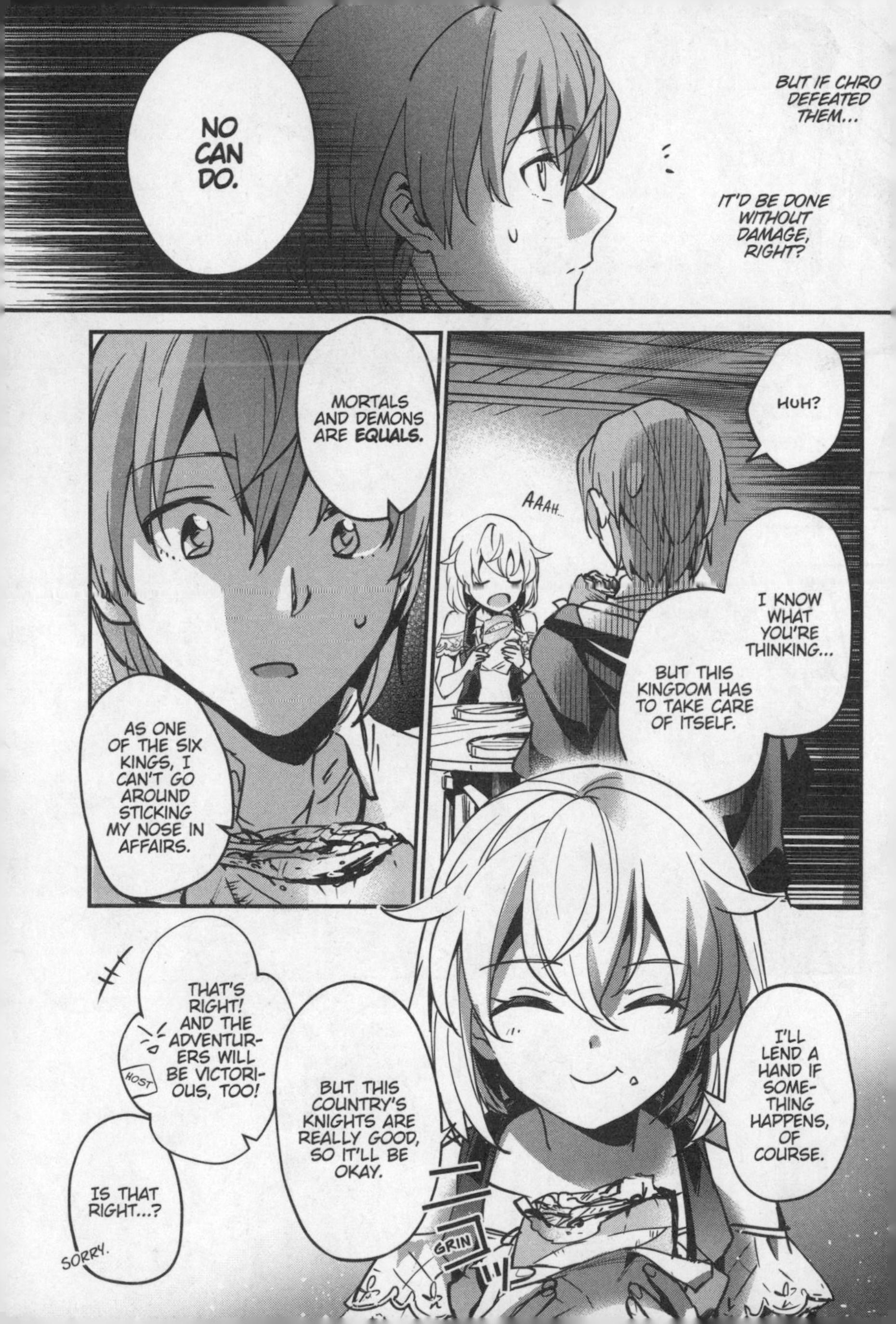
BUT IF CHRO DEFEATED THEM...
IT'D BE DONE WITHOUT DAMAGE, RIGHT?
NO CAN DO.
HUH?
AAAH...
I KNOW WHAT YOU'RE THINKING...
BUT THIS KINGDOM HAS TO TAKE CARE OF ITSELF.
MORTALS AND DEMONS ARE **EQUALS.**
AS ONE OF THE SIX KINGS, I CAN'T GO AROUND STICKING MY NOSE IN AFFAIRS.
I'LL LEND A HAND IF SOMETHING HAPPENS, OF COURSE.
GRIN
BUT THIS COUNTRY'S KNIGHTS ARE REALLY GOOD, SO IT'LL BE OKAY.
THAT'S RIGHT! AND THE ADVENTURERS WILL BE VICTORIOUS, TOO!
HOST
IS THAT RIGHT...?
SORRY.

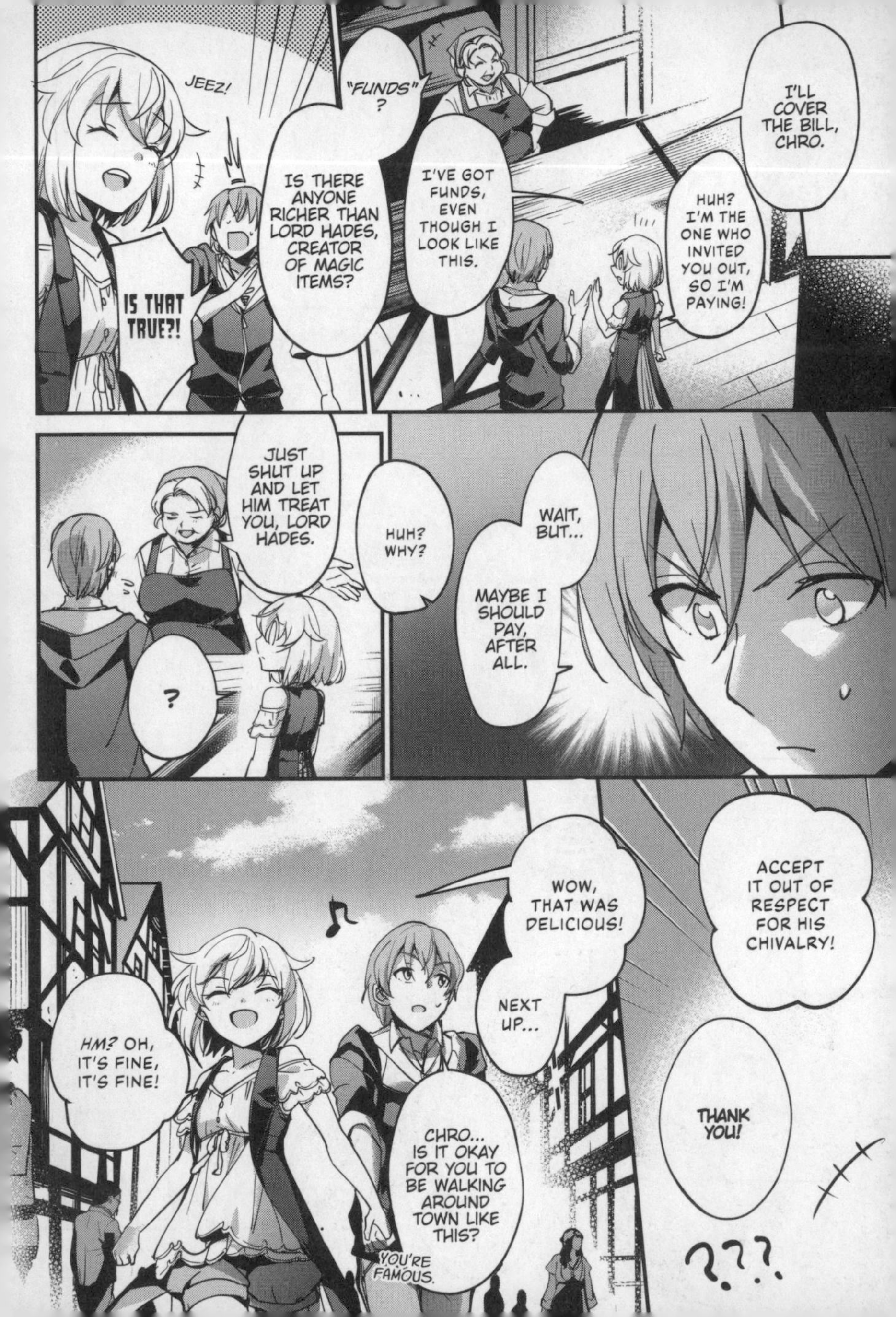
I'LL COVER THE BILL, CHRO.
HUH? I'M THE ONE WHO INVITED YOU OUT, SO I'M PAYING!
I'VE GOT FUNDS, EVEN THOUGH I LOOK LIKE THIS.
"FUNDS"?
IS THERE ANYONE RICHER THAN LORD HADES, CREATOR OF MAGIC ITEMS?
JEEZ!
IS THAT TRUE?!
...
WAIT, BUT...
MAYBE I SHOULD PAY, AFTER ALL.
JUST SHUT UP AND LET HIM TREAT YOU, LORD HADES.
HUH? WHY?
?
ACCEPT IT OUT OF RESPECT FOR HIS CHIVALRY!
THANK YOU!
???
WOW, THAT WAS DELICIOUS!
NEXT UP...
CHRO... IS IT OKAY FOR YOU TO BE WALKING AROUND TOWN LIKE THIS?
YOU'RE FAMOUS.
HM? OH, IT'S FINE, IT'S FINE!

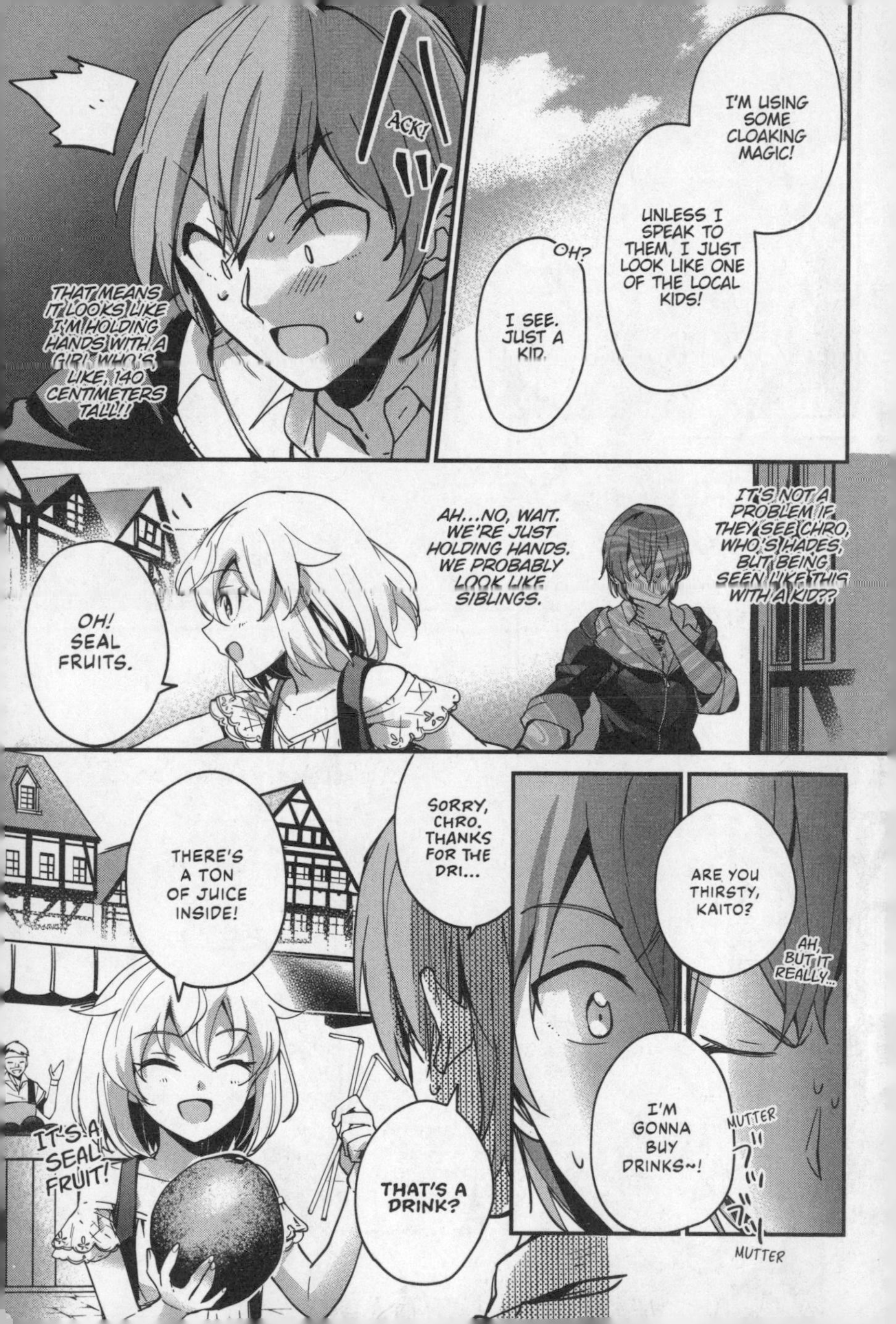
I'M USING SOME CLOAKING MAGIC!
UNLESS I SPEAK TO THEM, I JUST LOOK LIKE ONE OF THE LOCAL KIDS!
OH?
I SEE. JUST A KID.
ACK!
THAT MEANS IT LOOKS LIKE I'M HOLDING HANDS WITH A GIRL WHO'S, LIKE, 140 CENTIMETERS TALL!!
IT'S NOT A PROBLEM IF THEY SEE CHRO, WHO'S HADES, BUT BEING SEEN LIKE THIS WITH A KID??
AH...NO, WAIT. WE'RE JUST HOLDING HANDS. WE PROBABLY LOOK LIKE SIBLINGS.
OH! SEAL FRUITS.
ARE YOU THIRSTY, KAITO?
AH, BUT IT REALLY...
I'M GONNA BUY DRINKS~!
MUTTER
MUTTER
SORRY, CHRO. THANKS FOR THE DRI...
THERE'S A TON OF JUICE INSIDE!
IT'S A SEAL FRUIT!
THAT'S A DRINK?

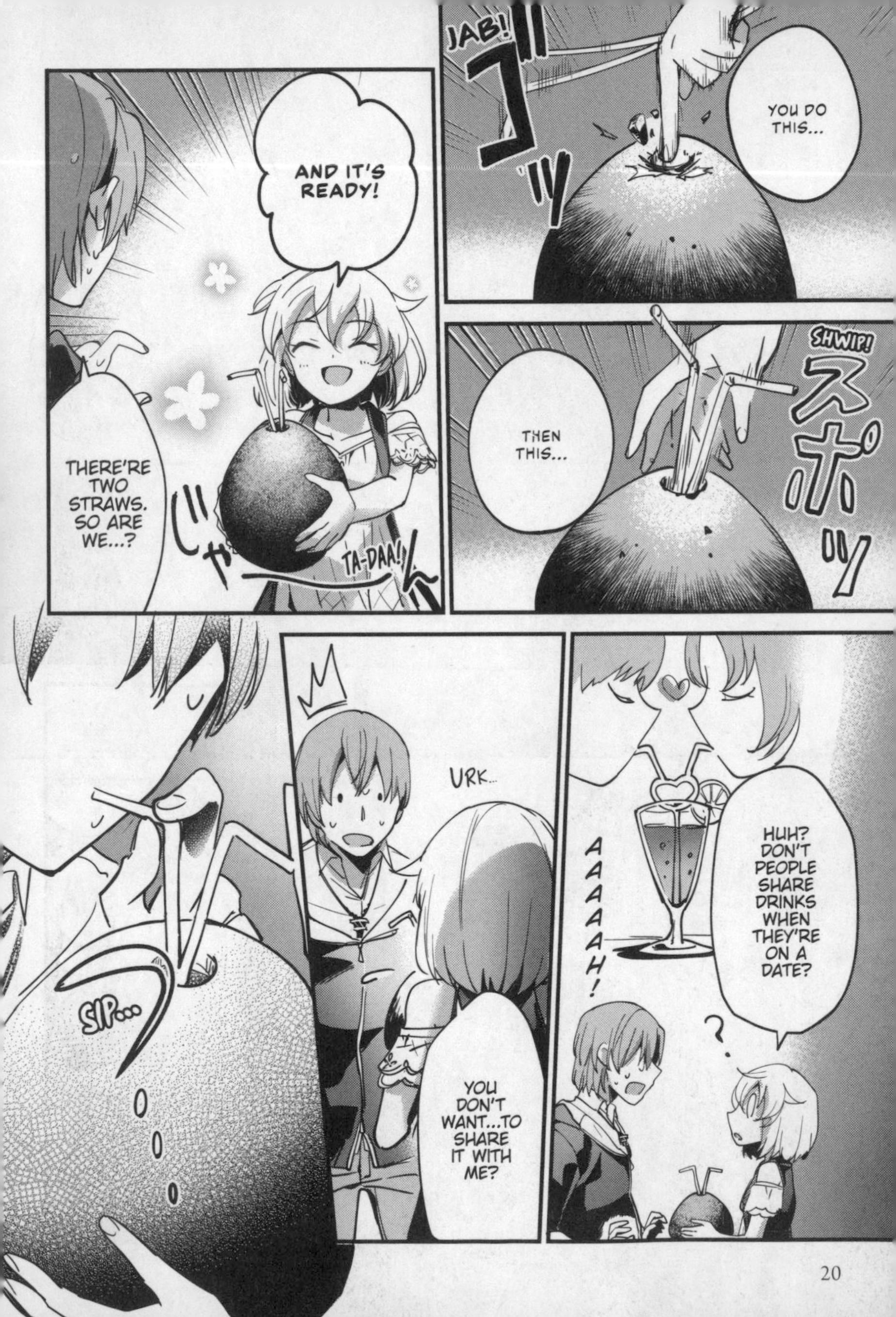
JAB!
ゴッ
YOU DO THIS...
SHWIP!
スポッ
THEN THIS...
AND IT'S READY!
TA-DAA!!
THERE'RE TWO STRAWS. SO ARE WE...?
HUH? DON'T PEOPLE SHARE DRINKS WHEN THEY'RE ON A DATE?
AAAAAAH!
URK...
YOU DON'T WANT...TO SHARE IT WITH ME?
SIP...

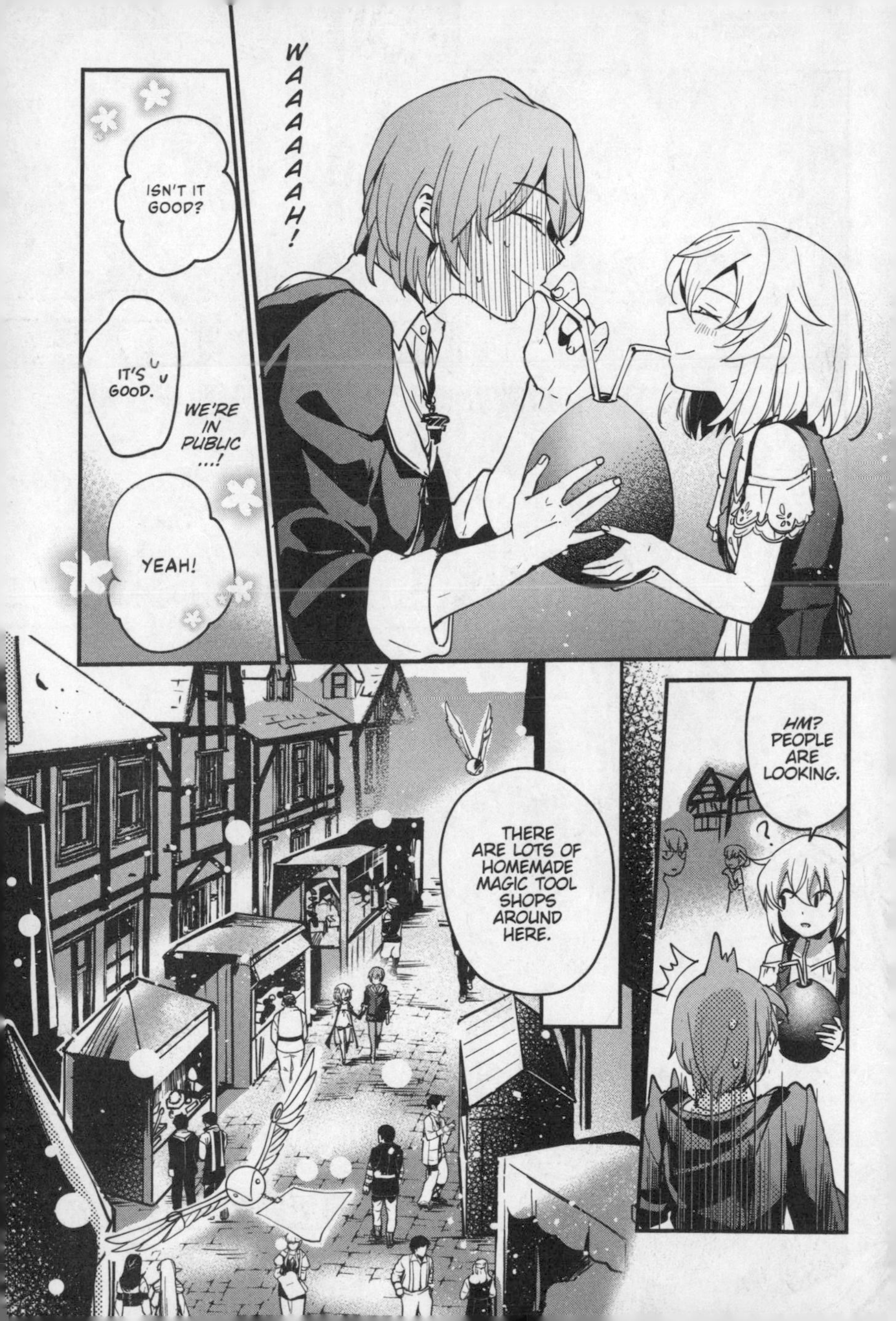
WAAAAAAAH!
ISN'T IT GOOD?
IT'S GOOD.
WE'RE IN PUBLIC...!
YEAH!
HM? PEOPLE ARE LOOKING.
THERE ARE LOTS OF HOMEMADE MAGIC TOOL SHOPS AROUND HERE.

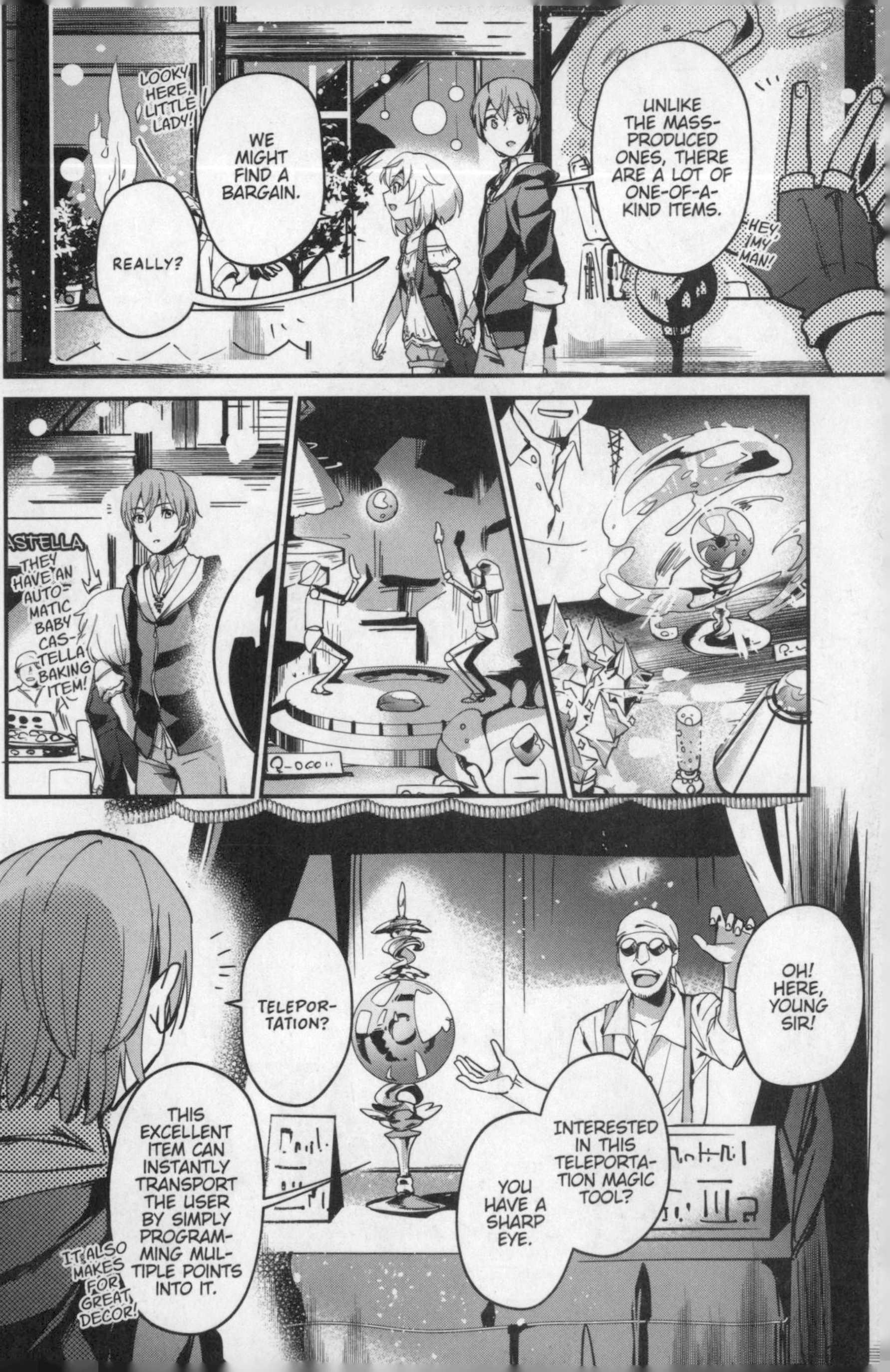
UNLIKE THE MASS-PRODUCED ONES, THERE ARE A LOT OF ONE-OF-A-KIND ITEMS.
HEY, MY MAN!
WE MIGHT FIND A BARGAIN.
LOOKY HERE, LITTLE LADY!
REALLY?
ASTELLA
THEY HAVE AN AUTOMATIC BABY CASTELLA BAKING ITEM!
OH! HERE, YOUNG SIR!
INTERESTED IN THIS TELEPORTATION MAGIC TOOL?
YOU HAVE A SHARP EYE.
TELEPORTATION?
THIS EXCELLENT ITEM CAN INSTANTLY TRANSPORT THE USER BY SIMPLY PROGRAMMING MULTIPLE POINTS INTO IT.
IT ALSO MAKES FOR GREAT DECOR!

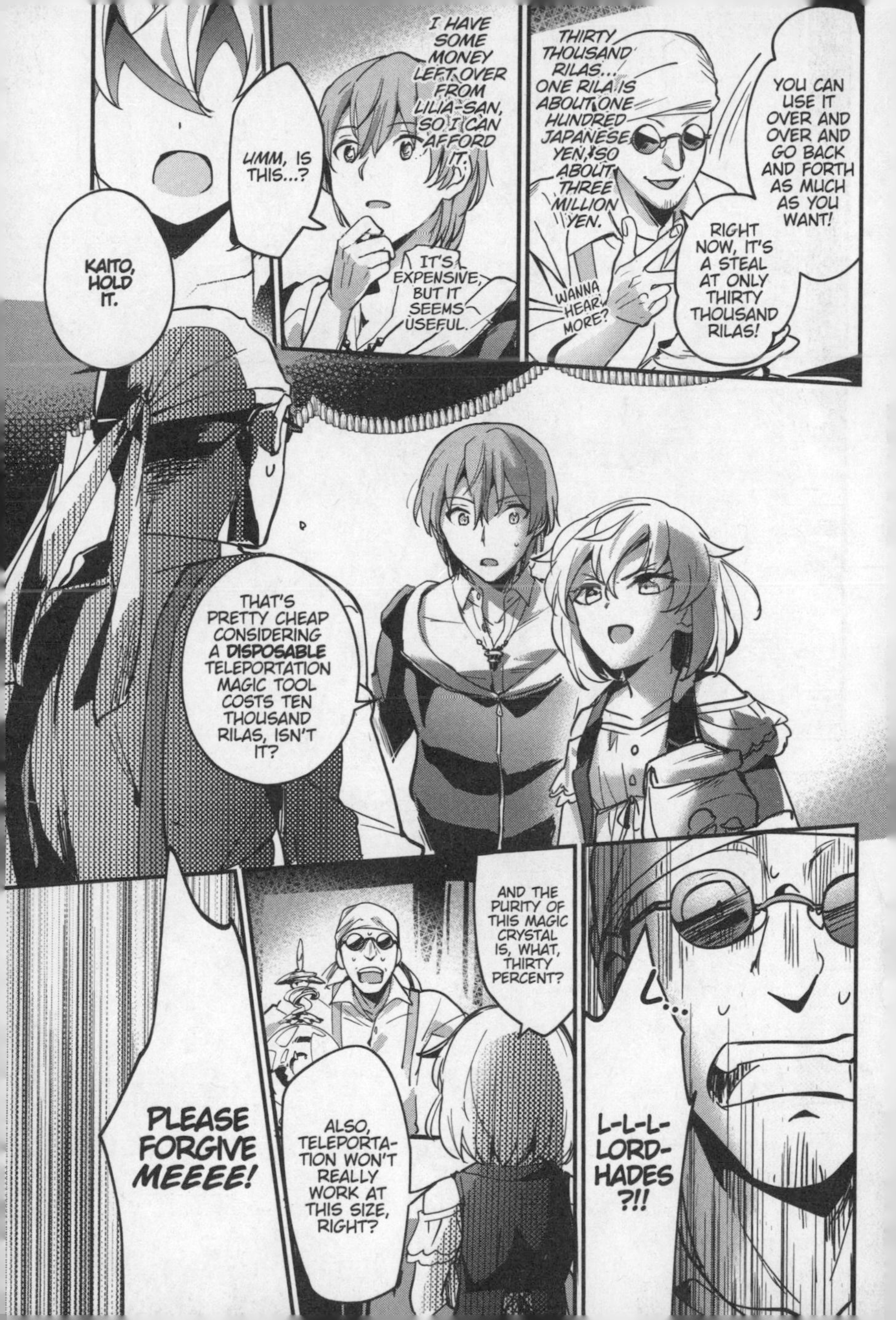
YOU CAN USE IT OVER AND OVER AND GO BACK AND FORTH AS MUCH AS YOU WANT!
RIGHT NOW, IT'S A STEAL AT ONLY THIRTY THOUSAND RILAS!
WANNA HEAR MORE?
THIRTY THOUSAND RILAS... ONE RILA IS ABOUT ONE HUNDRED JAPANESE YEN, SO ABOUT THREE MILLION YEN.
I HAVE SOME MONEY LEFT OVER FROM LILIA-SAN, SO I CAN AFFORD IT.
IT'S EXPENSIVE, BUT IT SEEMS USEFUL.
UMM, IS THIS...?
KAITO, HOLD IT.
THAT'S PRETTY CHEAP CONSIDERING A **DISPOSABLE** TELEPORTATION MAGIC TOOL COSTS TEN THOUSAND RILAS, ISN'T IT?
L...
L-L-L-LORD-HADES?!!
AND THE PURITY OF THIS MAGIC CRYSTAL IS, WHAT, THIRTY PERCENT?
ALSO, TELEPORTATION WON'T REALLY WORK AT THIS SIZE, RIGHT?
PLEASE FORGIVE MEEEE!

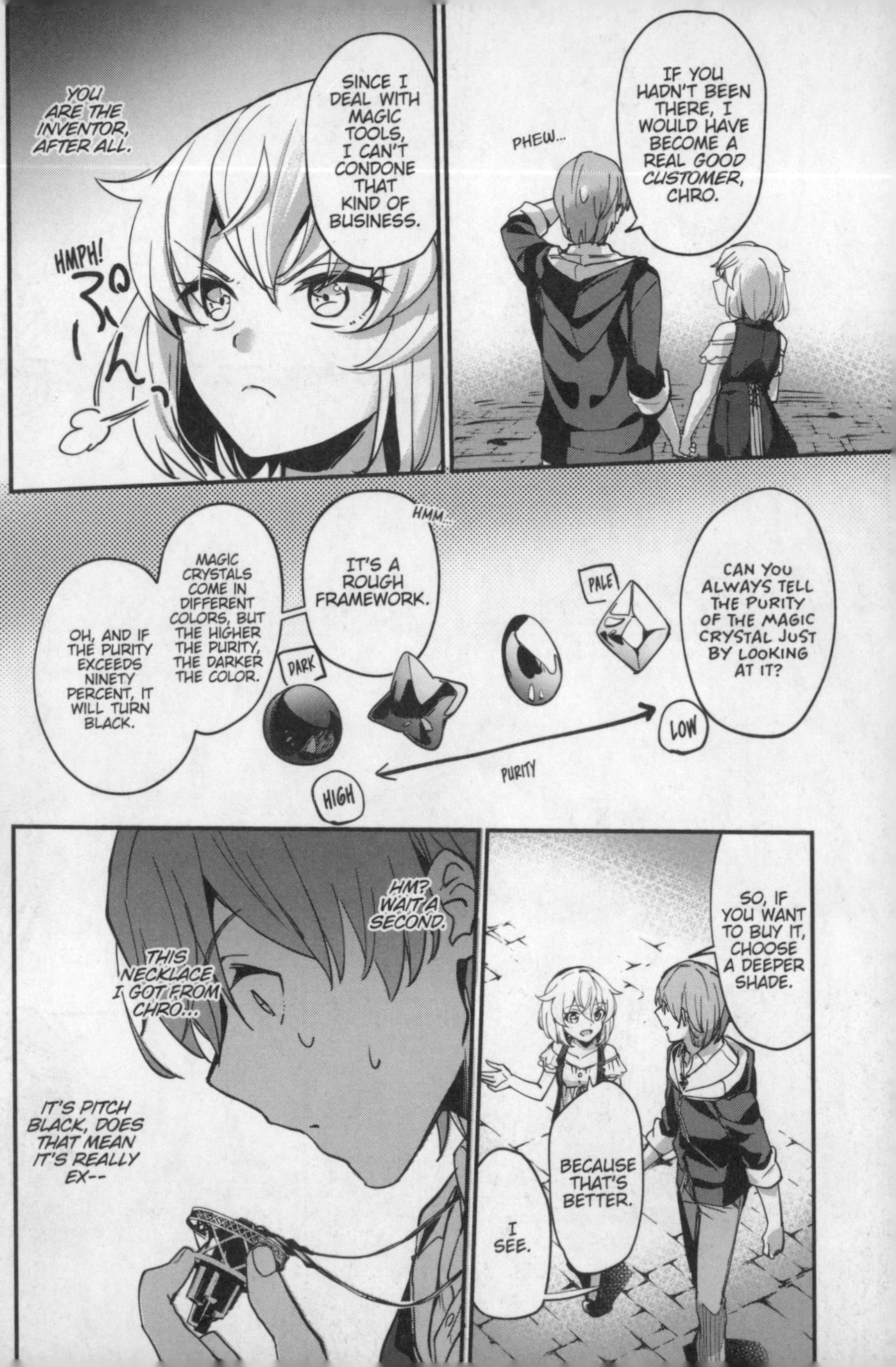
PHEW...
IF YOU HADN'T BEEN THERE, I WOULD HAVE BECOME A REAL GOOD CUSTOMER, CHRO.
SINCE I DEAL WITH MAGIC TOOLS, I CAN'T CONDONE THAT KIND OF BUSINESS.
HMPH!
YOU ARE THE INVENTOR, AFTER ALL.
CAN YOU ALWAYS TELL THE PURITY OF THE MAGIC CRYSTAL JUST BY LOOKING AT IT?
HMM
IT'S A ROUGH FRAMEWORK.
MAGIC CRYSTALS COME IN DIFFERENT COLORS, BUT THE HIGHER THE PURITY, THE DARKER THE COLOR.
OH, AND IF THE PURITY EXCEEDS NINETY PERCENT, IT WILL TURN BLACK.
PALE
DARK
LOW
PURITY
HIGH
SO, IF YOU WANT TO BUY IT, CHOOSE A DEEPER SHADE.
BECAUSE THAT'S BETTER.
I SEE.
HM? WAIT A SECOND.
THIS NECKLACE I GOT FROM CHRO...
IT'S PITCH BLACK, DOES THAT MEAN IT'S REALLY EX--

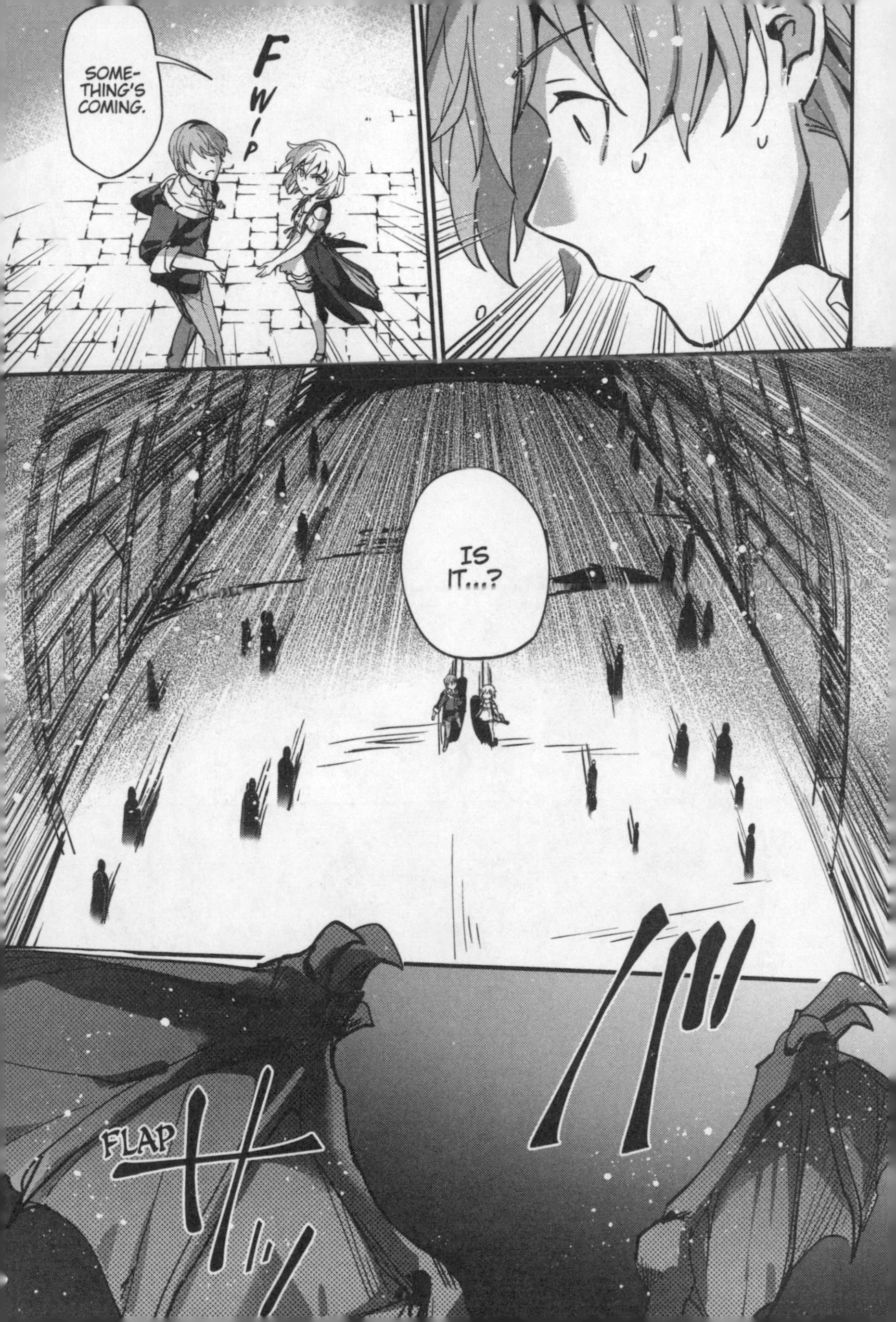
SOME-THING'S COMING.
FWIP
IS IT...?
FLAP

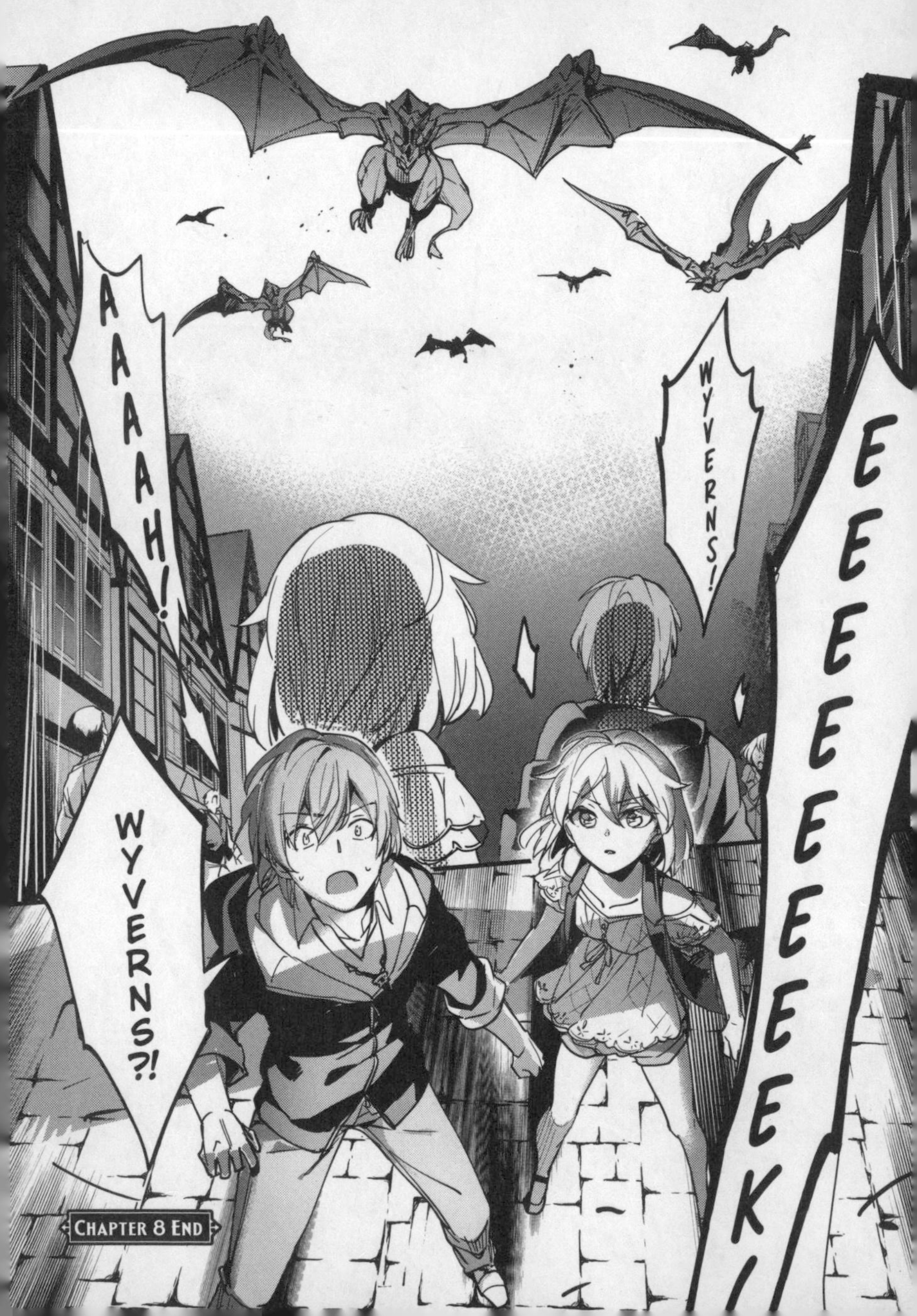
WYVERNS!
EEEEEEEEK!
AAAAH!
WYVERNS?!
CHAPTER 8 END

I GOT CAUGHT UP IN A HERO SUMMONS, BUT THE OTHER WORLD WAS AT PEACE!

I GOT CAUGHT UP IN A HERO SUMMONS, BUT THE OTHER WORLD WAS AT PEACE!

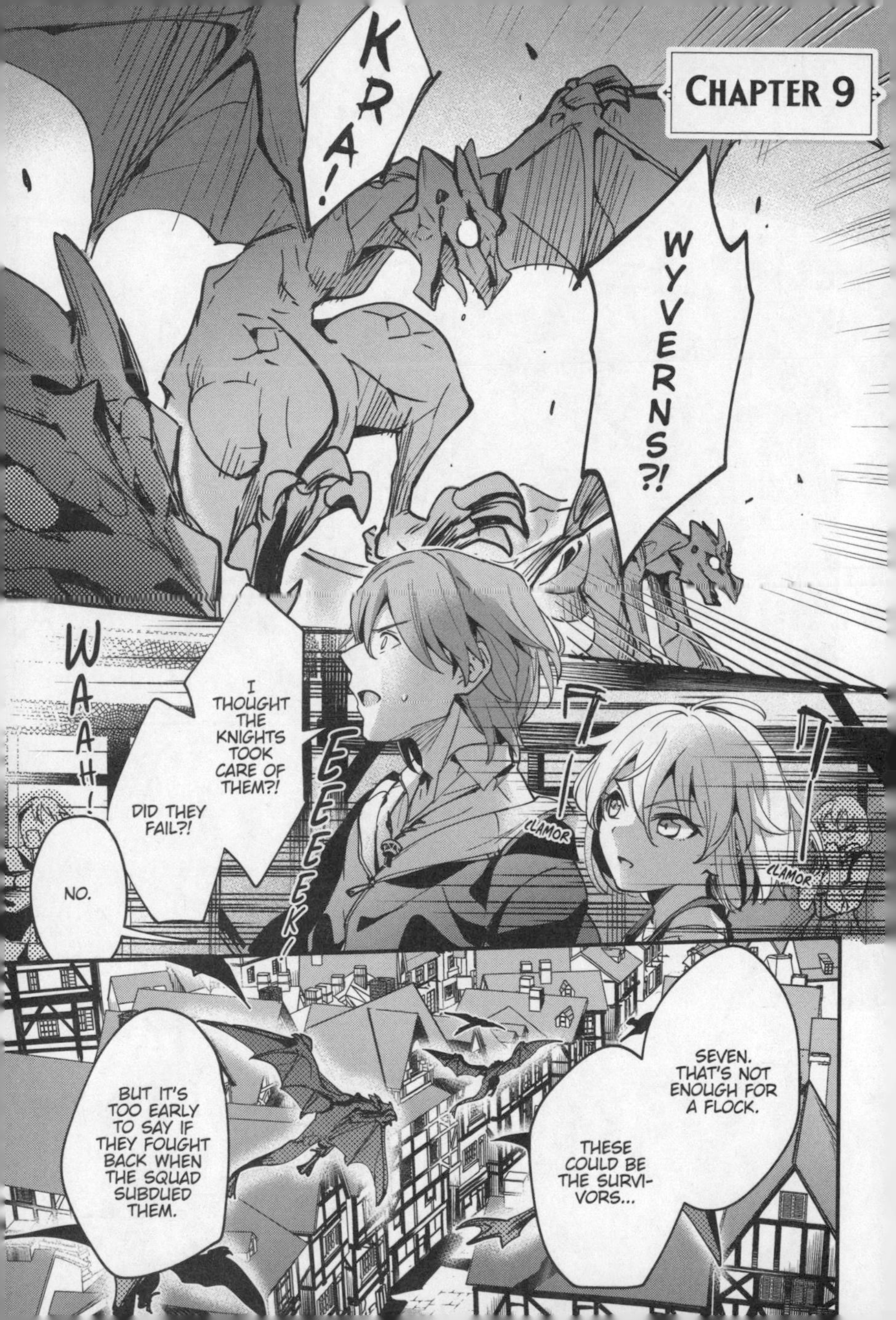

CHAPTER 9
WYVERNS?!
KRA!
CLAMOR
CLAMOR
I THOUGHT THE KNIGHTS TOOK CARE OF THEM?!
DID THEY FAIL?!
EEEEEK!
WAAAH!
NO.
SEVEN. THAT'S NOT ENOUGH FOR A FLOCK.
THESE COULD BE THE SURVIVORS...
BUT IT'S TOO EARLY TO SAY IF THEY FOUGHT BACK WHEN THE SQUAD SUBDUED THEM.

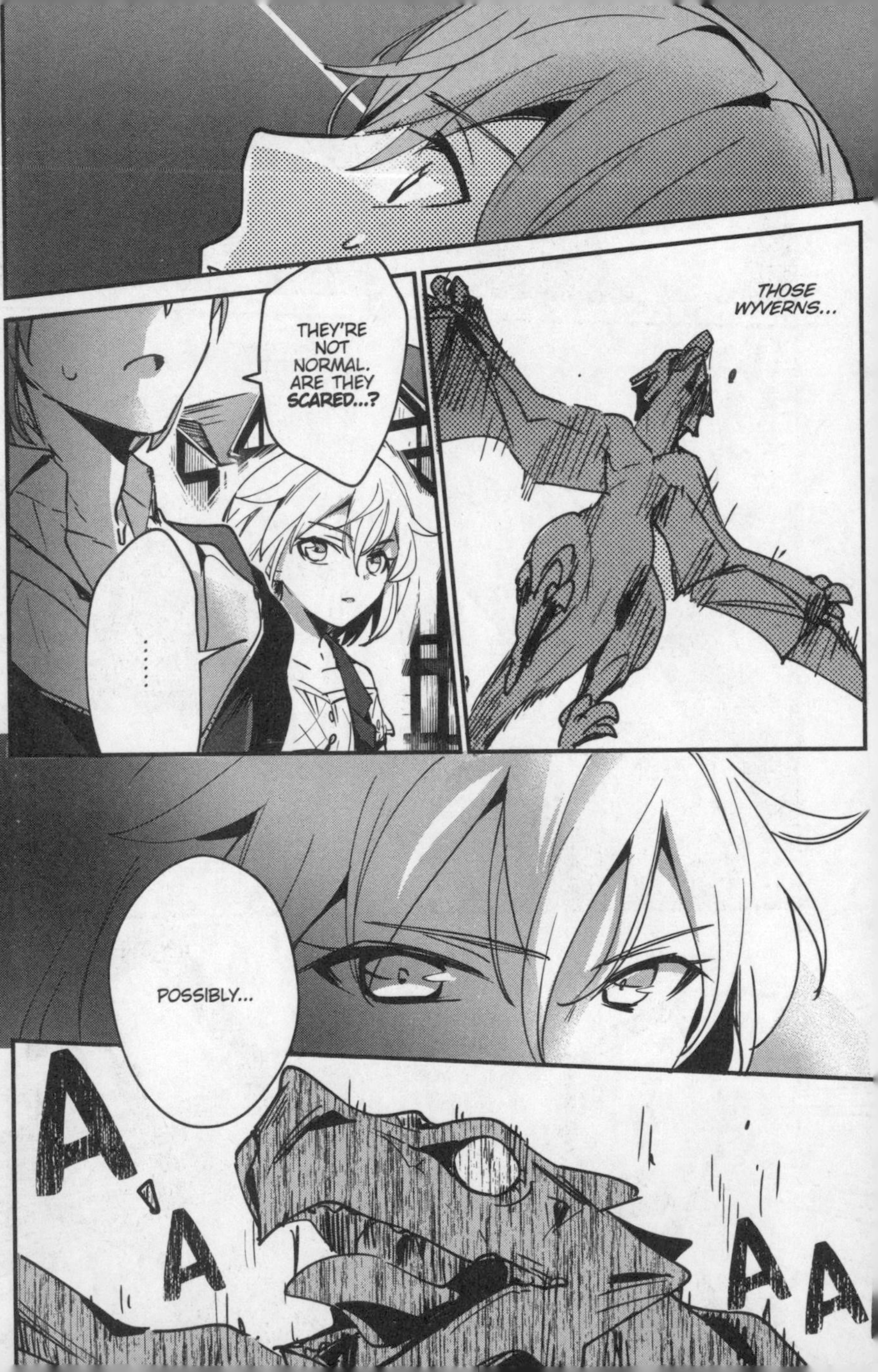
THOSE WYVERNS...
THEY'RE NOT NORMAL. ARE THEY SCARED...?
......
POSSIBLY...
AAAAA

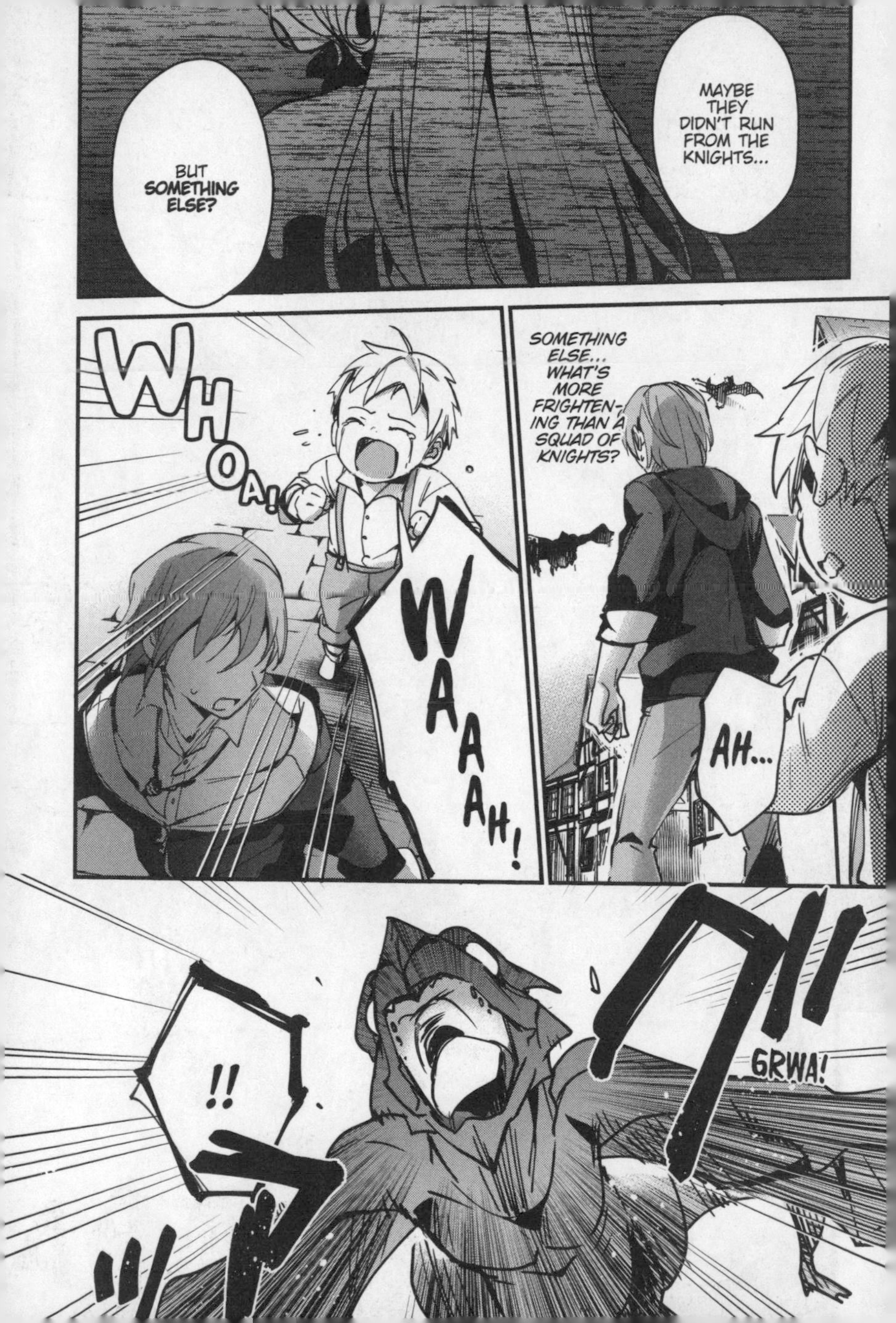
MAYBE THEY DIDN'T RUN FROM THE KNIGHTS...
BUT SOMETHING ELSE?
SOMETHING ELSE... WHAT'S MORE FRIGHTEN-ING THAN A SQUAD OF KNIGHTS?
AH...
WHOA!
WAAAAH!
GRWA!
!!

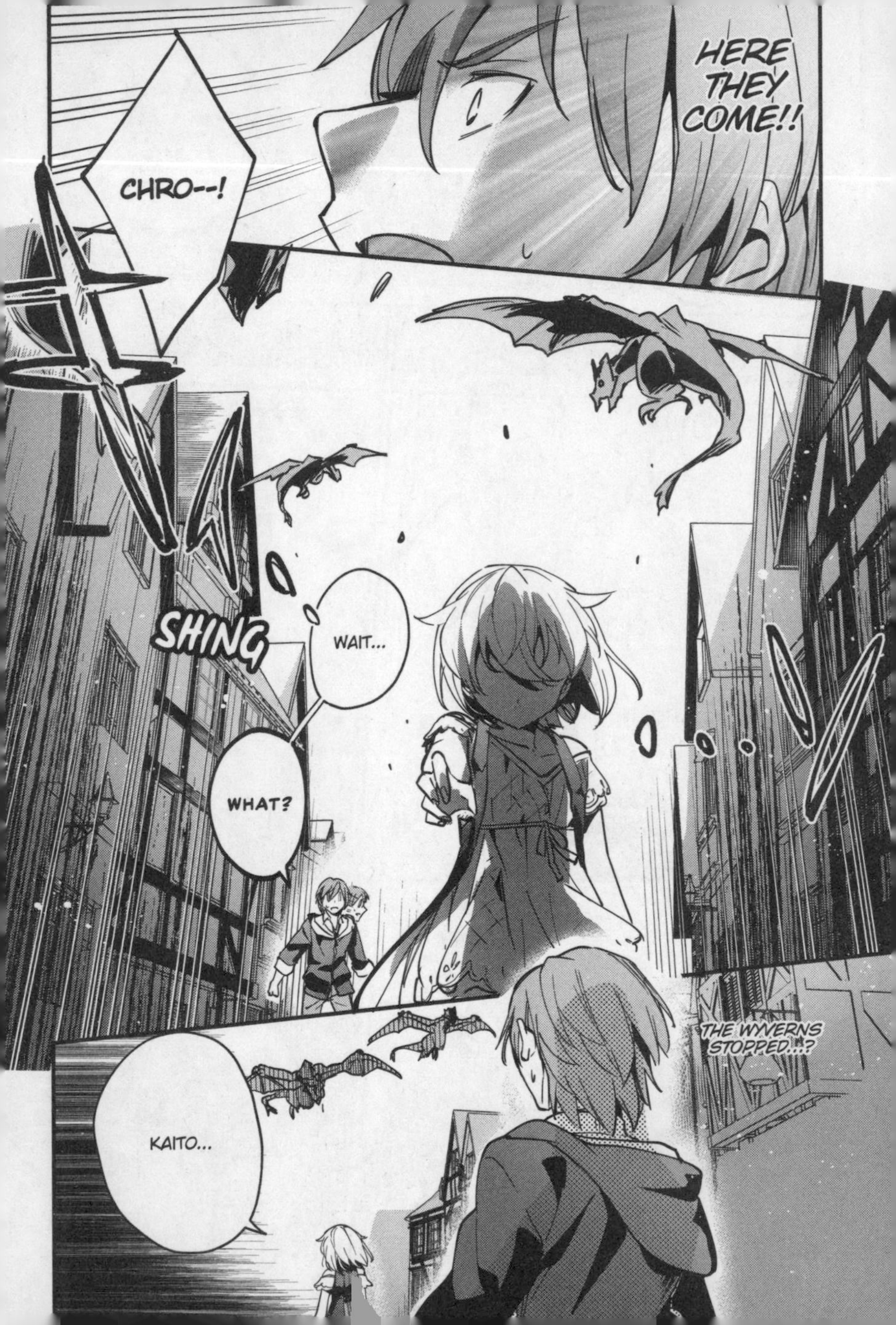
HERE THEY COME!!
CHRO--!
WAIT...
SHING
WHAT?
THE WYVERNS STOPPED...?
KAITO...

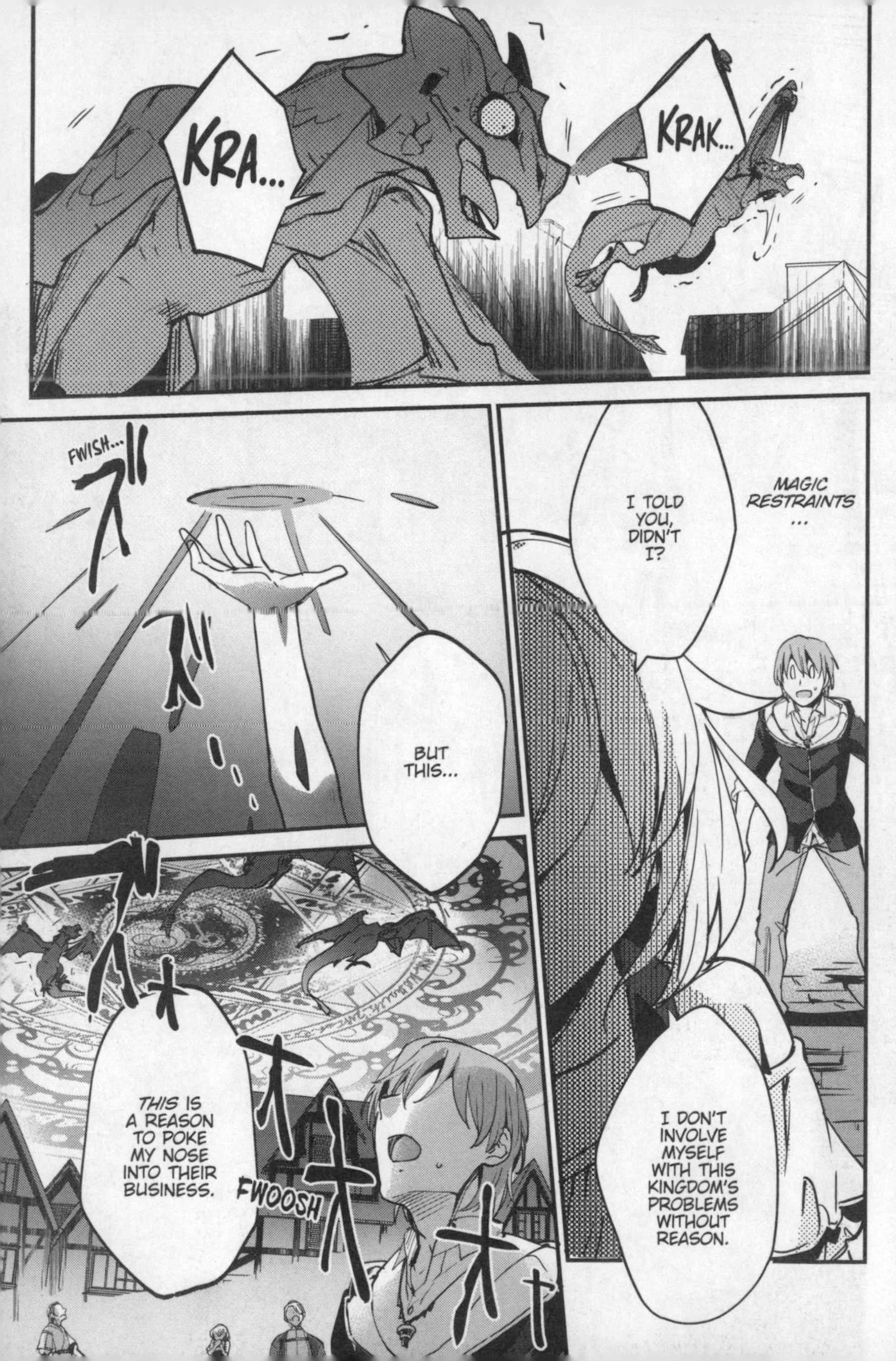
KRAK...
KRA...
MAGIC RESTRAINTS ...
I TOLD YOU, DIDN'T I?
I DON'T INVOLVE MYSELF WITH THIS KINGDOM'S PROBLEMS WITHOUT REASON.
FWISH...
BUT THIS...
THIS IS A REASON TO POKE MY NOSE INTO THEIR BUSINESS.
FWOOSH

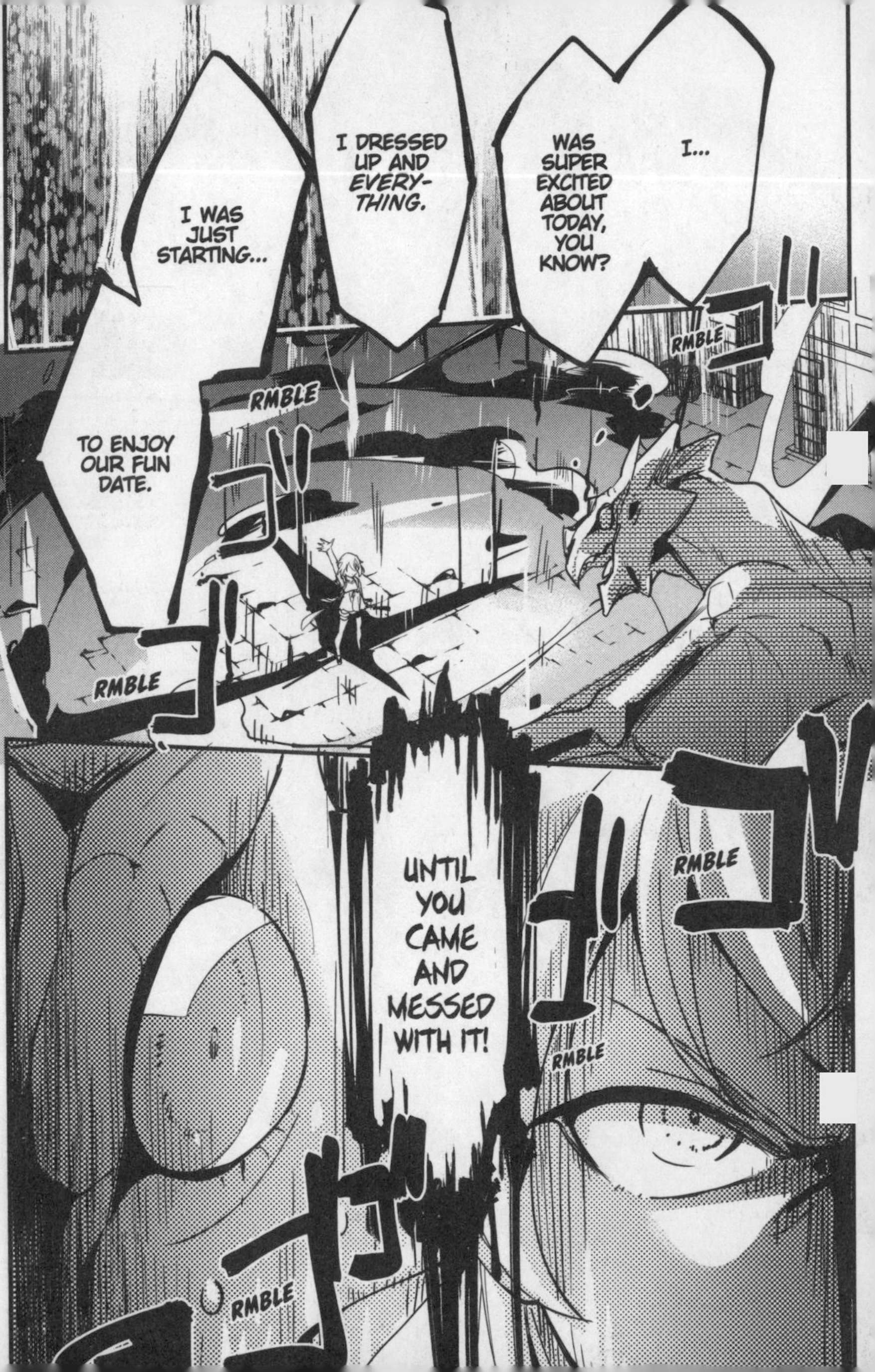
I...
WAS SUPER EXCITED ABOUT TODAY, YOU KNOW?
I DRESSED UP AND EVERYTHING.
I WAS JUST STARTING...
TO ENJOY OUR FUN DATE.
RMBLE
RMBLE
RMBLE
RMBLE
UNTIL YOU CAME AND MESSED WITH IT!
RMBLE
RMBLE

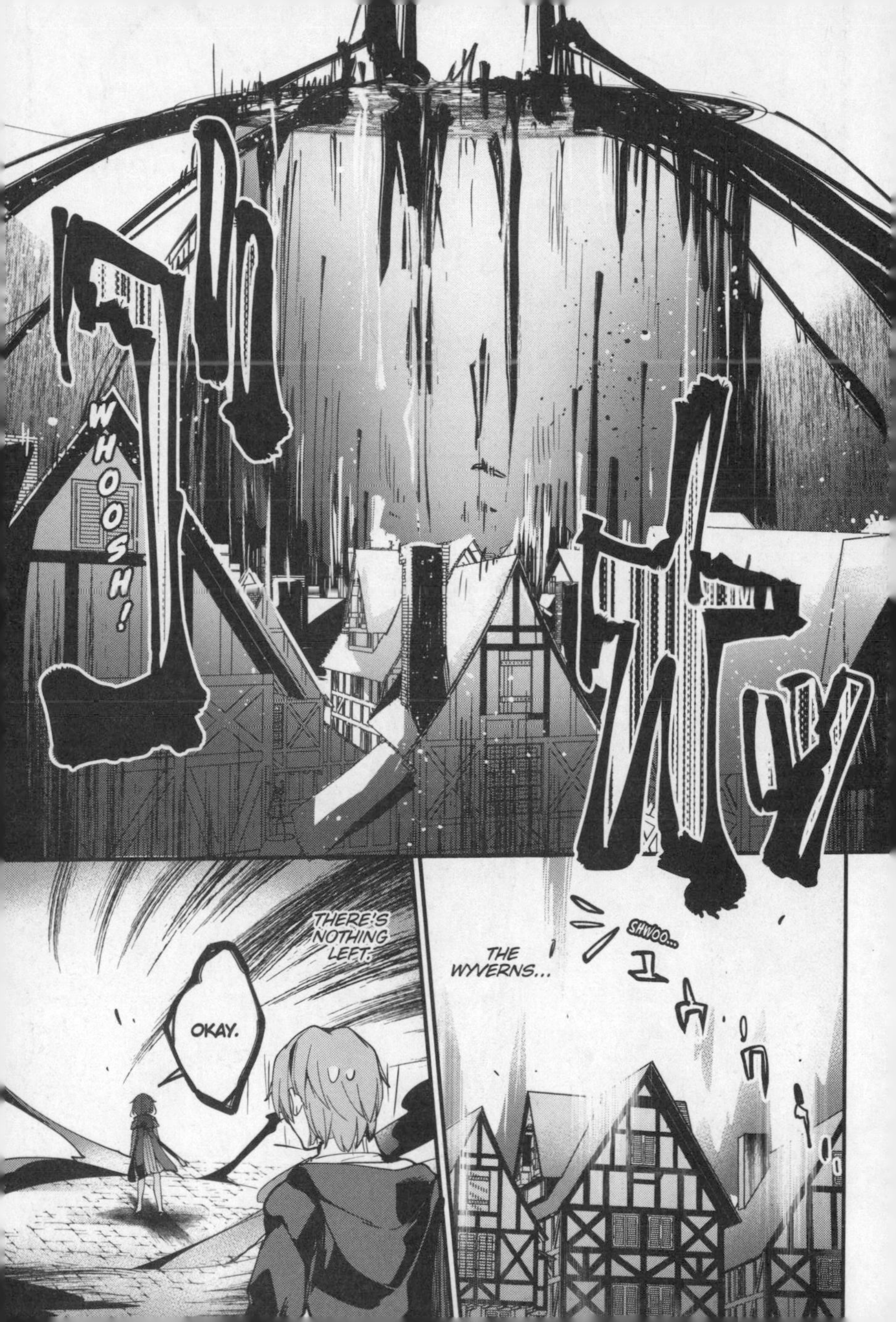
WHOOSH!
SHWOO...
THE WYVERNS...
THERE'S NOTHING LEFT.
OKAY.

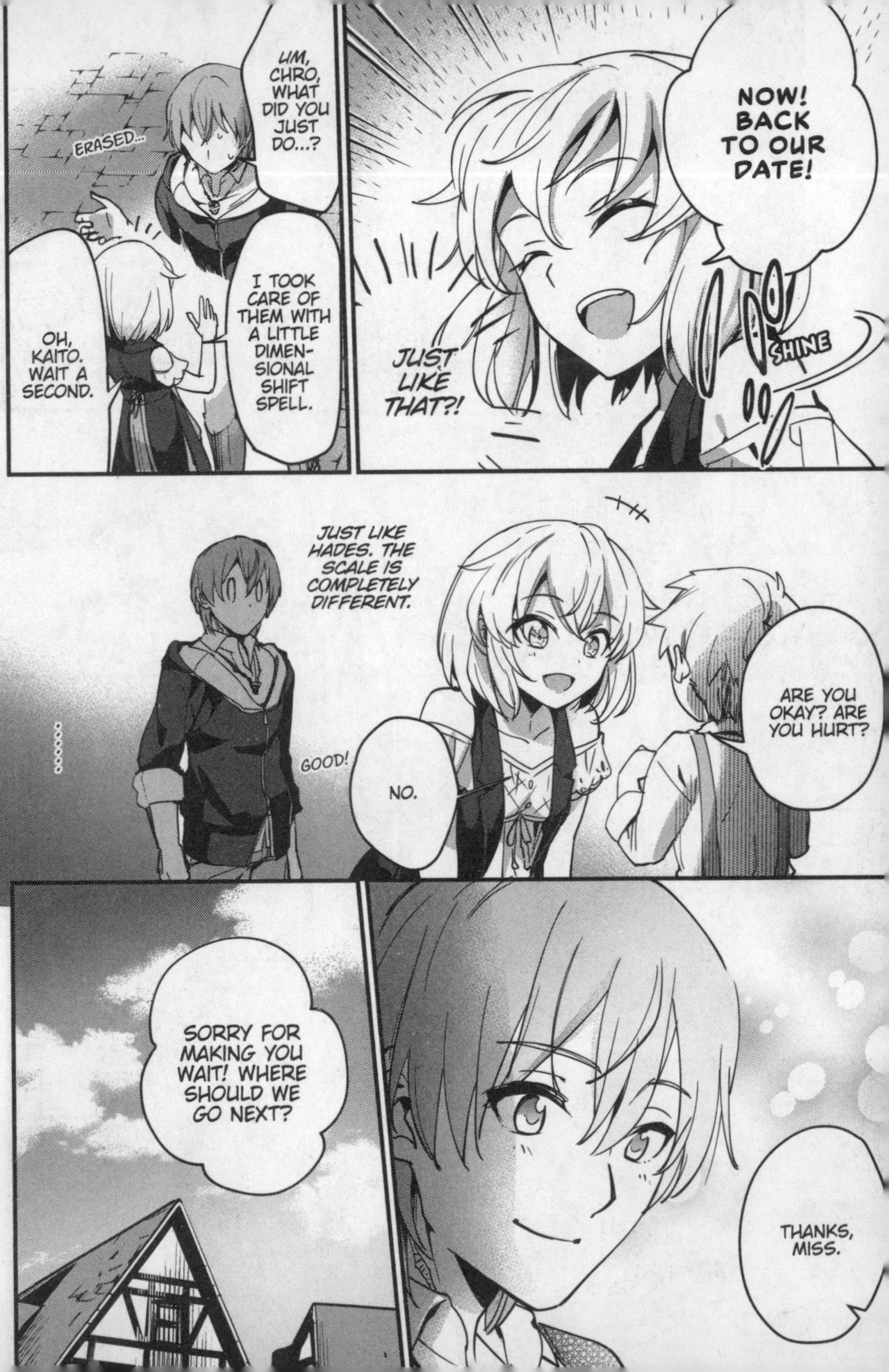
NOW! BACK TO OUR DATE!
SHINE
JUST LIKE THAT?!
UM, CHRO, WHAT DID YOU JUST DO...?
ERASED...
I TOOK CARE OF THEM WITH A LITTLE DIMENSIONAL SHIFT SPELL.
OH, KAITO. WAIT A SECOND.
ARE YOU OKAY? ARE YOU HURT?
NO.
GOOD!
JUST LIKE HADES. THE SCALE IS COMPLETELY DIFFERENT.
......
THANKS, MISS.
SORRY FOR MAKING YOU WAIT! WHERE SHOULD WE GO NEXT?

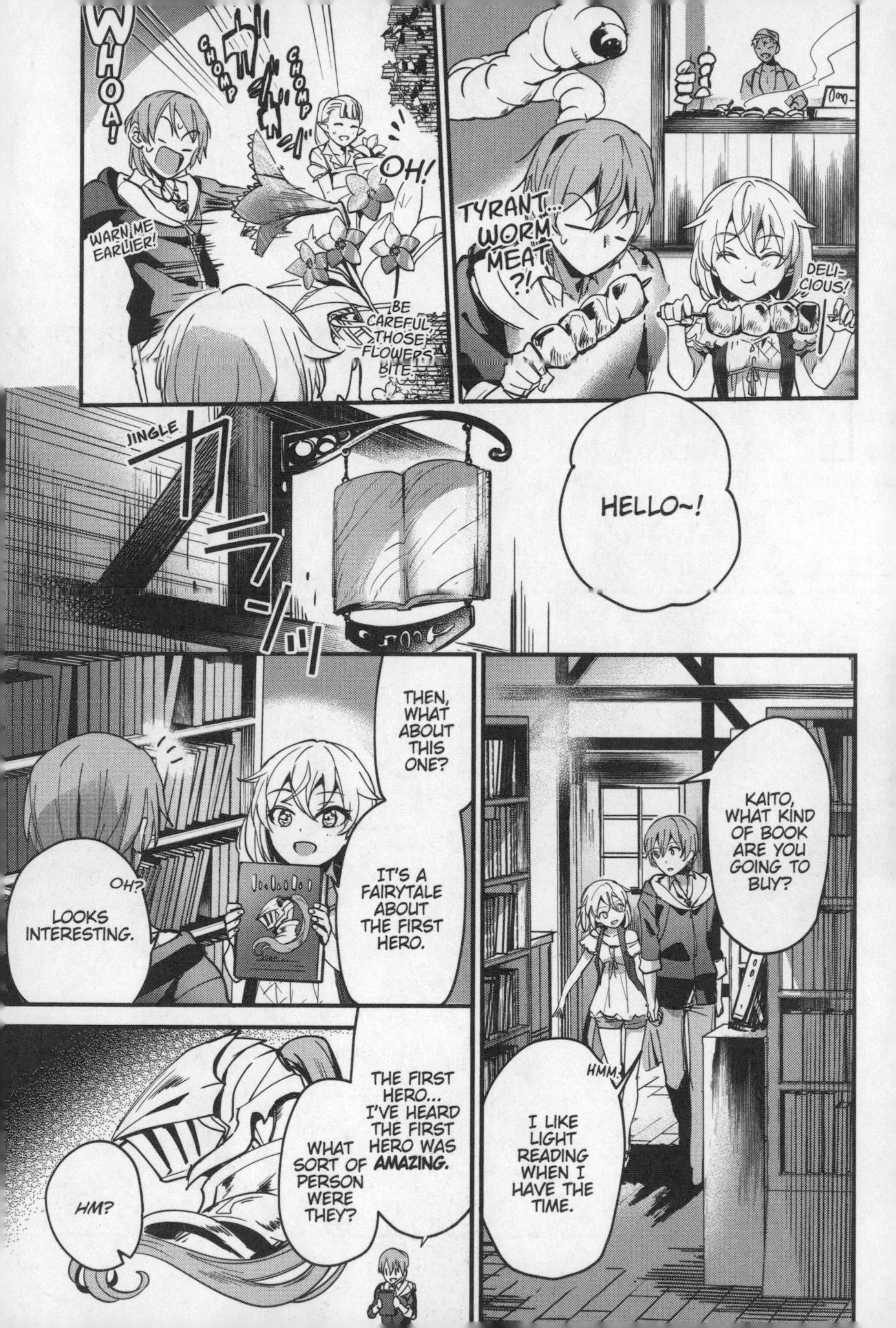
TYRANT... WORM MEAT ?!
DELI-CIOUS!
CHOMP
CHOMP
OH!
WHOA!
BE CAREFUL, THOSE FLOWERS BITE.
WARN ME EARLIER!
HELLO~!
JINGLE
KAITO, WHAT KIND OF BOOK ARE YOU GOING TO BUY?
HMM.
I LIKE LIGHT READING WHEN I HAVE THE TIME.
THEN, WHAT ABOUT THIS ONE?
IT'S A FAIRYTALE ABOUT THE FIRST HERO.
OH?
LOOKS INTERESTING.
THE FIRST HERO... I'VE HEARD THE FIRST HERO WAS **AMAZING**.
WHAT SORT OF PERSON WERE THEY?
HM?

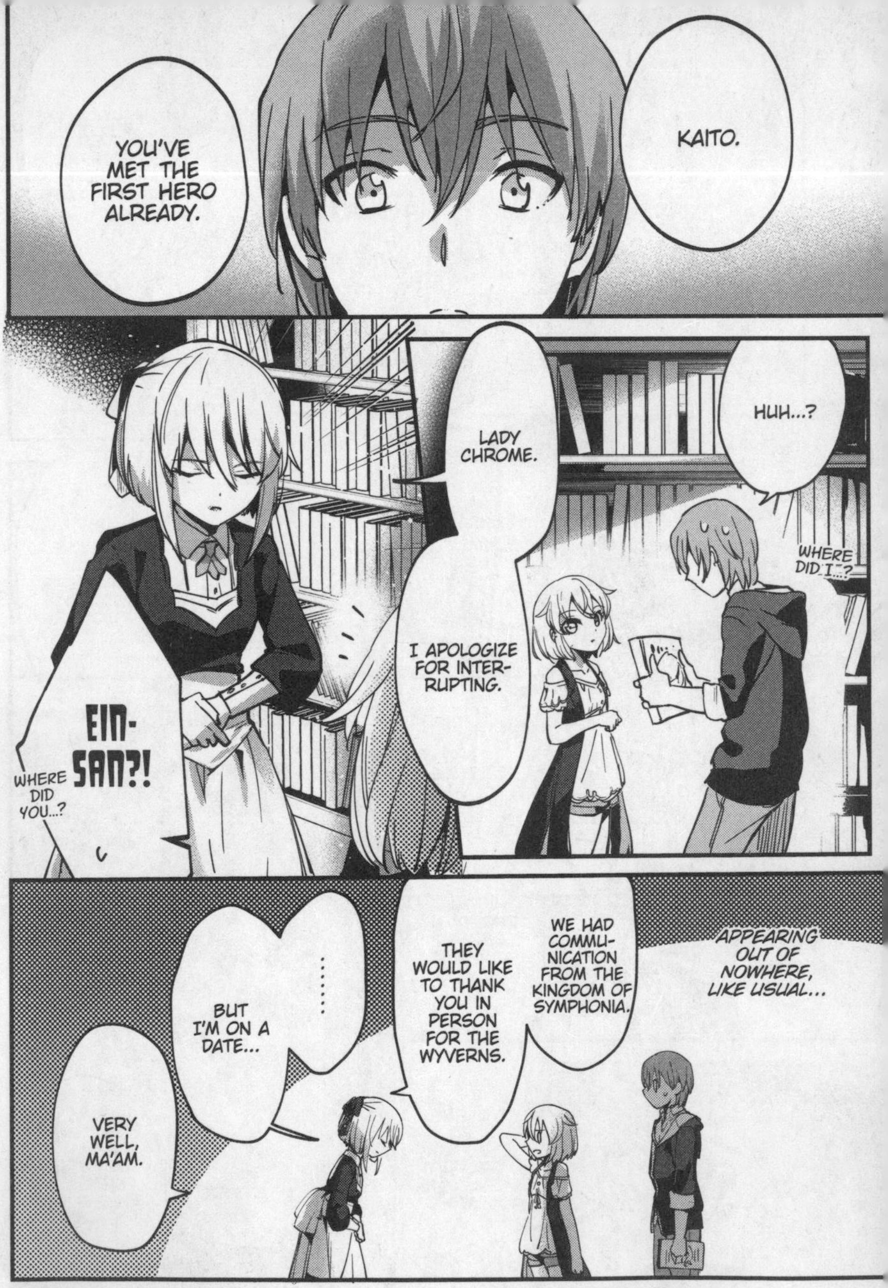
KAITO.
YOU'VE MET THE FIRST HERO ALREADY.
HUH...?
WHERE DID I...?
LADY CHROME.
I APOLOGIZE FOR INTER-RUPTING.
EIN-SAN?!
WHERE DID YOU...?
APPEARING OUT OF NOWHERE, LIKE USUAL...
WE HAD COMMUNICATION FROM THE KINGDOM OF SYMPHONIA.
THEY WOULD LIKE TO THANK YOU IN PERSON FOR THE WYVERNS.
......
BUT I'M ON A DATE...
VERY WELL, MA'AM.

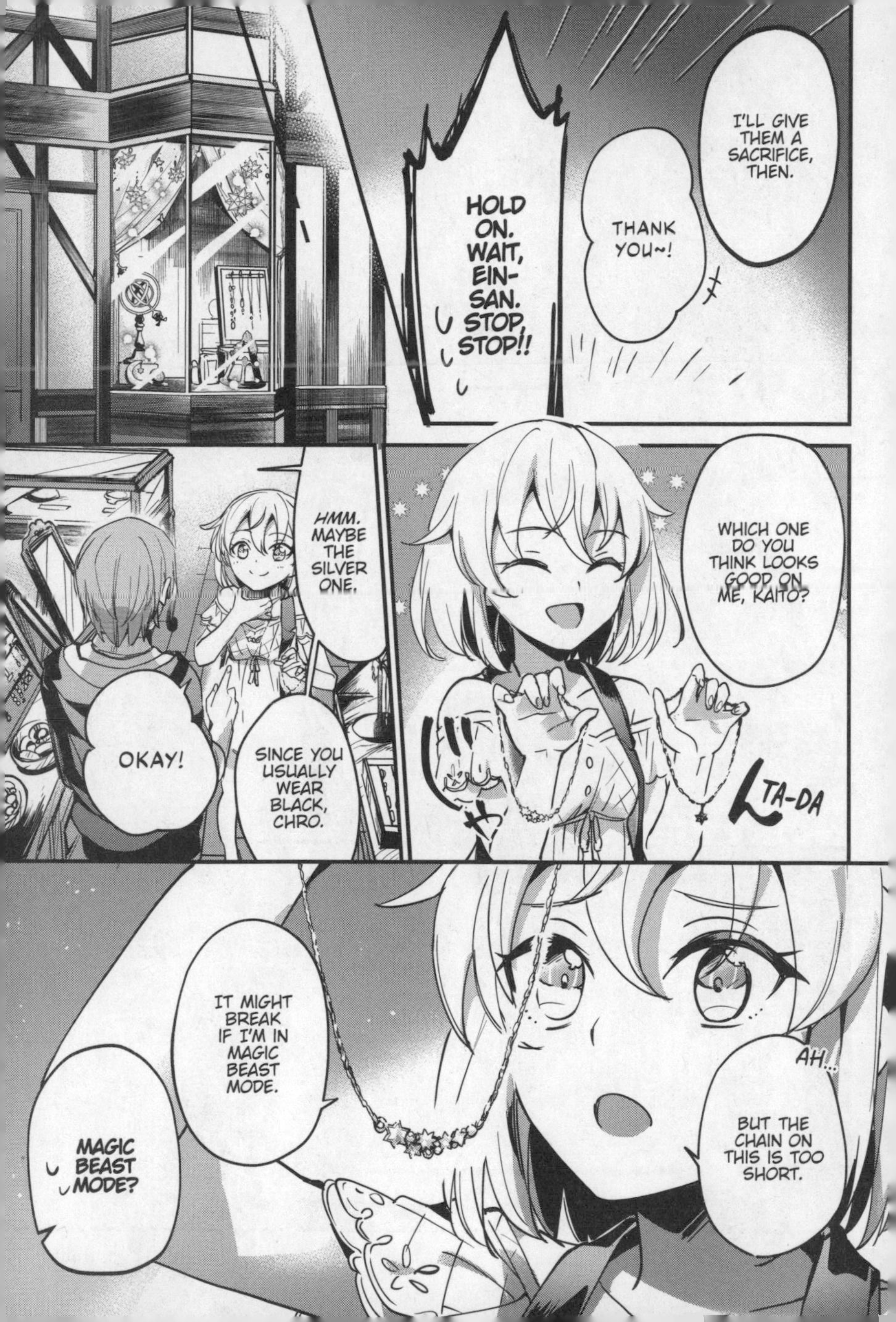
I'LL GIVE THEM A SACRIFICE, THEN.
THANK YOU~!
HOLD ON. WAIT, EIN-SAN. STOP, STOP!!
WHICH ONE DO YOU THINK LOOKS GOOD ON ME, KAITO?
TA-DA
HMM. MAYBE THE SILVER ONE.
SINCE YOU USUALLY WEAR BLACK, CHRO.
OKAY!
AH...
BUT THE CHAIN ON THIS IS TOO SHORT.
IT MIGHT BREAK IF I'M IN MAGIC BEAST MODE.
MAGIC BEAST MODE?

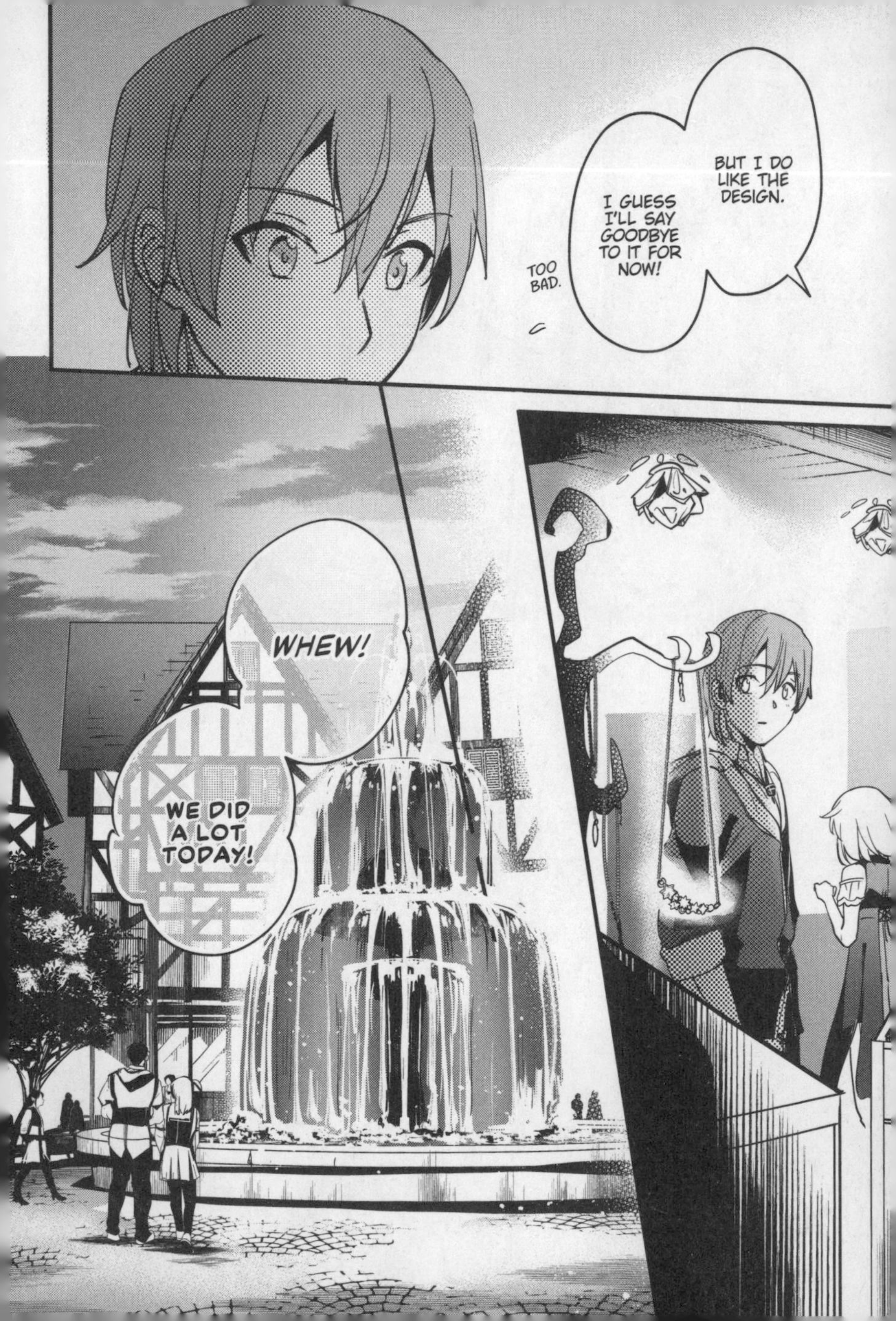
BUT I DO LIKE THE DESIGN.
I GUESS I'LL SAY GOODBYE TO IT FOR NOW!
TOO BAD.
WHEW!
WE DID A LOT TODAY!

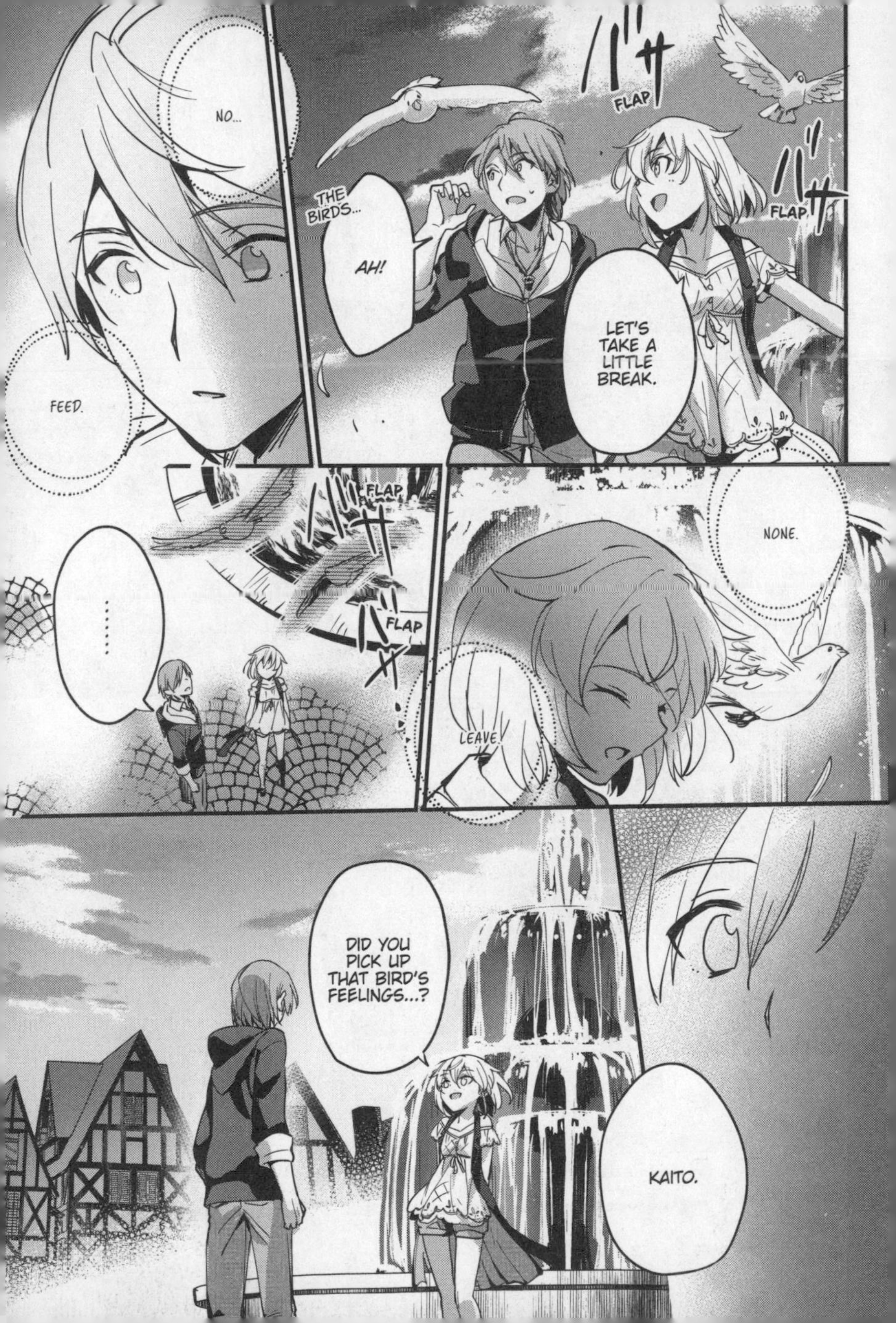
FLAP
FLAP
LET'S TAKE A LITTLE BREAK.
THE BIRDS...
AH!
NO...
FEED.
NONE.
LEAVE.
FLAP
FLAP
......
KAITO.
DID YOU PICK UP THAT BIRD'S FEELINGS...?

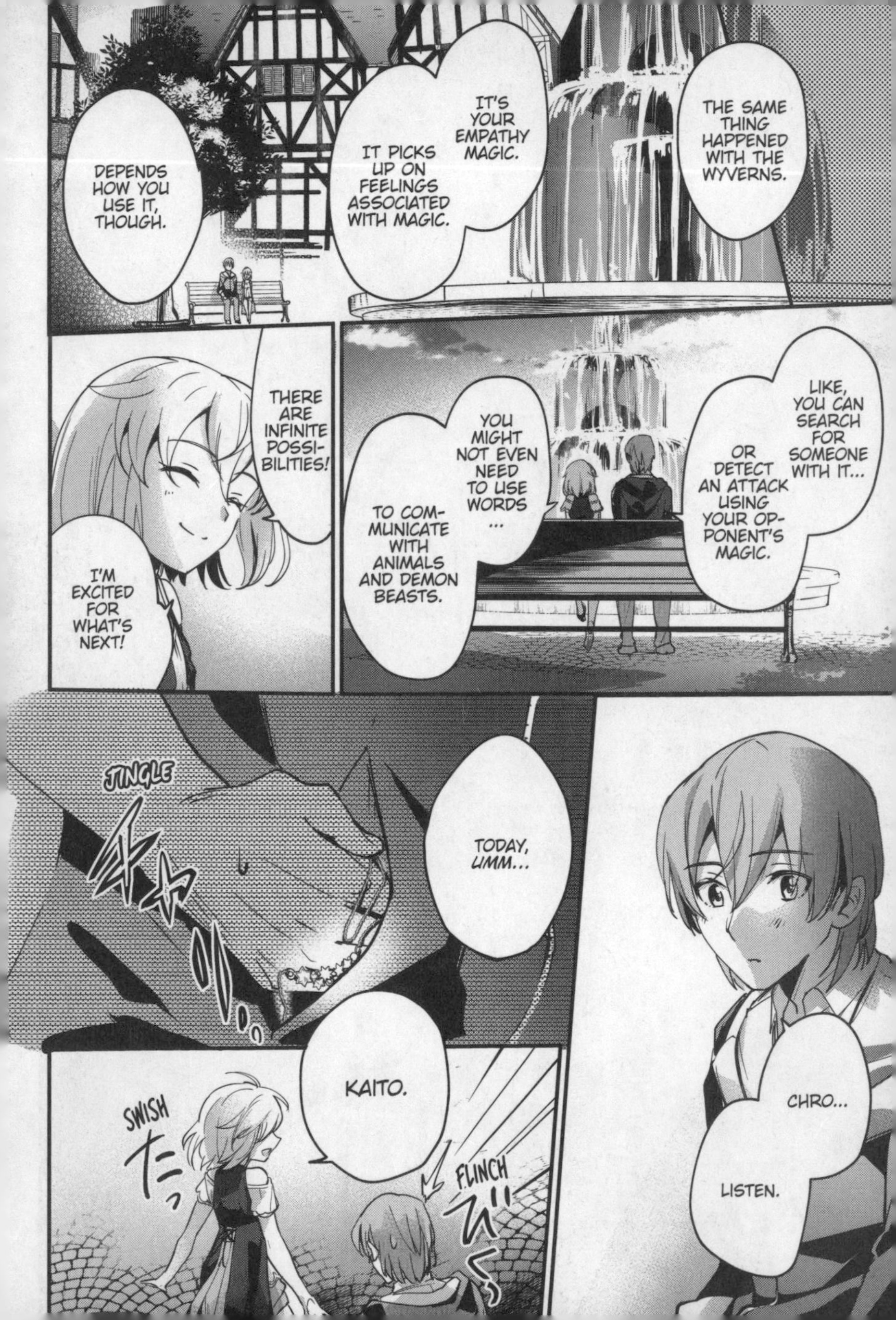
THE SAME THING HAPPENED WITH THE WYVERNS.
IT'S YOUR EMPATHY MAGIC.
IT PICKS UP ON FEELINGS ASSOCIATED WITH MAGIC.
DEPENDS HOW YOU USE IT, THOUGH.
LIKE, YOU CAN SEARCH FOR SOMEONE WITH IT...
OR DETECT AN ATTACK USING YOUR OPPONENT'S MAGIC.
YOU MIGHT NOT EVEN NEED TO USE WORDS...
TO COMMUNICATE WITH ANIMALS AND DEMON BEASTS.
THERE ARE INFINITE POSSIBILITIES!
I'M EXCITED FOR WHAT'S NEXT!
CHRO...
LISTEN.
JINGLE
TODAY, UMM...
KAITO.
SWISH
FLINCH

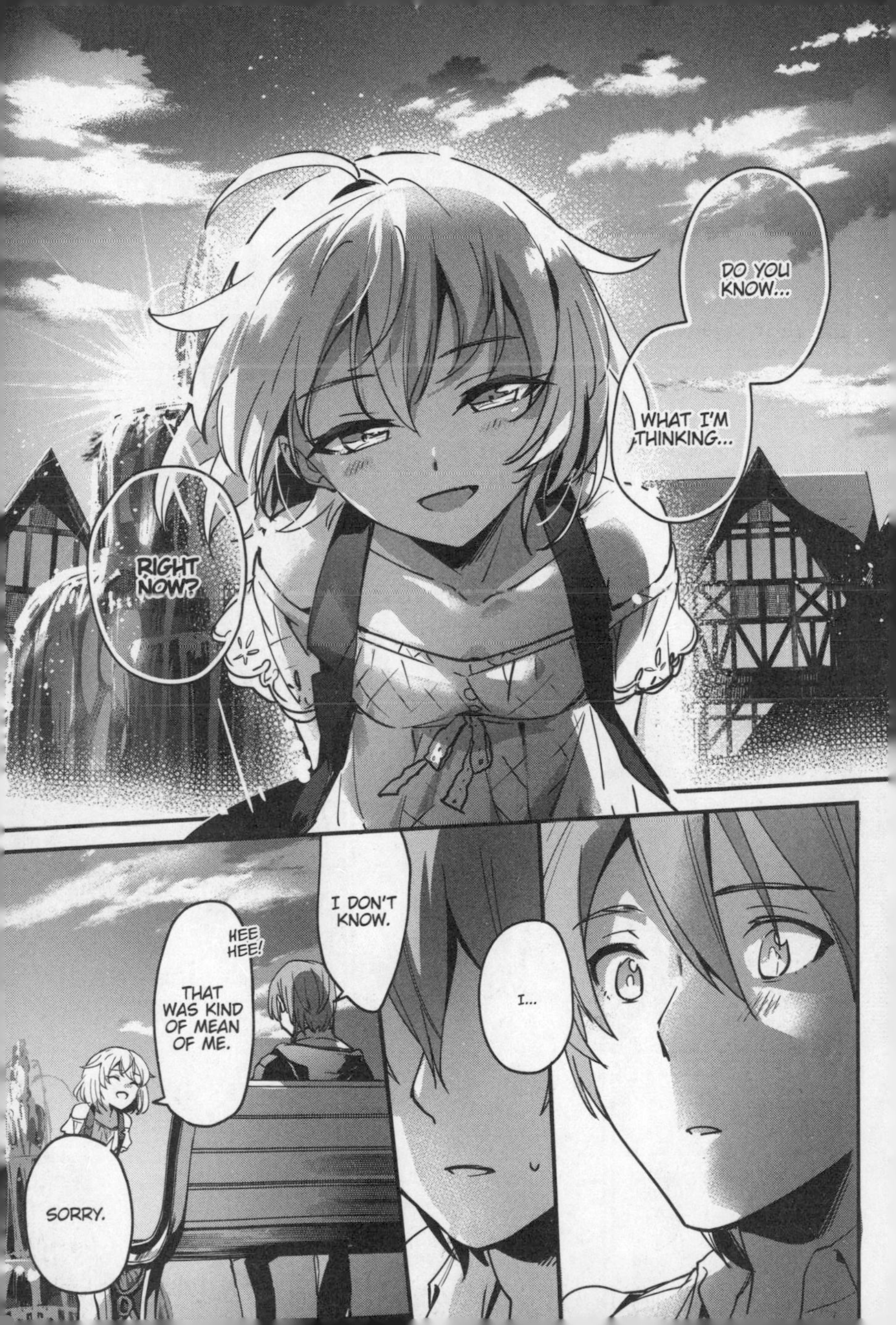
DO YOU KNOW...
WHAT I'M THINKING...
RIGHT NOW?
I...
I DON'T KNOW.
HEE HEE!
THAT WAS KIND OF MEAN OF ME.
SORRY.

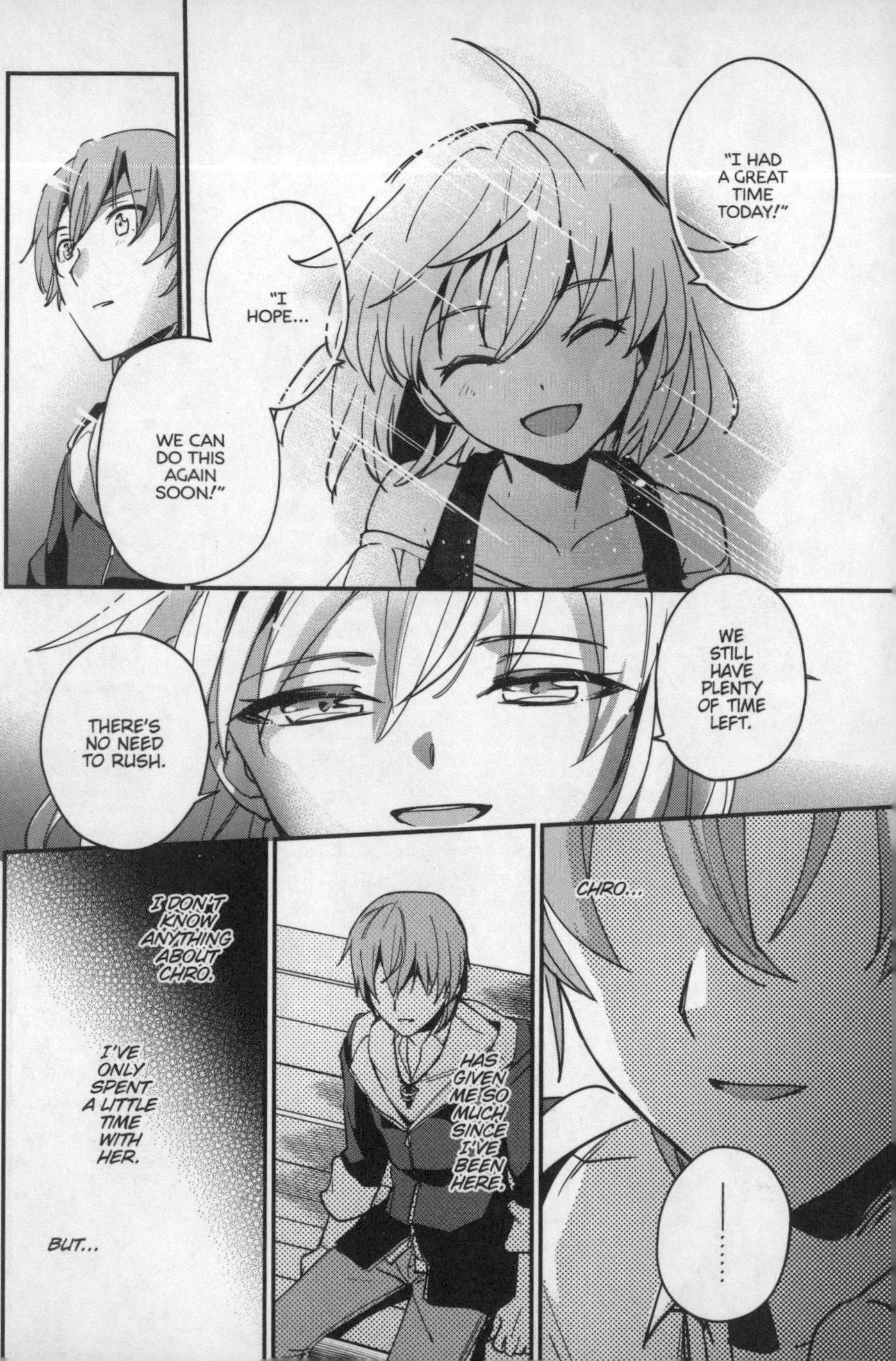
"I HAD A GREAT TIME TODAY!"
"I HOPE...
WE CAN DO THIS AGAIN SOON!"
WE STILL HAVE PLENTY OF TIME LEFT.
THERE'S NO NEED TO RUSH.
CHRO...
......
HAS GIVEN ME SO MUCH SINCE I'VE BEEN HERE.
I DON'T KNOW ANYTHING ABOUT CHRO.
I'VE ONLY SPENT A LITTLE TIME WITH HER.
BUT...

CHRO...
I... ALREADY REALLY LIKE HER.
THANK YOU FOR TODAY. REALLY.
I DON'T KNOW WHEN IT'LL BE...
I WANT TO KNOW MORE ABOUT CHRO.
BUT...
I DON'T WANT TO JUST GET A SENSE OF HER.
NEXT TIME...
CAN I ASK YOU OUT, INSTEAD...?
I WANT TO GIVE HER... SOMETHING.

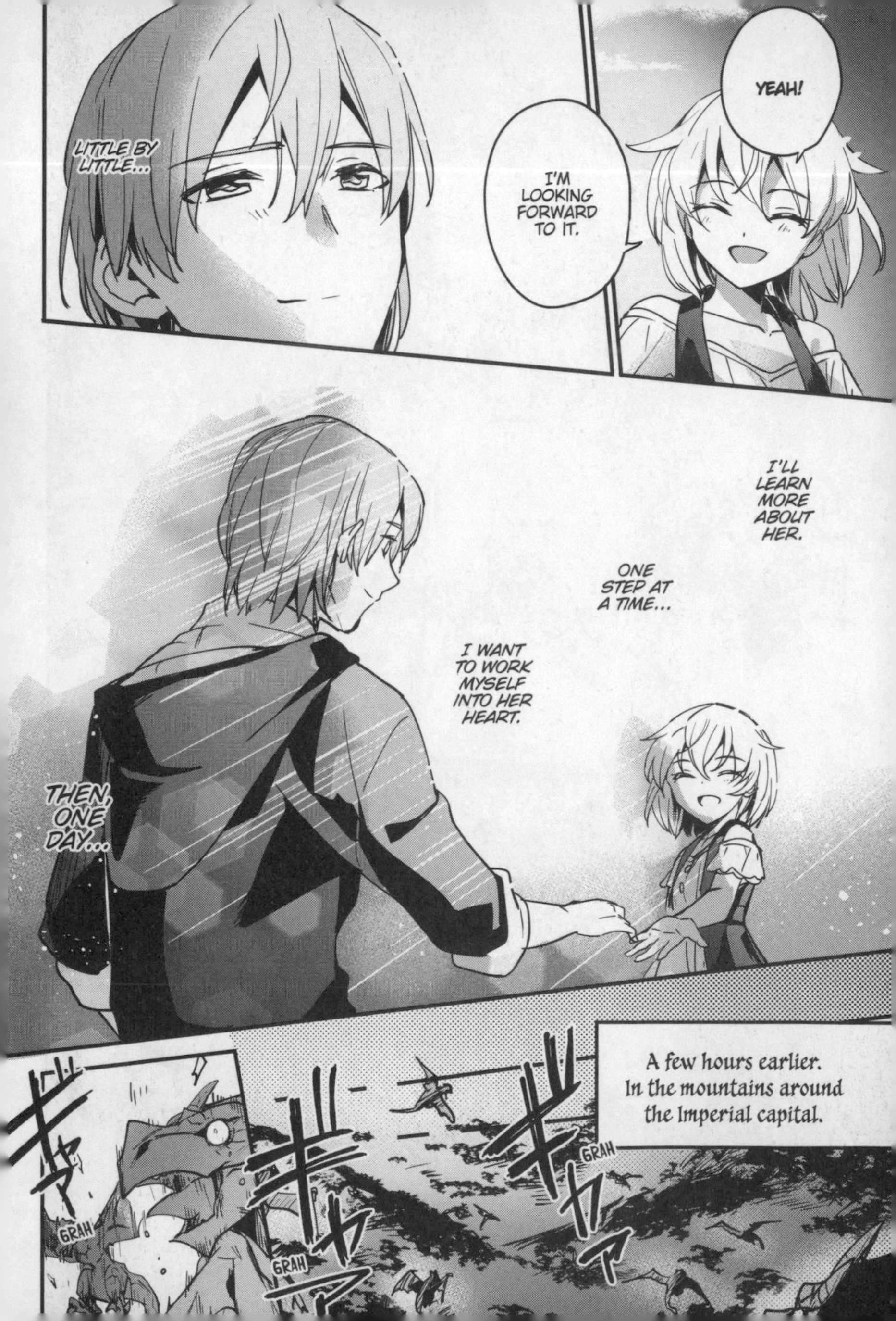
YEAH!
I'M LOOKING FORWARD TO IT.
LITTLE BY LITTLE...
I'LL LEARN MORE ABOUT HER.
ONE STEP AT A TIME...
I WANT TO WORK MYSELF INTO HER HEART.
THEN, ONE DAY...
A few hours earlier. In the mountains around the Imperial capital.
GRAH
GRAH
GRAH

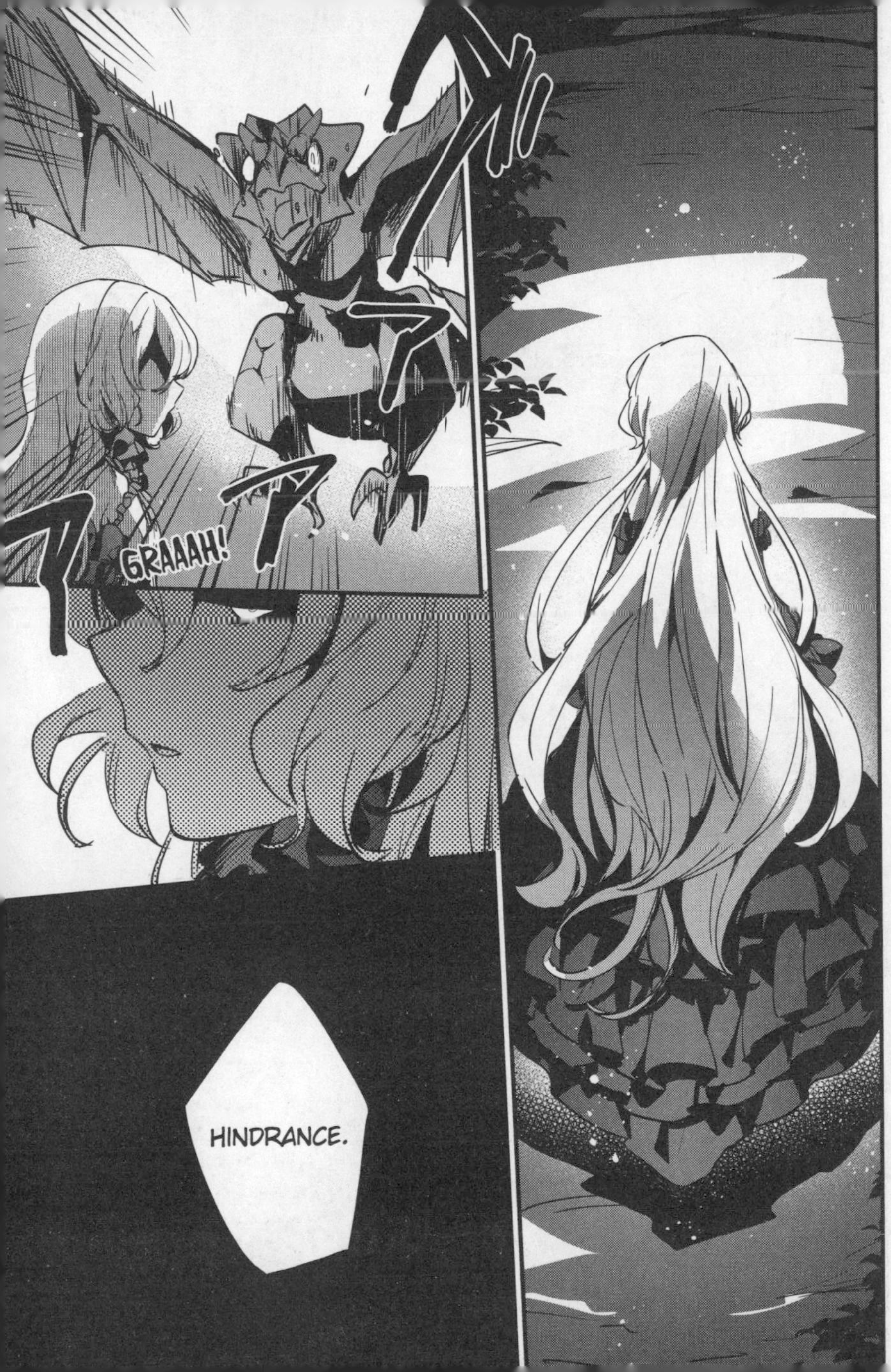
GRAAAH!
HINDRANCE.

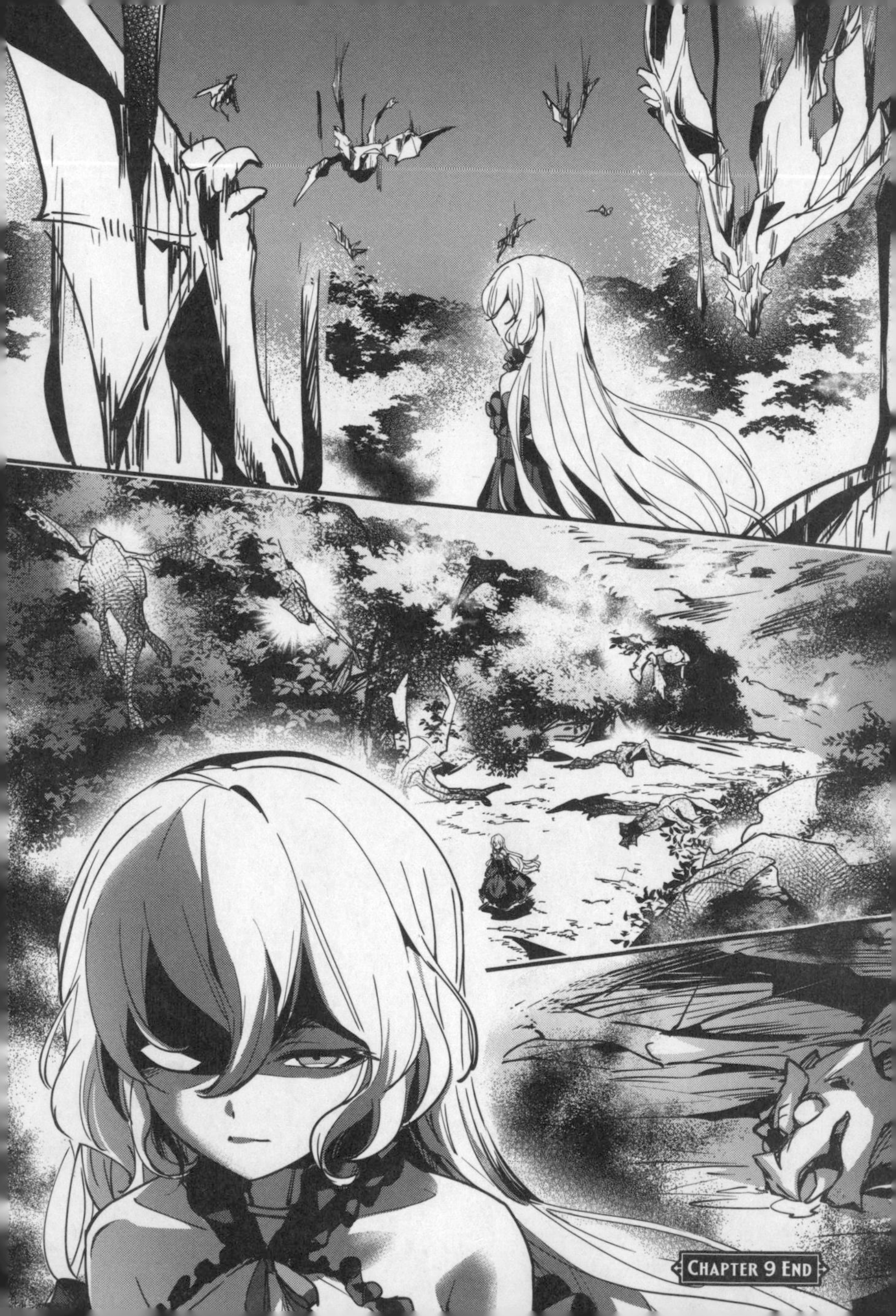
CHAPTER 9 END

I GOT CAUGHT
UP IN A HERO
SUMMONS,
BUT THE OTHER WORLD
WAS AT PEACE!

I GOT CAUGHT
UP IN A HERO
SUMMONS,
BUT THE OTHER WORLD
WAS AT PEACE!

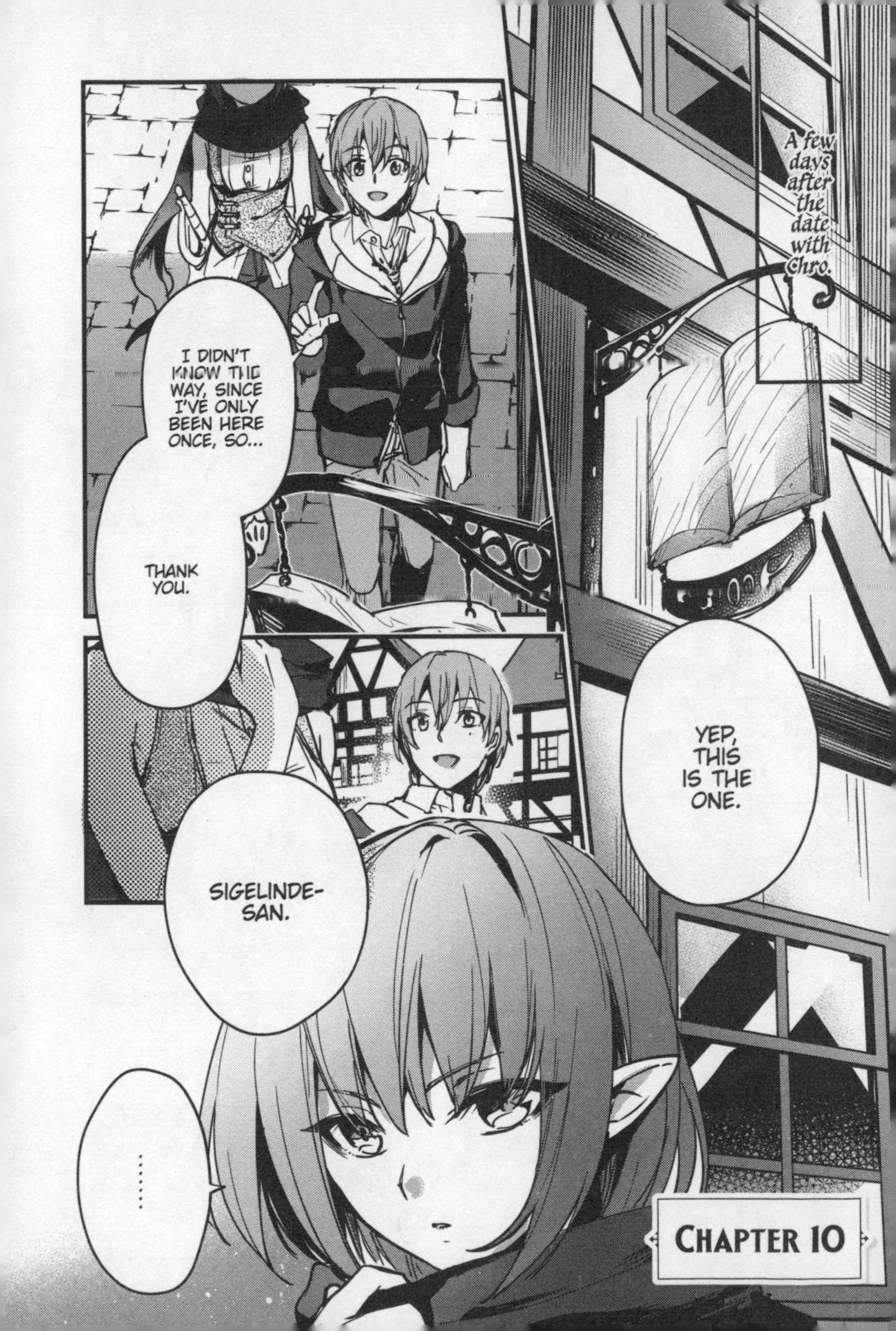
A few days after the date with Chro.
YEP, THIS IS THE ONE.
I DIDN'T KNOW THE WAY, SINCE I'VE ONLY BEEN HERE ONCE, SO...
THANK YOU.
SIGELINDE-SAN.
......
CHAPTER 10

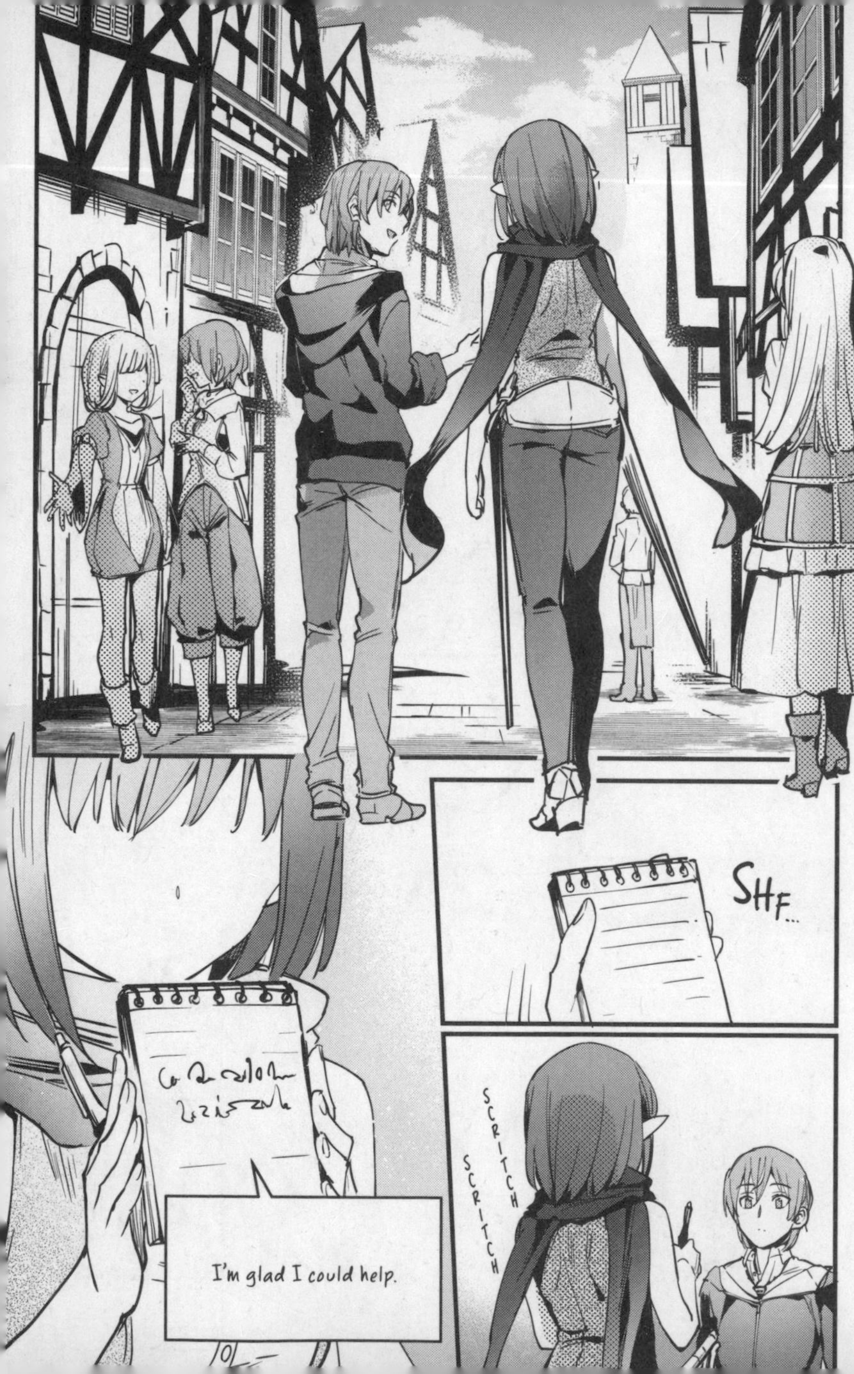
SHF...
SCRITCH
SCRITCH
I'm glad I could help.

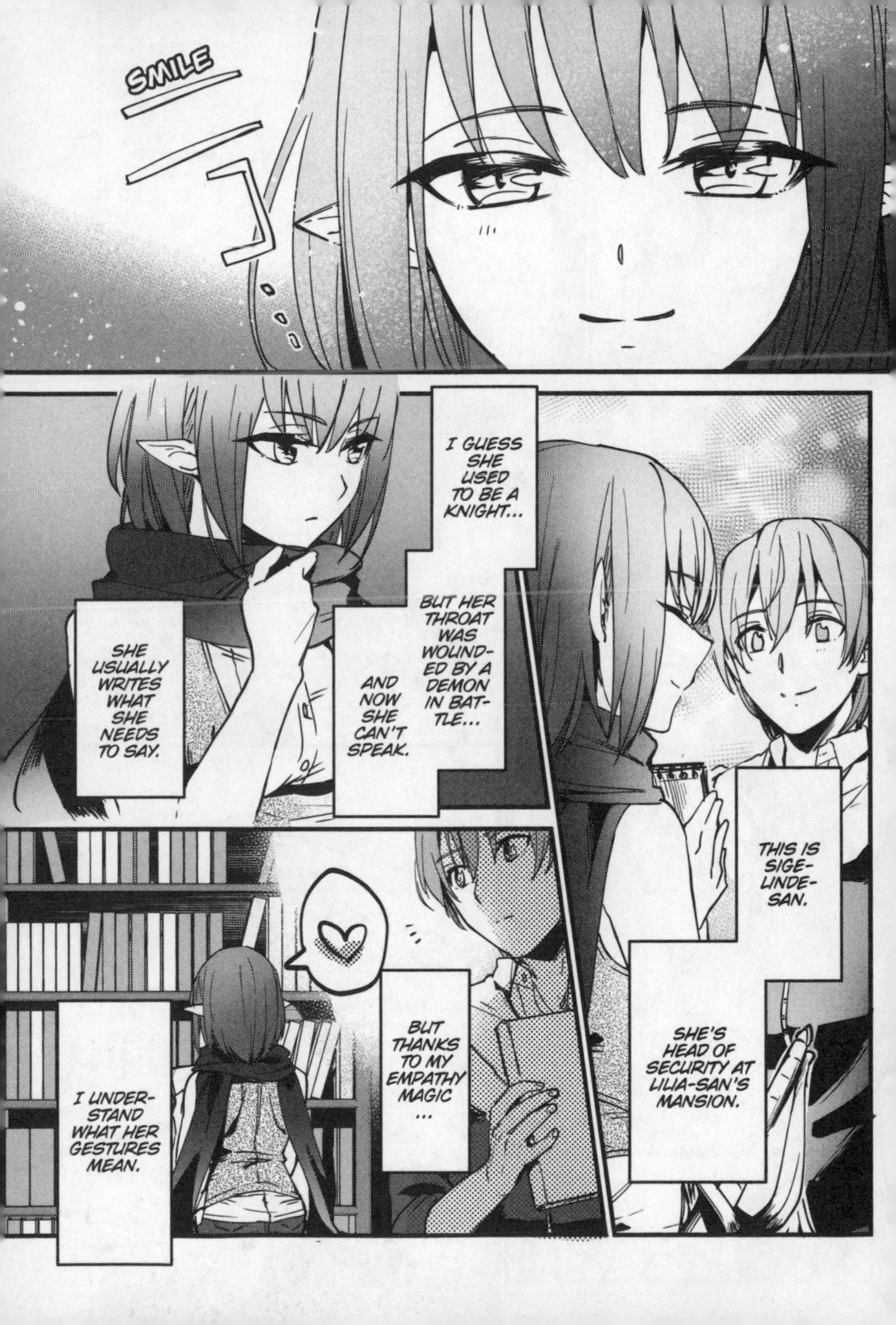
SMILE
THIS IS SIGE-LINDE-SAN.
SHE'S HEAD OF SECURITY AT LILIA-SAN'S MANSION.
I GUESS SHE USED TO BE A KNIGHT...
BUT HER THROAT WAS WOUND-ED BY A DEMON IN BAT-TLE...
AND NOW SHE CAN'T SPEAK.
SHE USUALLY WRITES WHAT SHE NEEDS TO SAY.
BUT THANKS TO MY EMPATHY MAGIC ...
I UNDER-STAND WHAT HER GESTURES MEAN.

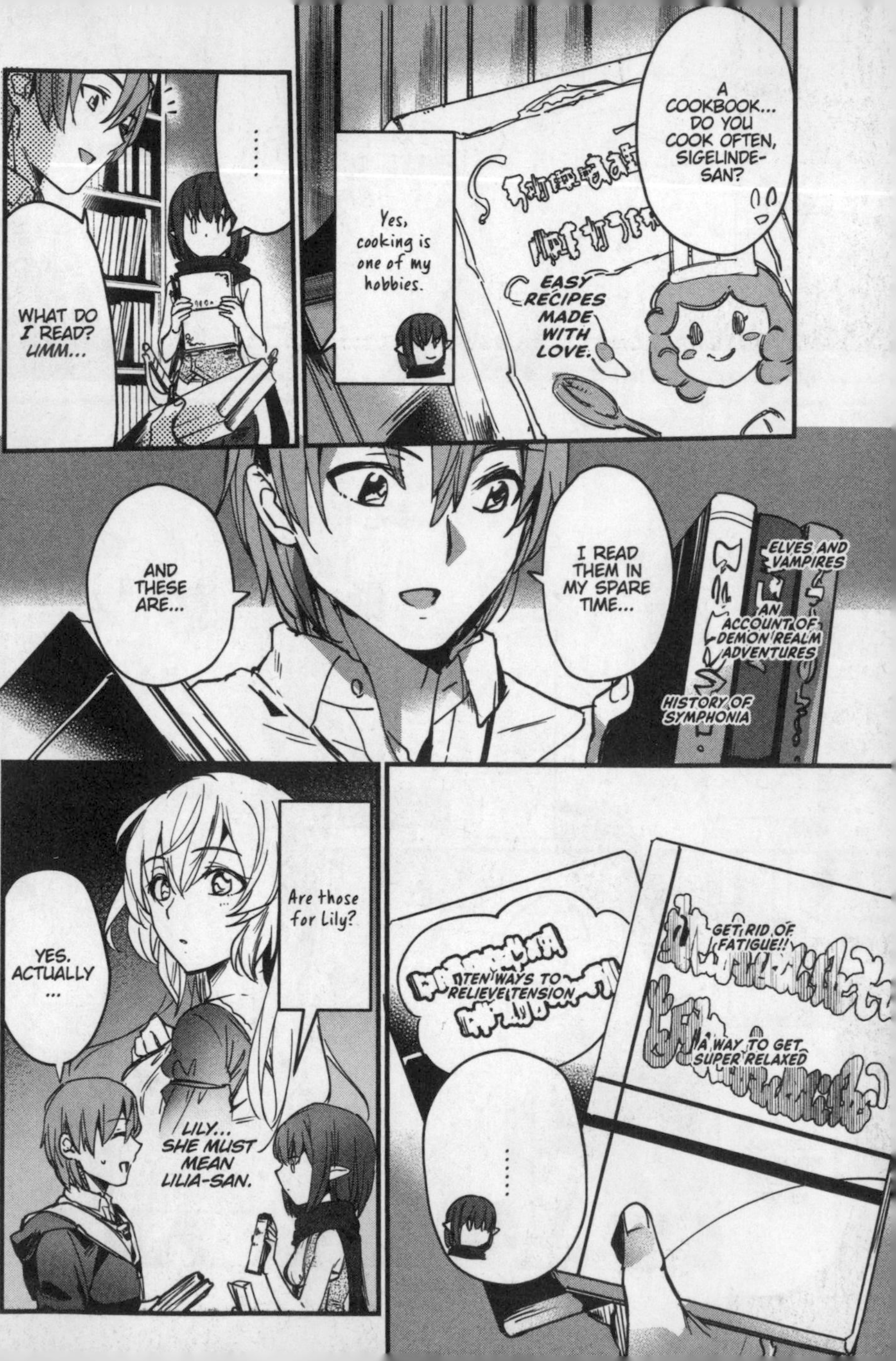
A COOKBOOK... DO YOU COOK OFTEN, SIGELINDE-SAN?
EASY RECIPES MADE WITH LOVE.
Yes, cooking is one of my hobbies.
......
WHAT DO I READ? UMM...
ELVES AND VAMPIRES
AN ACCOUNT OF DEMON REALM ADVENTURES
HISTORY OF SYMPHONIA
I READ THEM IN MY SPARE TIME...
AND THESE ARE...
GET RID OF FATIGUE!!
A WAY TO GET SUPER RELAXED
TEN WAYS TO RELIEVE TENSION
......
Are those for Lily?
YES. ACTUALLY ...
LILY... SHE MUST MEAN LILIA-SAN.

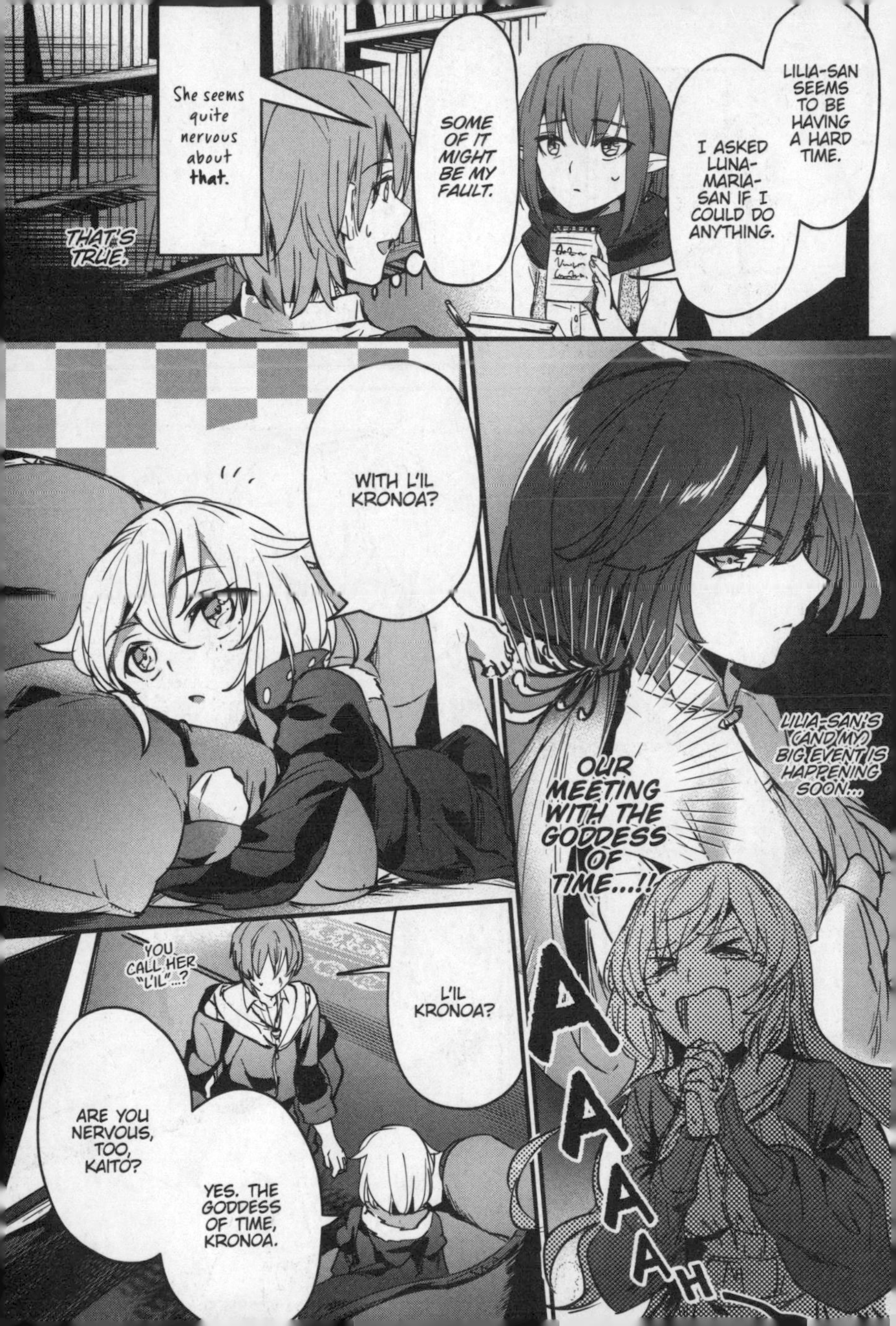
LILIA-SAN SEEMS TO BE HAVING A HARD TIME.
I ASKED LUNA-MARIA-SAN IF I COULD DO ANYTHING.
SOME OF IT MIGHT BE MY FAULT.
She seems quite nervous about **that**.
THAT'S TRUE.
LILIA-SAN'S (AND MY) BIG EVENT IS HAPPENING SOON...
OUR MEETING WITH THE GODDESS OF TIME...!!
AAAAH
WITH L'IL KRONOA?
L'IL KRONOA?
YOU CALL HER "L'IL"...?
ARE YOU NERVOUS, TOO, KAITO?
YES. THE GODDESS OF TIME, KRONOA.

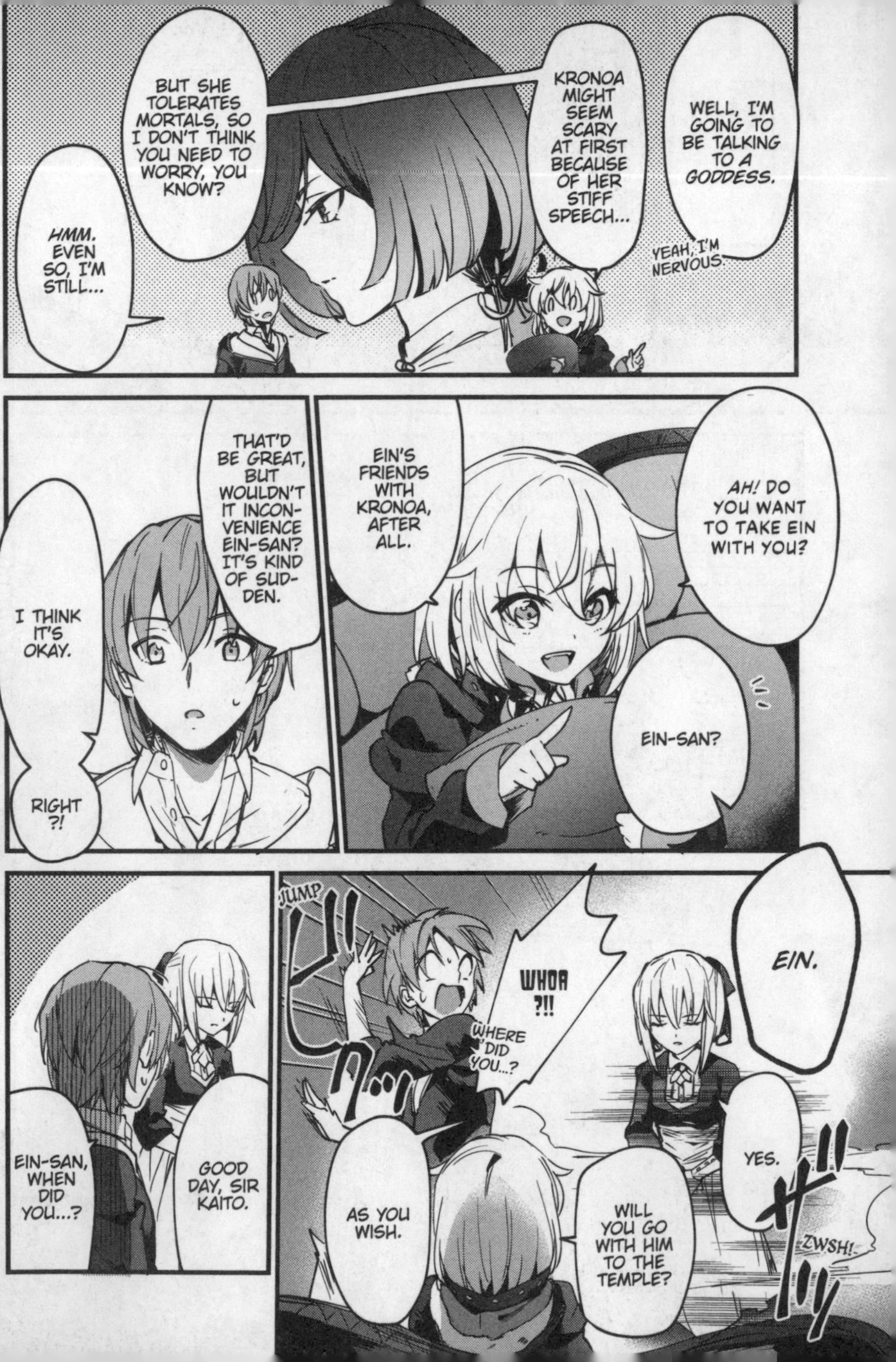
WELL, I'M GOING TO BE TALKING TO A GODDESS.
YEAH, I'M NERVOUS.
KRONOA MIGHT SEEM SCARY AT FIRST BECAUSE OF HER STIFF SPEECH...
BUT SHE TOLERATES MORTALS, SO I DON'T THINK YOU NEED TO WORRY, YOU KNOW?
HMM. EVEN SO, I'M STILL...
AH! DO YOU WANT TO TAKE EIN WITH YOU?
EIN'S FRIENDS WITH KRONOA, AFTER ALL.
EIN-SAN?
THAT'D BE GREAT, BUT WOULDN'T IT INCONVENIENCE EIN-SAN? IT'S KIND OF SUD-DEN.
I THINK IT'S OKAY.
RIGHT?!
EIN.
YES.
ZWSH!
WILL YOU GO WITH HIM TO THE TEMPLE?
AS YOU WISH.
JUMP
WHOA?!!
WHERE DID YOU...?
GOOD DAY, SIR KAITO.
EIN-SAN, WHEN DID YOU...?

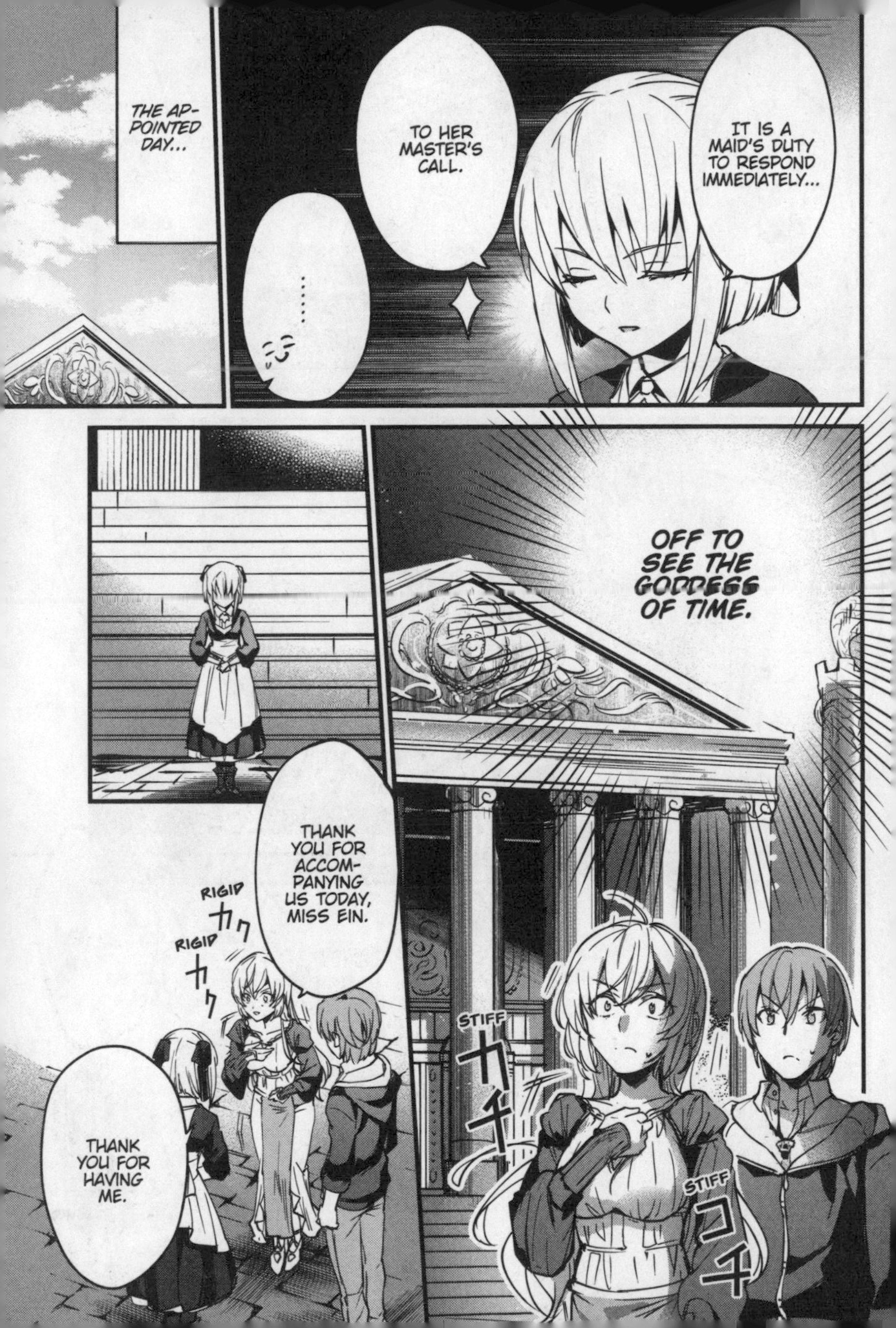
IT IS A MAID'S DUTY TO RESPOND IMMEDIATELY...
TO HER MASTER'S CALL.
......
THE AP-POINTED DAY...
OFF TO SEE THE GODDESS OF TIME.
STIFF
カチ
STIFF
コチ
THANK YOU FOR ACCOM-PANYING US TODAY, MISS EIN.
RIGID
カク
RIGID
カク
THANK YOU FOR HAVING ME.

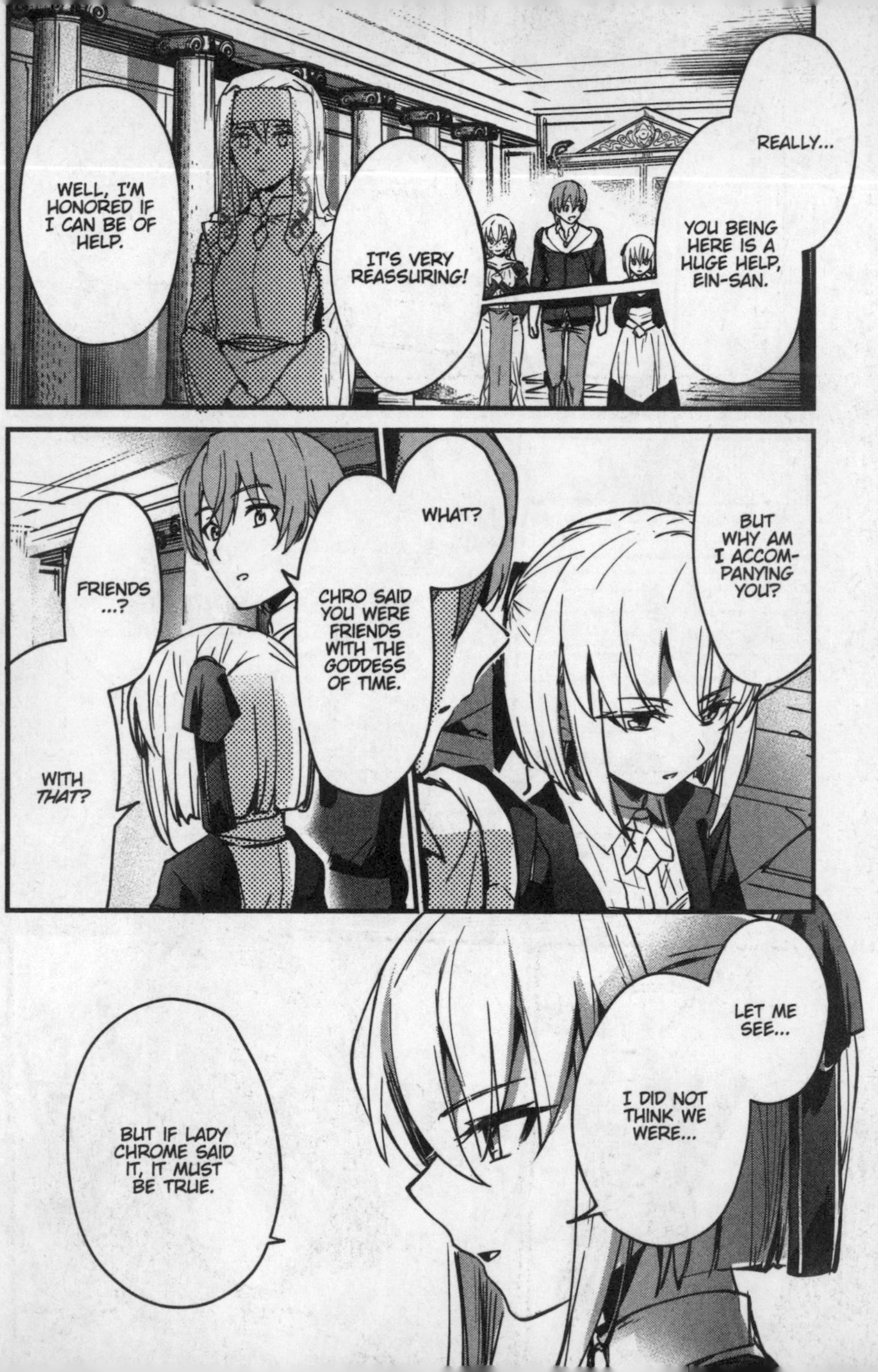
REALLY...
YOU BEING HERE IS A HUGE HELP, EIN-SAN.
IT'S VERY REASSURING!
WELL, I'M HONORED IF I CAN BE OF HELP.
BUT WHY AM I ACCOMPANYING YOU?
WHAT?
CHRO SAID YOU WERE FRIENDS WITH THE GODDESS OF TIME.
FRIENDS ...?
WITH *THAT*?
LET ME SEE...
I DID NOT THINK WE WERE...
BUT IF LADY CHROME SAID IT, IT MUST BE TRUE.

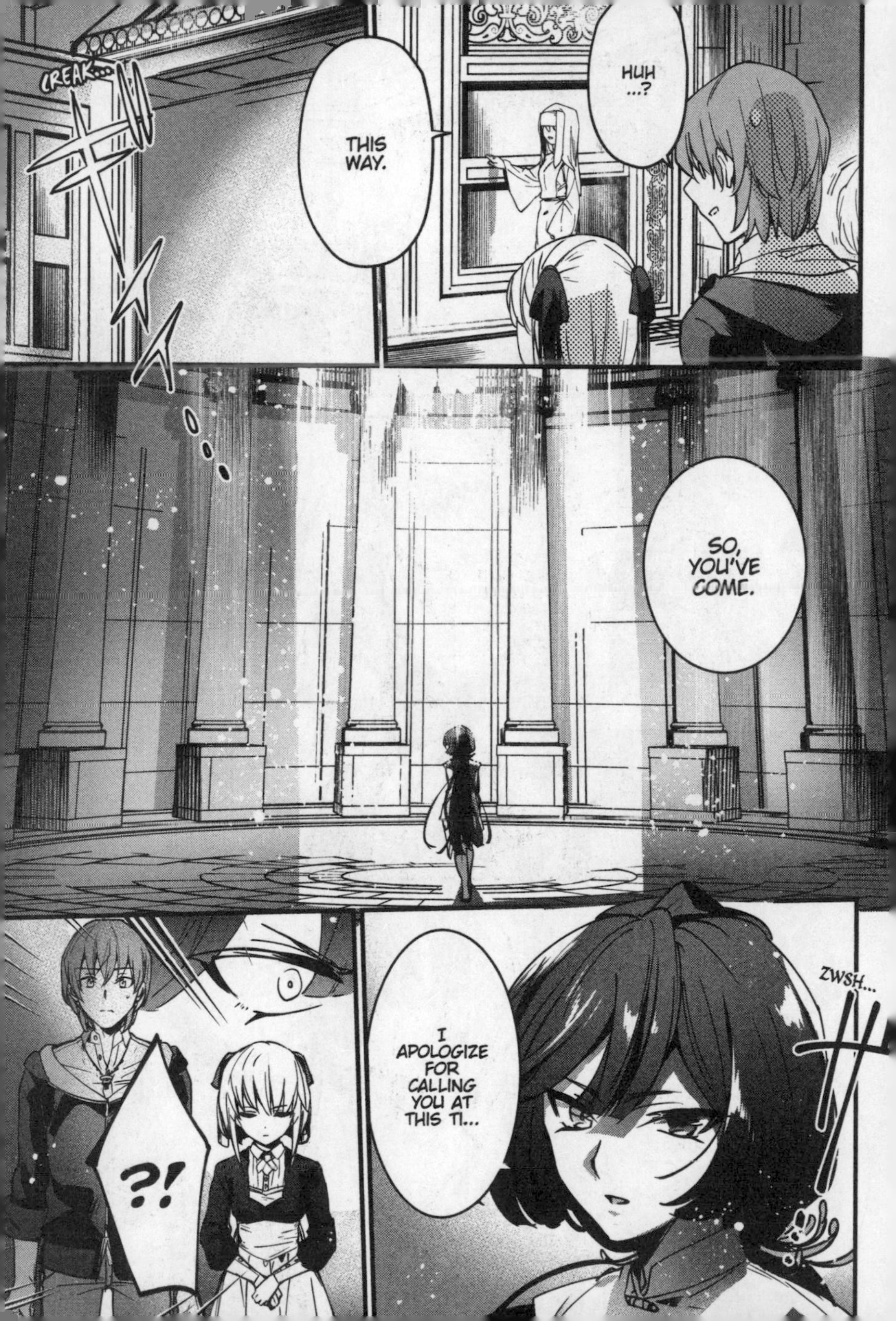
HUH ...?
THIS WAY.
CREAK...
SO, YOU'VE COME.
ZWSH...
I APOLOGIZE FOR CALLING YOU AT THIS TI...
?!

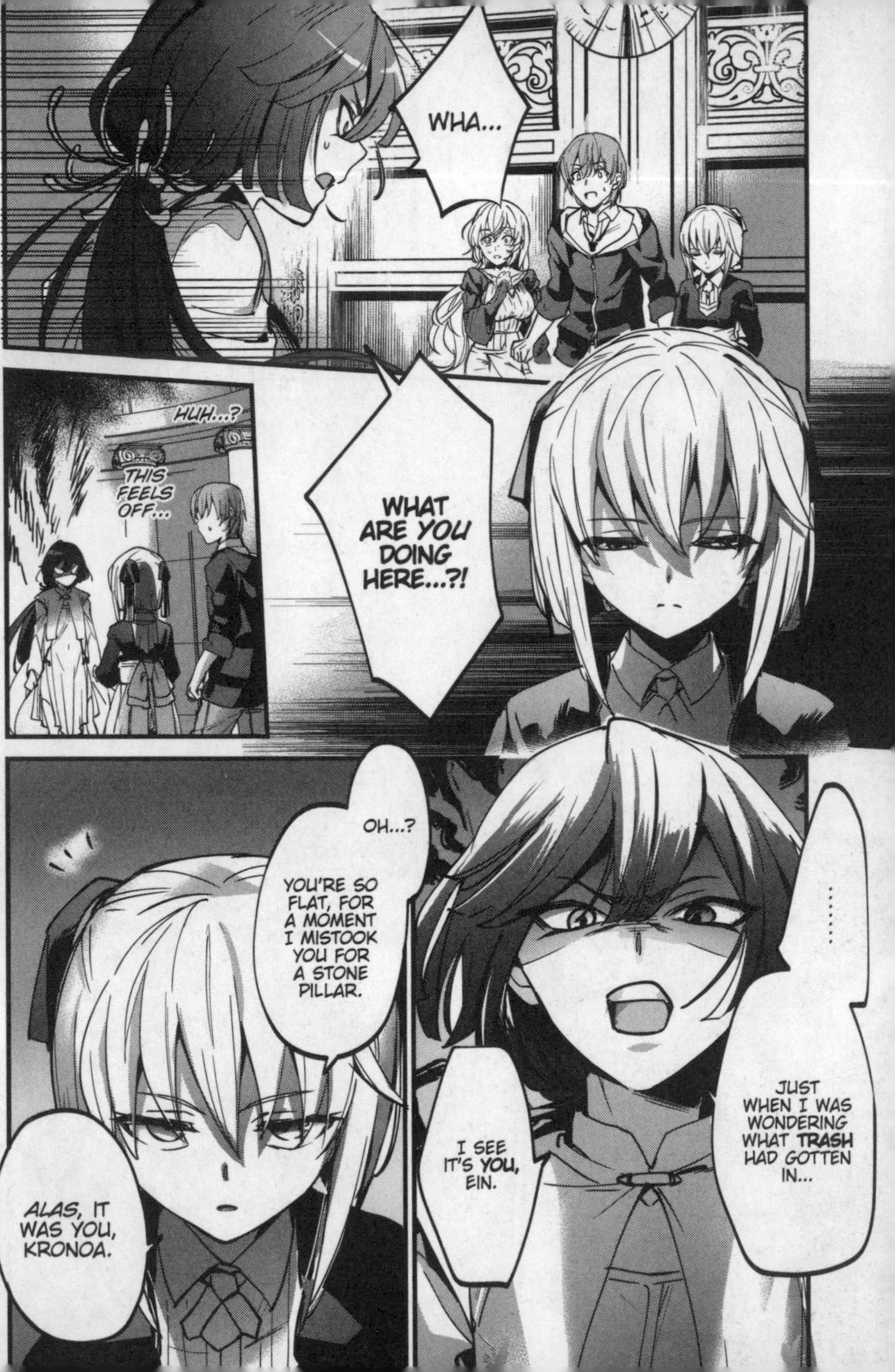
WHA...
WHAT ARE YOU DOING HERE...?!
HUH...?
THIS FEELS OFF...
......
JUST WHEN I WAS WONDERING WHAT TRASH HAD GOTTEN IN...
I SEE IT'S YOU, EIN.
OH...?
YOU'RE SO FLAT, FOR A MOMENT I MISTOOK YOU FOR A STONE PILLAR.
ALAS, IT WAS YOU, KRONOA.

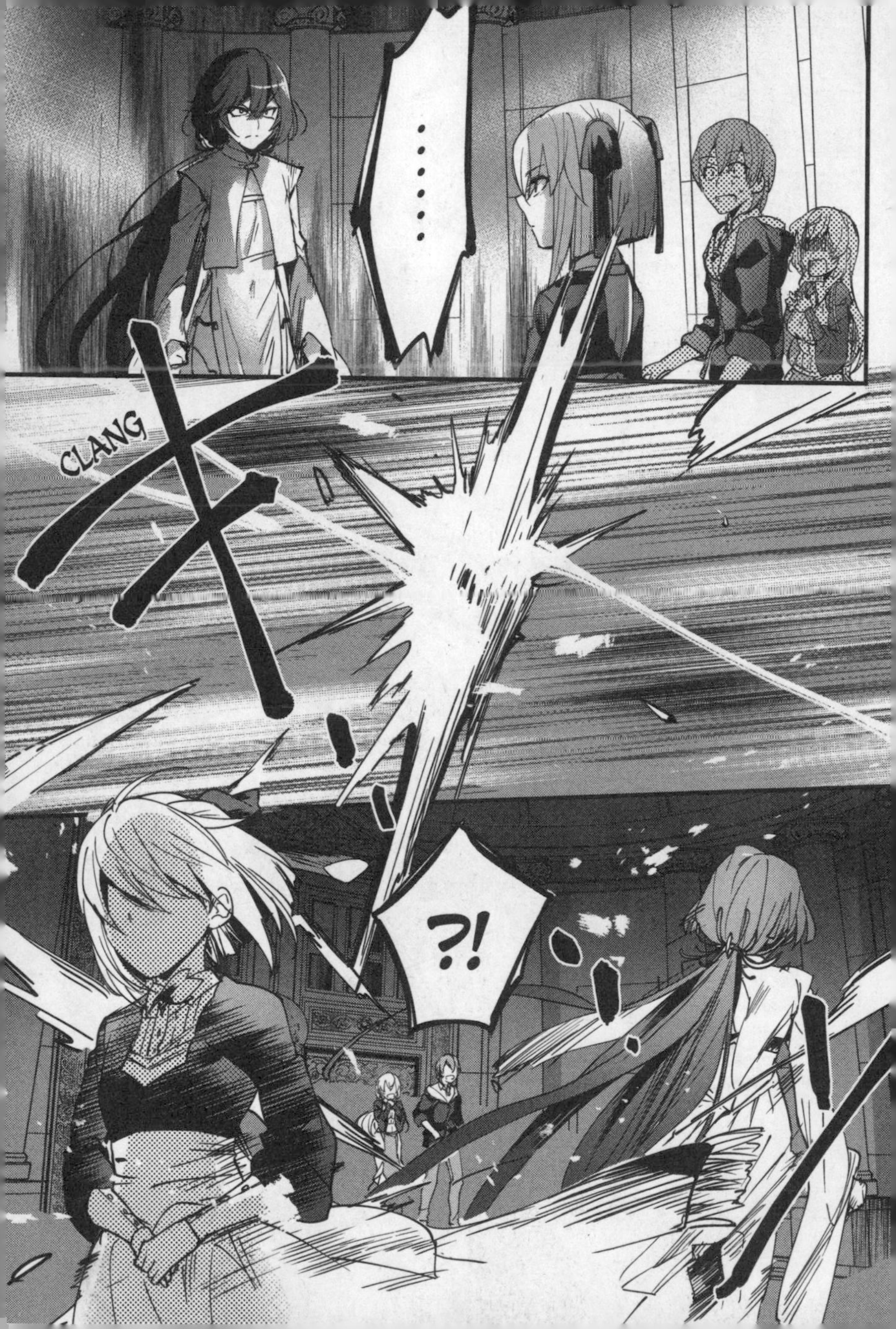
......
CLANG
?!

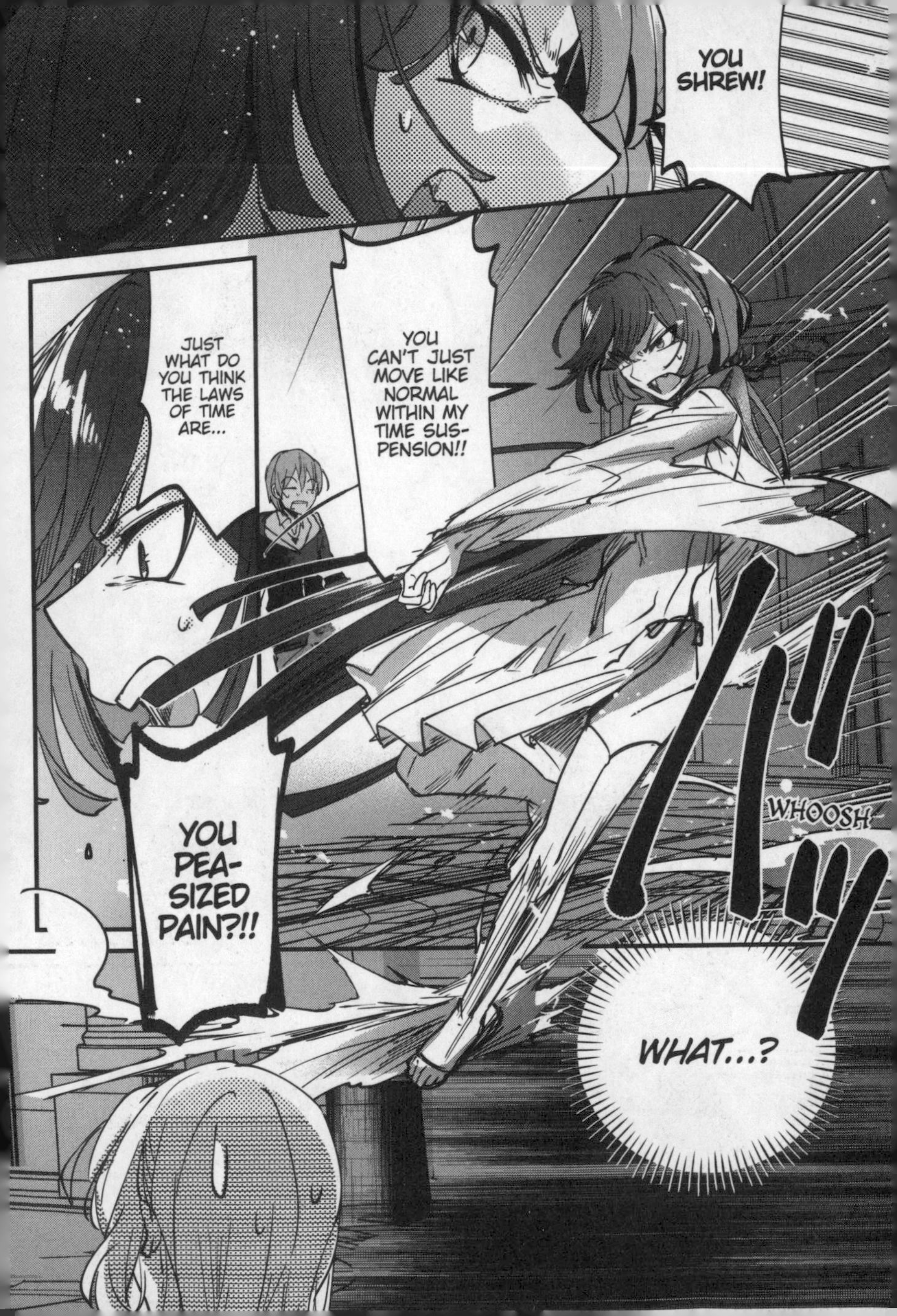
YOU SHREW!
YOU CAN'T JUST MOVE LIKE NORMAL WITHIN MY TIME SUS-PENSION!!
JUST WHAT DO YOU THINK THE LAWS OF TIME ARE...
YOU PEA-SIZED PAIN?!!
WHOOSH
WHAT...?

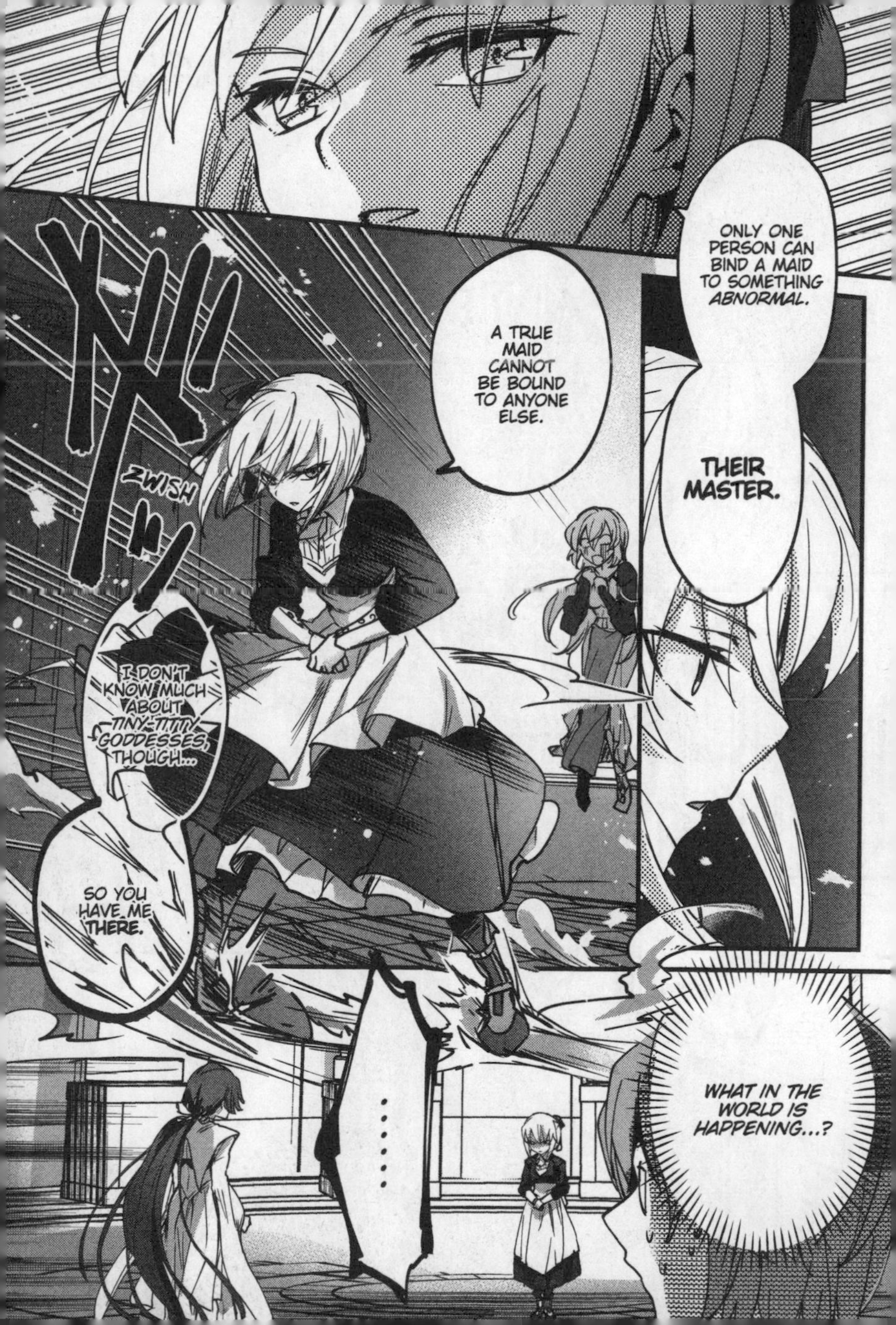
ONLY ONE PERSON CAN BIND A MAID TO SOMETHING ABNORMAL.
THEIR MASTER.
A TRUE MAID CANNOT BE BOUND TO ANYONE ELSE.
ZWISH
I DON'T KNOW MUCH ABOUT TINY-TITTY GODDESSES, THOUGH...
SO YOU HAVE ME THERE.
WHAT IN THE WORLD IS HAPPENING...?
......

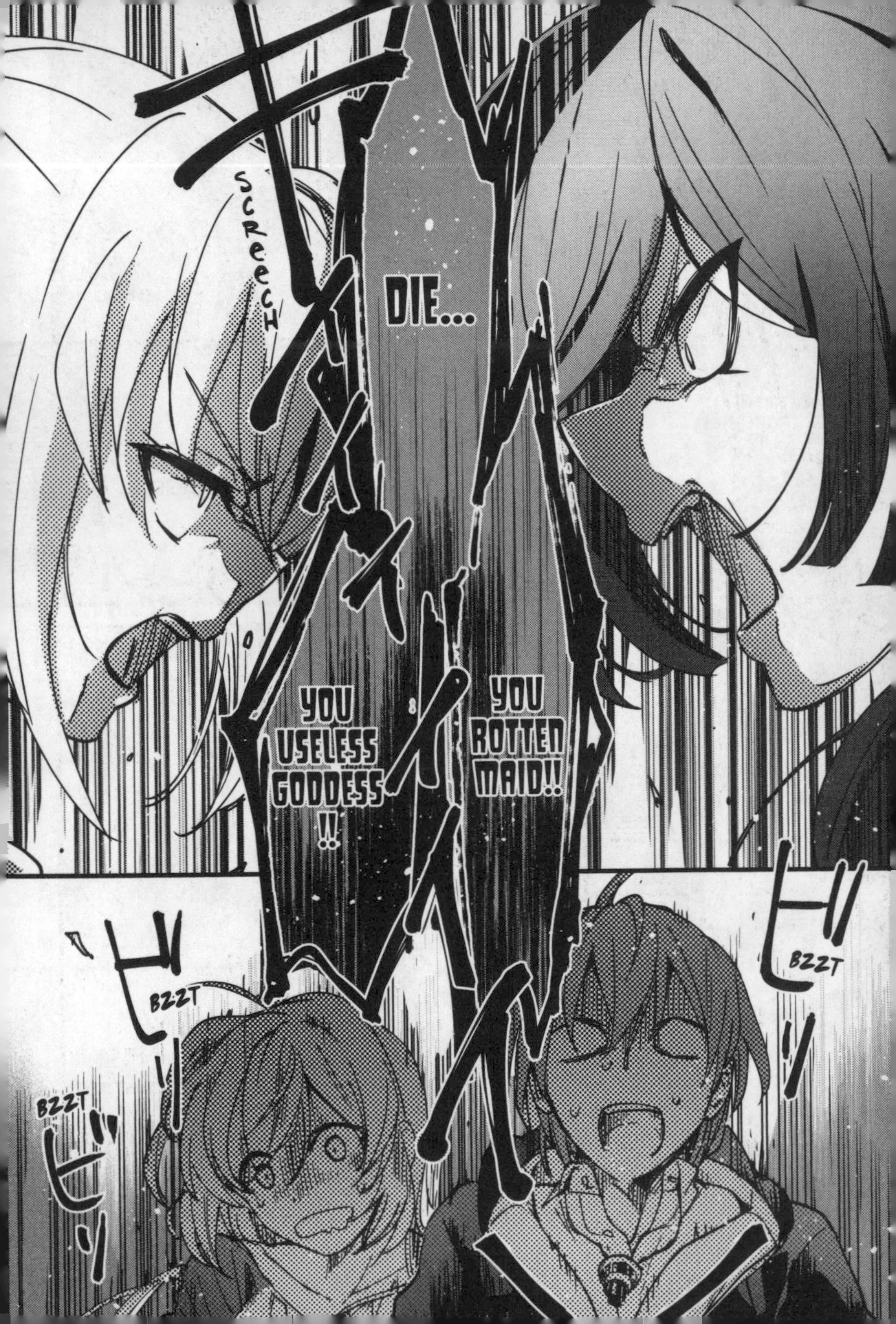
SCREECH
DIE...
YOU ROTTEN MAID!!
YOU USELESS GODDESS!!
BZZT
BZZT
BZZT

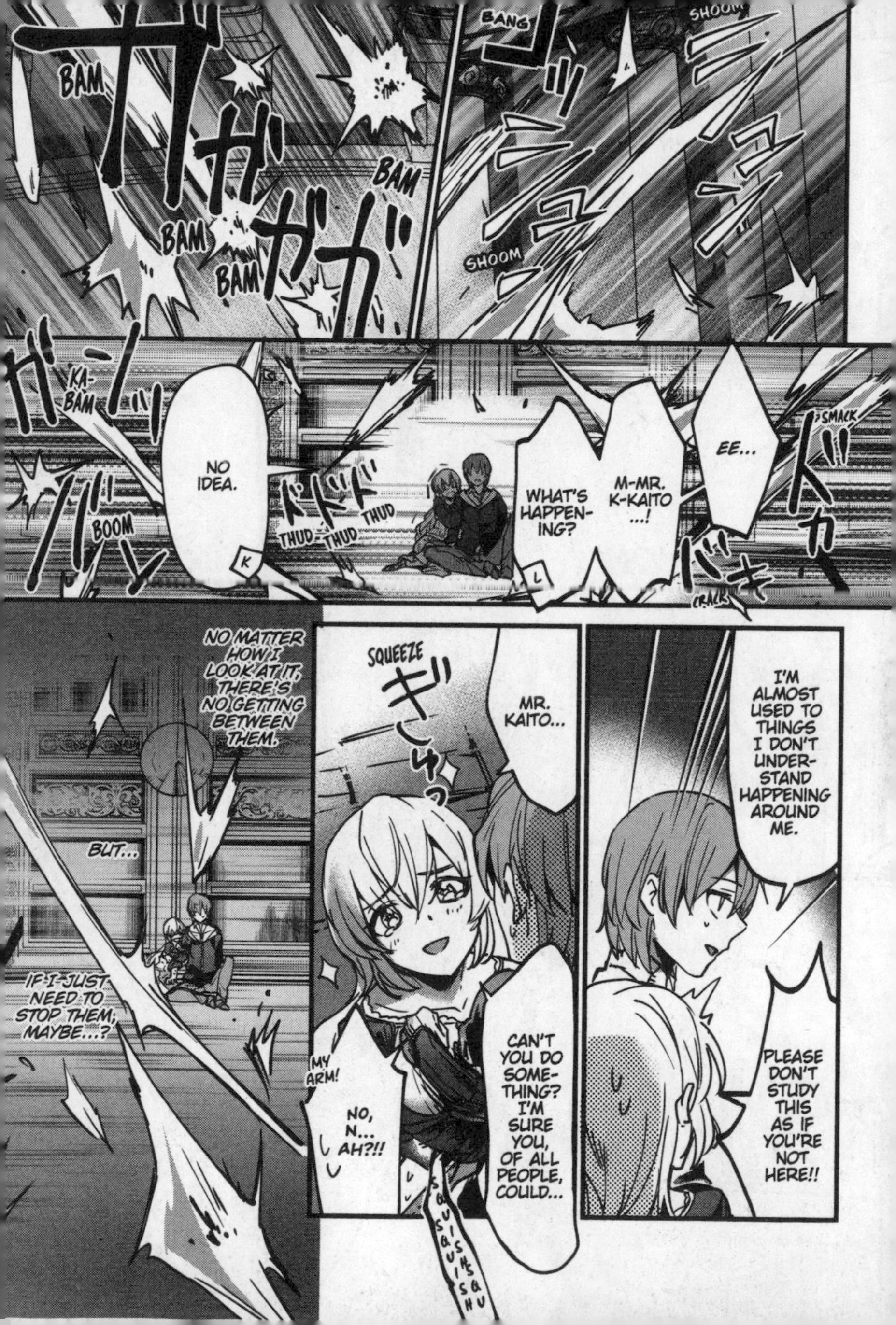
BANG
SHOOM
SHOOM
BAM
BAM
BAM
BAM
SMACK
EE...
M-MR. K-KAITO...!
WHAT'S HAPPEN-ING?
CRACK
NO IDEA.
THUD THUD THUD
KA-BAM
BOOM
I'M ALMOST USED TO THINGS I DON'T UNDER-STAND HAPPENING AROUND ME.
PLEASE DON'T STUDY THIS AS IF YOU'RE NOT HERE!!
SQUEEZE
MR. KAITO...
CAN'T YOU DO SOME-THING? I'M SURE YOU, OF ALL PEOPLE, COULD...
NO, N... AH?!!
MY ARM!
SQUISH SQUISH
NO MATTER HOW I LOOK AT IT, THERE'S NO GETTING BETWEEN THEM.
BUT...
IF I JUST NEED TO STOP THEM, MAYBE...?

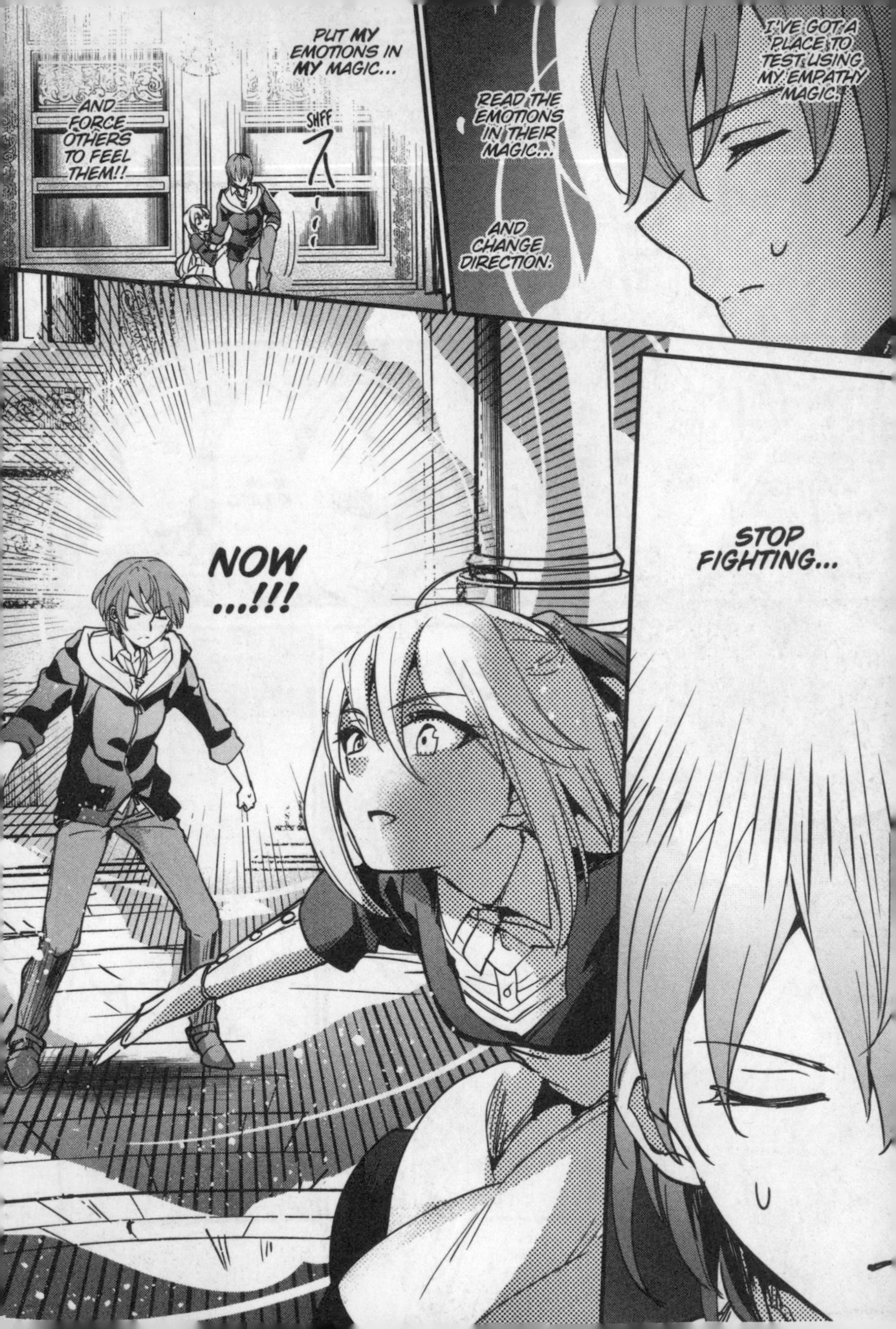
I'VE GOT A PLACE TO TEST USING MY EMPATHY MAGIC.
READ THE EMOTIONS IN THEIR MAGIC...
AND CHANGE DIRECTION.
PUT MY EMOTIONS IN MY MAGIC...
AND FORCE OTHERS TO FEEL THEM!!
SHFF
STOP FIGHTING...
NOW ...!!!

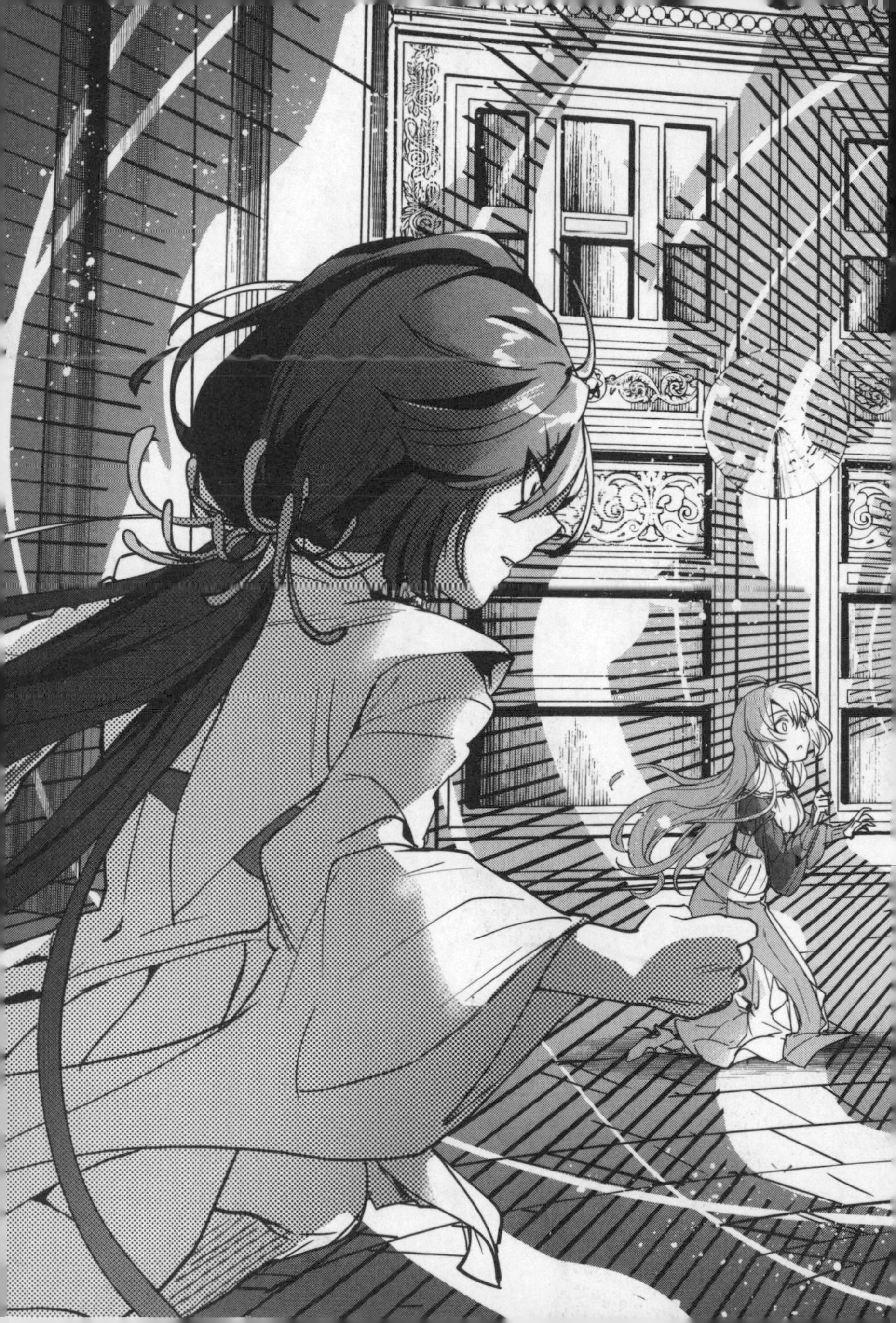

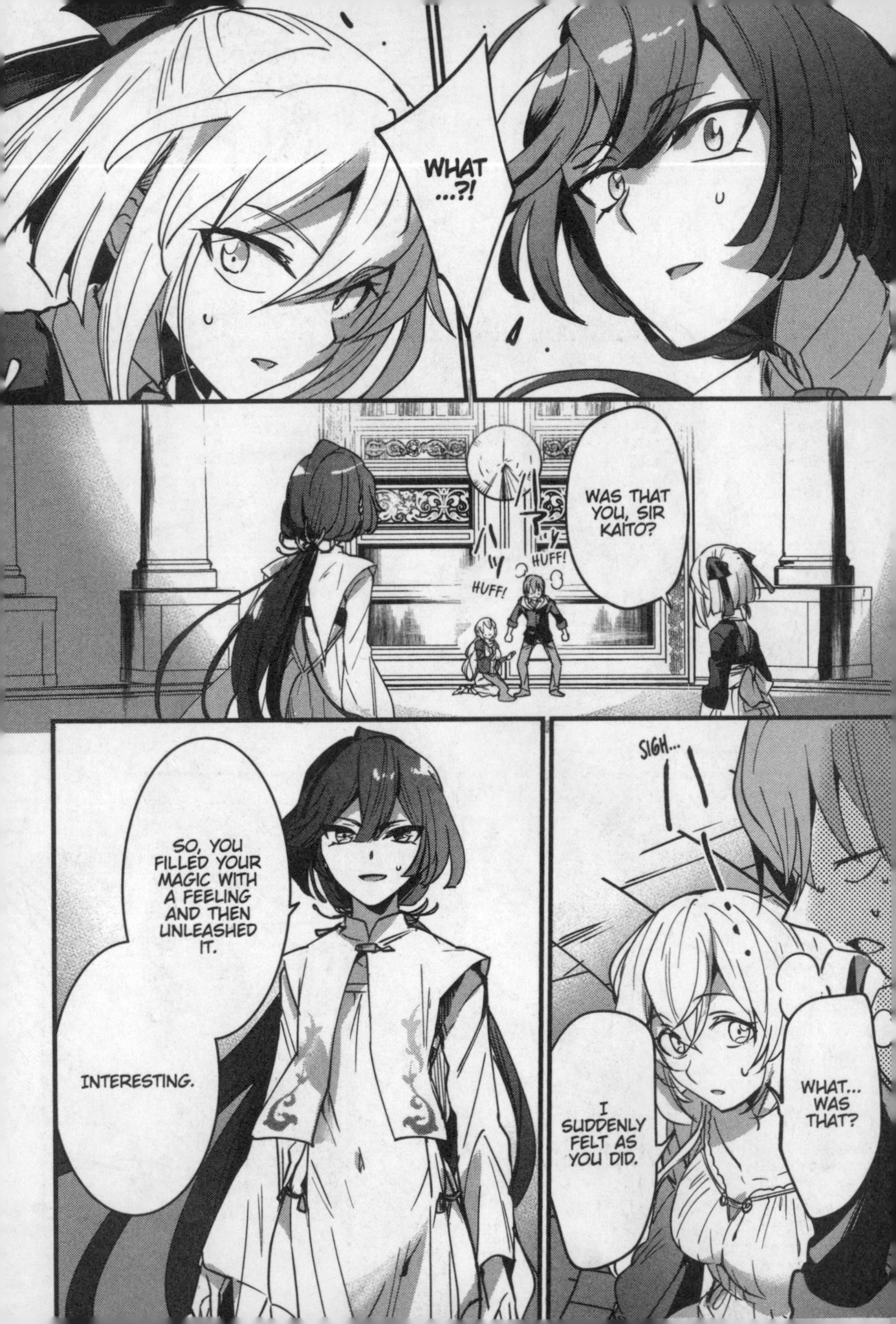
WHAT ...?!
WAS THAT YOU, SIR KAITO?
HUFF!
HUFF!
SIGH...
WHAT... WAS THAT?
I SUDDENLY FELT AS YOU DID.
SO, YOU FILLED YOUR MAGIC WITH A FEELING AND THEN UNLEASHED IT.
INTERESTING.

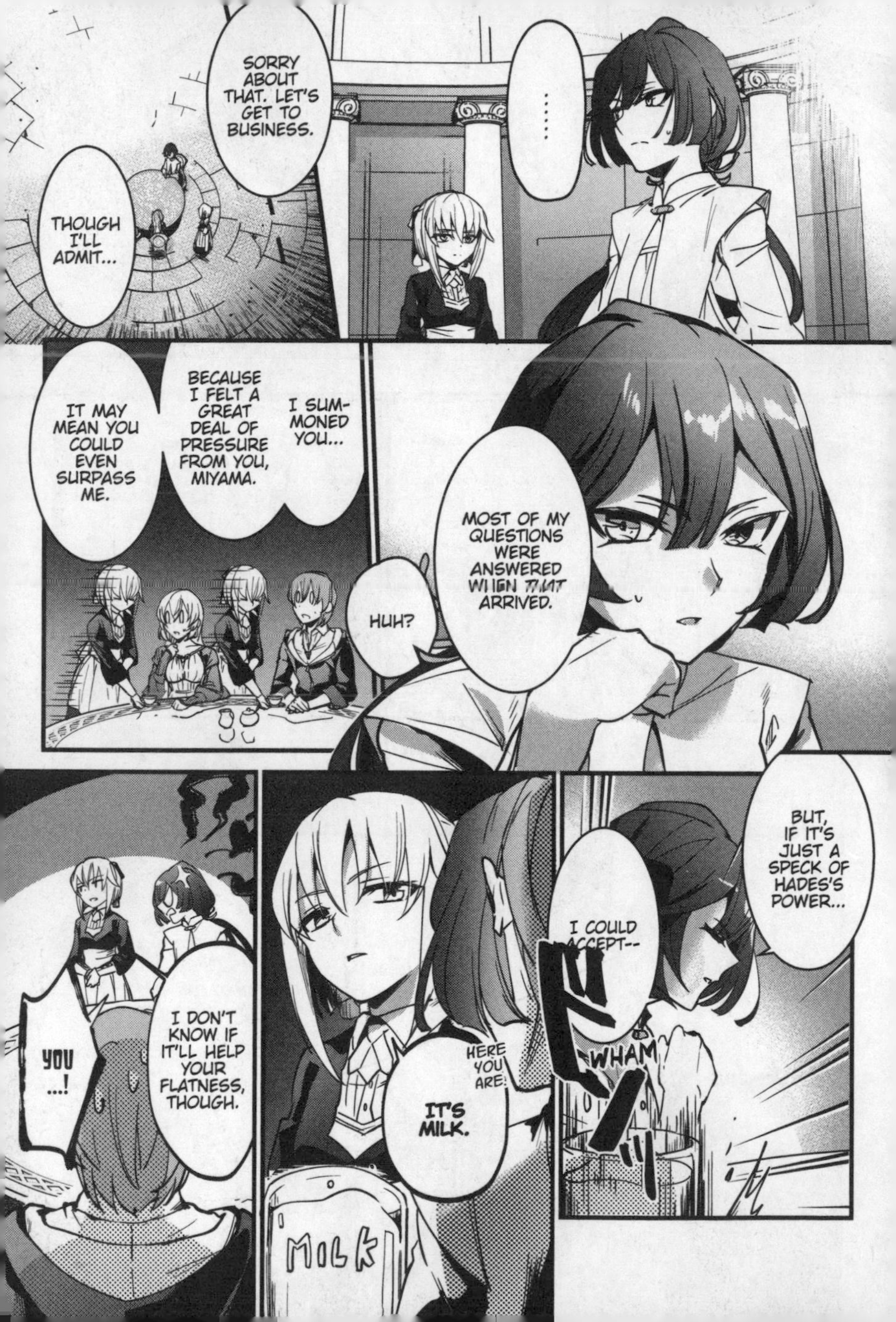
……
SORRY ABOUT THAT. LET'S GET TO BUSINESS.
THOUGH I'LL ADMIT...
MOST OF MY QUESTIONS WERE ANSWERED WHEN THAT ARRIVED.
HUH?
I SUM-MONED YOU...
BECAUSE I FELT A GREAT DEAL OF PRESSURE FROM YOU, MIYAMA.
IT MAY MEAN YOU COULD EVEN SURPASS ME.
BUT, IF IT'S JUST A SPECK OF HADES'S POWER...
I COULD ACCEPT--
WHAM
HERE YOU ARE!
IT'S MILK.
MILK
I DON'T KNOW IF IT'LL HELP YOUR FLATNESS, THOUGH.
YOU ...!

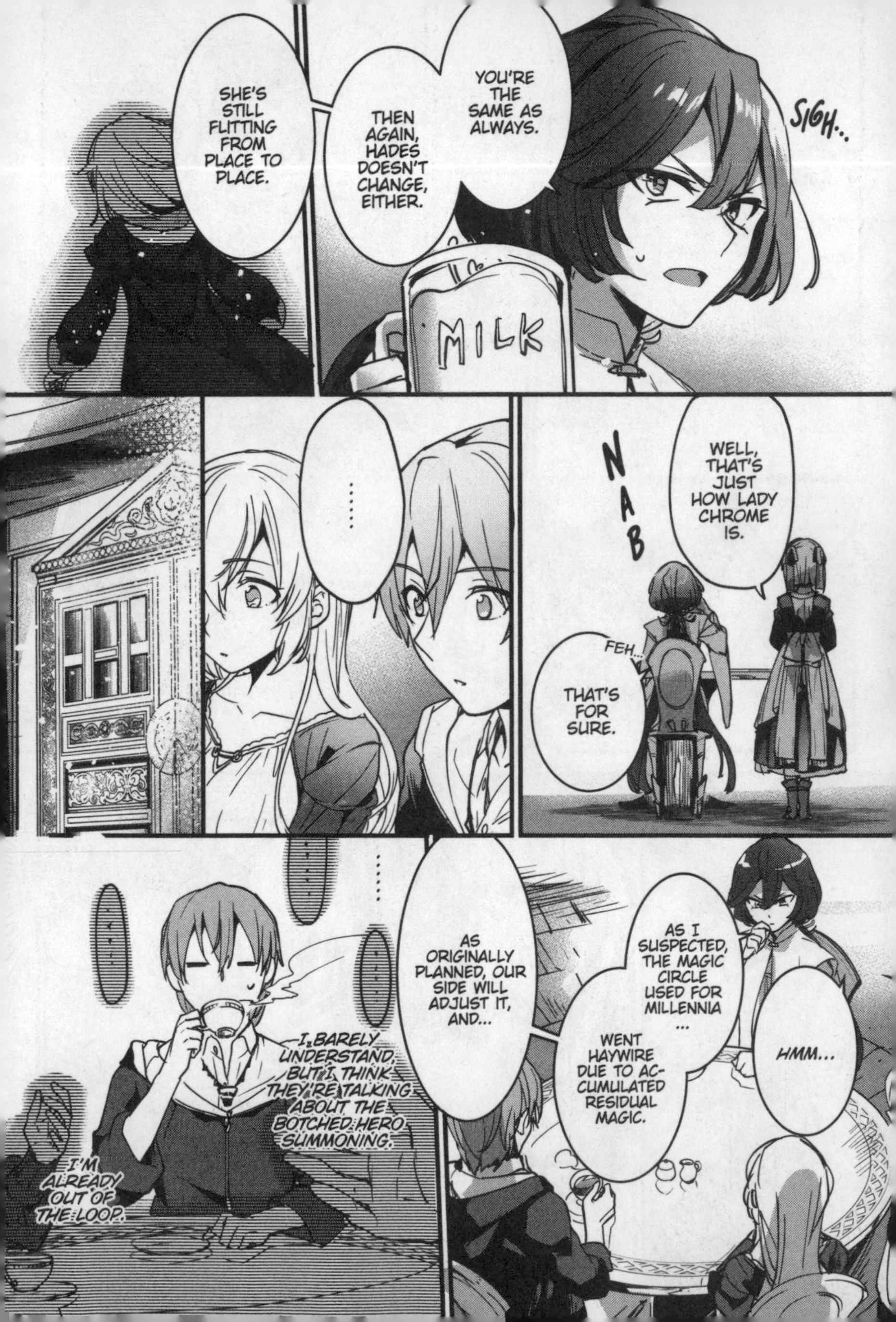
SIGH...
YOU'RE THE SAME AS ALWAYS.
THEN AGAIN, HADES DOESN'T CHANGE, EITHER.
SHE'S STILL FLITTING FROM PLACE TO PLACE.
MILK
NAB
WELL, THAT'S JUST HOW LADY CHROME IS.
FEH...
THAT'S FOR SURE.
......
AS I SUSPECTED, THE MAGIC CIRCLE USED FOR MILLENNIA ...
WENT HAYWIRE DUE TO AC-CUMULATED RESIDUAL MAGIC.
HMM...
AS ORIGINALLY PLANNED, OUR SIDE WILL ADJUST IT, AND...
......
......
......
I BARELY UNDERSTAND, BUT I THINK THEY'RE TALKING ABOUT THE BOTCHED HERO SUMMONING.
I'M ALREADY OUT OF THE LOOP.

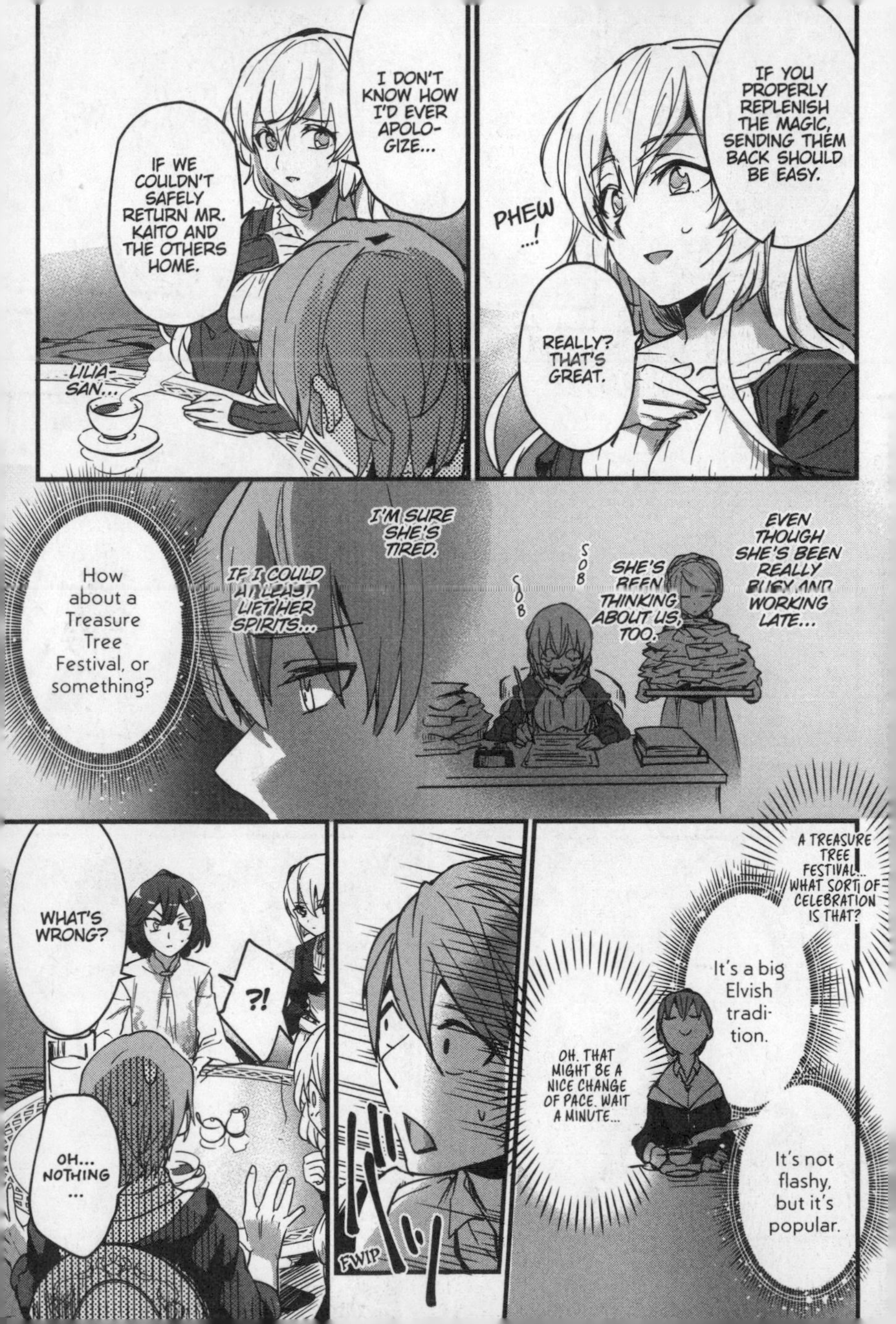
IF YOU PROPERLY REPLENISH THE MAGIC, SENDING THEM BACK SHOULD BE EASY.
PHEW ...!
REALLY? THAT'S GREAT.
I DON'T KNOW HOW I'D EVER APOLOGIZE...
IF WE COULDN'T SAFELY RETURN MR. KAITO AND THE OTHERS HOME.
LILIA-SAN...
EVEN THOUGH SHE'S BEEN REALLY BUSY AND WORKING LATE...
SHE'S BEEN THINKING ABOUT US, TOO.
SOB
SOB
I'M SURE SHE'S TIRED.
IF I COULD AT LEAST LIFT HER SPIRITS...
How about a Treasure Tree Festival, or something?
A TREASURE TREE FESTIVAL... WHAT SORT OF CELEBRATION IS THAT?
It's a big Elvish tradition.
It's not flashy, but it's popular.
OH. THAT MIGHT BE A NICE CHANGE OF PACE. WAIT A MINUTE...
FWIP
WHAT'S WRONG?
?!
OH... NOTHING...

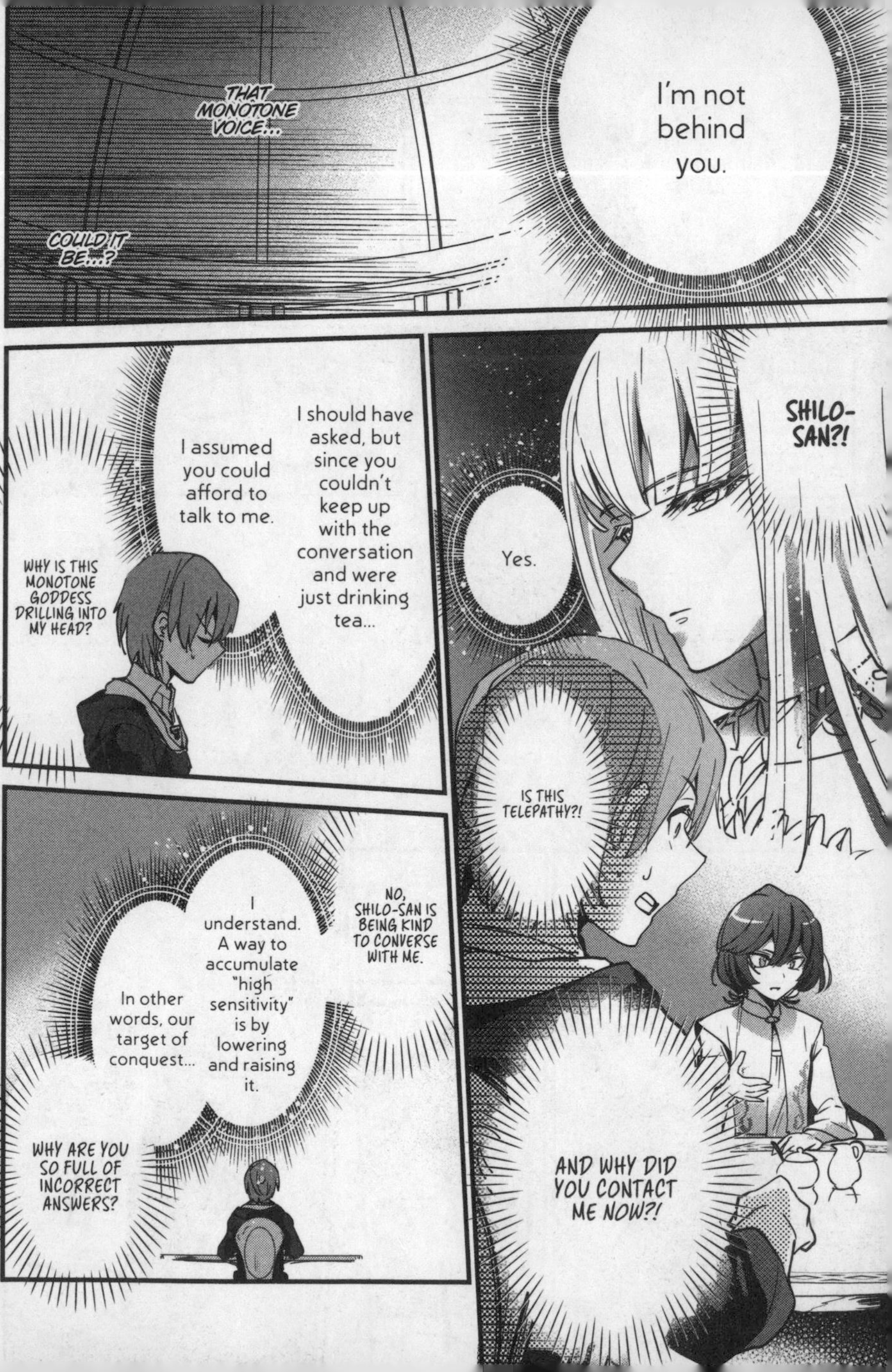
I'm not behind you.
THAT MONOTONE VOICE...
COULD IT BE...?
SHILO-SAN?!
Yes.
IS THIS TELEPATHY?!
AND WHY DID YOU CONTACT ME NOW?!
I should have asked, but since you couldn't keep up with the conversation and were just drinking tea...
I assumed you could afford to talk to me.
WHY IS THIS MONOTONE GODDESS DRILLING INTO MY HEAD?
NO, SHILO-SAN IS BEING KIND TO CONVERSE WITH ME.
I understand. A way to accumulate "high sensitivity" is by lowering and raising it.
In other words, our target of conquest...
WHY ARE YOU SO FULL OF INCORRECT ANSWERS?

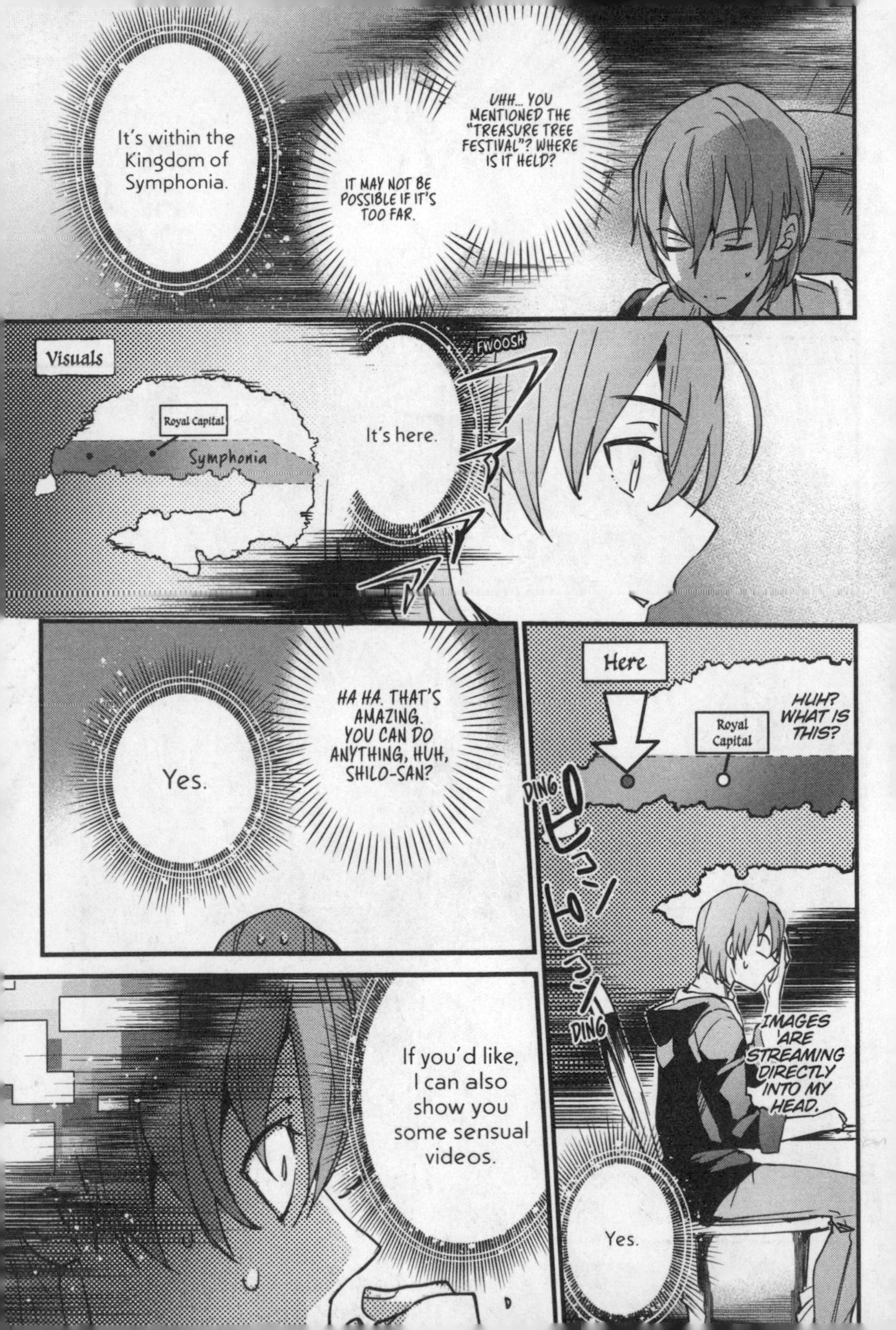
UHH... YOU MENTIONED THE "TREASURE TREE FESTIVAL"? WHERE IS IT HELD?
IT MAY NOT BE POSSIBLE IF IT'S TOO FAR.
It's within the Kingdom of Symphonia.
FWOOSH
It's here.
Visuals
Royal Capital
Symphonia
Here
Royal Capital
HUH? WHAT IS THIS?
DING
DING
IMAGES ARE STREAMING DIRECTLY INTO MY HEAD.
Yes.
HA HA. THAT'S AMAZING. YOU CAN DO ANYTHING, HUH, SHILO-SAN?
Yes.
If you'd like, I can also show you some sensual videos.

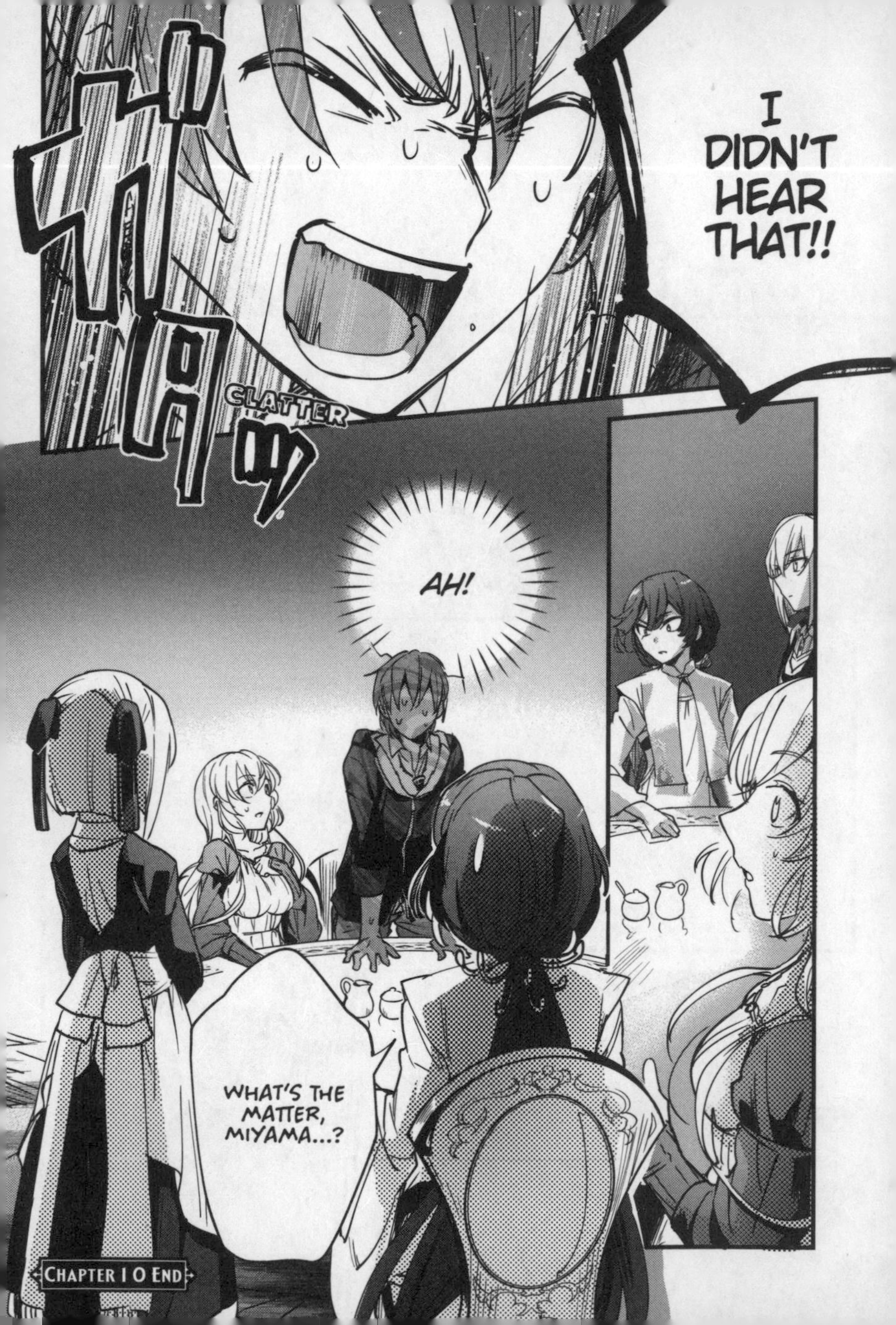
I DIDN'T HEAR THAT!!
CLATTER
AH!
WHAT'S THE MATTER, MIYAMA...?
CHAPTER 10 END

I GOT CAUGHT
UP IN A HERO
SUMMONS,
BUT THE OTHER WORLD
WAS AT PEACE!

I GOT CAUGHT UP IN A HERO SUMMONS,

BUT THE OTHER WORLD WAS AT PEACE!

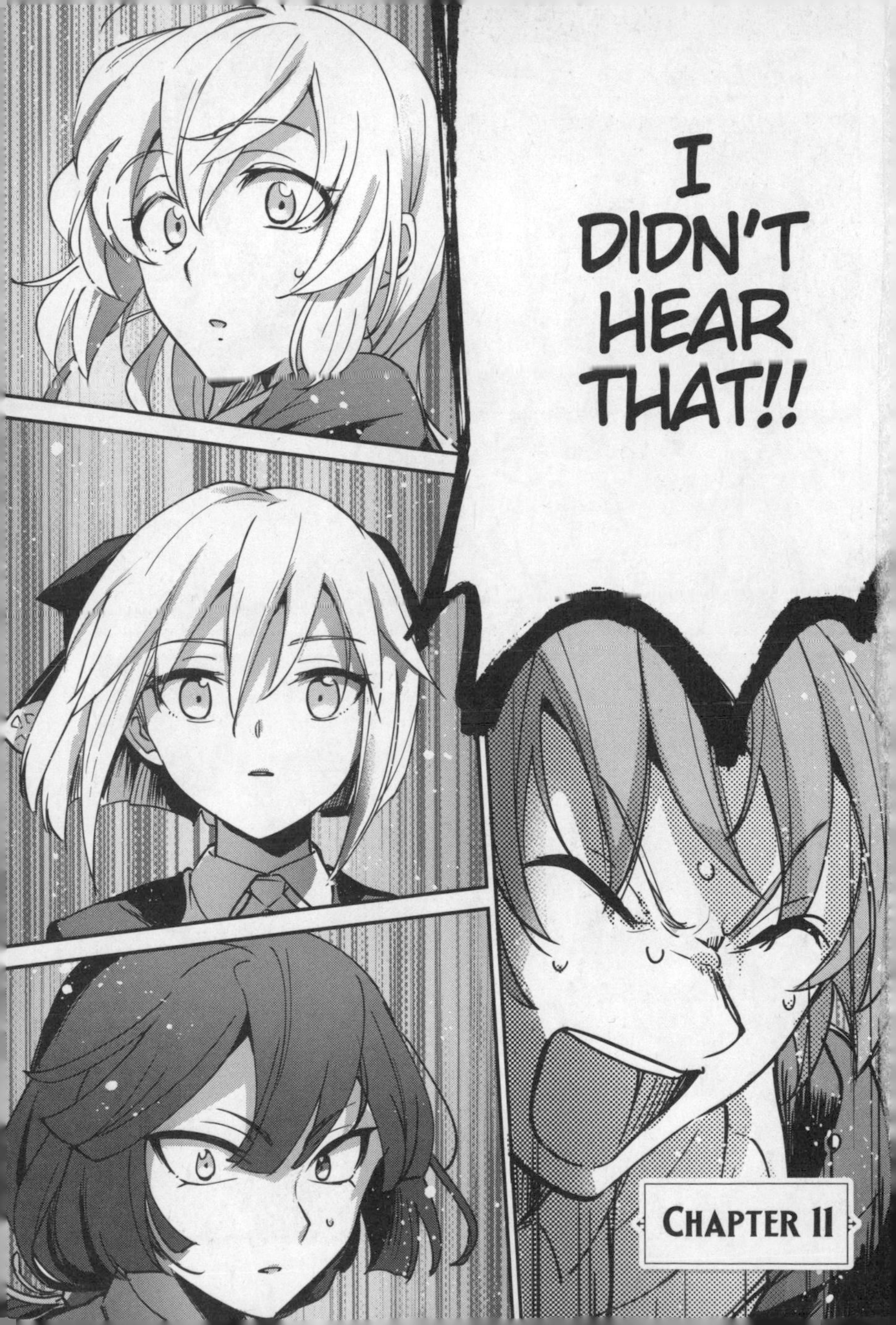
I DIDN'T HEAR THAT!!
CHAPTER 11

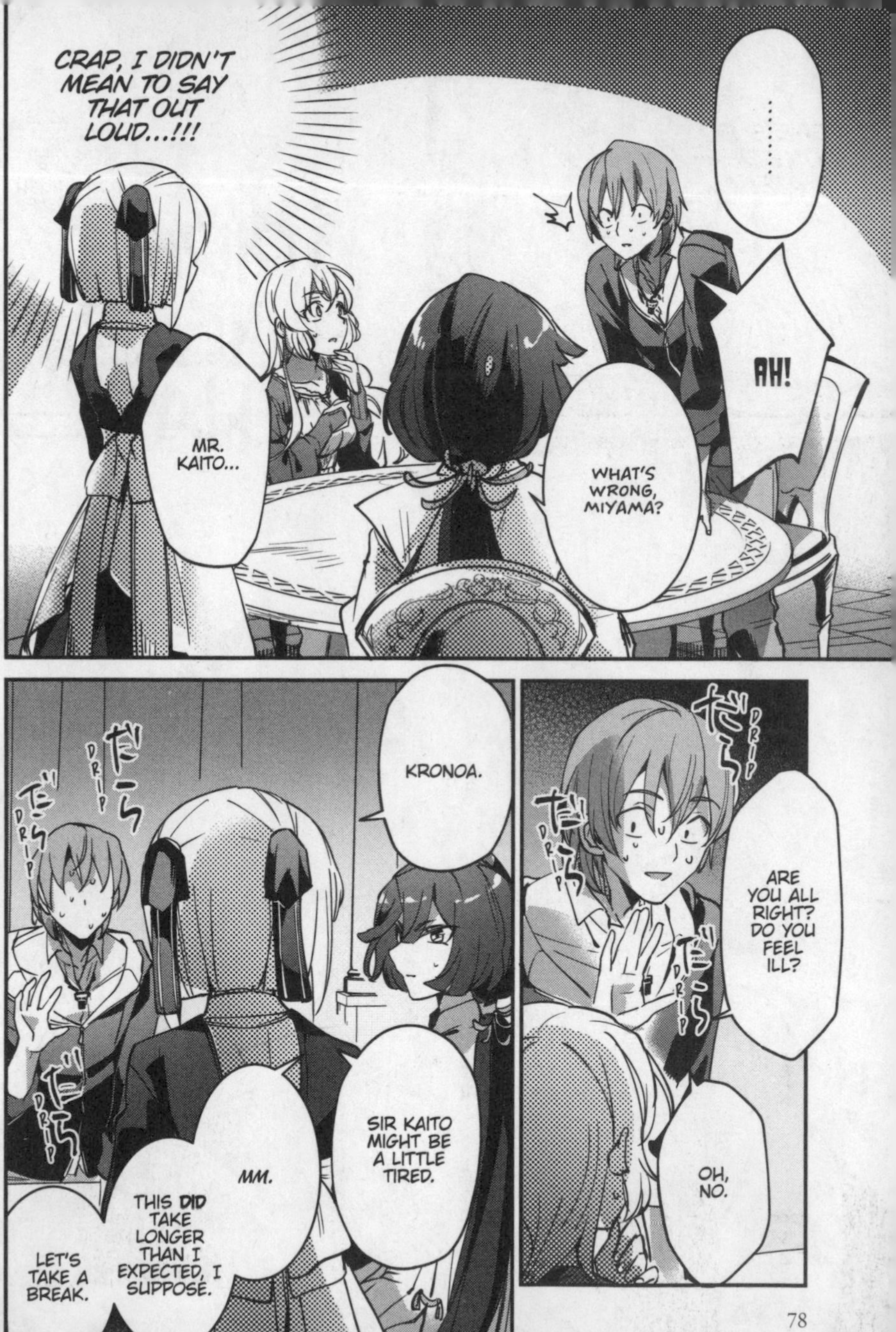
......
AH!
CRAP, I DIDN'T MEAN TO SAY THAT OUT LOUD...!!!
WHAT'S WRONG, MIYAMA?
MR. KAITO...
だら DRIP
だら DRIP
ARE YOU ALL RIGHT? DO YOU FEEL ILL?
だら DRIP
OH, NO.
KRONOA.
だら DRIP
だら DRIP
SIR KAITO MIGHT BE A LITTLE TIRED.
だら DRIP
MM.
THIS DID TAKE LONGER THAN I EXPECTED, I SUPPOSE.
LET'S TAKE A BREAK.

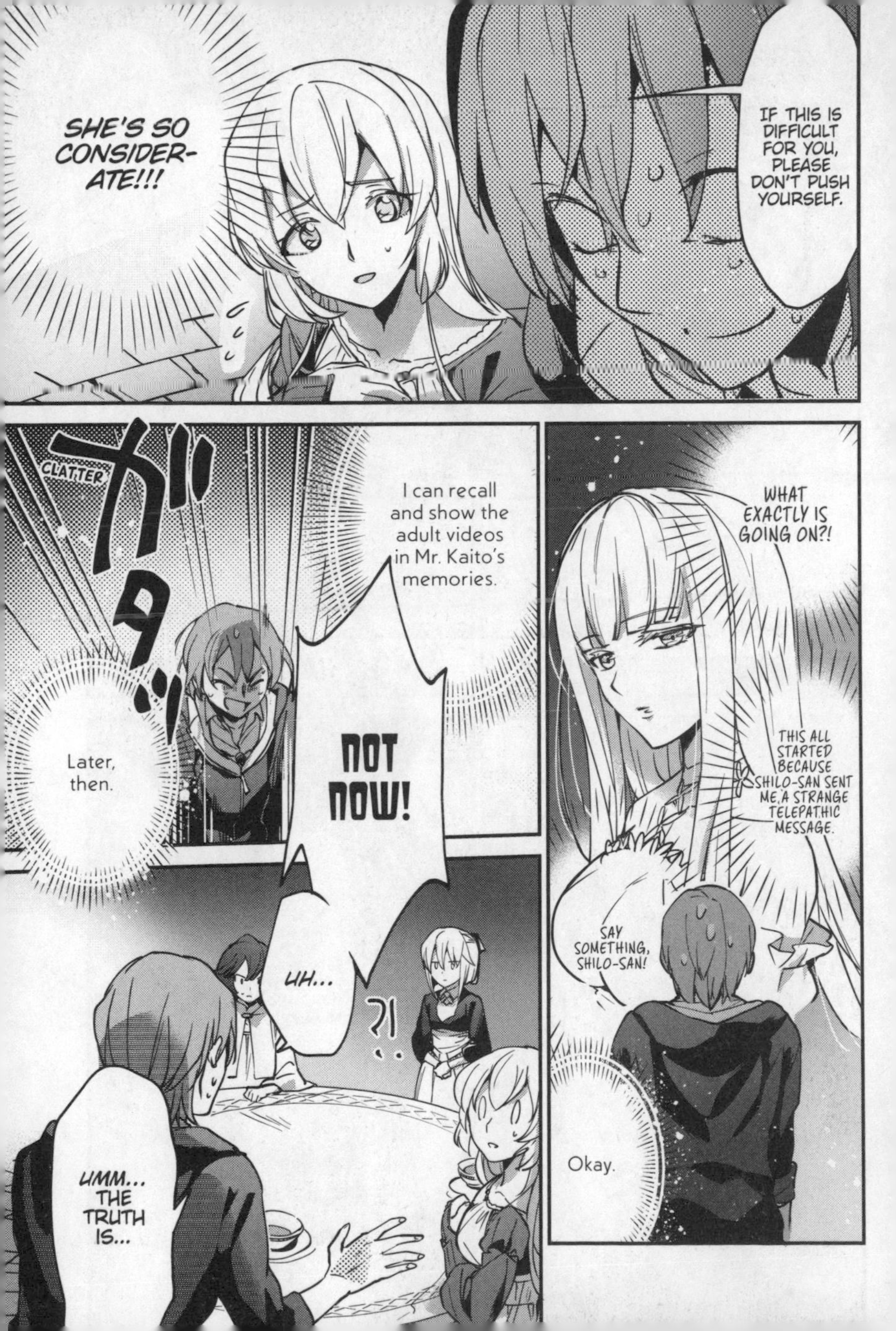

IF THIS IS DIFFICULT FOR YOU, PLEASE DON'T PUSH YOURSELF.
SHE'S SO CONSIDERATE!!!
WHAT EXACTLY IS GOING ON?!
THIS ALL STARTED BECAUSE SHILO-SAN SENT ME A STRANGE TELEPATHIC MESSAGE.
SAY SOMETHING, SHILO-SAN!
Okay.
I can recall and show the adult videos in Mr. Kaito's memories.
ガタッ
CLATTER
NOT NOW!
Later, then.
UH...
?!
UMM... THE TRUTH IS...

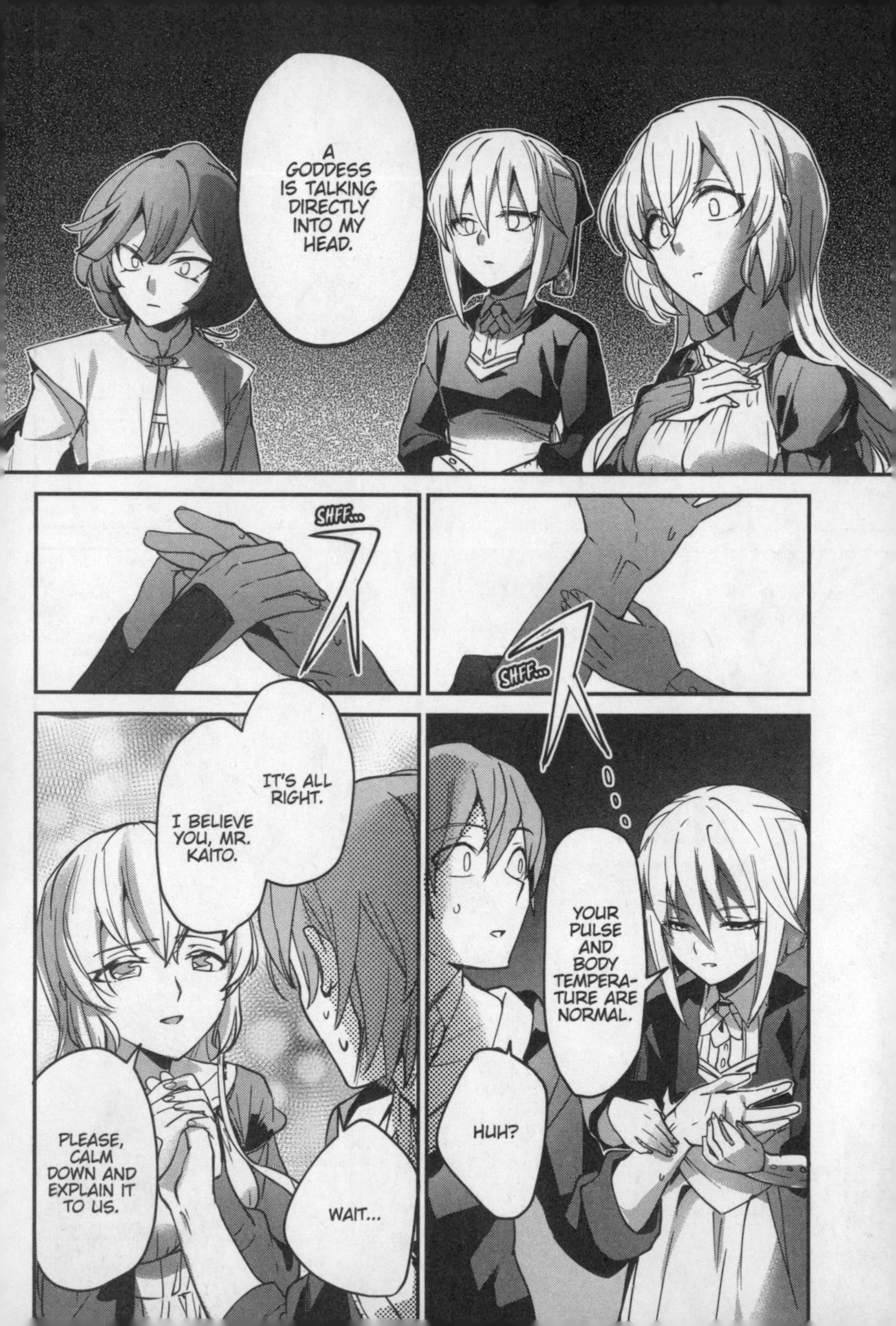
A GODDESS IS TALKING DIRECTLY INTO MY HEAD.
SHFF...
SHFF...
YOUR PULSE AND BODY TEMPERA-TURE ARE NORMAL.
HUH?
IT'S ALL RIGHT.
I BELIEVE YOU, MR. KAITO.
WAIT...
PLEASE, CALM DOWN AND EXPLAIN IT TO US.

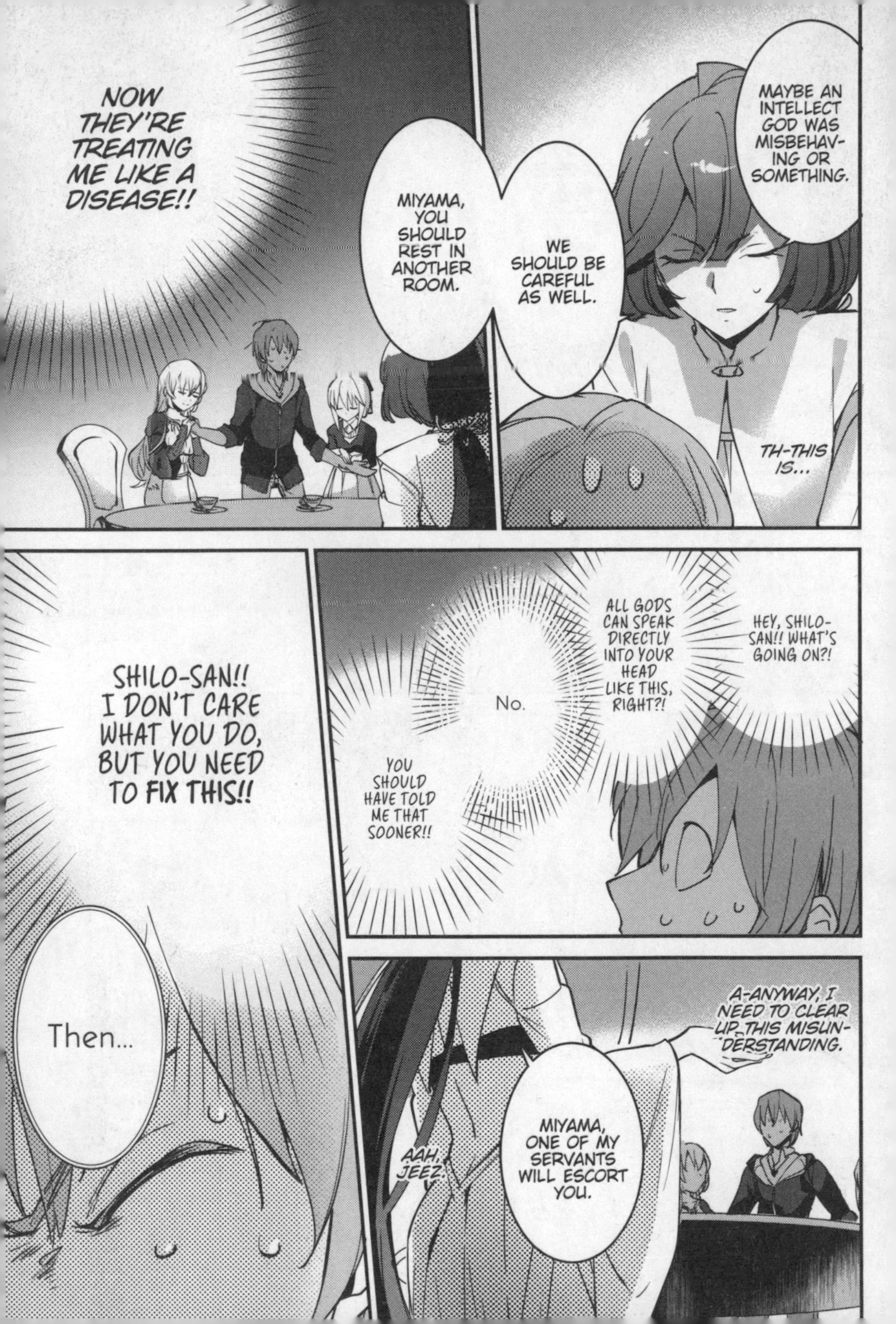
MAYBE AN INTELLECT GOD WAS MISBEHAVING OR SOMETHING.
TH-THIS IS...
WE SHOULD BE CAREFUL AS WELL.
MIYAMA, YOU SHOULD REST IN ANOTHER ROOM.
NOW THEY'RE TREATING ME LIKE A DISEASE!!
HEY, SHILO-SAN!! WHAT'S GOING ON?!
ALL GODS CAN SPEAK DIRECTLY INTO YOUR HEAD LIKE THIS, RIGHT?!
No.
YOU SHOULD HAVE TOLD ME THAT SOONER!!
SHILO-SAN!! I DON'T CARE WHAT YOU DO, BUT YOU NEED TO FIX THIS!!
A-ANYWAY, I NEED TO CLEAR UP THIS MISUNDERSTANDING.
MIYAMA, ONE OF MY SERVANTS WILL ESCORT YOU.
AAH, JEEZ.
Then...

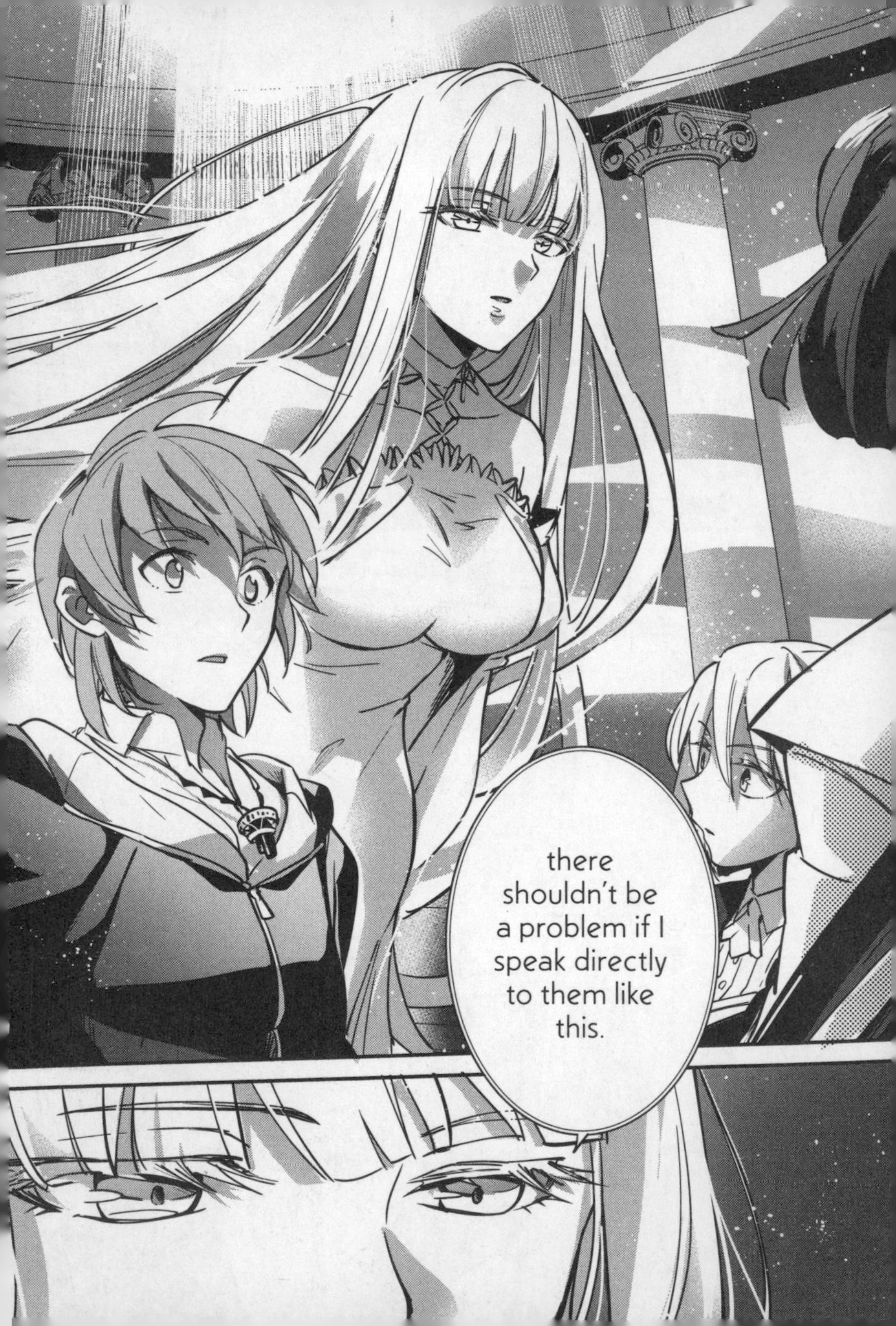
there shouldn't be a problem if I speak directly to them like this.

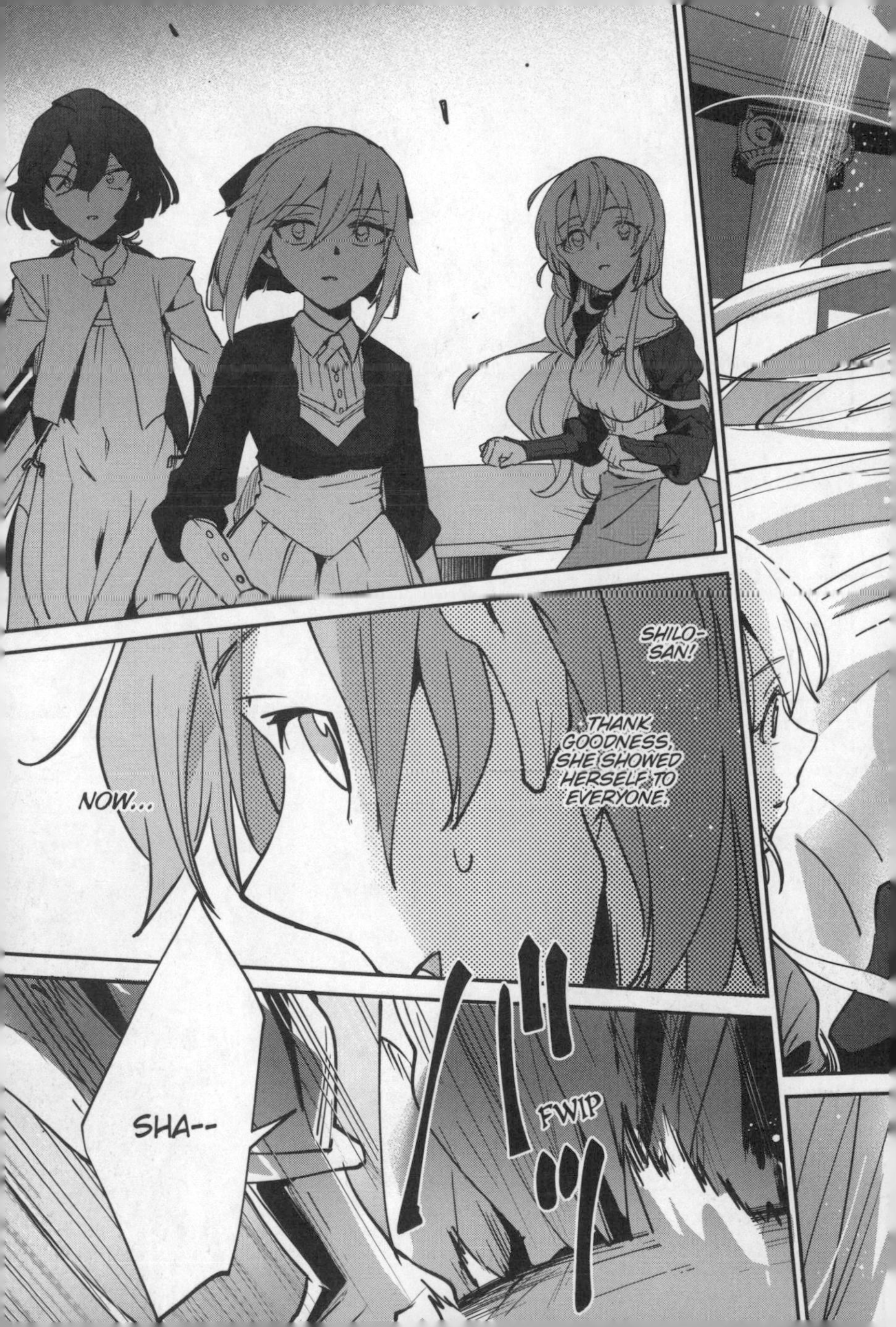
SHILO-SAN!
THANK GOODNESS, SHE SHOWED HERSELF TO EVERYONE.
NOW...
FWIP
SHA--

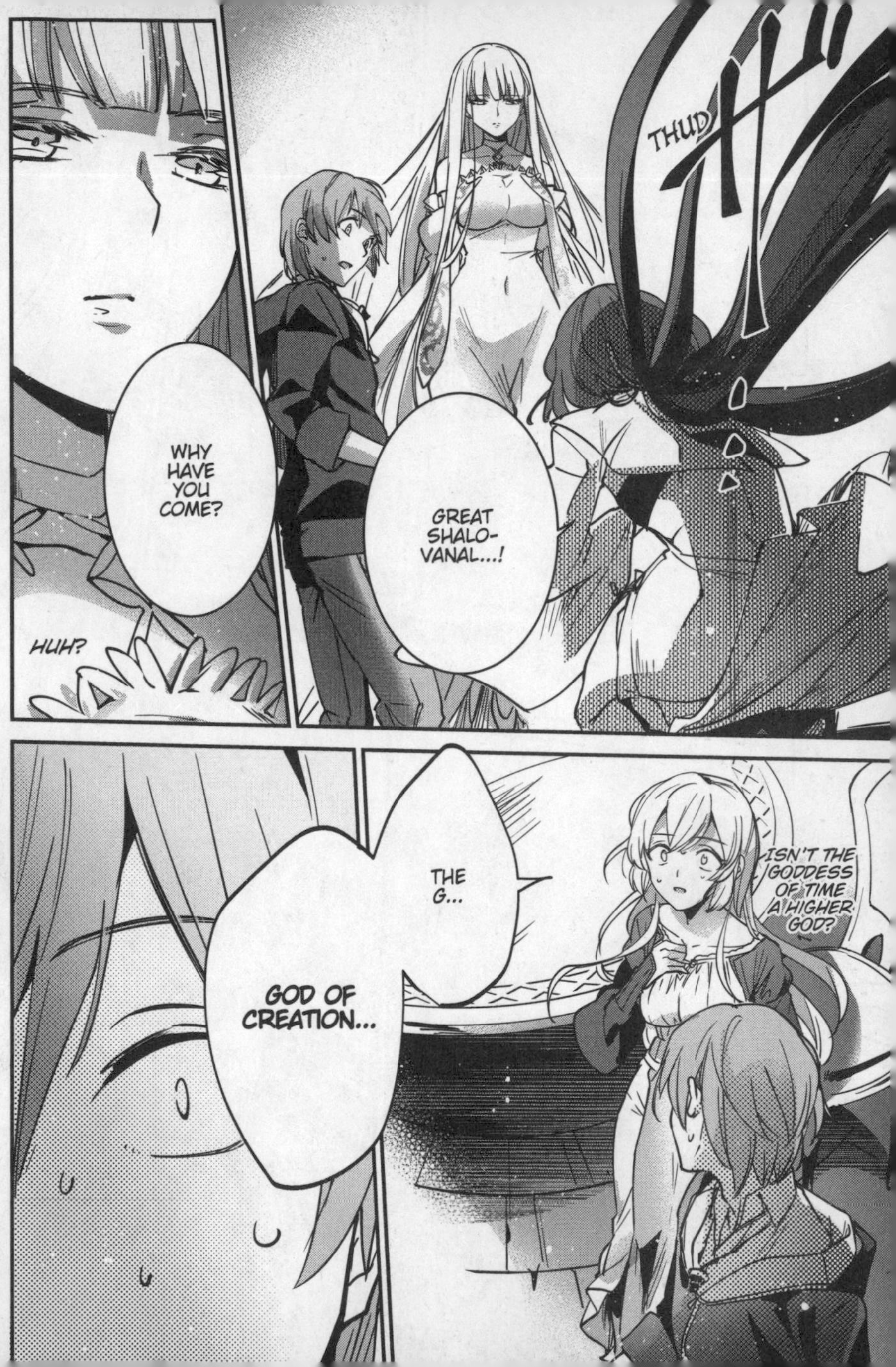
THUD
GREAT SHALO-VANAL...!
WHY HAVE YOU COME?
HUH?
ISN'T THE GODDESS OF TIME A HIGHER GOD?
THE G...
GOD OF CREATION...

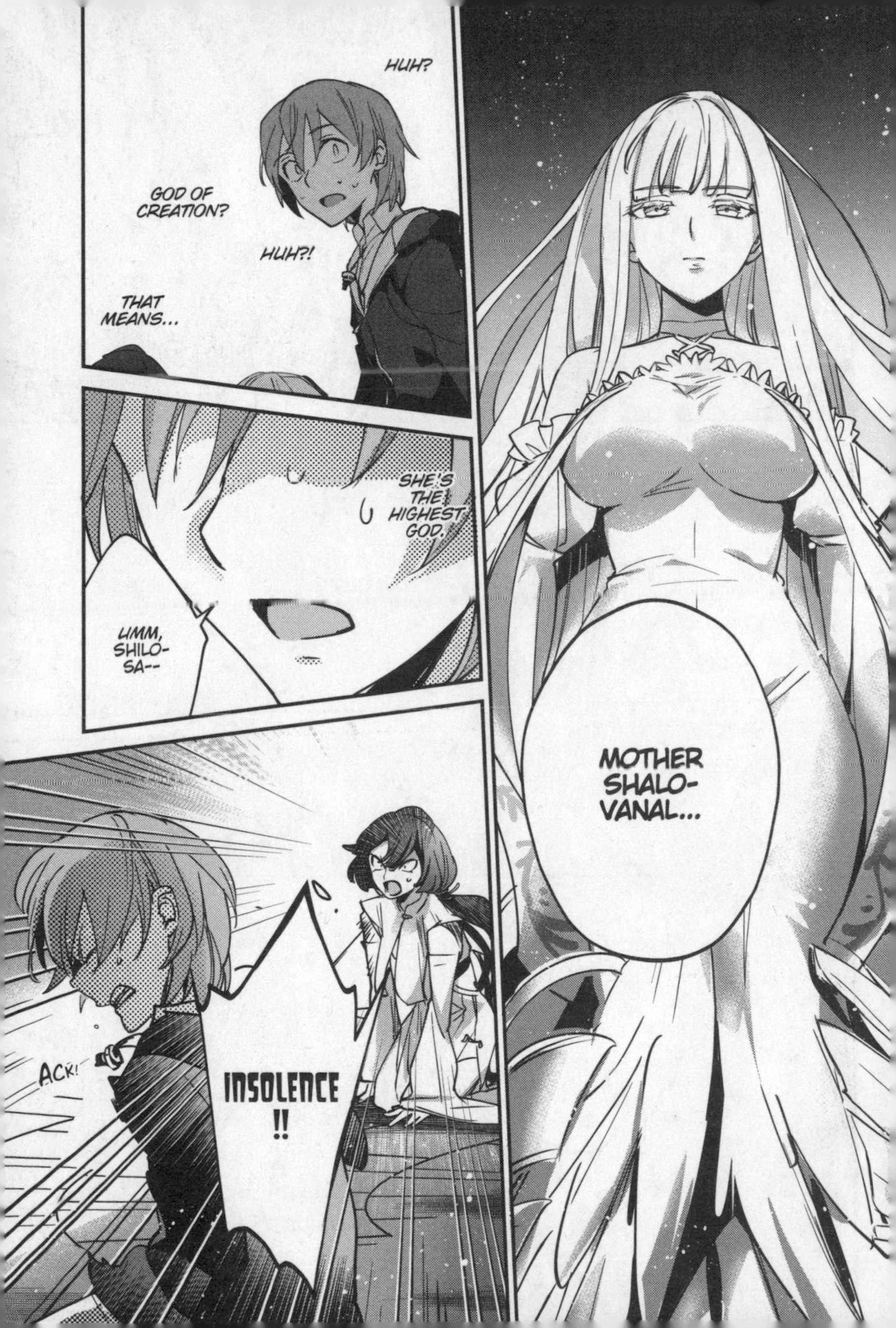
MOTHER SHALO-VANAL...
HUH?
GOD OF CREATION?
HUH?!
THAT MEANS...
SHE'S THE HIGHEST GOD.
UMM, SHILO-SA--
INSOLENCE !!
ACK!

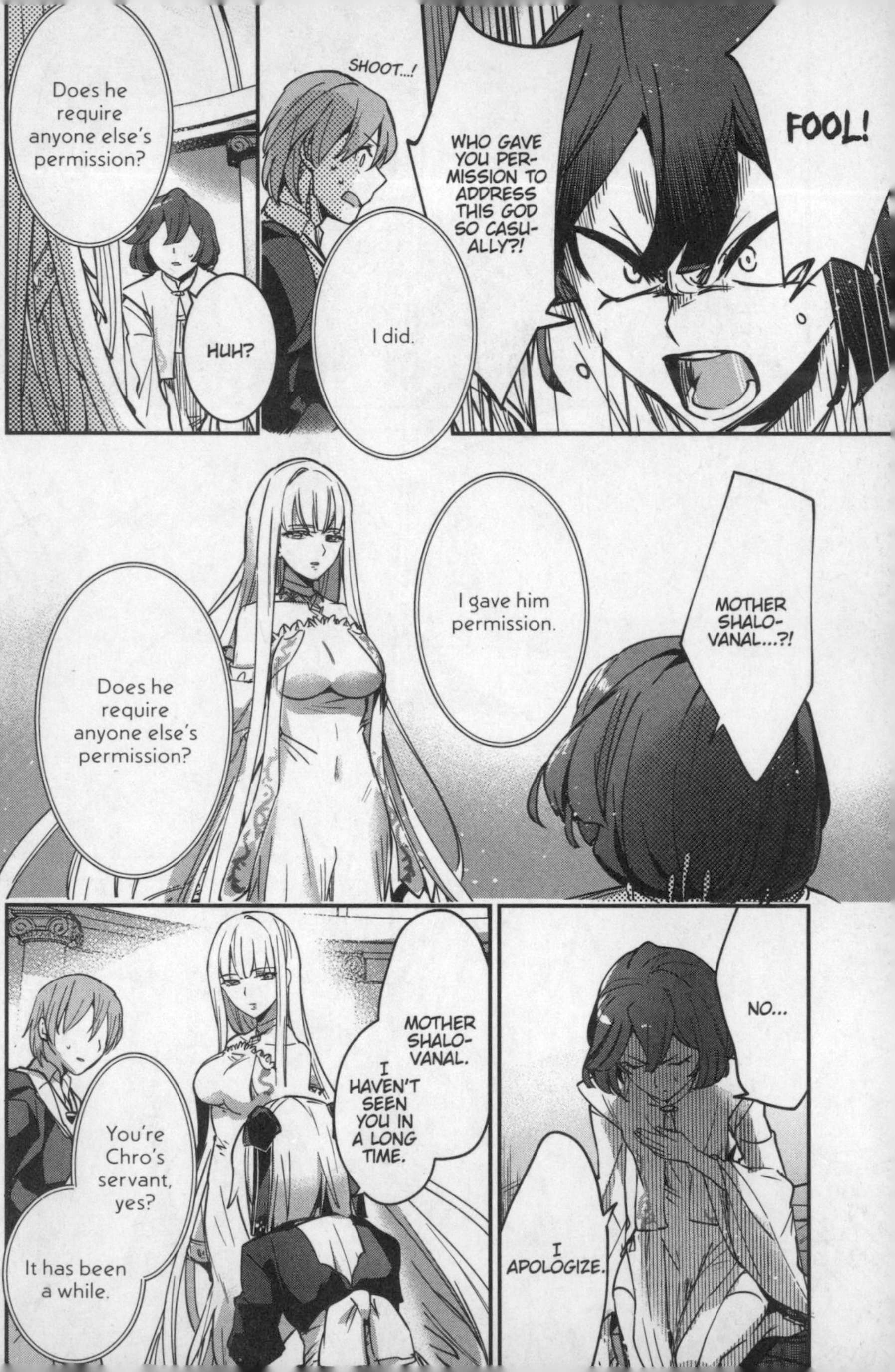
FOOL!
WHO GAVE YOU PERMISSION TO ADDRESS THIS GOD SO CASUALLY?!
SHOOT...!
I did.
HUH?
Does he require anyone else's permission?
MOTHER SHALOVANAL...?!
I gave him permission.
Does he require anyone else's permission?
NO...
I APOLOGIZE.
MOTHER SHALOVANAL.
I HAVEN'T SEEN YOU IN A LONG TIME.
You're Chro's servant, yes?
It has been a while.

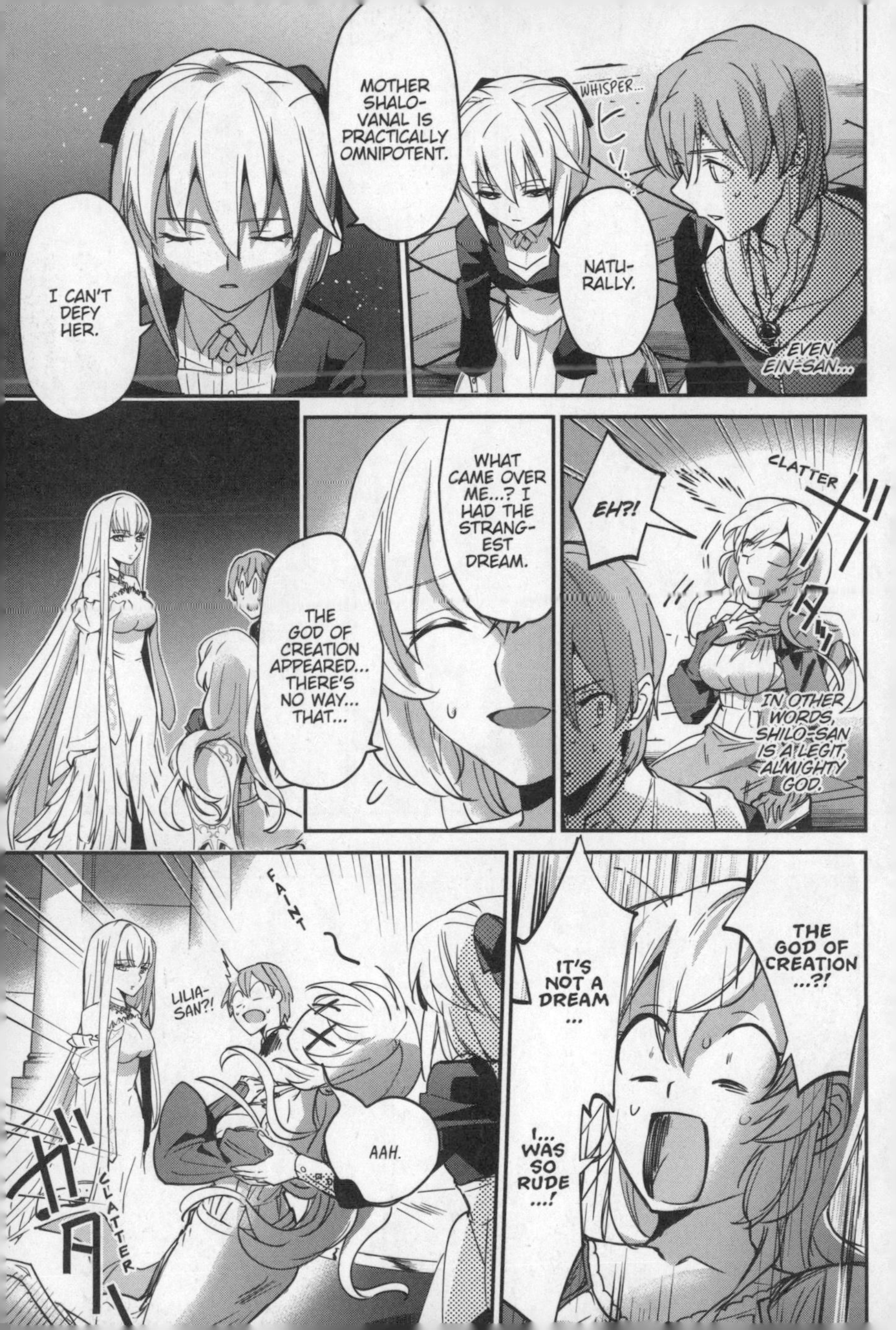
WHISPER...
EVEN EIN-SAN...
NATU-RALLY.
MOTHER SHALO-VANAL IS PRACTICALLY OMNIPOTENT.
I CAN'T DEFY HER.
CLATTER
EH?!
IN OTHER WORDS, SHILO-SAN IS A LEGIT, ALMIGHTY GOD.
WHAT CAME OVER ME...? I HAD THE STRANG-EST DREAM.
THE GOD OF CREATION APPEARED... THERE'S NO WAY... THAT...
THE GOD OF CREATION ...?!
IT'S NOT A DREAM ...
I... WAS SO RUDE ...!
FAINT
LILIA-SAN?!
AAH.
CLATTER

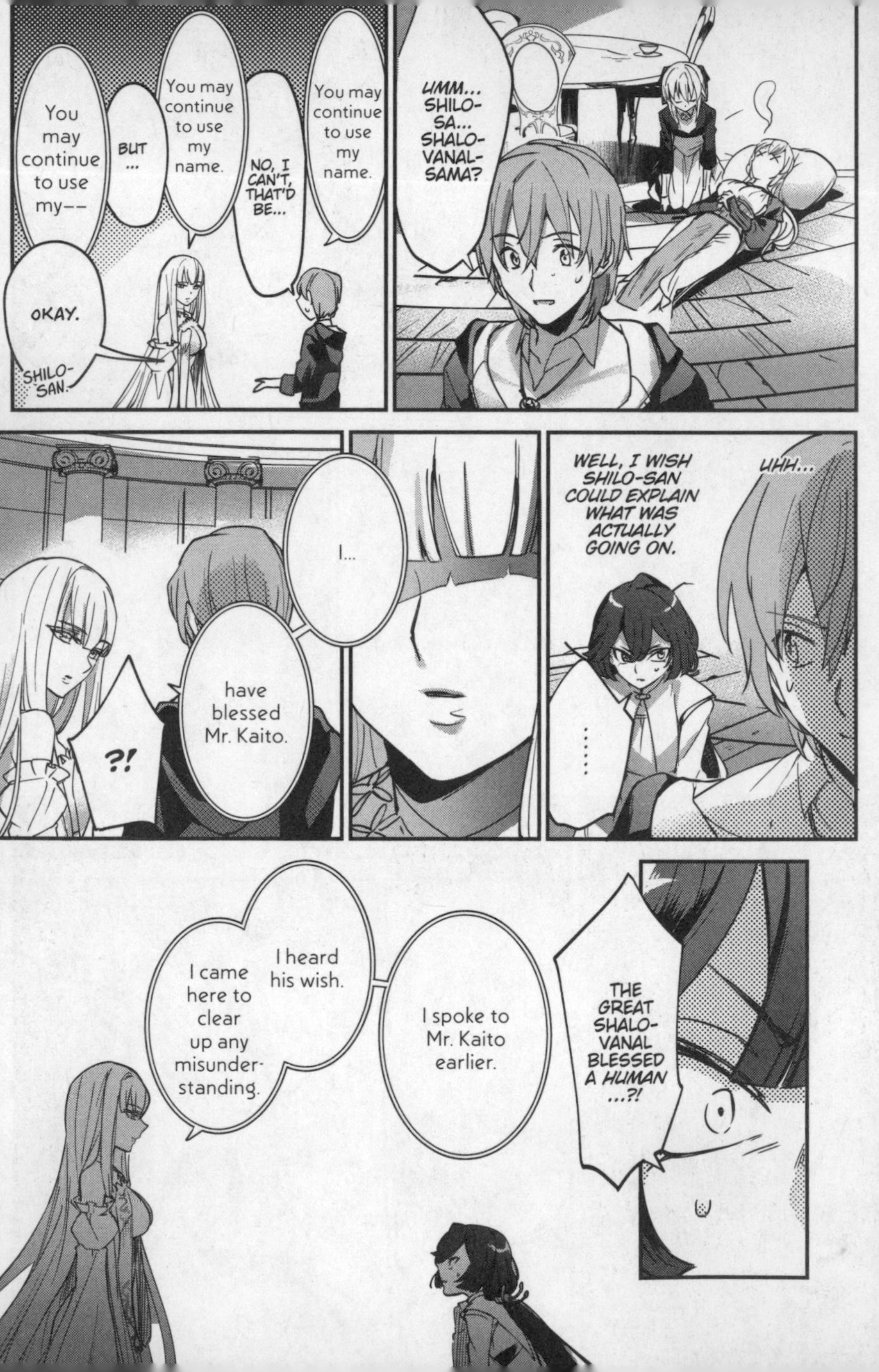

UMM... SHILO-SA... SHALO-VANAL-SAMA?
You may continue to use my name.
NO, I CAN'T, THAT'D BE...
You may continue to use my name.
BUT...
You may continue to use my--
OKAY.
SHILO-SAN.
UHH...
WELL, I WISH SHILO-SAN COULD EXPLAIN WHAT WAS ACTUALLY GOING ON.
......
I...
have blessed Mr. Kaito.
?!
THE GREAT SHALO-VANAL BLESSED A HUMAN...?!
I spoke to Mr. Kaito earlier.
I heard his wish.
I came here to clear up any misunderstanding.

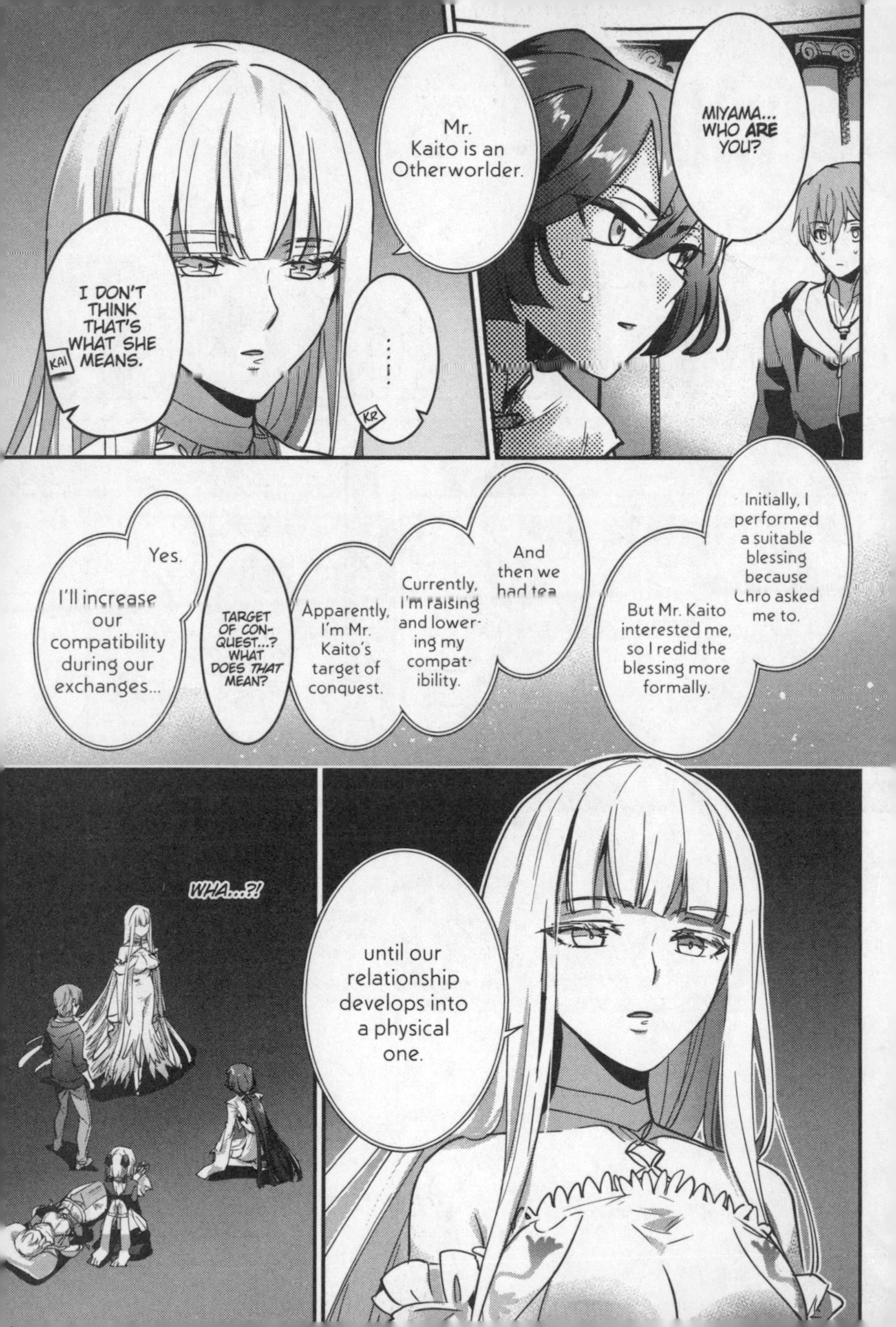
MIYAMA... WHO **ARE** YOU?
Mr. Kaito is an Otherworlder.
…!
KR
I DON'T THINK THAT'S WHAT SHE MEANS.
KAI
Initially, I performed a suitable blessing because Chro asked me to.
But Mr. Kaito interested me, so I redid the blessing more formally.
And then we had tea
Currently, I'm raising and lowering my compatibility.
Apparently, I'm Mr. Kaito's target of conquest.
TARGET OF CONQUEST...? WHAT DOES *THAT* MEAN?
Yes.
I'll increase our compatibility during our exchanges...
until our relationship develops into a physical one.
WHA...?!

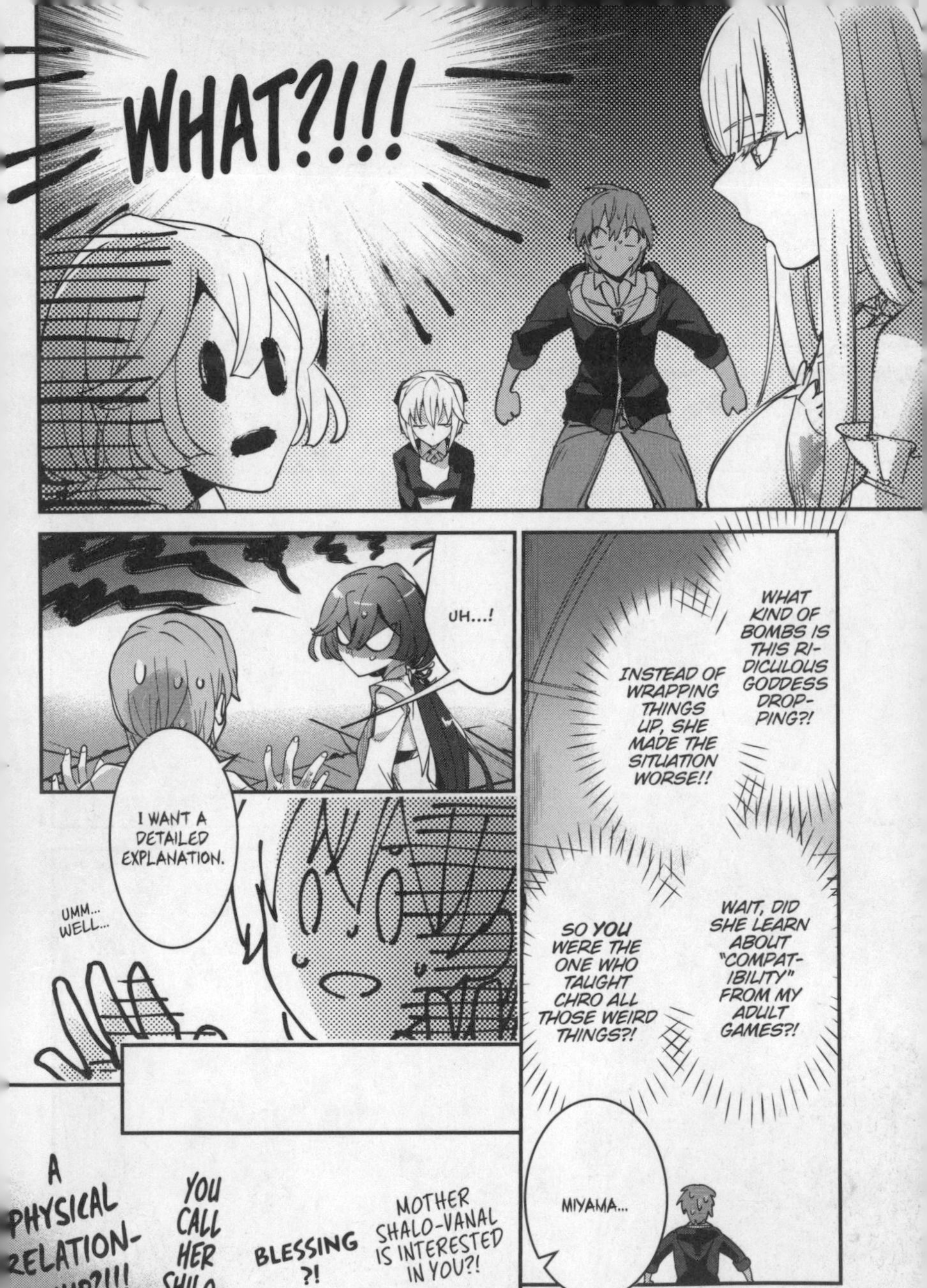
WHAT?!!!
WHAT KIND OF BOMBS IS THIS RI-DICULOUS GODDESS DROP-PING?!
INSTEAD OF WRAPPING THINGS UP, SHE MADE THE SITUATION WORSE!!
WAIT, DID SHE LEARN ABOUT "COMPAT-IBILITY" FROM MY ADULT GAMES?!
SO YOU WERE THE ONE WHO TAUGHT CHRO ALL THOSE WEIRD THINGS?!
MIYAMA...
UH...!
I WANT A DETAILED EXPLANATION.
UMM... WELL...
MOTHER SHALO-VANAL IS INTERESTED IN YOU?!
BLESSING?!
YOU CALL HER SHILO-SAN?!!
A PHYSICAL RELATION-SHIP?!!!

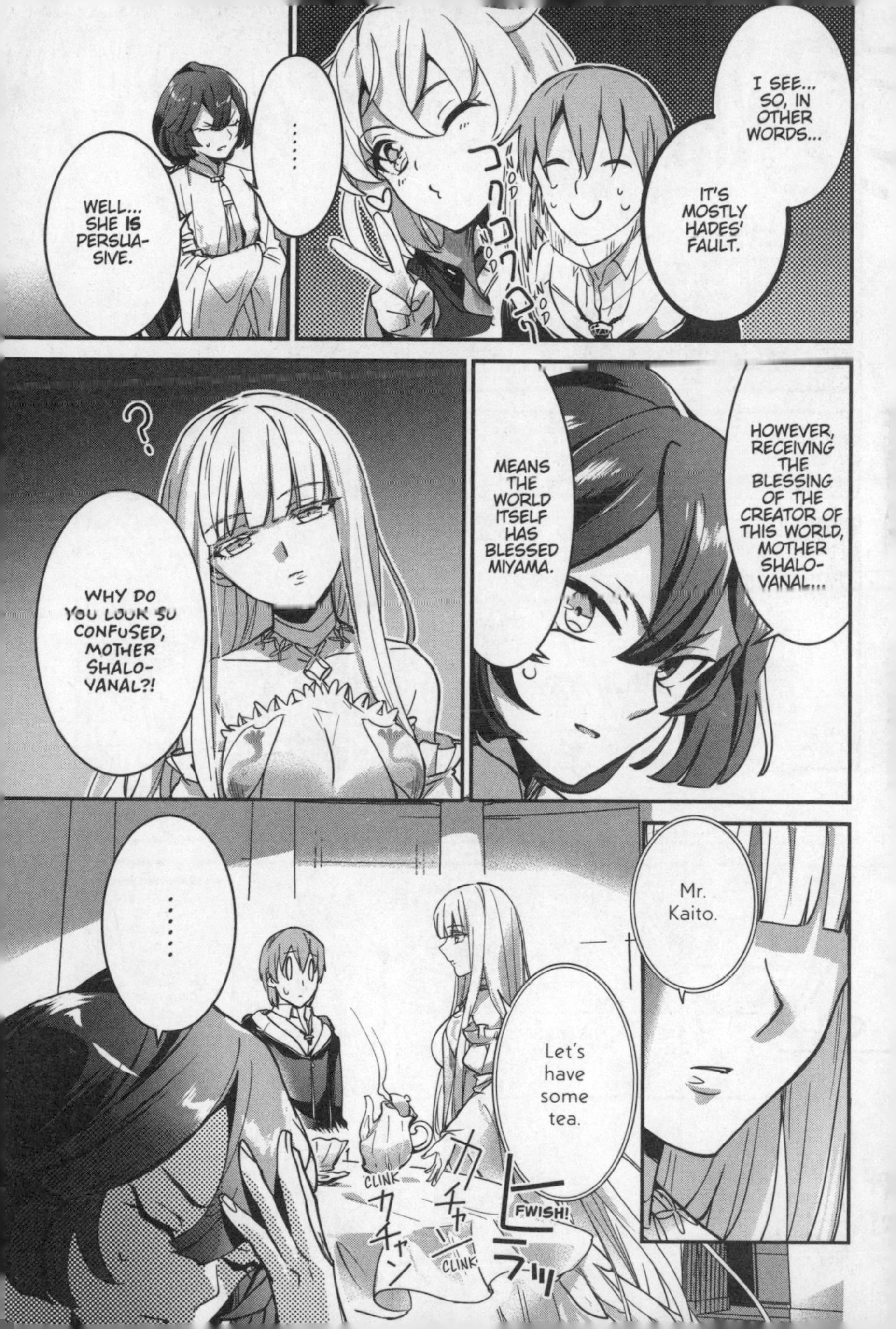
I SEE... SO, IN OTHER WORDS...
IT'S MOSTLY HADES' FAULT.
NOD NOD NOD
......
WELL... SHE IS PERSUA-SIVE.
HOWEVER, RECEIVING THE BLESSING OF THE CREATOR OF THIS WORLD, MOTHER SHALO-VANAL...
MEANS THE WORLD ITSELF HAS BLESSED MIYAMA.
?
WHY DO YOU LOOK SO CONFUSED, MOTHER SHALO-VANAL?!
Mr. Kaito.
Let's have some tea.
FWISH!
CLINK
CLINK
......

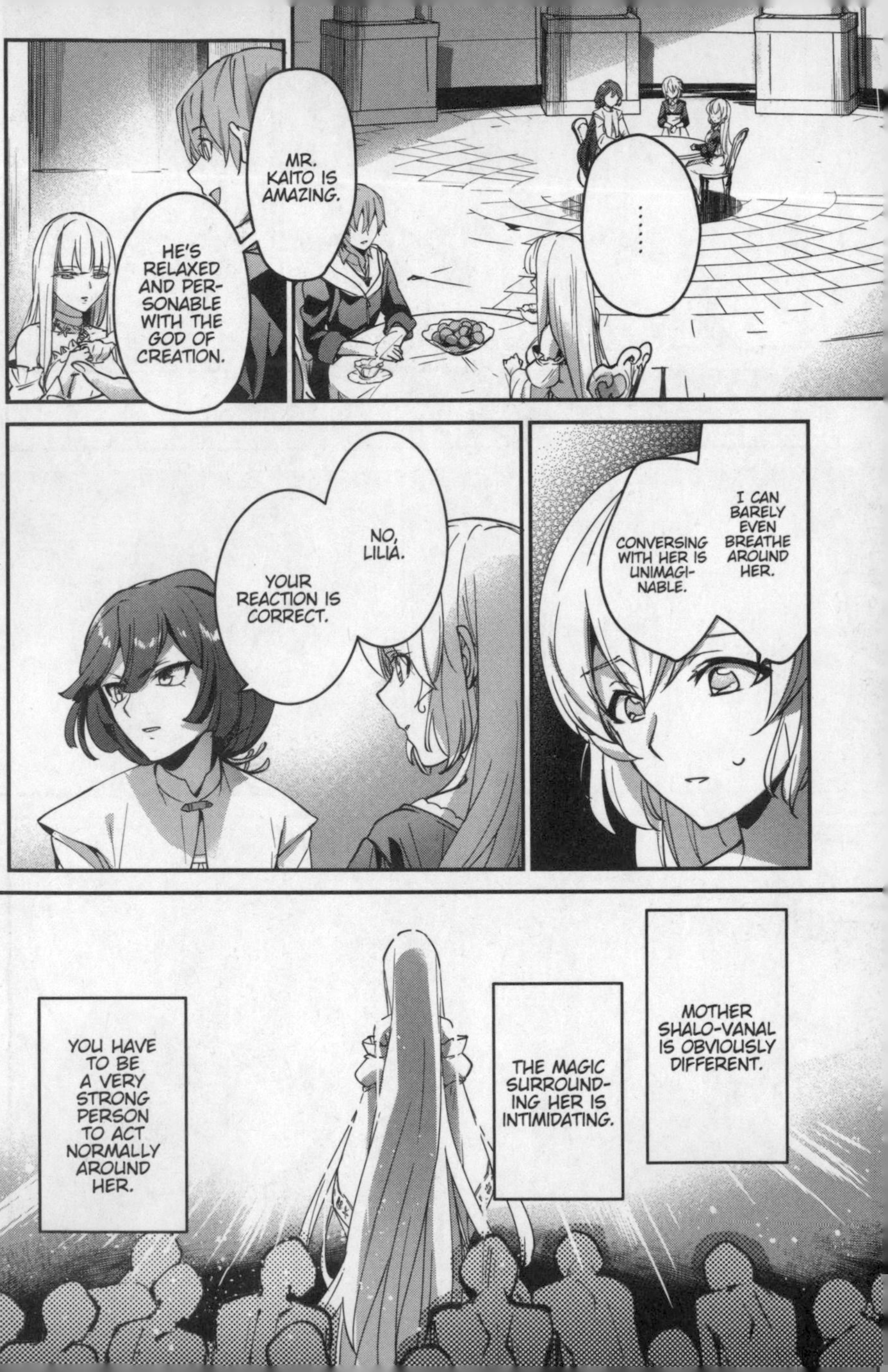
……
MR. KAITO IS AMAZING.
HE'S RELAXED AND PERSONABLE WITH THE GOD OF CREATION.
I CAN BARELY EVEN BREATHE AROUND HER.
CONVERSING WITH HER IS UNIMAGINABLE.
NO, LILIA.
YOUR REACTION IS CORRECT.
MOTHER SHALO-VANAL IS OBVIOUSLY DIFFERENT.
THE MAGIC SURROUNDING HER IS INTIMIDATING.
YOU HAVE TO BE A VERY STRONG PERSON TO ACT NORMALLY AROUND HER.

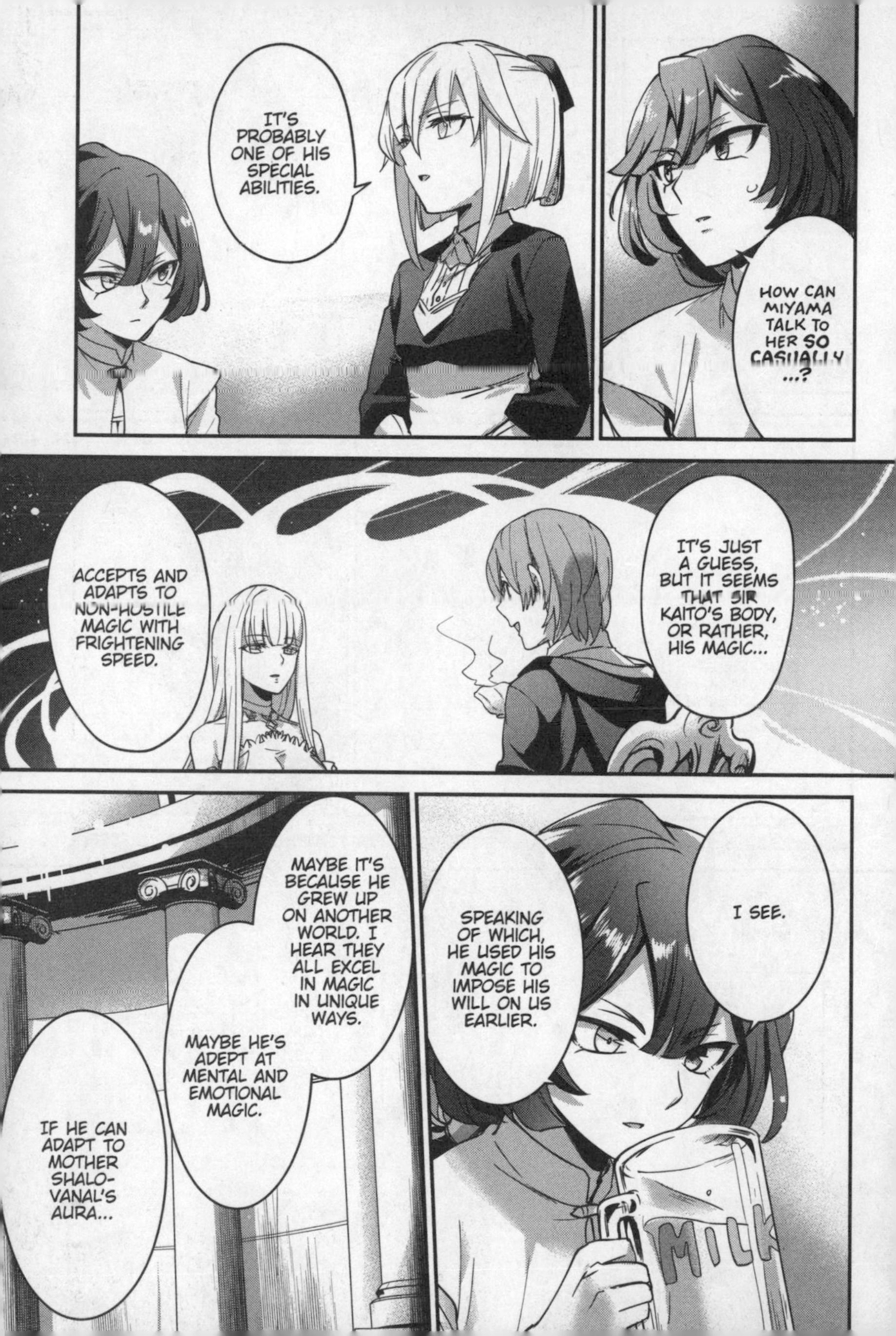
HOW CAN MIYAMA TALK TO HER SO CASUALLY ...?
IT'S PROBABLY ONE OF HIS SPECIAL ABILITIES.
IT'S JUST A GUESS, BUT IT SEEMS THAT SIR KAITO'S BODY, OR RATHER, HIS MAGIC...
ACCEPTS AND ADAPTS TO NON-HOSTILE MAGIC WITH FRIGHTENING SPEED.
I SEE.
SPEAKING OF WHICH, HE USED HIS MAGIC TO IMPOSE HIS WILL ON US EARLIER.
MILK
MAYBE IT'S BECAUSE HE GREW UP ON ANOTHER WORLD. I HEAR THEY ALL EXCEL IN MAGIC IN UNIQUE WAYS.
MAYBE HE'S ADEPT AT MENTAL AND EMOTIONAL MAGIC.
IF HE CAN ADAPT TO MOTHER SHALO-VANAL'S AURA...

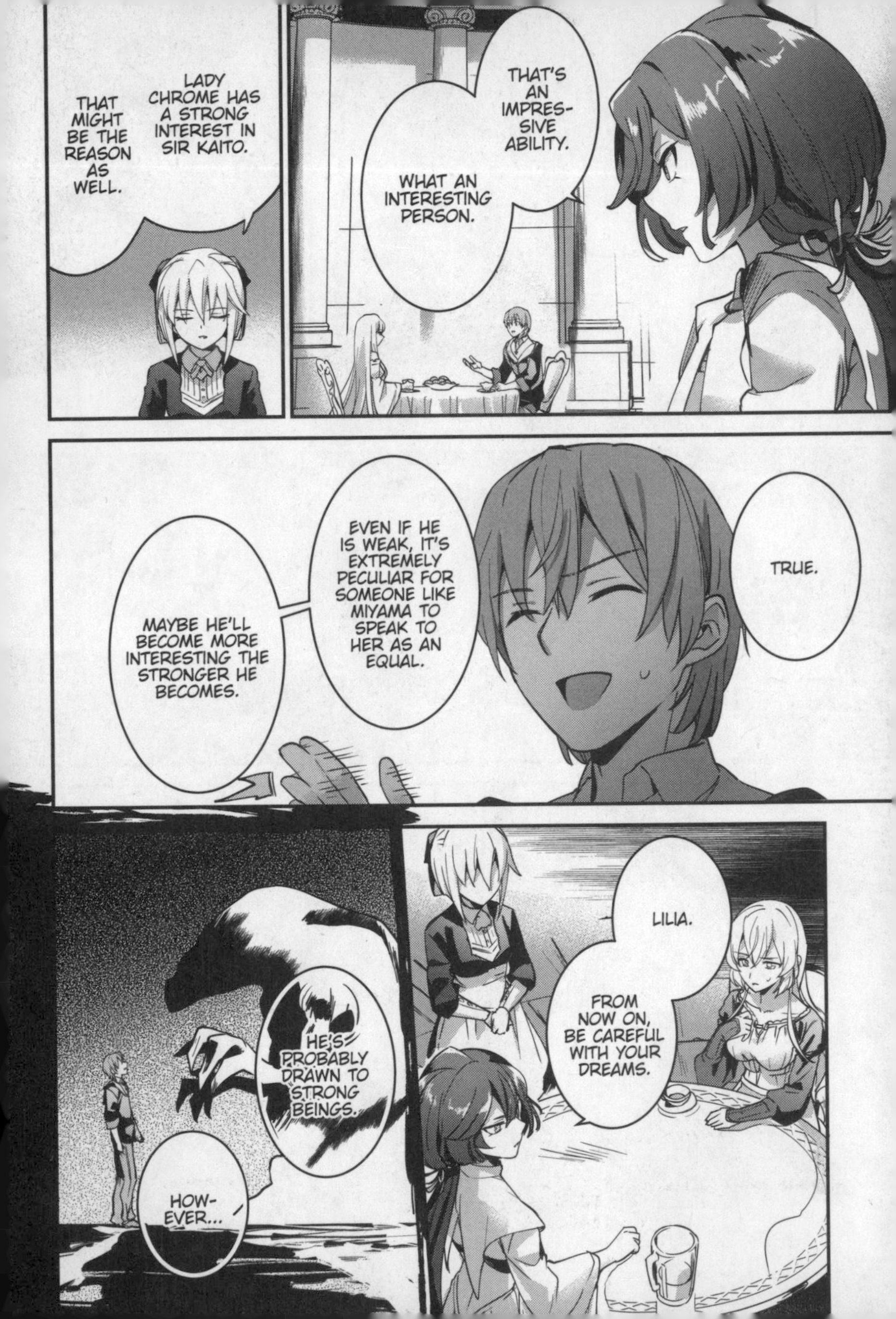
THAT'S AN IMPRES-SIVE ABILITY.
WHAT AN INTERESTING PERSON.
LADY CHROME HAS A STRONG INTEREST IN SIR KAITO.
THAT MIGHT BE THE REASON AS WELL.
TRUE.
EVEN IF HE IS WEAK, IT'S EXTREMELY PECULIAR FOR SOMEONE LIKE MIYAMA TO SPEAK TO HER AS AN EQUAL.
MAYBE HE'LL BECOME MORE INTERESTING THE STRONGER HE BECOMES.
LILIA.
FROM NOW ON, BE CAREFUL WITH YOUR DREAMS.
HE'S PROBABLY DRAWN TO STRONG BEINGS.
HOW-EVER...

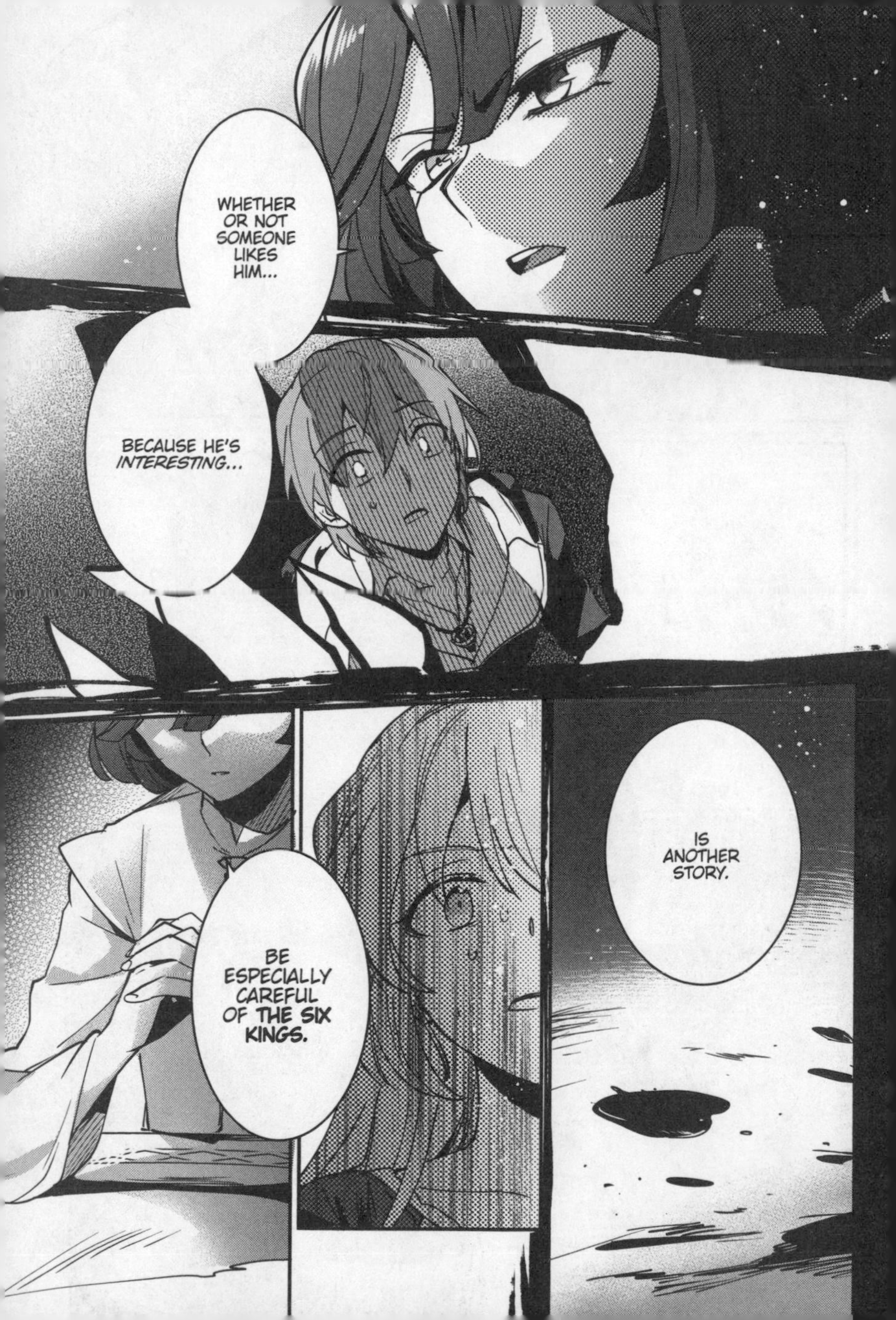
WHETHER OR NOT SOMEONE LIKES HIM...
BECAUSE HE'S *INTERESTING*...
IS ANOTHER STORY.
BE ESPECIALLY CAREFUL OF **THE SIX KINGS.**

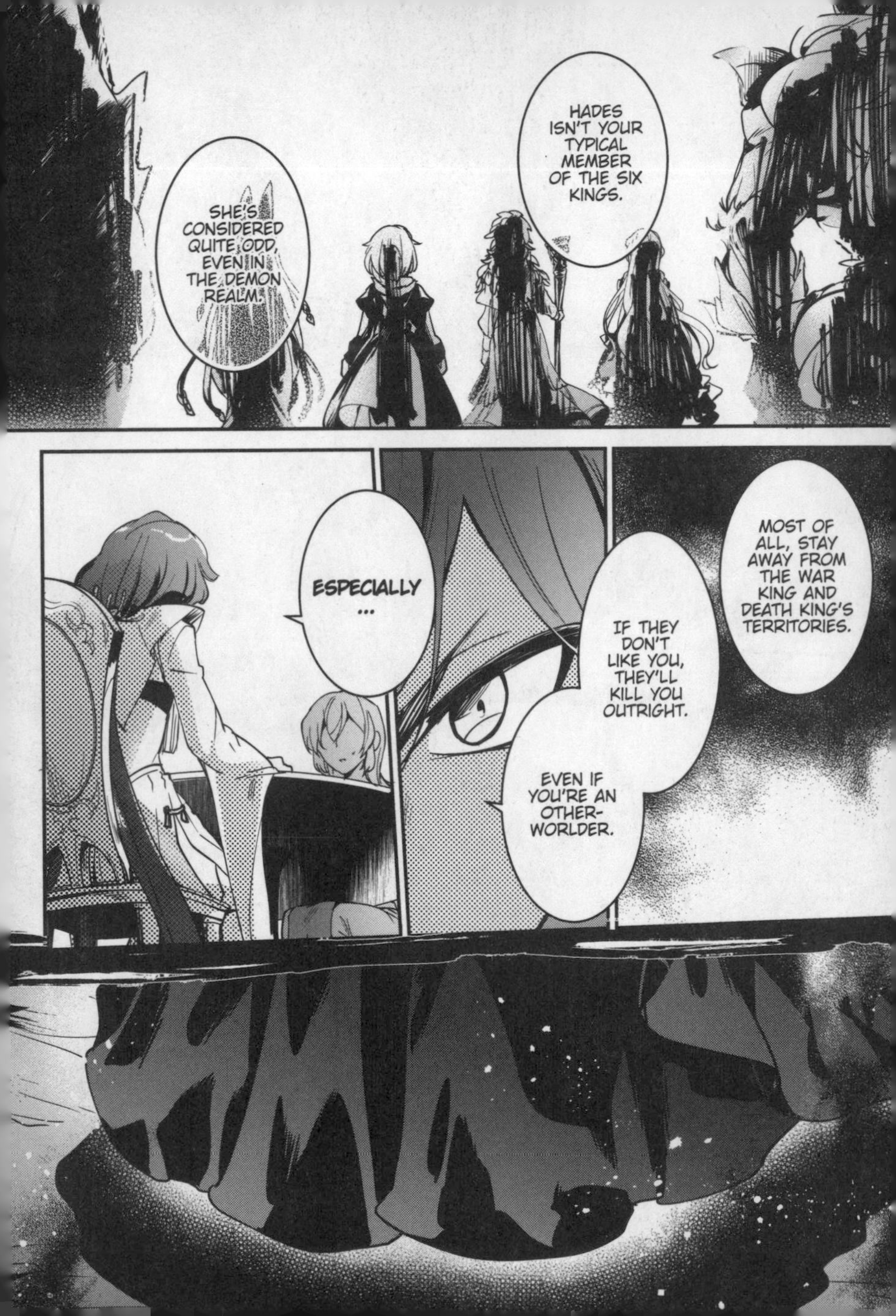
HADES ISN'T YOUR TYPICAL MEMBER OF THE SIX KINGS.
SHE'S CONSIDERED QUITE ODD, EVEN IN THE DEMON REALM.
MOST OF ALL, STAY AWAY FROM THE WAR KING AND DEATH KING'S TERRITORIES.
IF THEY DON'T LIKE YOU, THEY'LL KILL YOU OUTRIGHT.
EVEN IF YOU'RE AN OTHER-WORLDER.
ESPECIALLY...

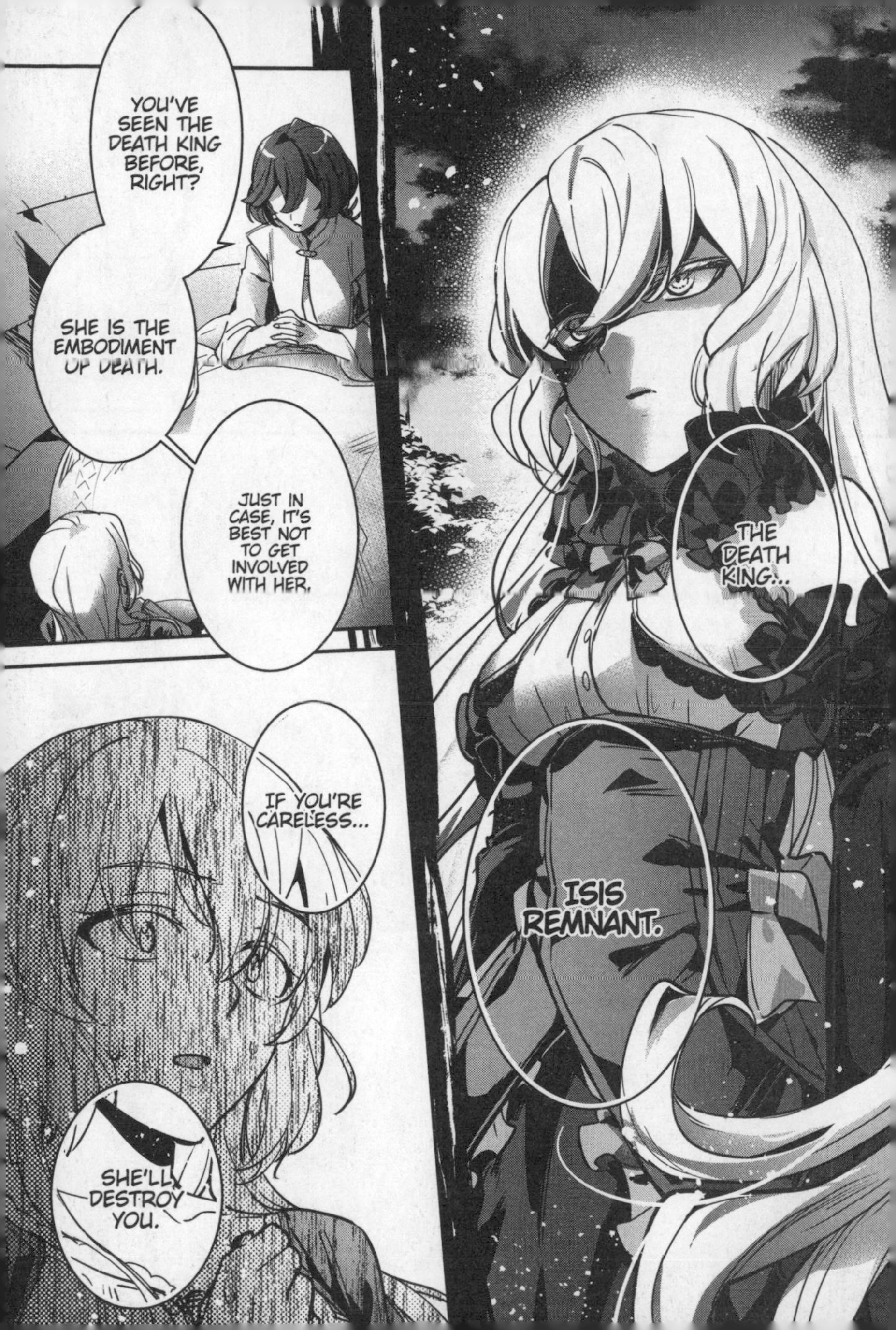
THE DEATH KING...
ISIS REMNANT.
YOU'VE SEEN THE DEATH KING BEFORE, RIGHT?
SHE IS THE EMBODIMENT OF DEATH.
JUST IN CASE, IT'S BEST NOT TO GET INVOLVED WITH HER.
IF YOU'RE CARELESS...
SHE'LL DESTROY YOU.

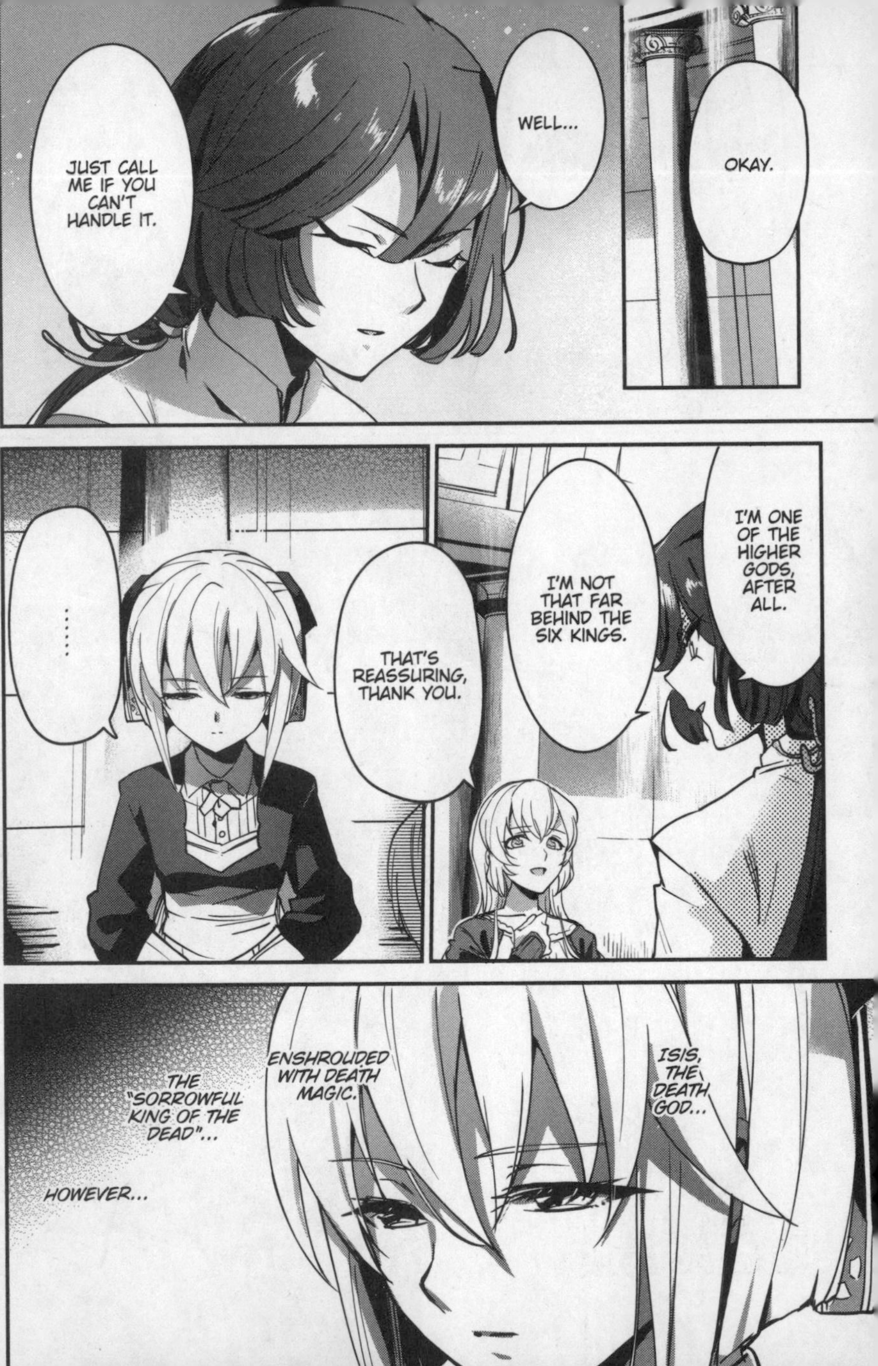
OKAY.
WELL...
JUST CALL ME IF YOU CAN'T HANDLE IT.
I'M ONE OF THE HIGHER GODS, AFTER ALL.
I'M NOT THAT FAR BEHIND THE SIX KINGS.
THAT'S REASSURING, THANK YOU.
......
ISIS, THE DEATH GOD...
ENSHROUDED WITH DEATH MAGIC.
THE "SORROWFUL KING OF THE DEAD"...
HOWEVER...

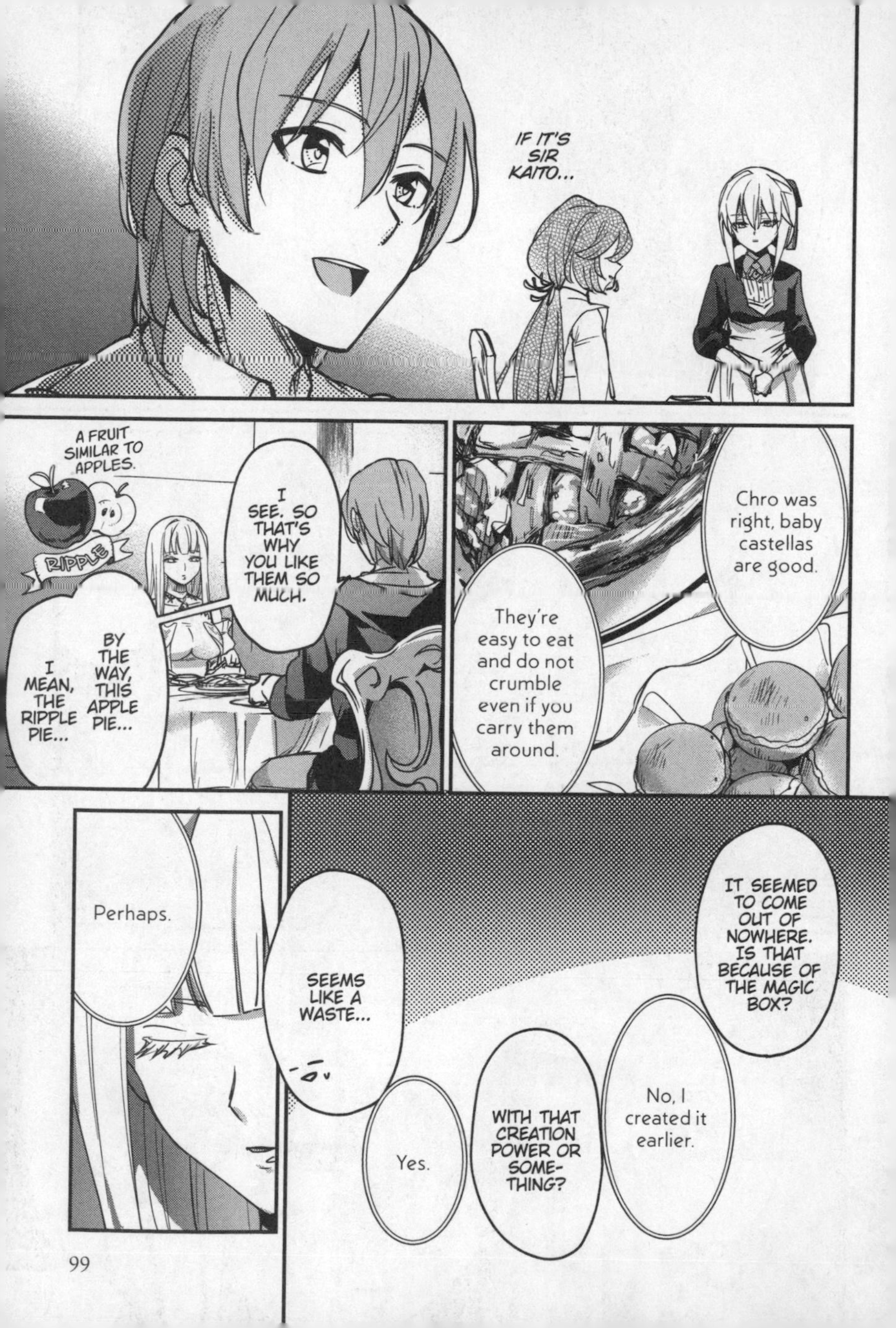

IF IT'S SIR KAITO...
Chro was right, baby castellas are good.
They're easy to eat and do not crumble even if you carry them around.
I SEE. SO THAT'S WHY YOU LIKE THEM SO MUCH.
A FRUIT SIMILAR TO APPLES.
RIPPLE
BY THE WAY, THIS APPLE PIE...
I MEAN, THE RIPPLE PIE...
IT SEEMED TO COME OUT OF NOWHERE. IS THAT BECAUSE OF THE MAGIC BOX?
No, I created it earlier.
WITH THAT CREATION POWER OR SOME-THING?
Yes.
SEEMS LIKE A WASTE...
Perhaps.

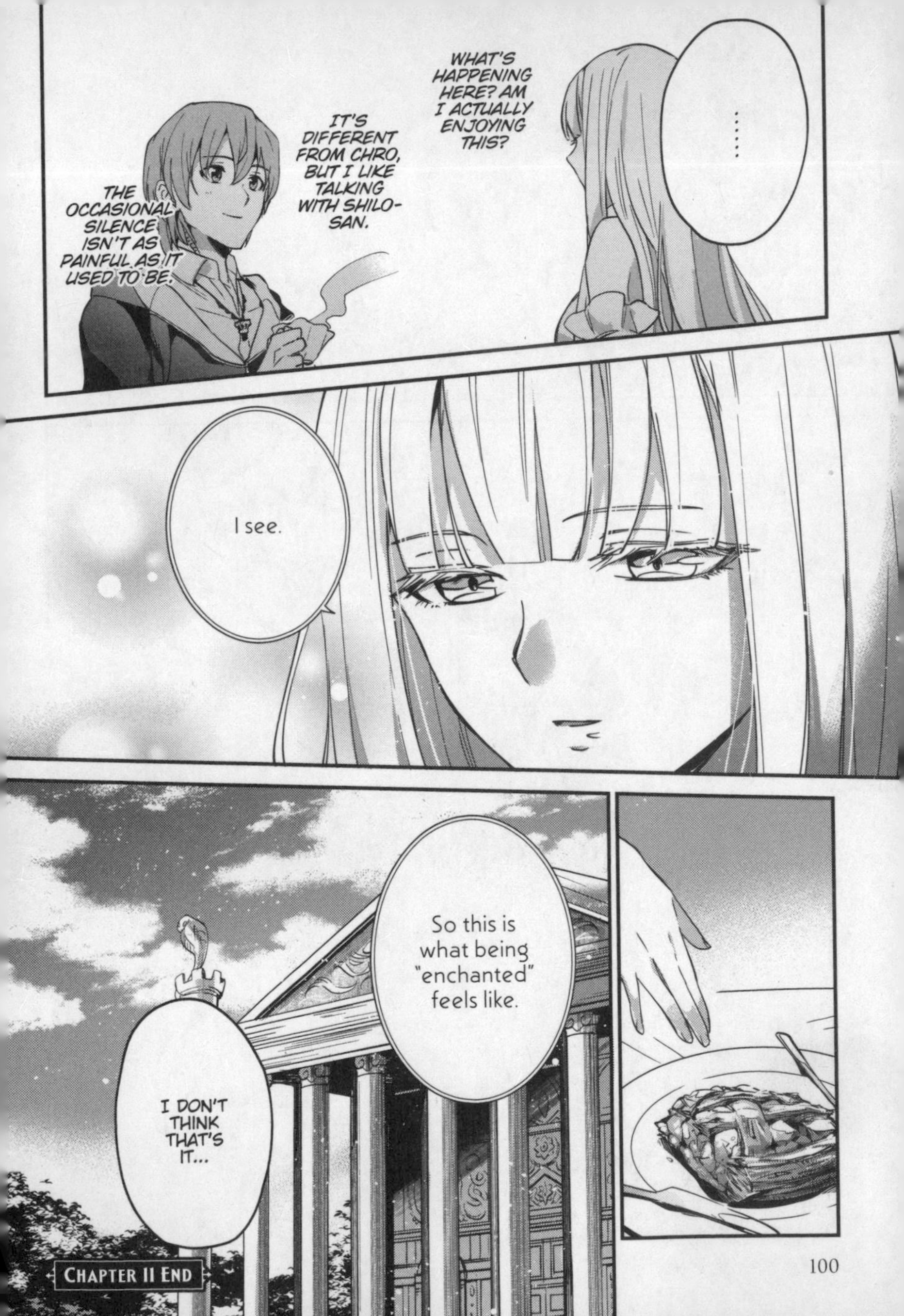
......
WHAT'S HAPPENING HERE? AM I ACTUALLY ENJOYING THIS?
IT'S DIFFERENT FROM CHRO, BUT I LIKE TALKING WITH SHILO-SAN.
THE OCCASIONAL SILENCE ISN'T AS PAINFUL AS IT USED TO BE.
I see.
So this is what being "enchanted" feels like.
I DON'T THINK THAT'S IT...
CHAPTER II END

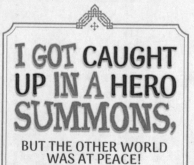

I GOT CAUGHT
UP IN A HERO
SUMMONS,
BUT THE OTHER WORLD
WAS AT PEACE!

I GOT CAUGHT UP IN A HERO SUMMONS,

BUT THE OTHER WORLD WAS AT PEACE!

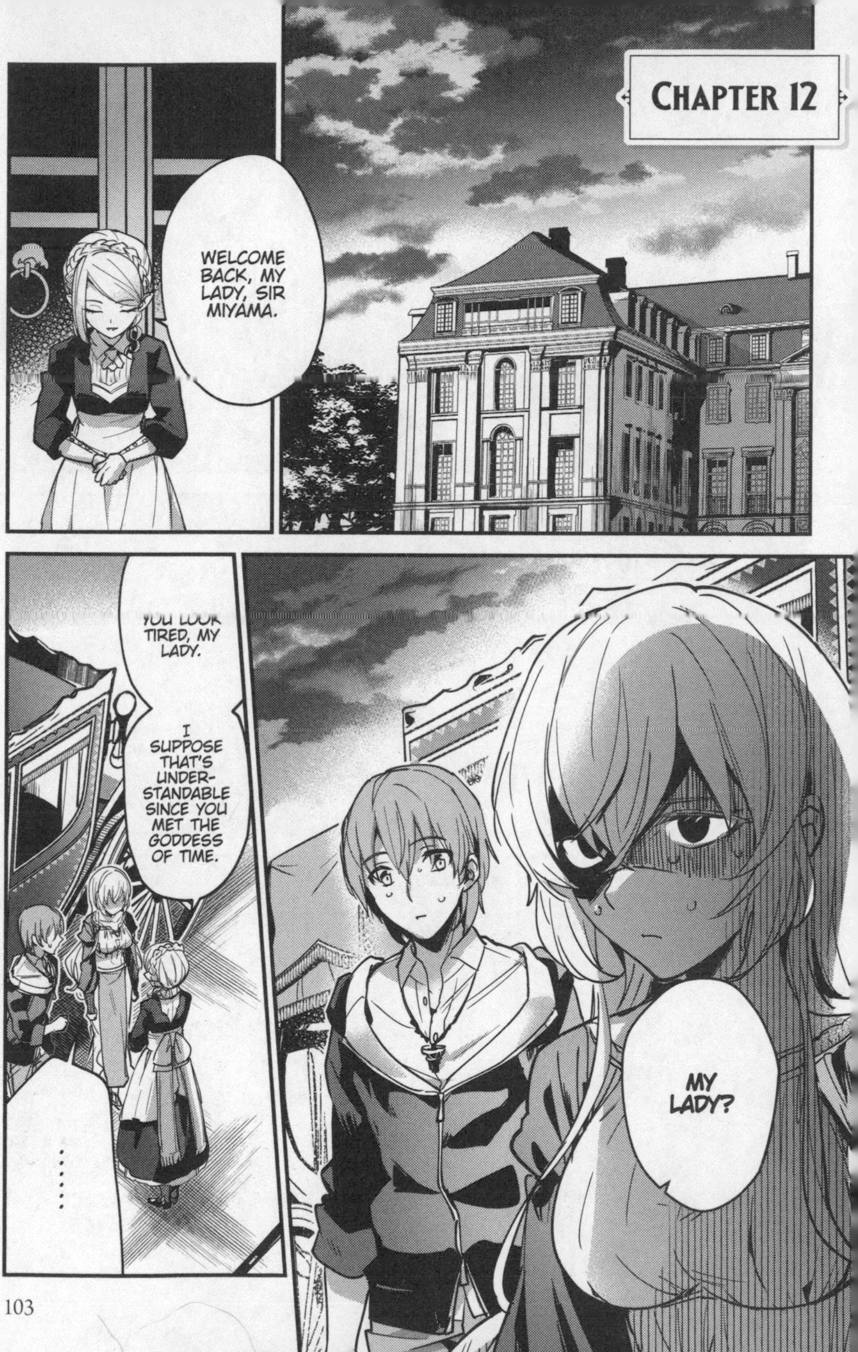
Chapter 12
WELCOME BACK, MY LADY, SIR MIYAMA.
MY LADY?
YOU LOOK TIRED, MY LADY.
I SUPPOSE THAT'S UNDER-STANDABLE SINCE YOU MET THE GODDESS OF TIME.
......

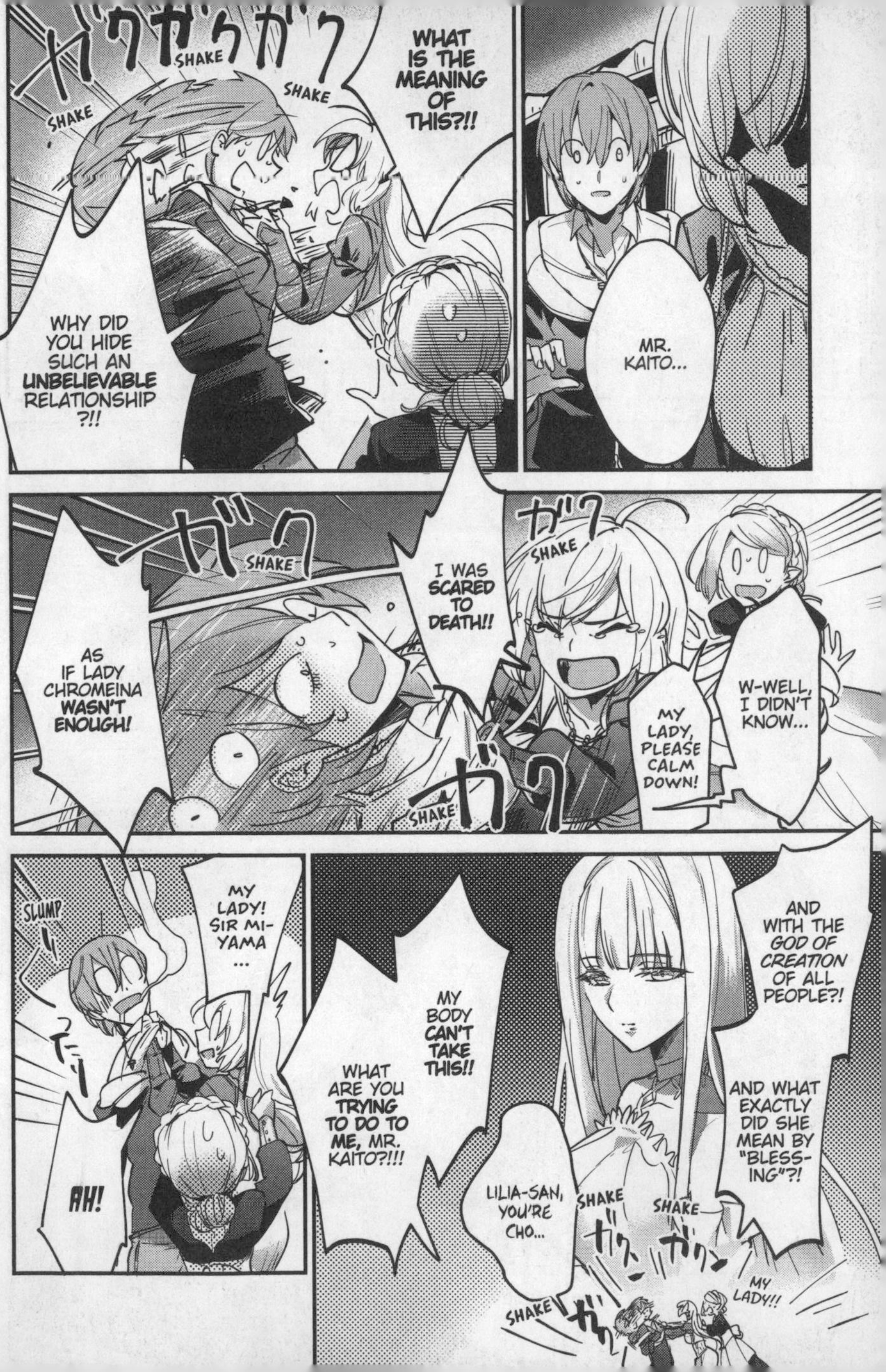
MR. KAITO...
SHAKE
SHAKE
SHAKE
WHAT IS THE MEANING OF THIS?!!
WHY DID YOU HIDE SUCH AN UNBELIEVABLE RELATIONSHIP?!!
SHAKE
W-WELL, I DIDN'T KNOW...
MY LADY, PLEASE CALM DOWN!
I WAS SCARED TO DEATH!!
SHAKE
SHAKE
AS IF LADY CHROMEINA WASN'T ENOUGH!
AND WITH THE GOD OF CREATION OF ALL PEOPLE?!
AND WHAT EXACTLY DID SHE MEAN BY "BLESSING"?!
MY BODY CAN'T TAKE THIS!!
WHAT ARE YOU TRYING TO DO TO ME, MR. KAITO?!!!
LILIA-SAN, YOU'RE CHO...
SHAKE
SHAKE
MY LADY!!
SHAKE
MY LADY! SIR MIYAMA ...
SLUMP
AH!

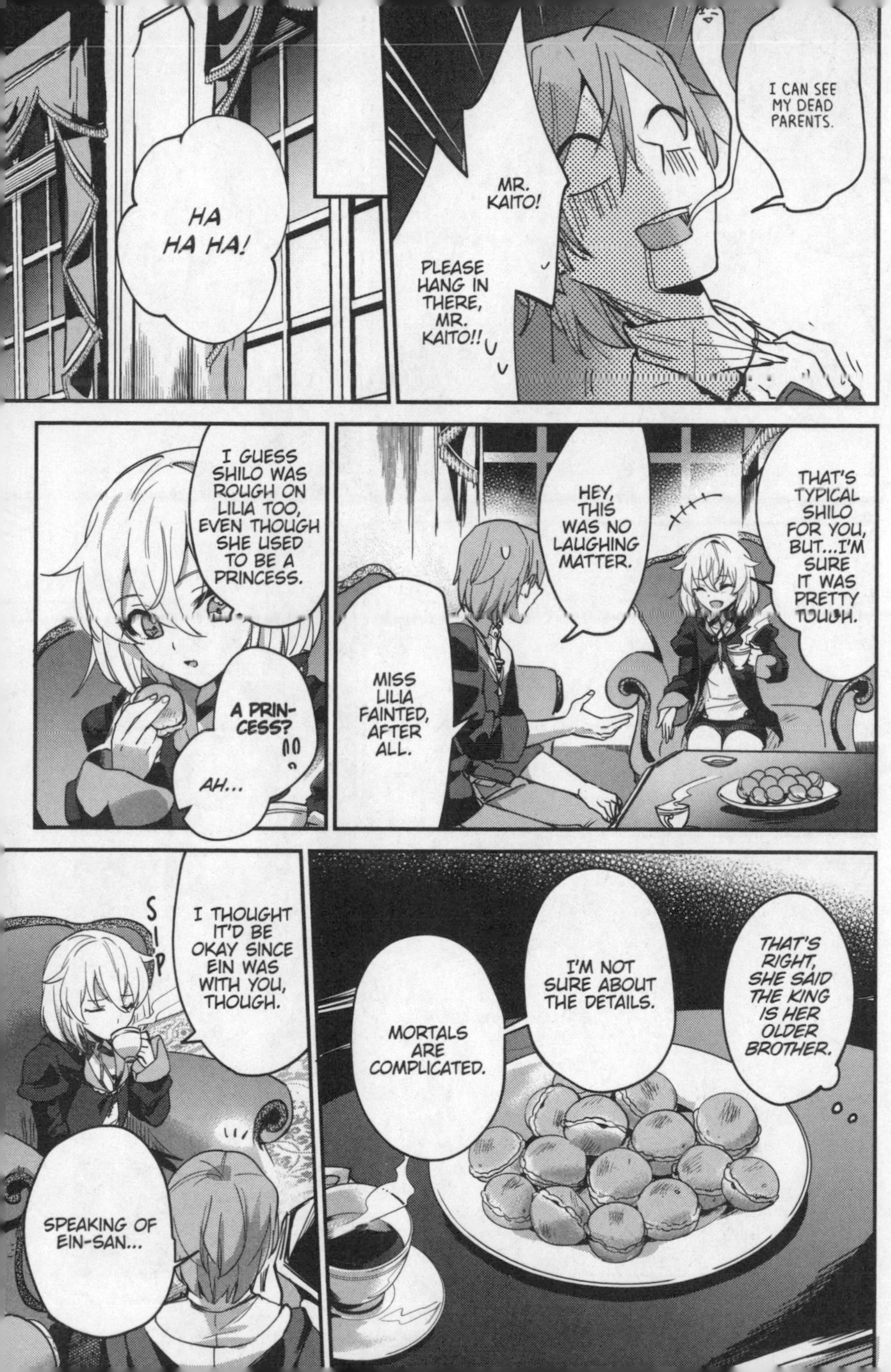
I CAN SEE MY DEAD PARENTS.
MR. KAITO!
PLEASE HANG IN THERE, MR. KAITO!!
HA HA HA!
THAT'S TYPICAL SHILO FOR YOU, BUT...I'M SURE IT WAS PRETTY TOUGH.
HEY, THIS WAS NO LAUGHING MATTER.
MISS LILIA FAINTED, AFTER ALL.
I GUESS SHILO WAS ROUGH ON LILIA TOO, EVEN THOUGH SHE USED TO BE A PRINCESS.
A PRINCESS?
AH...
THAT'S RIGHT, SHE SAID THE KING IS HER OLDER BROTHER.
I'M NOT SURE ABOUT THE DETAILS.
MORTALS ARE COMPLICATED.
SIP
I THOUGHT IT'D BE OKAY SINCE EIN WAS WITH YOU, THOUGH.
SPEAKING OF EIN-SAN...

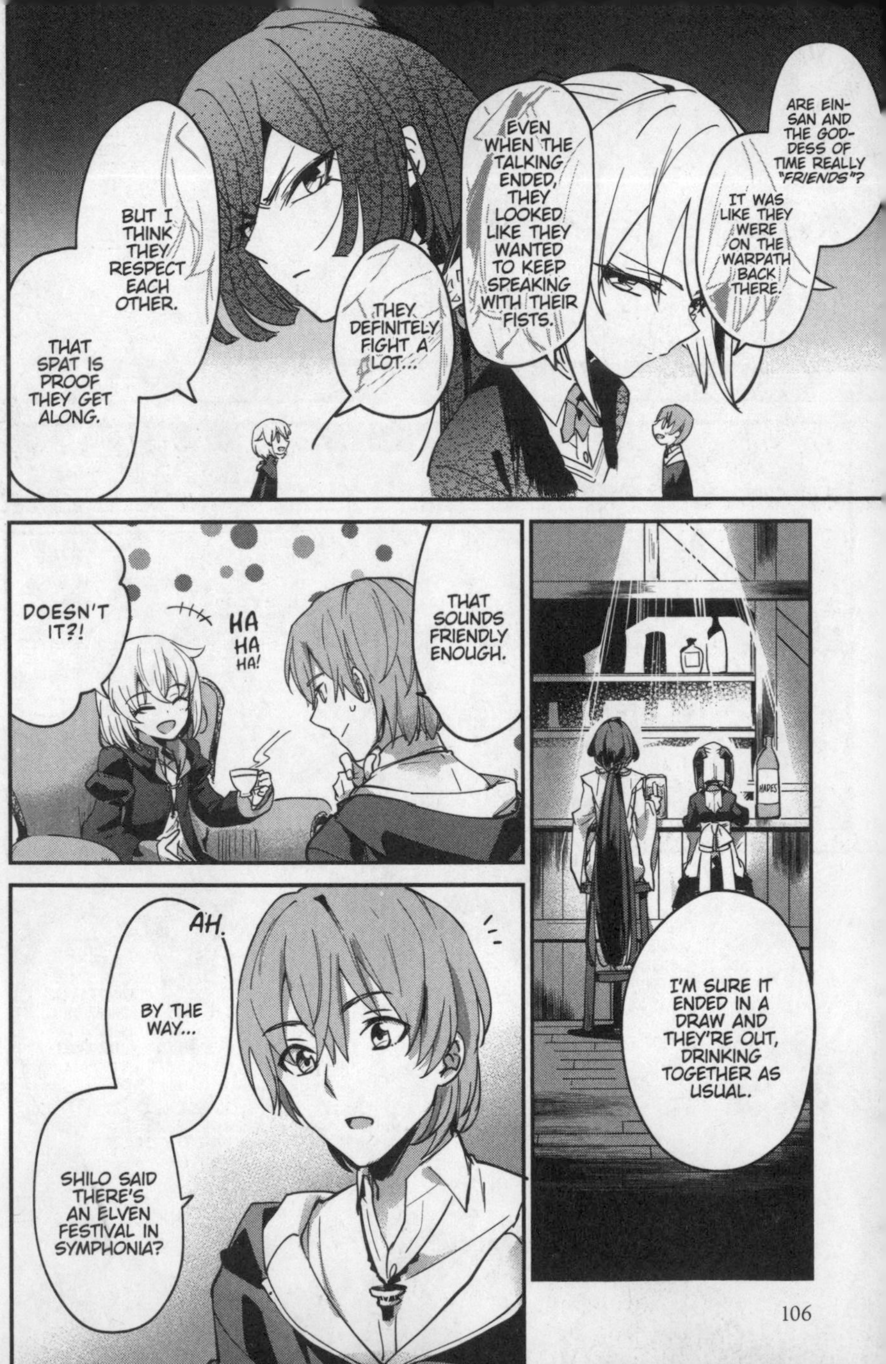
ARE EIN-SAN AND THE GOD-DESS OF TIME REALLY "FRIENDS"?
IT WAS LIKE THEY WERE ON THE WARPATH BACK THERE.
EVEN WHEN THE TALKING ENDED, THEY LOOKED LIKE THEY WANTED TO KEEP SPEAKING WITH THEIR FISTS.
THEY DEFINITELY FIGHT A LOT...
BUT I THINK THEY RESPECT EACH OTHER.
THAT SPAT IS PROOF THEY GET ALONG.
HADES
I'M SURE IT ENDED IN A DRAW AND THEY'RE OUT, DRINKING TOGETHER AS USUAL.
THAT SOUNDS FRIENDLY ENOUGH.
HA HA HA!
DOESN'T IT?!
AH.
BY THE WAY...
SHILO SAID THERE'S AN ELVEN FESTIVAL IN SYMPHONIA?

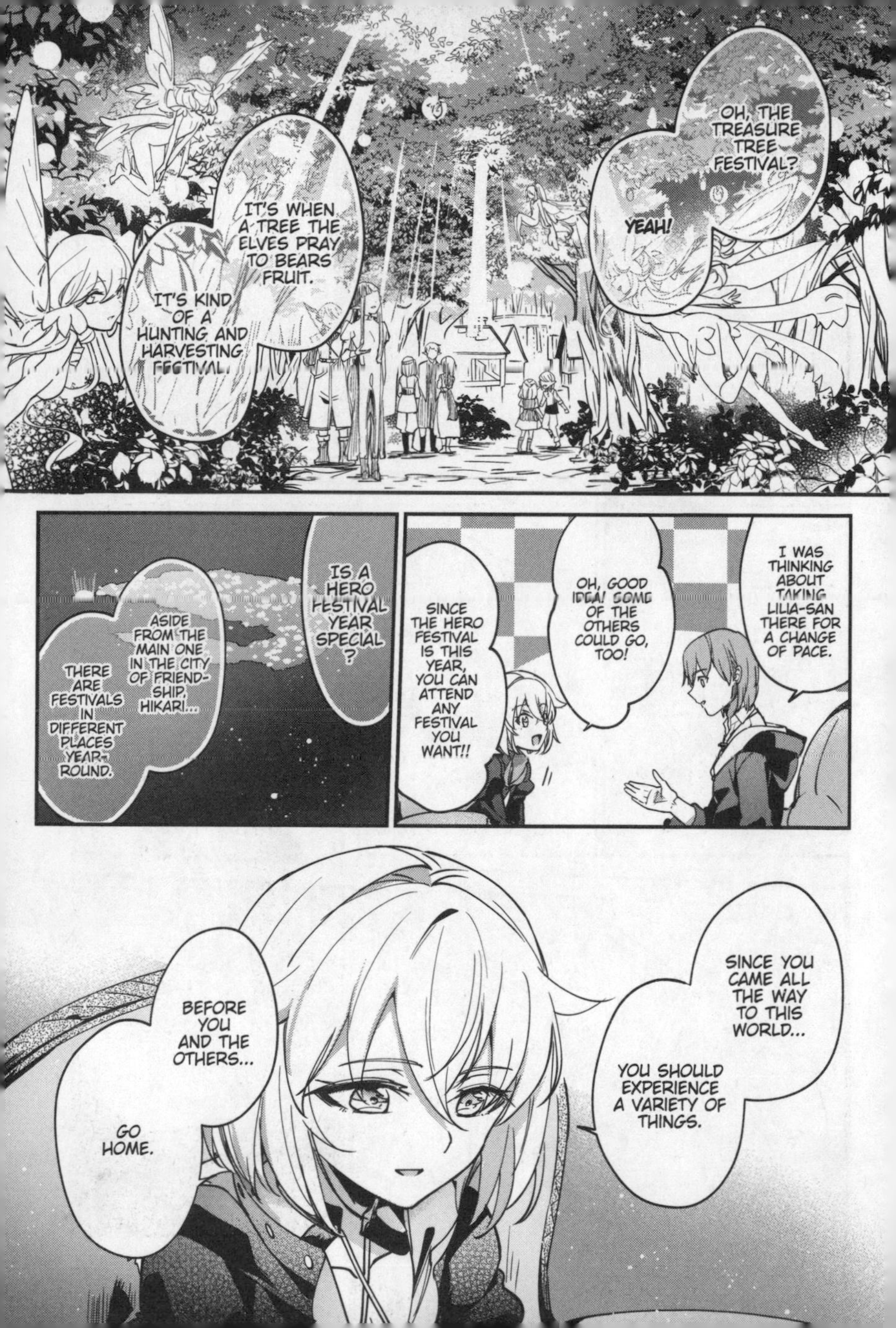
OH, THE TREASURE TREE FESTIVAL?
YEAH!
IT'S WHEN A TREE THE ELVES PRAY TO BEARS FRUIT.
IT'S KIND OF A HUNTING AND HARVESTING FESTIVAL.
I WAS THINKING ABOUT TAKING LILIA-SAN THERE FOR A CHANGE OF PACE.
OH, GOOD IDEA! SOME OF THE OTHERS COULD GO, TOO!
SINCE THE HERO FESTIVAL IS THIS YEAR, YOU CAN ATTEND ANY FESTIVAL YOU WANT!!
IS A HERO FESTIVAL YEAR SPECIAL?
ASIDE FROM THE MAIN ONE IN THE CITY OF FRIENDSHIP, HIKARI...
THERE ARE FESTIVALS IN DIFFERENT PLACES YEAR-ROUND.
SINCE YOU CAME ALL THE WAY TO THIS WORLD...
YOU SHOULD EXPERIENCE A VARIETY OF THINGS.
BEFORE YOU AND THE OTHERS...
GO HOME.

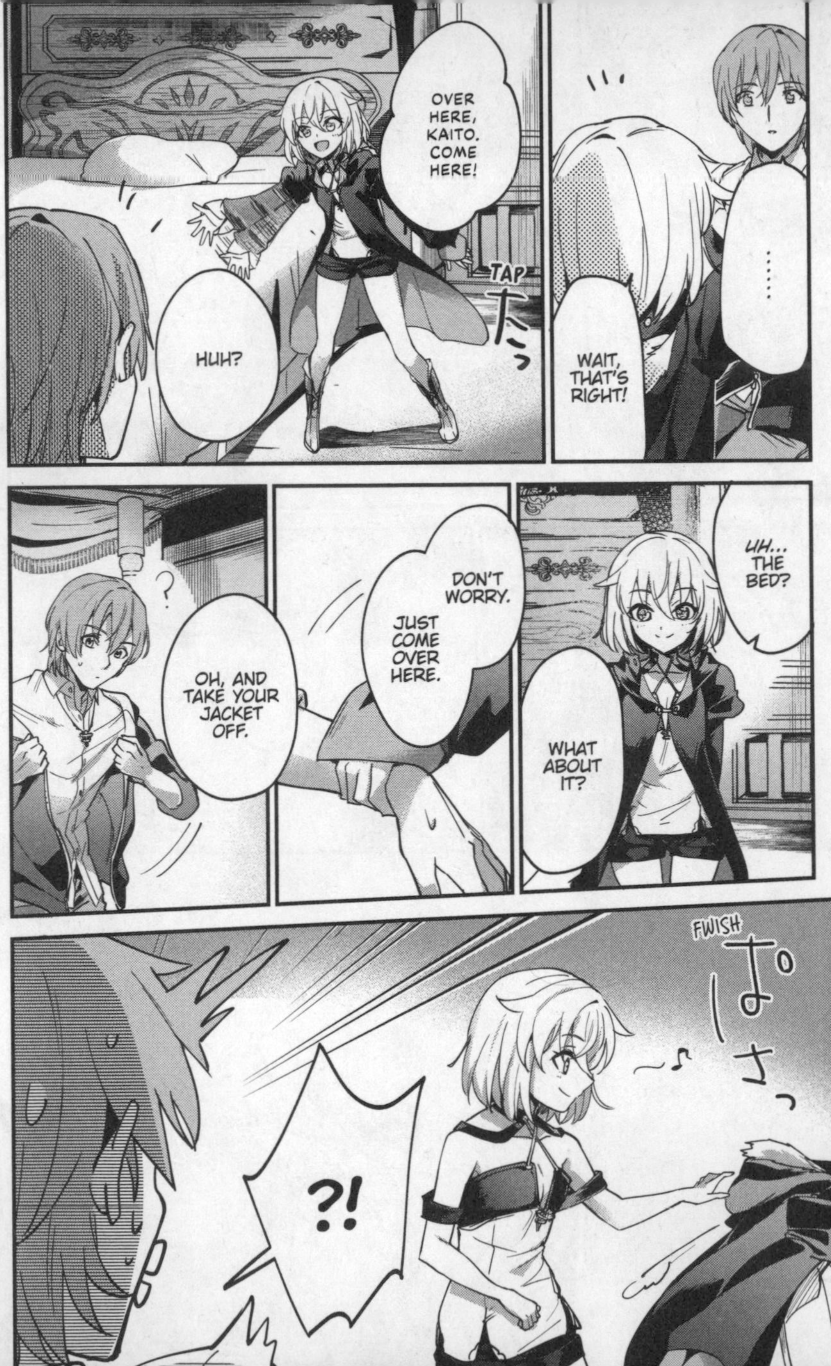
......
WAIT, THAT'S RIGHT!
OVER HERE, KAITO. COME HERE!
TAP
HUH?
UH... THE BED?
WHAT ABOUT IT?
DON'T WORRY.
JUST COME OVER HERE.
?
OH, AND TAKE YOUR JACKET OFF.
FWISH
?!

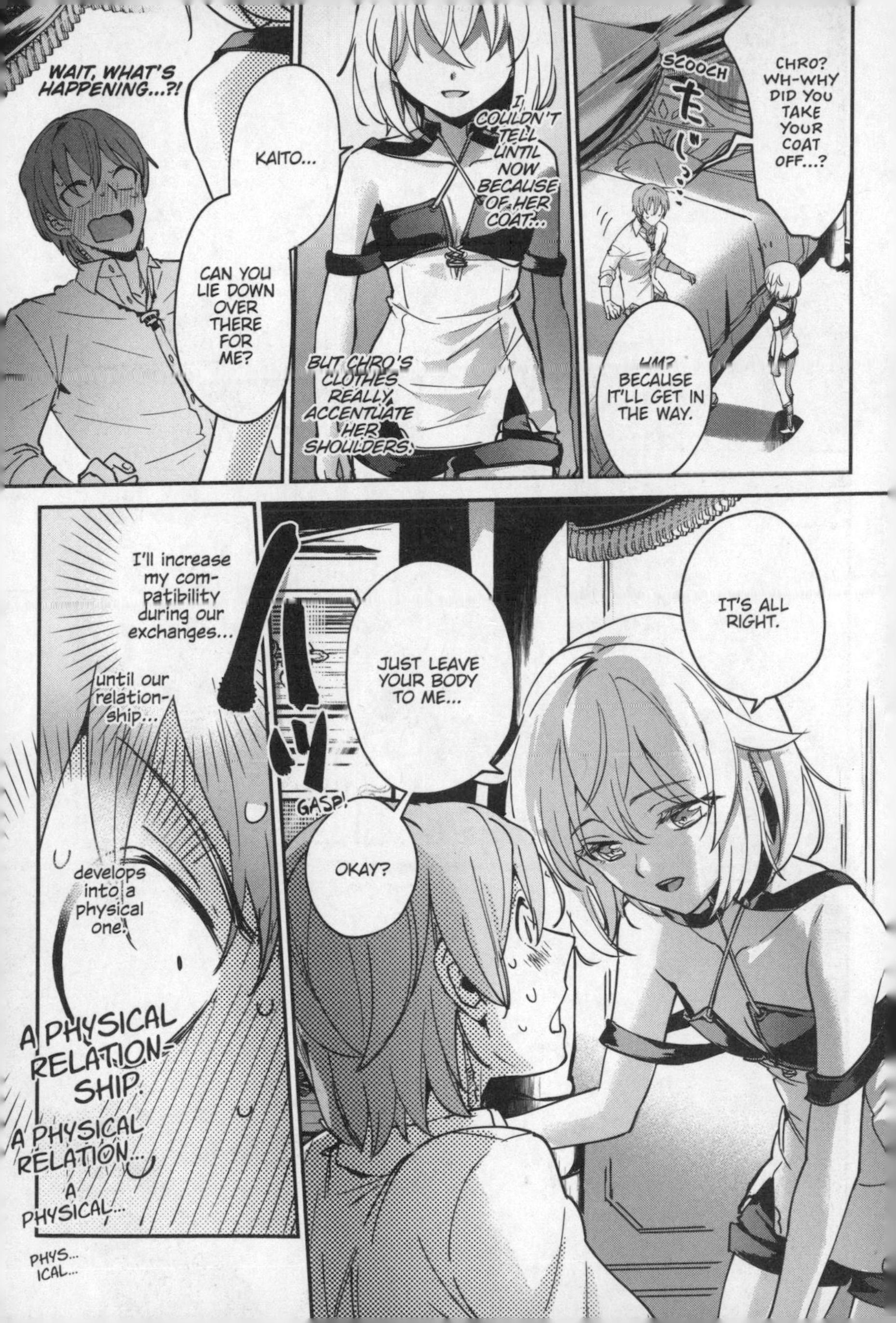
CHRO? WH-WHY DID YOU TAKE YOUR COAT OFF...?
SCOOCH
HM? BECAUSE IT'LL GET IN THE WAY.
KAITO...
CAN YOU LIE DOWN OVER THERE FOR ME?
I COULDN'T TELL UNTIL NOW BECAUSE OF HER COAT...
BUT CHRO'S CLOTHES REALLY ACCENTUATE HER SHOULDERS.
WAIT, WHAT'S HAPPENING...?!
IT'S ALL RIGHT.
JUST LEAVE YOUR BODY TO ME...
OKAY?
GASP!
I'll increase my com-patibility during our exchanges...
until our relation-ship...
develops into a physical one!
A PHYSICAL RELATION-SHIP.
A PHYSICAL RELATION...
A PHYSICAL...
PHYS... ICAL...

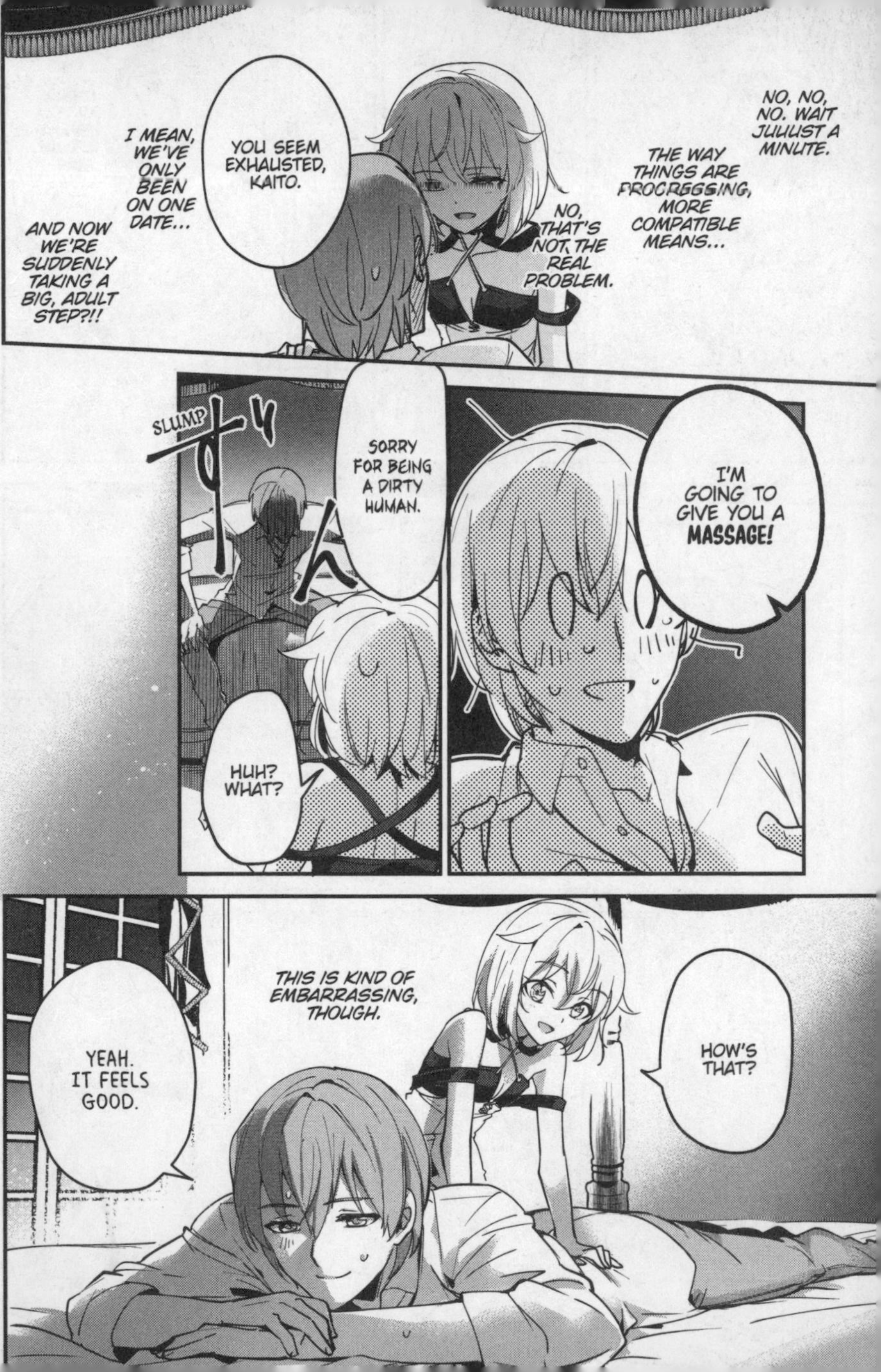
NO, NO, NO. WAIT JUUUST A MINUTE.
THE WAY THINGS ARE PROGRESSING, MORE COMPATIBLE MEANS...
NO, THAT'S NOT THE REAL PROBLEM.
YOU SEEM EXHAUSTED, KAITO.
I MEAN, WE'VE ONLY BEEN ON ONE DATE...
AND NOW WE'RE SUDDENLY TAKING A BIG, ADULT STEP?!!
I'M GOING TO GIVE YOU A **MASSAGE!**
SORRY FOR BEING A DIRTY HUMAN.
SLUMP
HUH? WHAT?
HOW'S THAT?
THIS IS KIND OF EMBARRASSING, THOUGH.
YEAH. IT FEELS GOOD.

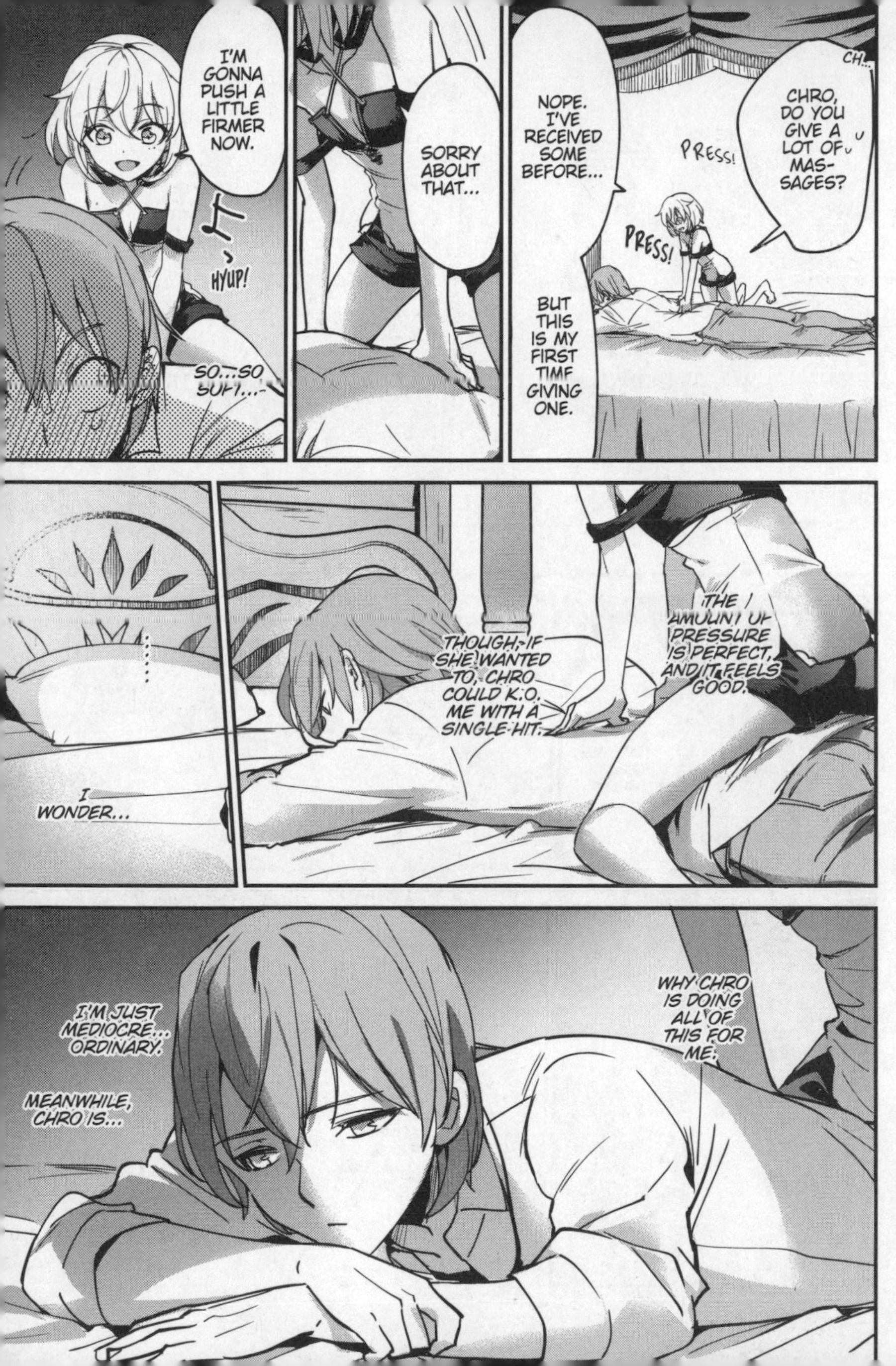
CH...
CHRO, DO YOU GIVE A LOT OF MAS-SAGES?
PRESS!
PRESS!
NOPE. I'VE RECEIVED SOME BEFORE...
BUT THIS IS MY FIRST TIME GIVING ONE.
SORRY ABOUT THAT...
I'M GONNA PUSH A LITTLE FIRMER NOW.
HYUP!
SO... SO SOFT...
THE AMOUNT OF PRESSURE IS PERFECT, AND IT FEELS GOOD.
THOUGH, IF SHE WANTED TO, CHRO COULD K.O. ME WITH A SINGLE HIT.
......
I WONDER...
WHY CHRO IS DOING ALL OF THIS FOR ME.
I'M JUST MEDIOCRE... ORDINARY.
MEANWHILE, CHRO IS...

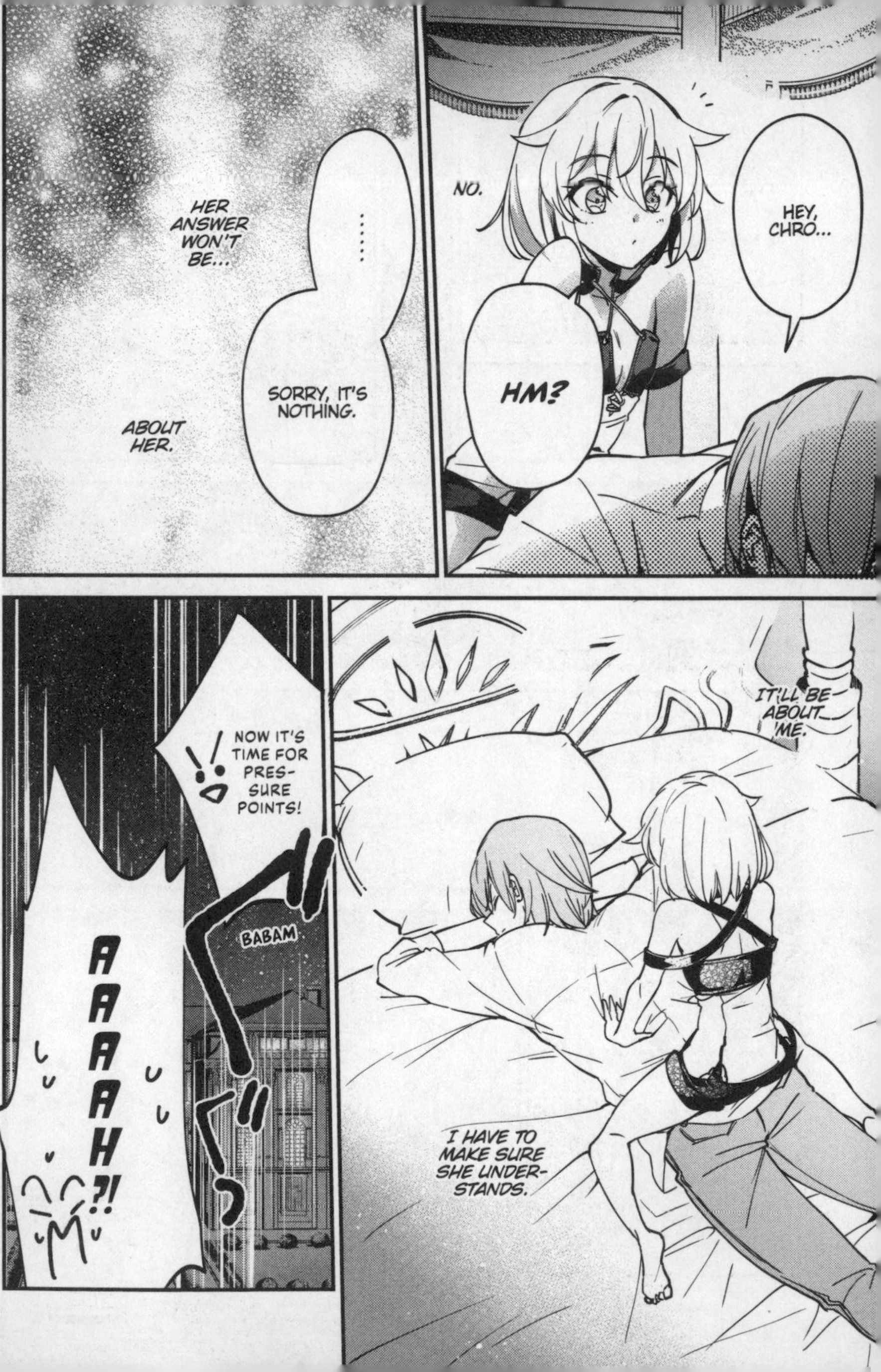
HEY, CHRO...
NO.
HM?
......
SORRY, IT'S NOTHING.
HER ANSWER WON'T BE...
ABOUT HER.
IT'LL BE ABOUT ME.
I HAVE TO MAKE SURE SHE UNDERSTANDS.
NOW IT'S TIME FOR PRES-SURE POINTS!
BABAM
AAAAAH?!

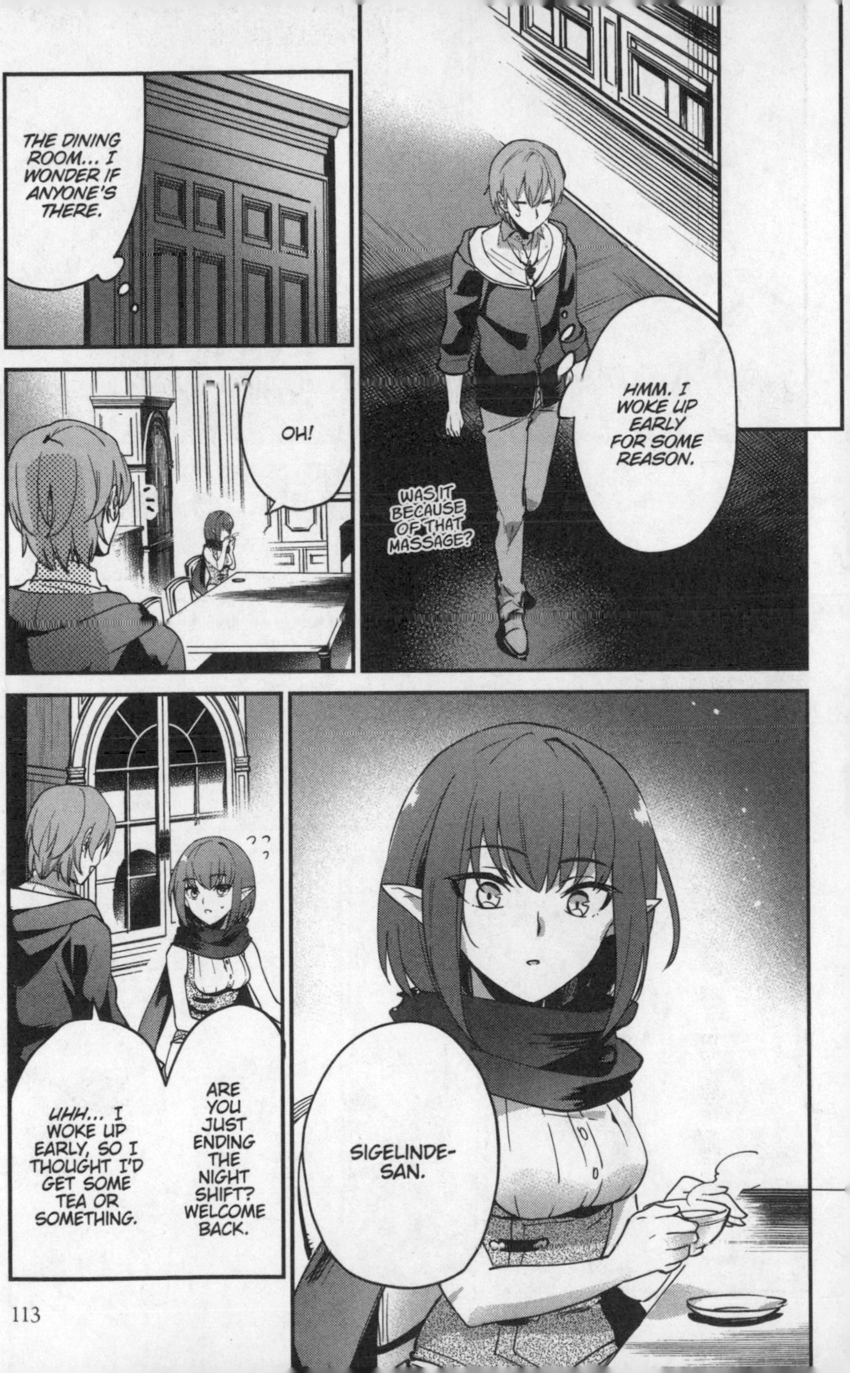
HMM. I WOKE UP EARLY FOR SOME REASON.
WAS IT BECAUSE OF THAT MASSAGE?
THE DINING ROOM... I WONDER IF ANYONE'S THERE.
OH!
SIGELINDE-SAN.
ARE YOU JUST ENDING THE NIGHT SHIFT? WELCOME BACK.
UHH... I WOKE UP EARLY, SO I THOUGHT I'D GET SOME TEA OR SOMETHING.

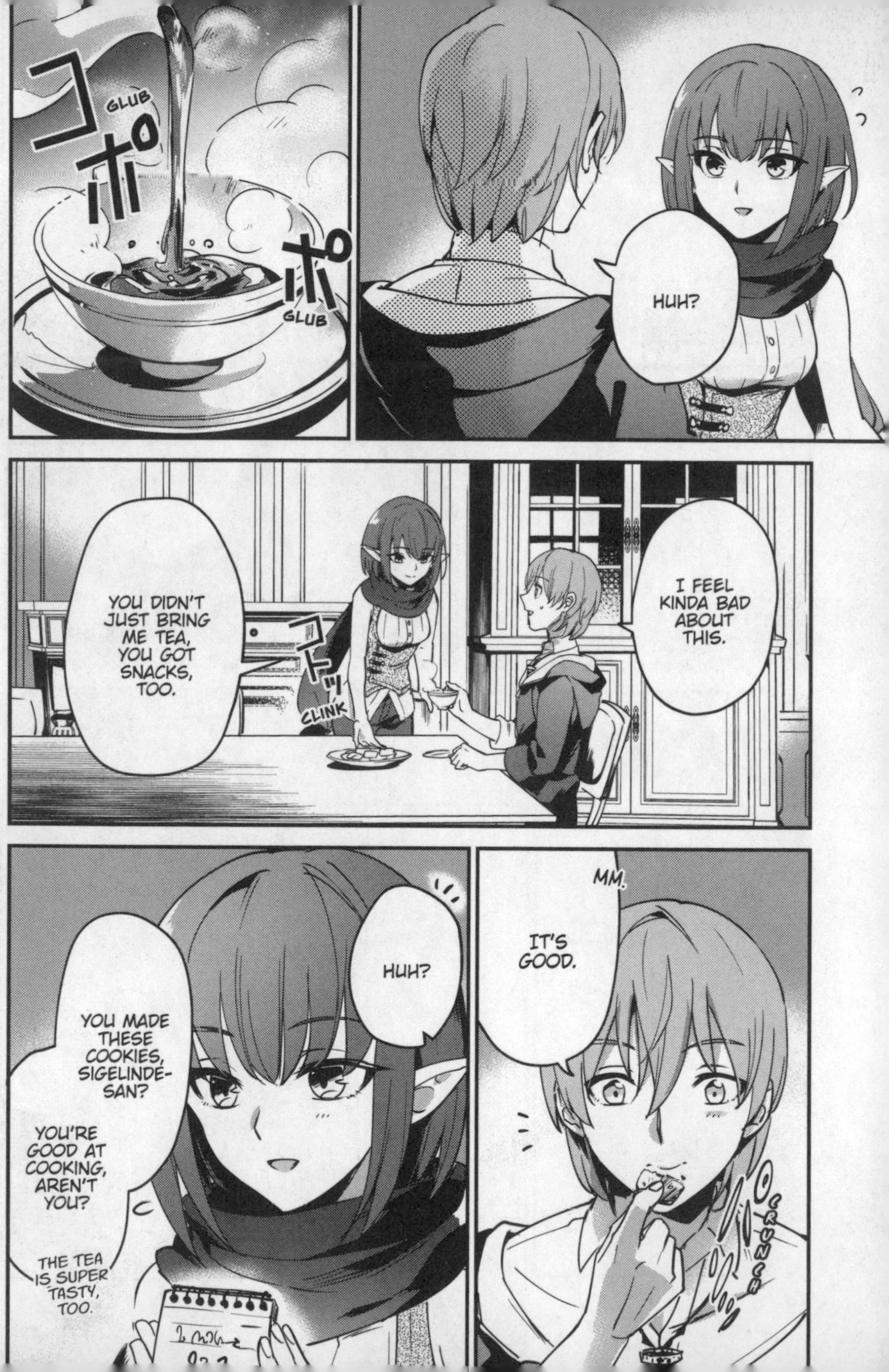
HUH?
GLUB
GLUB
I FEEL KINDA BAD ABOUT THIS.
YOU DIDN'T JUST BRING ME TEA, YOU GOT SNACKS, TOO.
CLINK
MM.
IT'S GOOD.
CRUNCH
HUH?
YOU MADE THESE COOKIES, SIGELINDE-SAN?
YOU'RE GOOD AT COOKING, AREN'T YOU?
THE TEA IS SUPER TASTY, TOO.

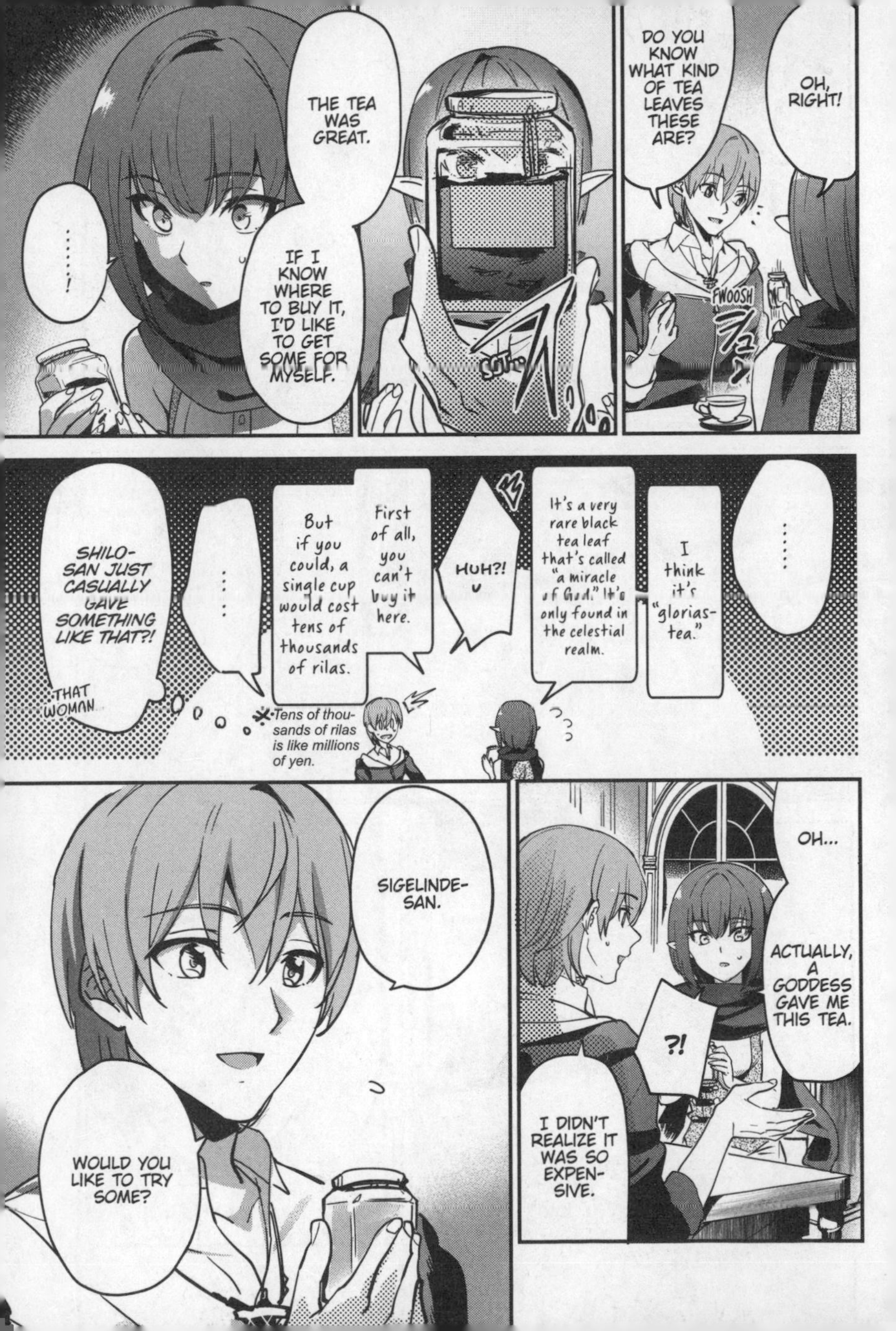
OH, RIGHT!
DO YOU KNOW WHAT KIND OF TEA LEAVES THESE ARE?
FWOOSH
THE TEA WAS GREAT.
IF I KNOW WHERE TO BUY IT, I'D LIKE TO GET SOME FOR MYSELF.
......!
......
I think it's "glorias-tea."
It's a very rare black tea leaf that's called "a miracle of God." It's only found in the celestial realm.
HUH?!
First of all, you can't buy it here.
But if you could, a single cup would cost tens of thousands of rilas.
......
SHILO-SAN JUST CASUALLY GAVE SOMETHING LIKE THAT?!
THAT WOMAN...
※Tens of thousands of rilas is like millions of yen.
OH...
ACTUALLY, A GODDESS GAVE ME THIS TEA.
?!
I DIDN'T REALIZE IT WAS SO EXPENSIVE.
SIGELINDE-SAN.
WOULD YOU LIKE TO TRY SOME?

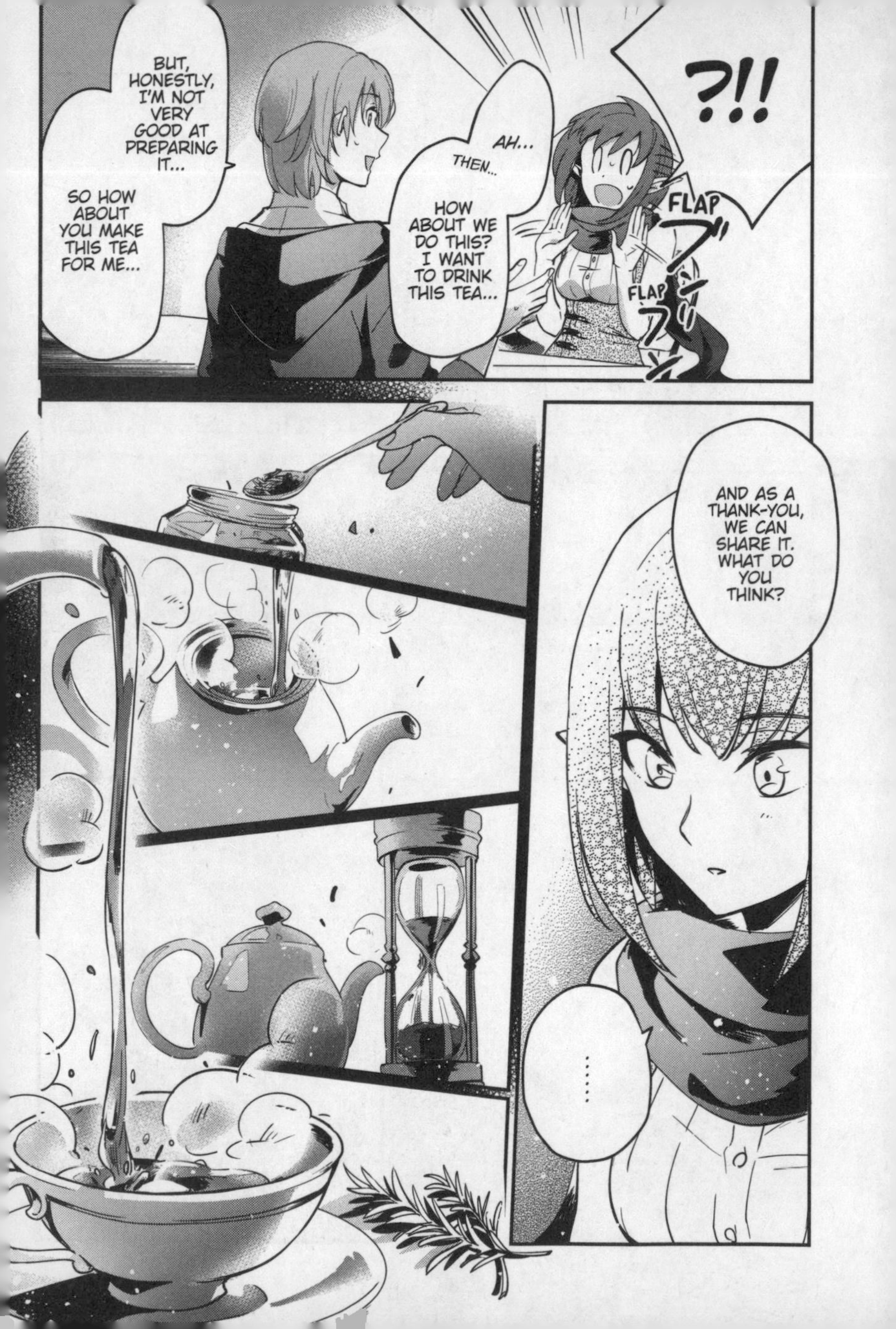
?!!
FLAP
FLAP
AH... THEN... HOW ABOUT WE DO THIS? I WANT TO DRINK THIS TEA...
BUT, HONESTLY, I'M NOT VERY GOOD AT PREPARING IT...
SO HOW ABOUT YOU MAKE THIS TEA FOR ME...
AND AS A THANK-YOU, WE CAN SHARE IT. WHAT DO YOU THINK?
......

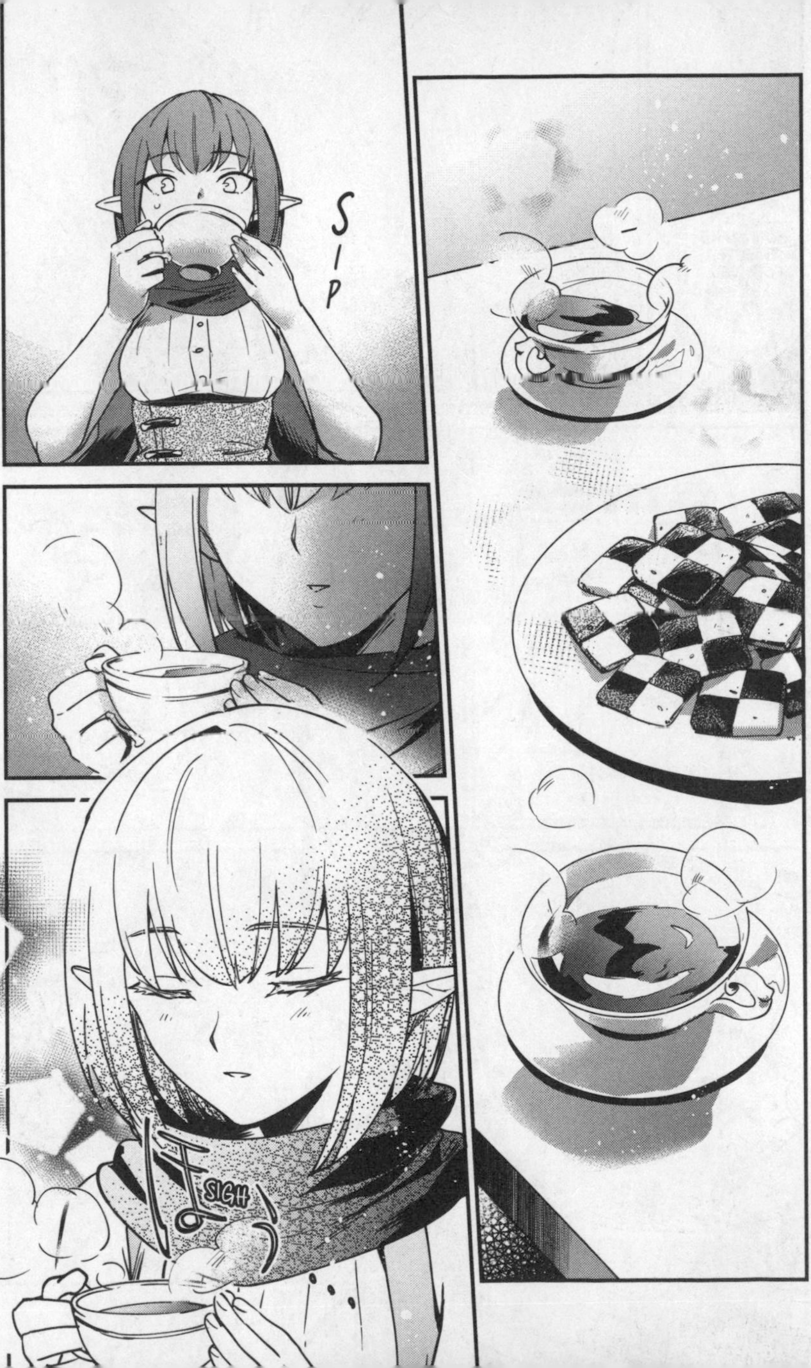
SIP
SIGH

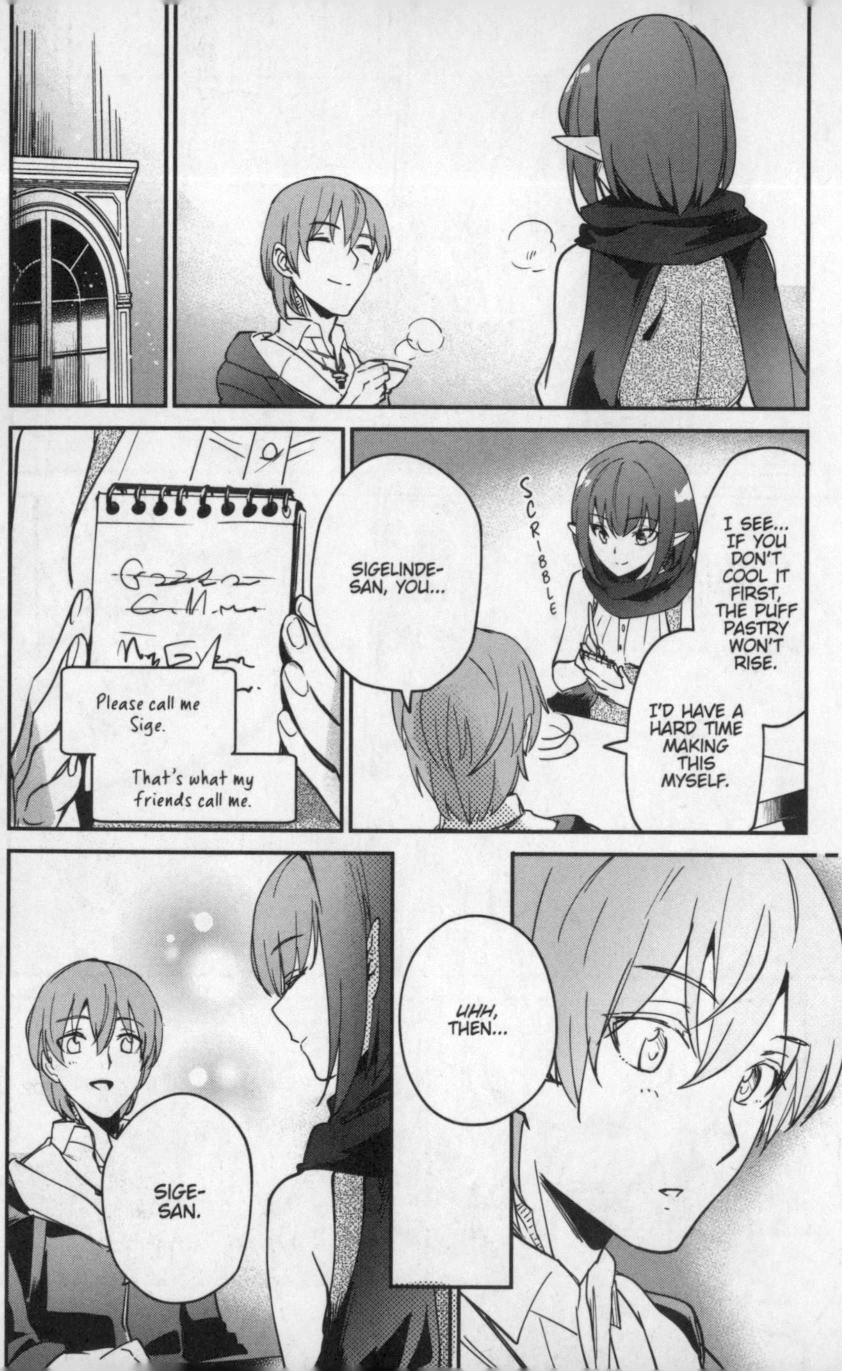
SCRIBBLE
I SEE... IF YOU DON'T COOL IT FIRST, THE PUFF PASTRY WON'T RISE.
I'D HAVE A HARD TIME MAKING THIS MYSELF.
SIGELINDE-SAN, YOU...
Please call me Sige.
That's what my friends call me.
UHH, THEN...
SIGE-SAN.

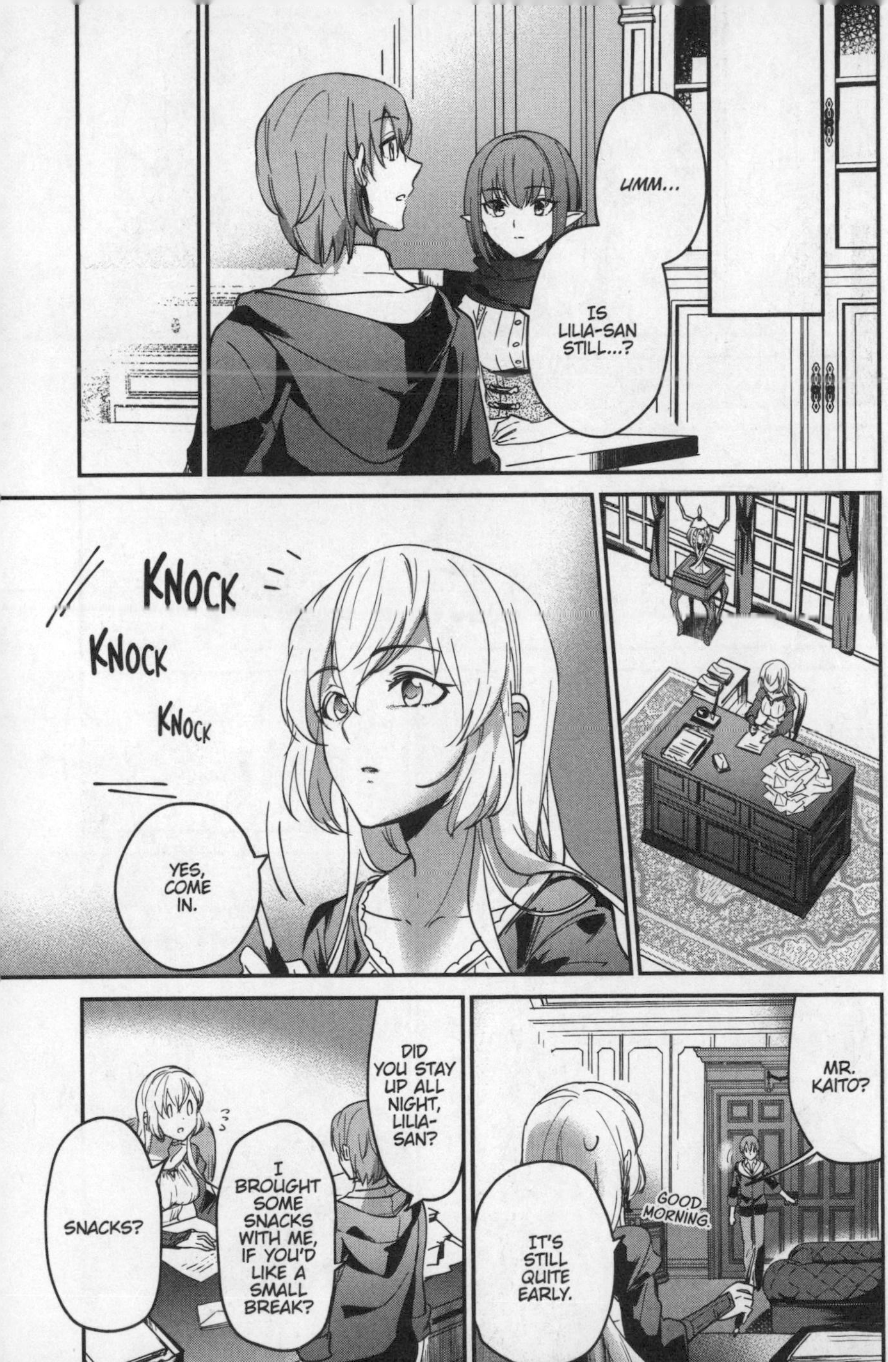
UMM...
IS LILIA-SAN STILL...?
KNOCK
KNOCK
KNOCK
YES, COME IN.
MR. KAITO?
GOOD MORNING.
IT'S STILL QUITE EARLY.
DID YOU STAY UP ALL NIGHT, LILIA-SAN?
I BROUGHT SOME SNACKS WITH ME, IF YOU'D LIKE A SMALL BREAK?
SNACKS?

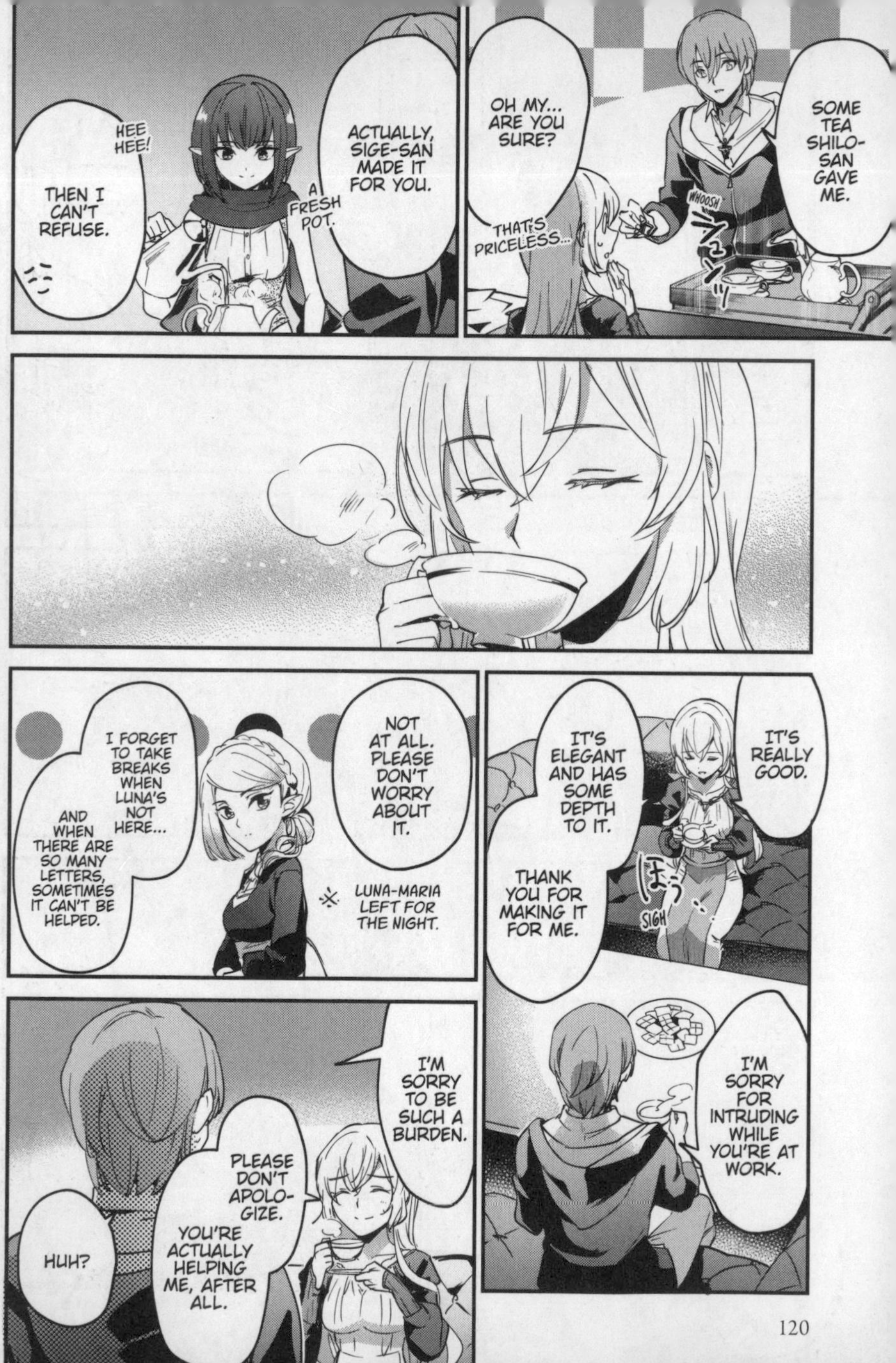
SOME TEA SHILO-SAN GAVE ME.
WHOOSH
OH MY... ARE YOU SURE?
THAT'S PRICELESS...
ACTUALLY, SIGE-SAN MADE IT FOR YOU.
A FRESH POT.
HEE HEE!
THEN I CAN'T REFUSE.
IT'S REALLY GOOD.
IT'S ELEGANT AND HAS SOME DEPTH TO IT.
SIGH
THANK YOU FOR MAKING IT FOR ME.
NOT AT ALL. PLEASE DON'T WORRY ABOUT IT.
※ LUNA-MARIA LEFT FOR THE NIGHT.
I FORGET TO TAKE BREAKS WHEN LUNA'S NOT HERE...
AND WHEN THERE ARE SO MANY LETTERS, SOMETIMES IT CAN'T BE HELPED.
I'M SORRY FOR INTRUDING WHILE YOU'RE AT WORK.
I'M SORRY TO BE SUCH A BURDEN.
PLEASE DON'T APOLOGIZE.
YOU'RE ACTUALLY HELPING ME, AFTER ALL.
HUH?

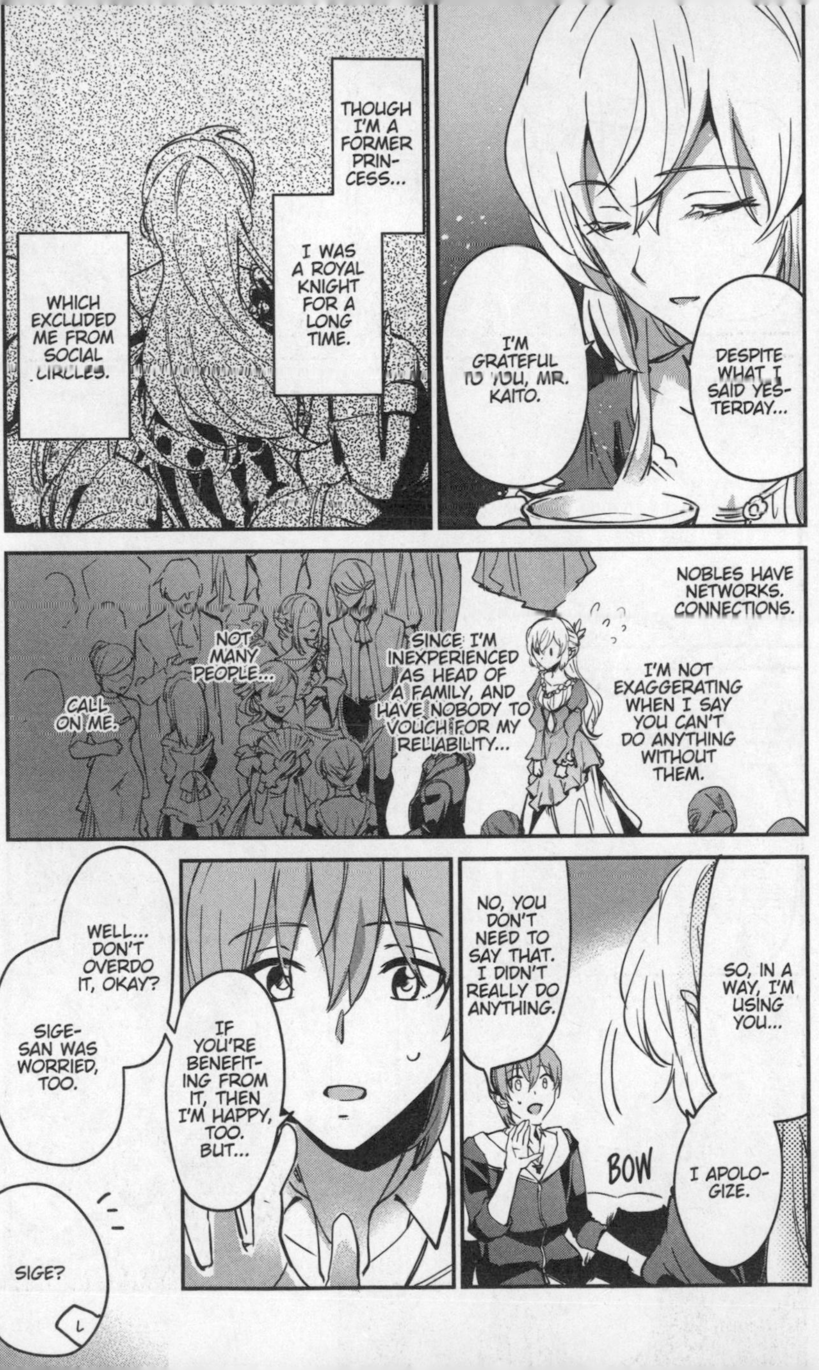
DESPITE WHAT I SAID YESTERDAY...
I'M GRATEFUL TO YOU, MR. KAITO.
THOUGH I'M A FORMER PRINCESS...
I WAS A ROYAL KNIGHT FOR A LONG TIME.
WHICH EXCLUDED ME FROM SOCIAL CIRCLES.
NOBLES HAVE NETWORKS. CONNECTIONS.
I'M NOT EXAGGERATING WHEN I SAY YOU CAN'T DO ANYTHING WITHOUT THEM.
SINCE I'M INEXPERIENCED AS HEAD OF A FAMILY, AND HAVE NOBODY TO VOUCH FOR MY RELIABILITY...
NOT MANY PEOPLE...
CALL ON ME.
SO, IN A WAY, I'M USING YOU...
I APOLOGIZE.
BOW
NO, YOU DON'T NEED TO SAY THAT. I DIDN'T REALLY DO ANYTHING.
IF YOU'RE BENEFITING FROM IT, THEN I'M HAPPY, TOO. BUT...
WELL... DON'T OVERDO IT, OKAY?
SIGE-SAN WAS WORRIED, TOO.
SIGE?

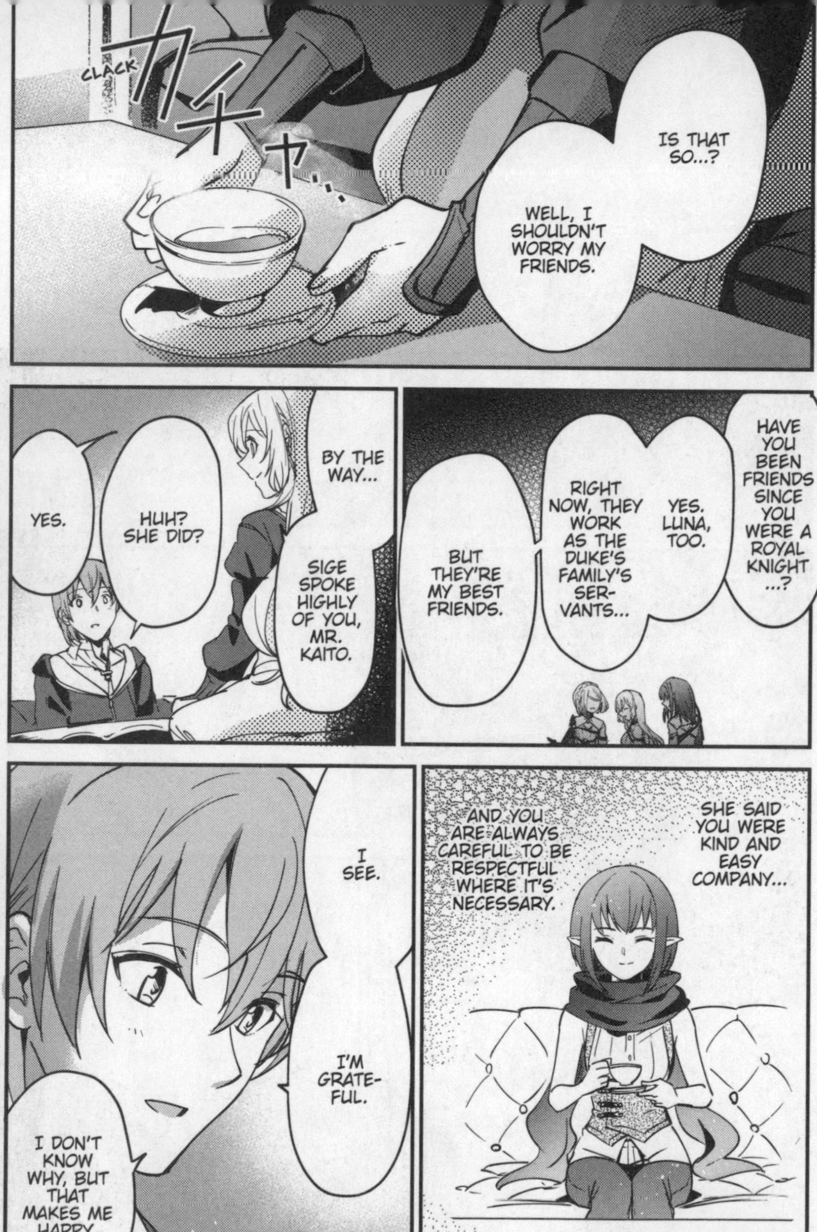
CLACK
IS THAT SO...?
WELL, I SHOULDN'T WORRY MY FRIENDS.
HAVE YOU BEEN FRIENDS SINCE YOU WERE A ROYAL KNIGHT ...?
YES. LUNA, TOO.
RIGHT NOW, THEY WORK AS THE DUKE'S FAMILY'S SER-VANTS...
BUT THEY'RE MY BEST FRIENDS.
BY THE WAY...
SIGE SPOKE HIGHLY OF YOU, MR. KAITO.
HUH? SHE DID?
YES.
SHE SAID YOU WERE KIND AND EASY COMPANY...
AND YOU ARE ALWAYS CAREFUL TO BE RESPECTFUL WHERE IT'S NECESSARY.
I SEE.
I'M GRATE-FUL.
I DON'T KNOW WHY, BUT THAT MAKES ME HAPPY.

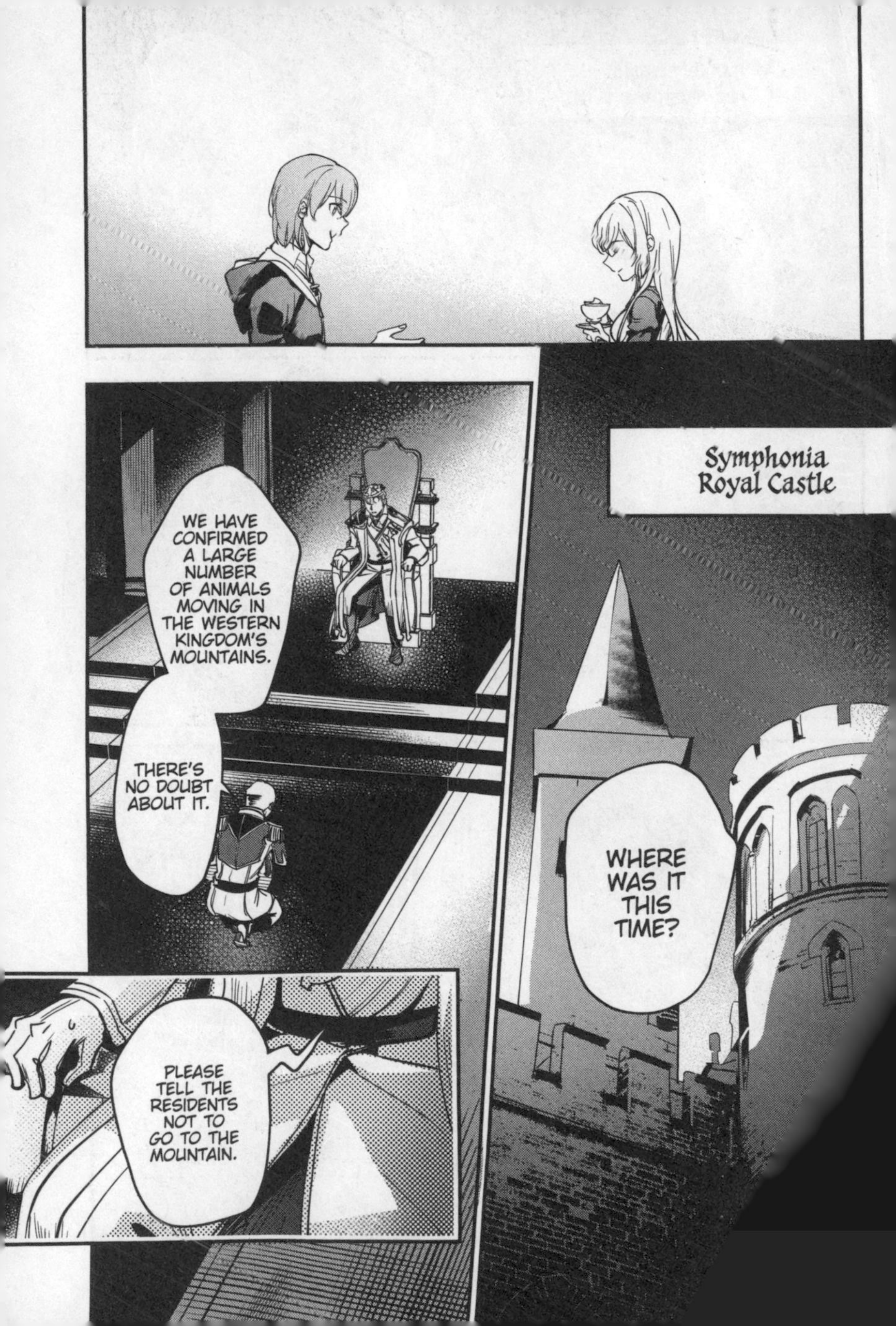
Symphonia Royal Castle
WHERE WAS IT THIS TIME?
WE HAVE CONFIRMED A LARGE NUMBER OF ANIMALS MOVING IN THE WESTERN KINGDOM'S MOUNTAINS.
THERE'S NO DOUBT ABOUT IT.
PLEASE TELL THE RESIDENTS NOT TO GO TO THE MOUNTAIN.

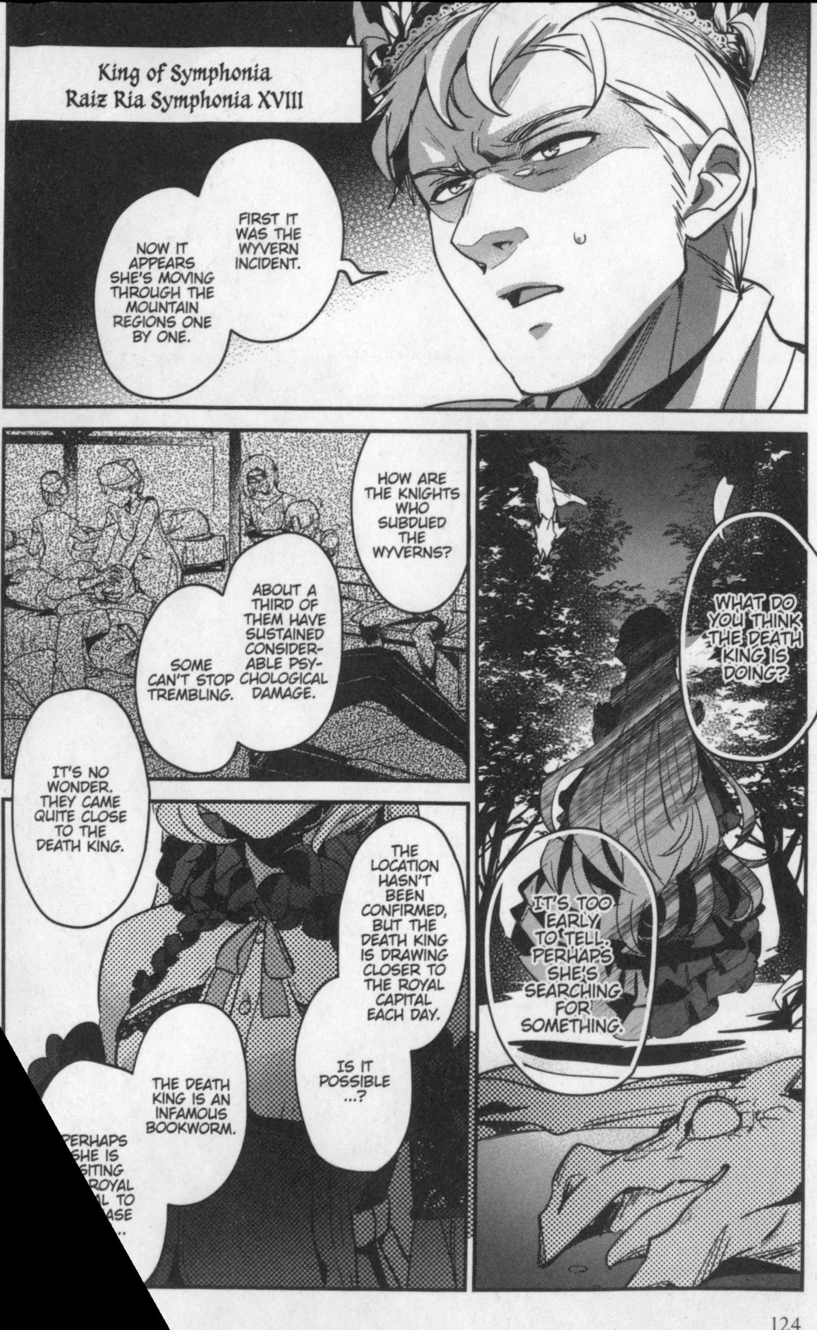
King of Symphonia
Raiz Ria Symphonia XVIII
FIRST IT WAS THE WYVERN INCIDENT.
NOW IT APPEARS SHE'S MOVING THROUGH THE MOUNTAIN REGIONS ONE BY ONE.
WHAT DO YOU THINK THE DEATH KING IS DOING?
IT'S TOO EARLY TO TELL. PERHAPS SHE'S SEARCHING FOR SOMETHING.
HOW ARE THE KNIGHTS WHO SUBDUED THE WYVERNS?
ABOUT A THIRD OF THEM HAVE SUSTAINED CONSIDERABLE PSYCHOLOGICAL DAMAGE.
SOME CAN'T STOP TREMBLING.
IT'S NO WONDER. THEY CAME QUITE CLOSE TO THE DEATH KING.
THE LOCATION HASN'T BEEN CONFIRMED, BUT THE DEATH KING IS DRAWING CLOSER TO THE ROYAL CAPITAL EACH DAY.
IS IT POSSIBLE ...?
THE DEATH KING IS AN INFAMOUS BOOKWORM.
PERHAPS SHE IS

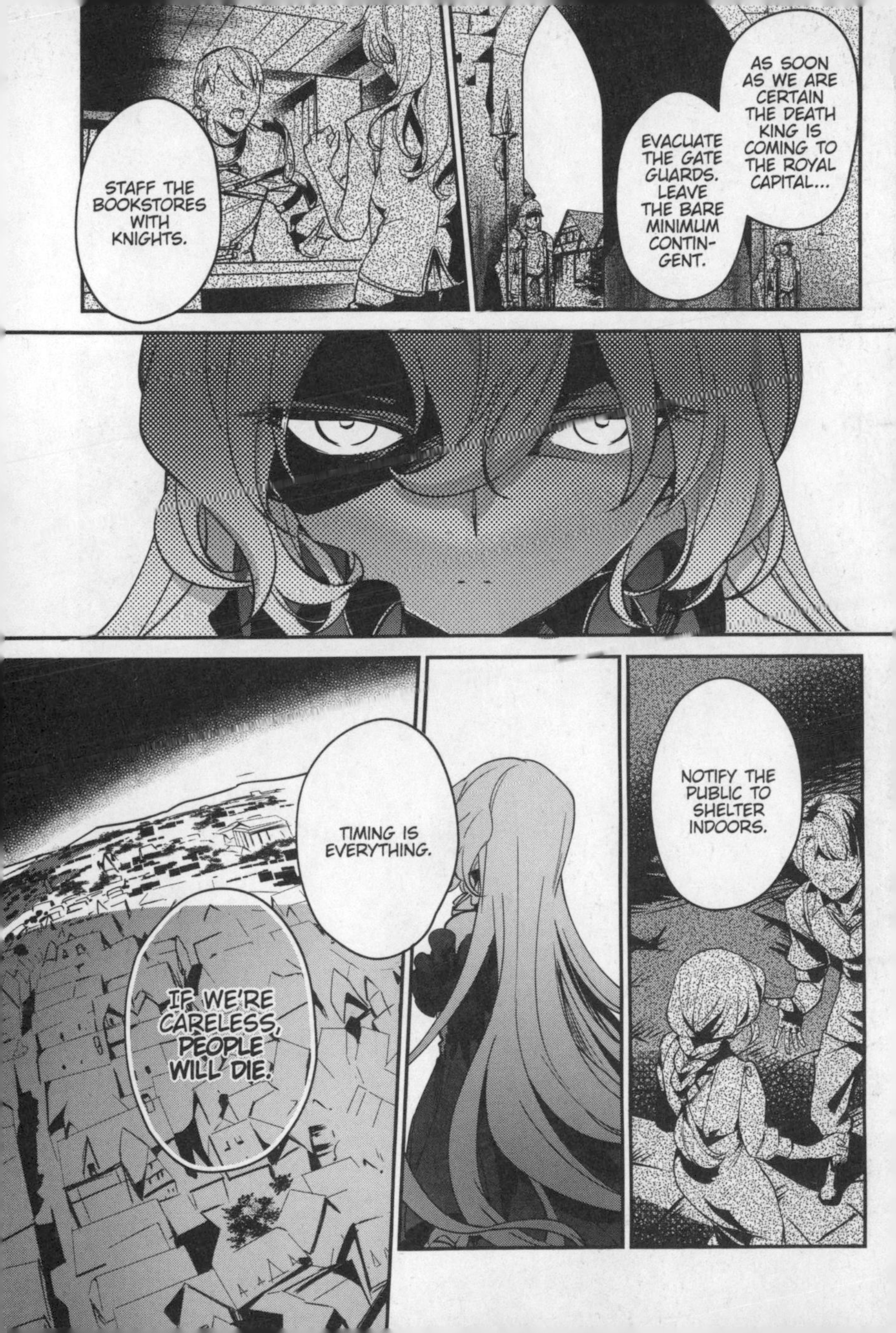
AS SOON AS WE ARE CERTAIN THE DEATH KING IS COMING TO THE ROYAL CAPITAL...
EVACUATE THE GATE GUARDS. LEAVE THE BARE MINIMUM CONTIN-GENT.
STAFF THE BOOKSTORES WITH KNIGHTS.
NOTIFY THE PUBLIC TO SHELTER INDOORS.
TIMING IS EVERYTHING.
IF WE'RE CARELESS, PEOPLE WILL DIE.

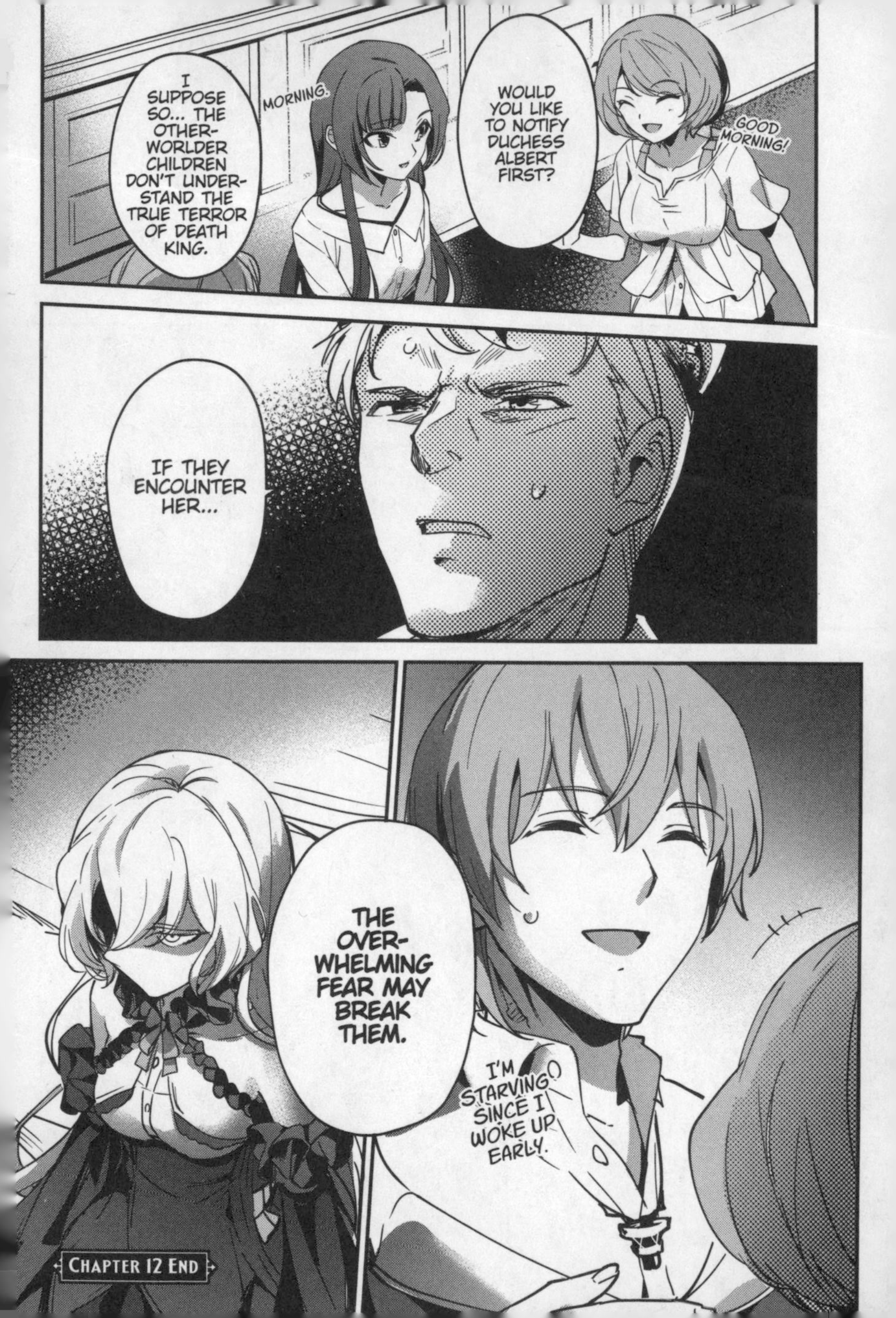
GOOD MORNING!
WOULD YOU LIKE TO NOTIFY DUCHESS ALBERT FIRST?
MORNING.
I SUPPOSE SO... THE OTHER-WORLDER CHILDREN DON'T UNDER-STAND THE TRUE TERROR OF DEATH KING.
IF THEY ENCOUNTER HER...
THE OVER-WHELMING FEAR MAY BREAK THEM.
I'M STARVING SINCE I WOKE UP EARLY.
CHAPTER 12 END

I GOT CAUGHT UP IN A HERO SUMMONS, BUT THE OTHER WORLD WAS AT PEACE!

I GOT CAUGHT UP IN A HERO SUMMONS,

BUT THE OTHER WORLD
WAS AT PEACE!

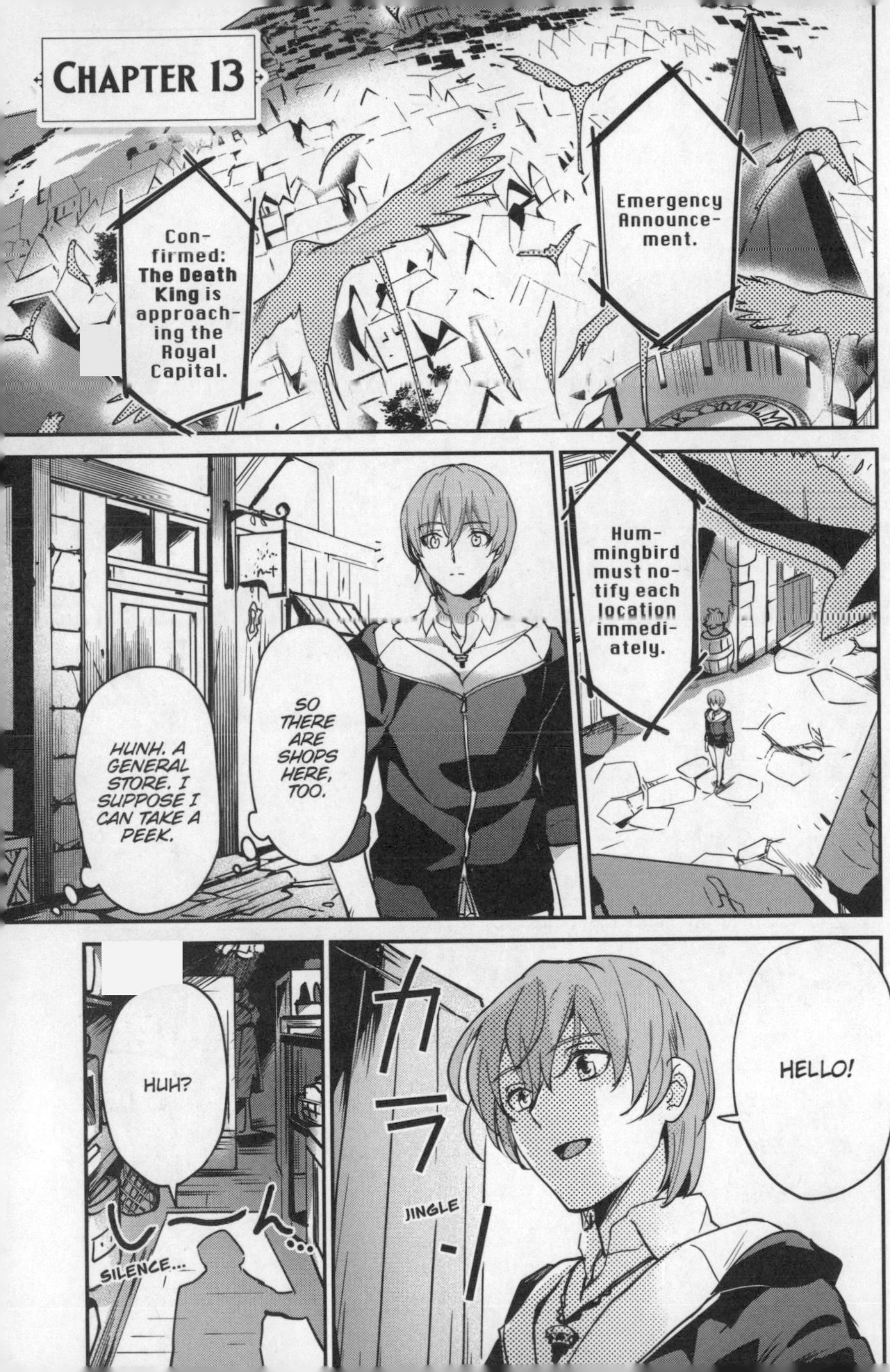
CHAPTER 13
Emergency Announcement.
Confirmed: The Death King is approaching the Royal Capital.
Hummingbird must notify each location immediately.
SO THERE ARE SHOPS HERE, TOO.
HUNH. A GENERAL STORE. I SUPPOSE I CAN TAKE A PEEK.
HELLO!
カラ
JINGLE
HUH?
しーん…
SILENCE...

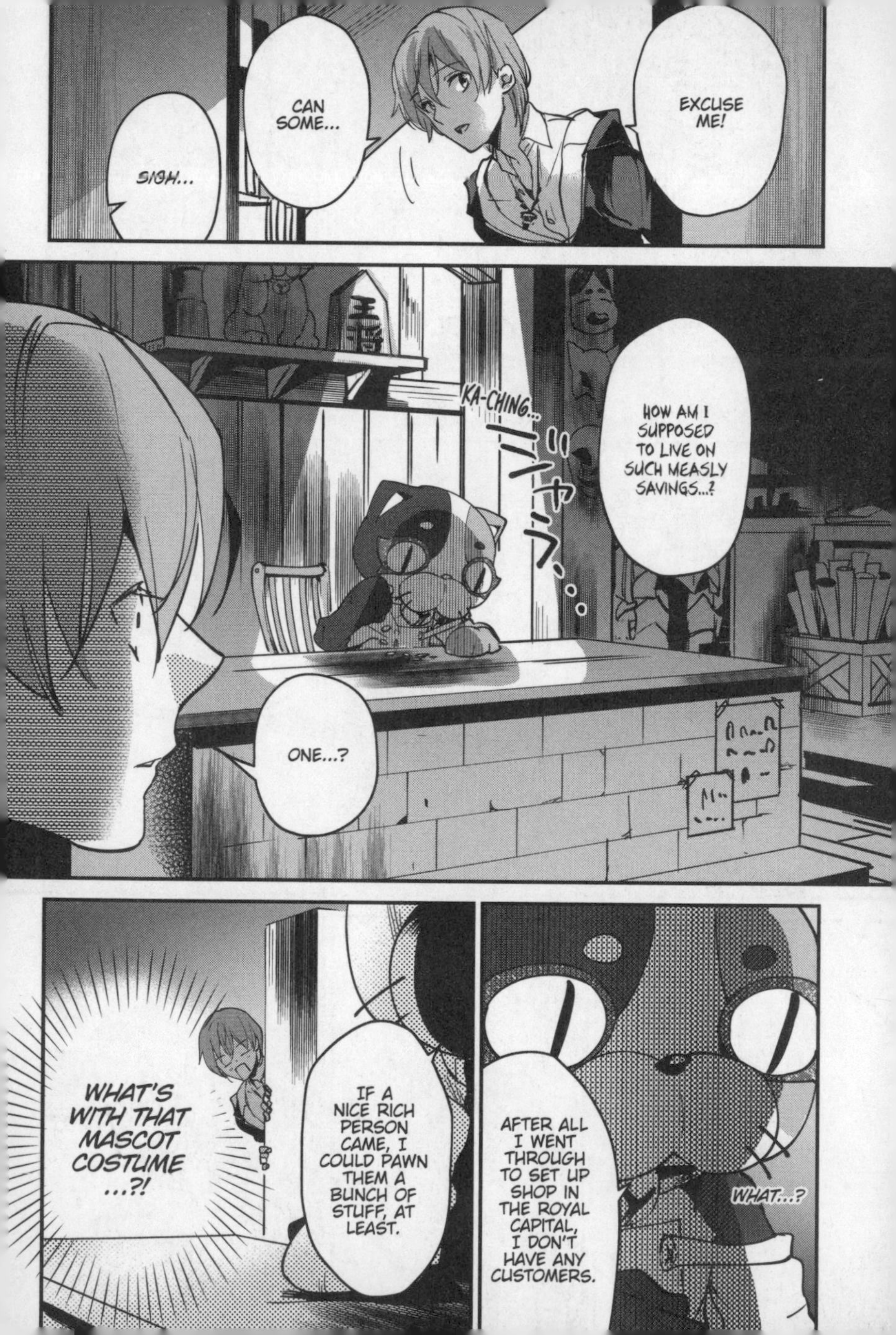
EXCUSE ME!
CAN SOME...
SIGH...
HOW AM I SUPPOSED TO LIVE ON SUCH MEASLY SAVINGS...?
KA-CHING...
ONE...?
WHAT...?
AFTER ALL I WENT THROUGH TO SET UP SHOP IN THE ROYAL CAPITAL, I DON'T HAVE ANY CUSTOMERS.
IF A NICE RICH PERSON CAME, I COULD PAWN THEM A BUNCH OF STUFF, AT LEAST.
WHAT'S WITH THAT MASCOT COSTUME ...?!

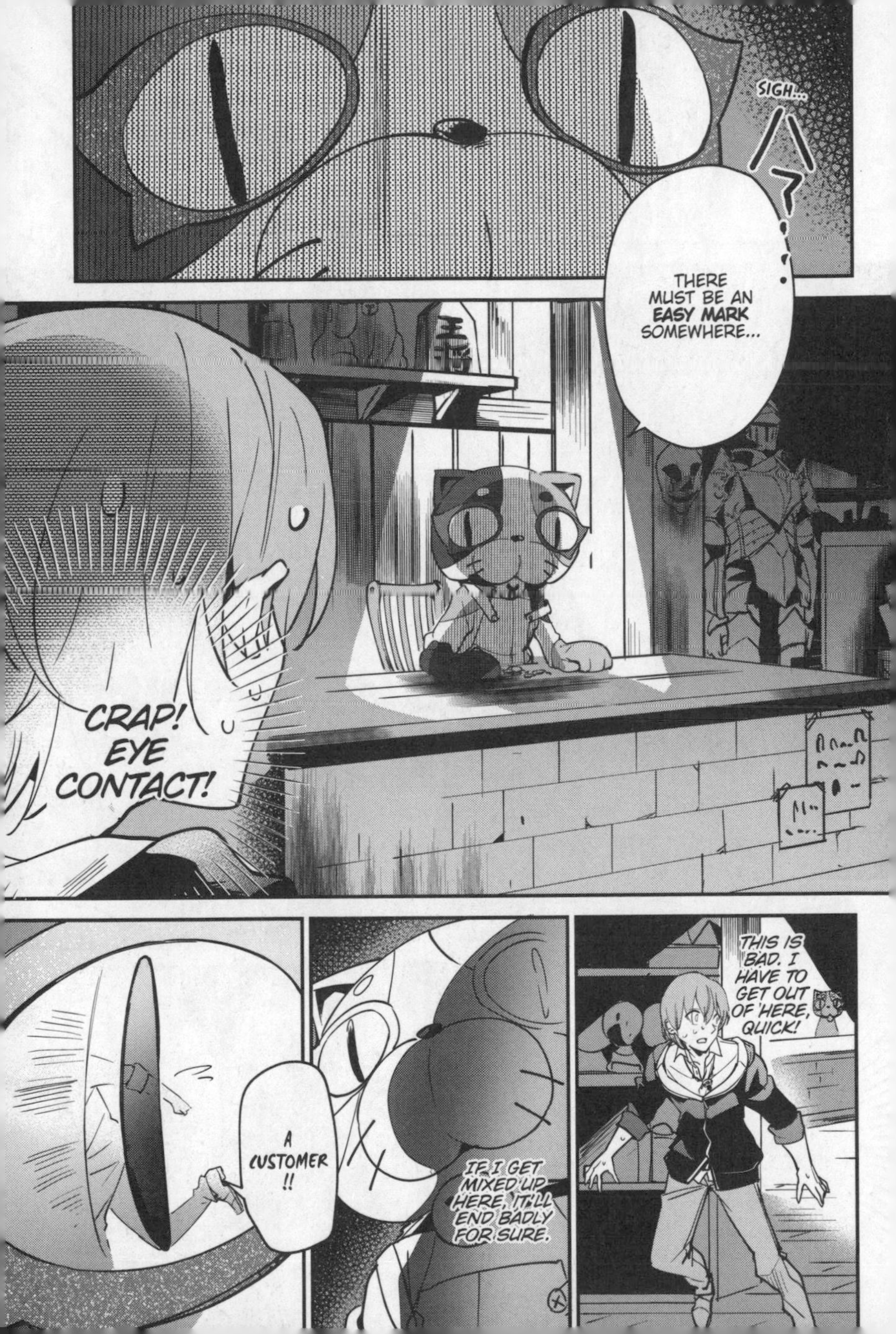
SIGH...
THERE MUST BE AN EASY MARK SOMEWHERE...
CRAP! EYE CONTACT!
THIS IS BAD. I HAVE TO GET OUT OF HERE, QUICK!
IF I GET MIXED UP HERE, IT'LL END BADLY FOR SURE.
A CUSTOMER !!

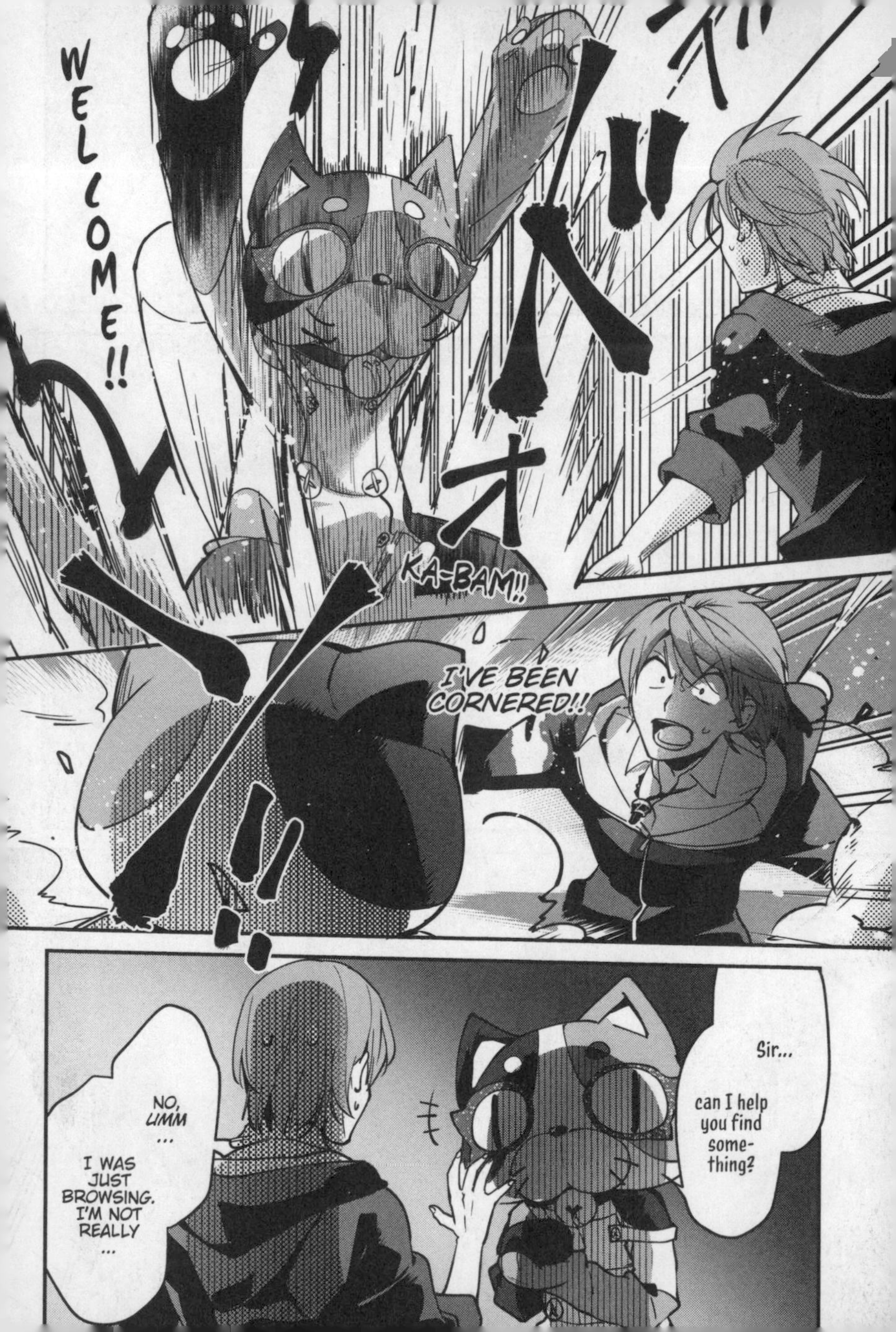
WELLCOME!!
KA-BAM!!
I'VE BEEN CORNERED!!
Sir...
can I help you find some-thing?
NO, UMM...
I WAS JUST BROWSING. I'M NOT REALLY...

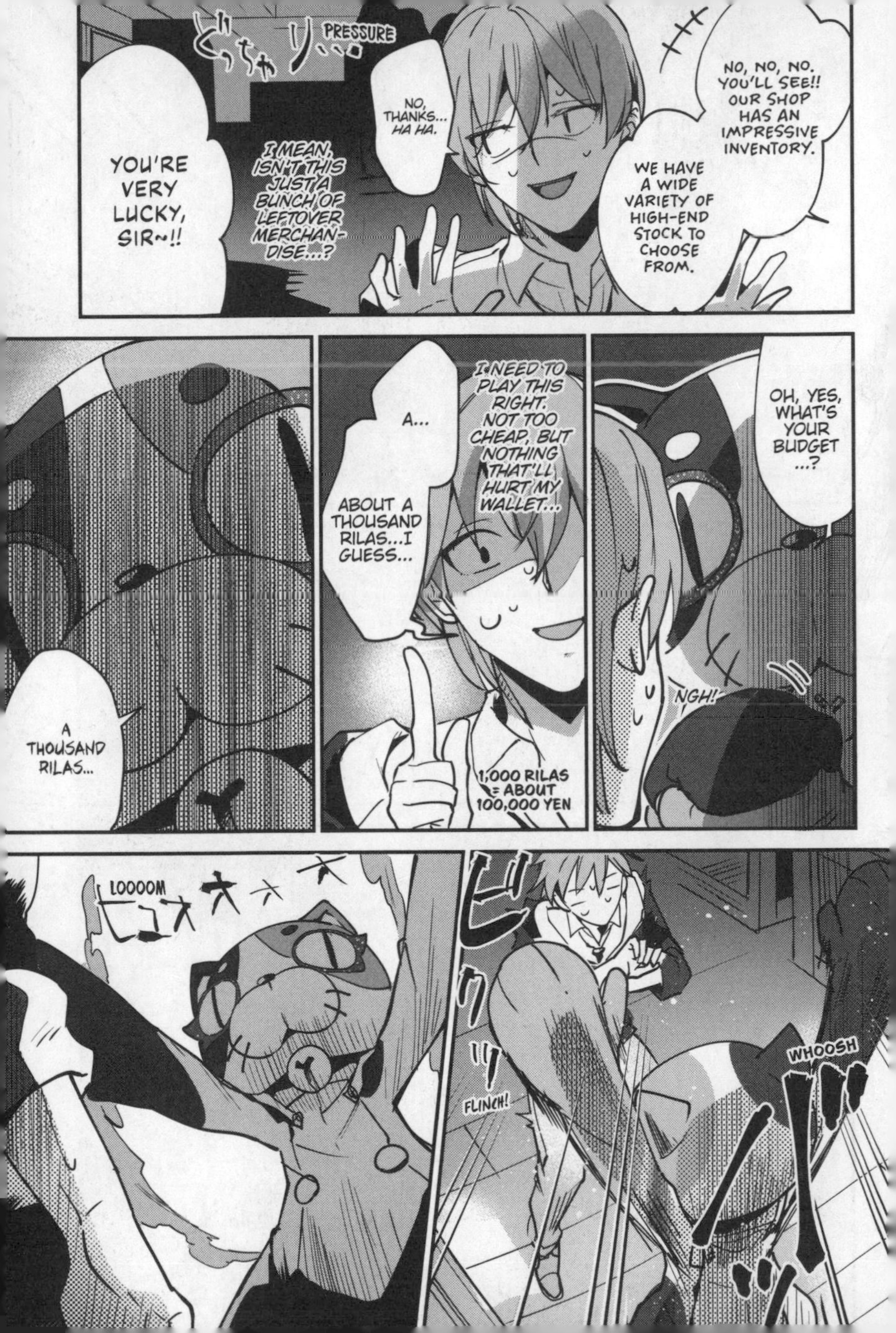
NO, NO, NO. YOU'LL SEE!! OUR SHOP HAS AN IMPRESSIVE INVENTORY.
WE HAVE A WIDE VARIETY OF HIGH-END STOCK TO CHOOSE FROM.
NO, THANKS... HA HA.
PRESSURE
I MEAN, ISN'T THIS JUST A BUNCH OF LEFTOVER MERCHANDISE...?
YOU'RE VERY LUCKY, SIR~!!
OH, YES, WHAT'S YOUR BUDGET ...?
NGH!
I NEED TO PLAY THIS RIGHT. NOT TOO CHEAP, BUT NOTHING THAT'LL HURT MY WALLET...
A...
ABOUT A THOUSAND RILAS...I GUESS...
1,000 RILAS = ABOUT 100,000 YEN
A THOUSAND RILAS...
WHOOSH
FLINCH!
LOOOOM

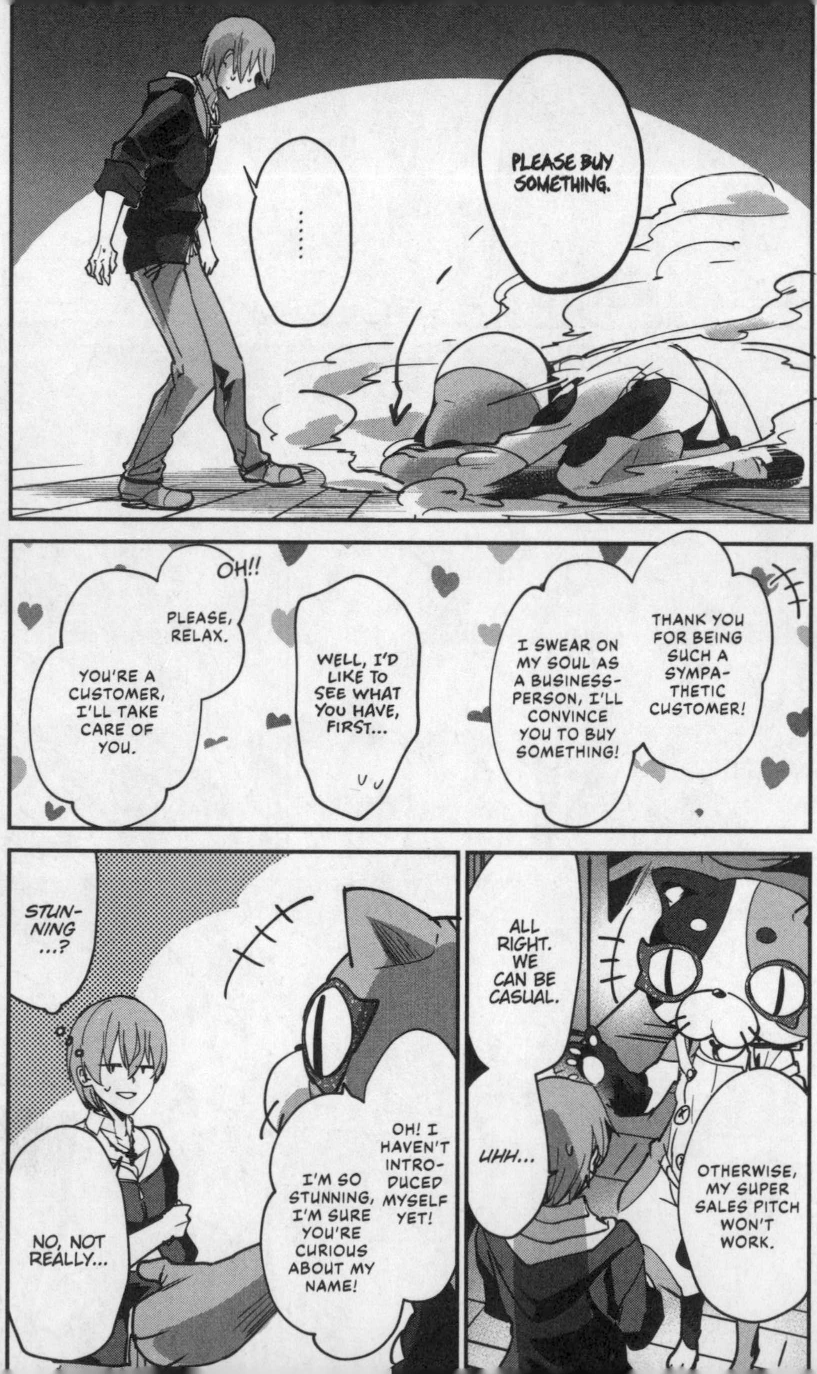
PLEASE BUY SOMETHING.
......
THANK YOU FOR BEING SUCH A SYMPA-THETIC CUSTOMER!
I SWEAR ON MY SOUL AS A BUSINESS-PERSON, I'LL CONVINCE YOU TO BUY SOMETHING!
WELL, I'D LIKE TO SEE WHAT YOU HAVE, FIRST...
OH!!
PLEASE, RELAX.
YOU'RE A CUSTOMER, I'LL TAKE CARE OF YOU.
ALL RIGHT. WE CAN BE CASUAL.
OTHERWISE, MY SUPER SALES PITCH WON'T WORK.
UHH...
OH! I HAVEN'T INTRO-DUCED MYSELF YET!
I'M SO STUNNING, I'M SURE YOU'RE CURIOUS ABOUT MY NAME!
STUN-NING ...?
NO, NOT REALLY...

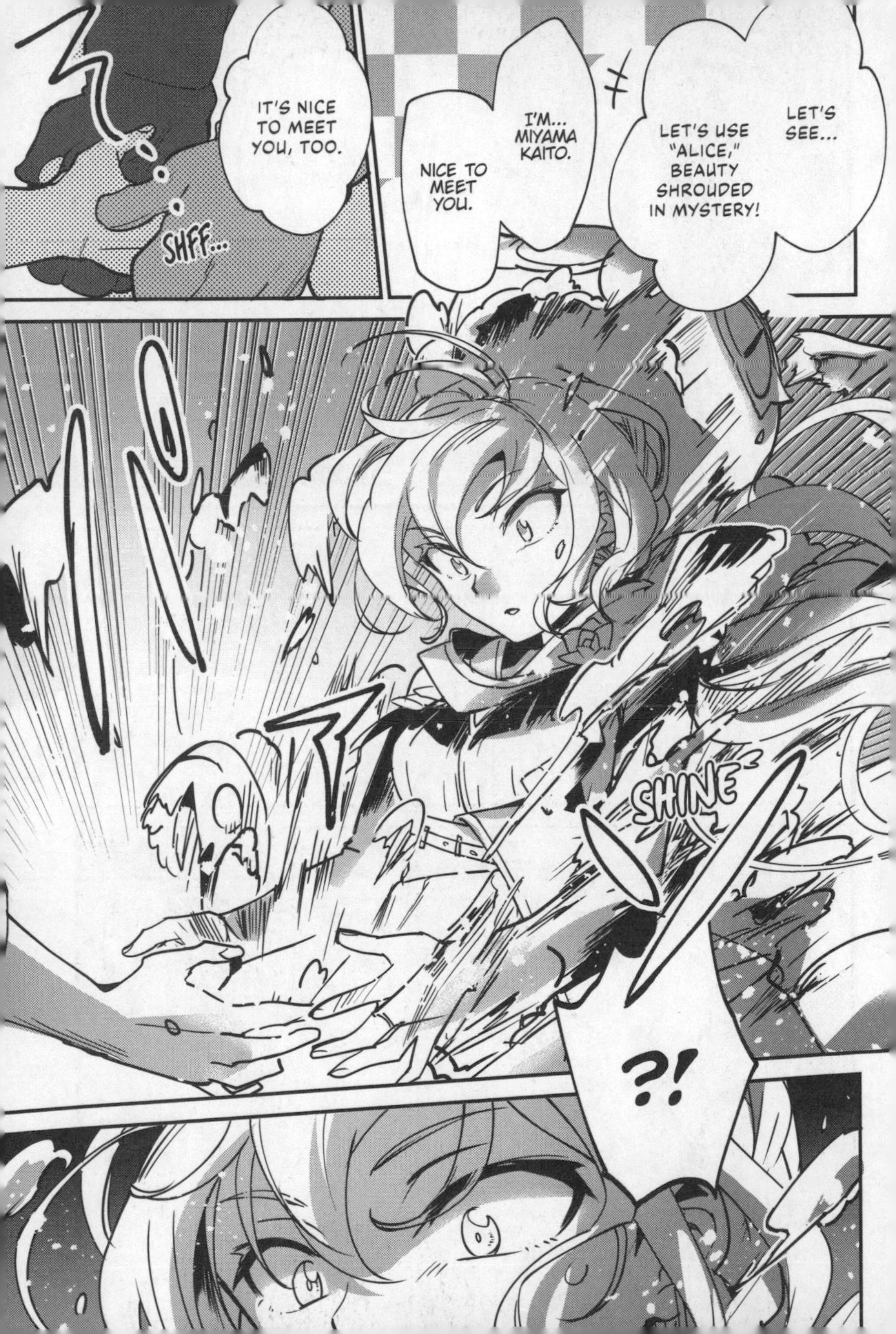
LET'S SEE...
LET'S USE "ALICE," BEAUTY SHROUDED IN MYSTERY!
I'M... MIYAMA KAITO.
NICE TO MEET YOU.
IT'S NICE TO MEET YOU, TOO.
SHFF...
SHINE
?!

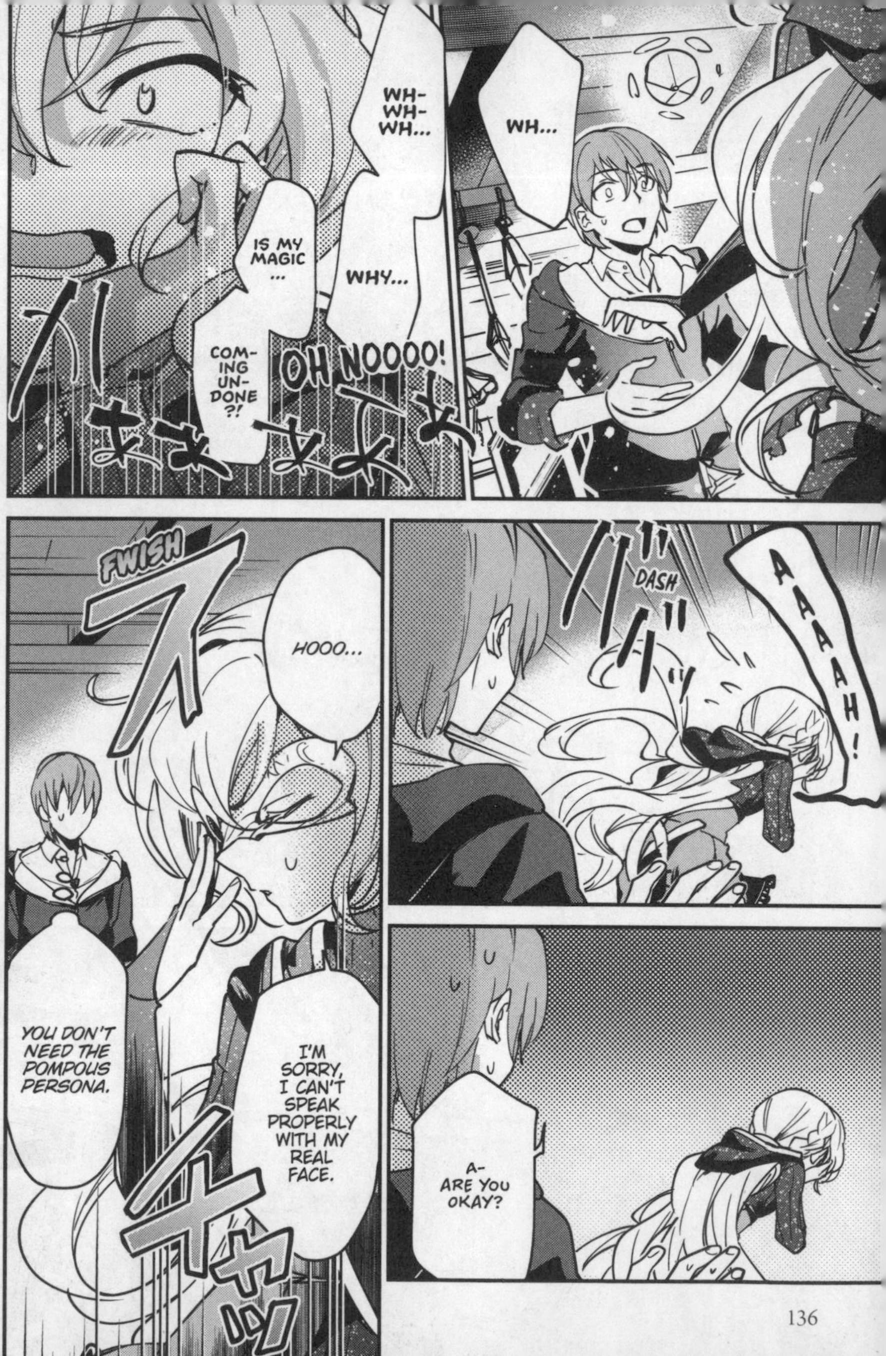
WH...
WH-WH-WH...
IS MY MAGIC ...
WHY...
COMING UNDONE ?!
OH NOOOO!
AAAAAH!
DASH
A- ARE YOU OKAY?
FWISH
HOOO...
I'M SORRY, I CAN'T SPEAK PROPERLY WITH MY REAL FACE.
YOU DON'T NEED THE POMPOUS PERSONA.

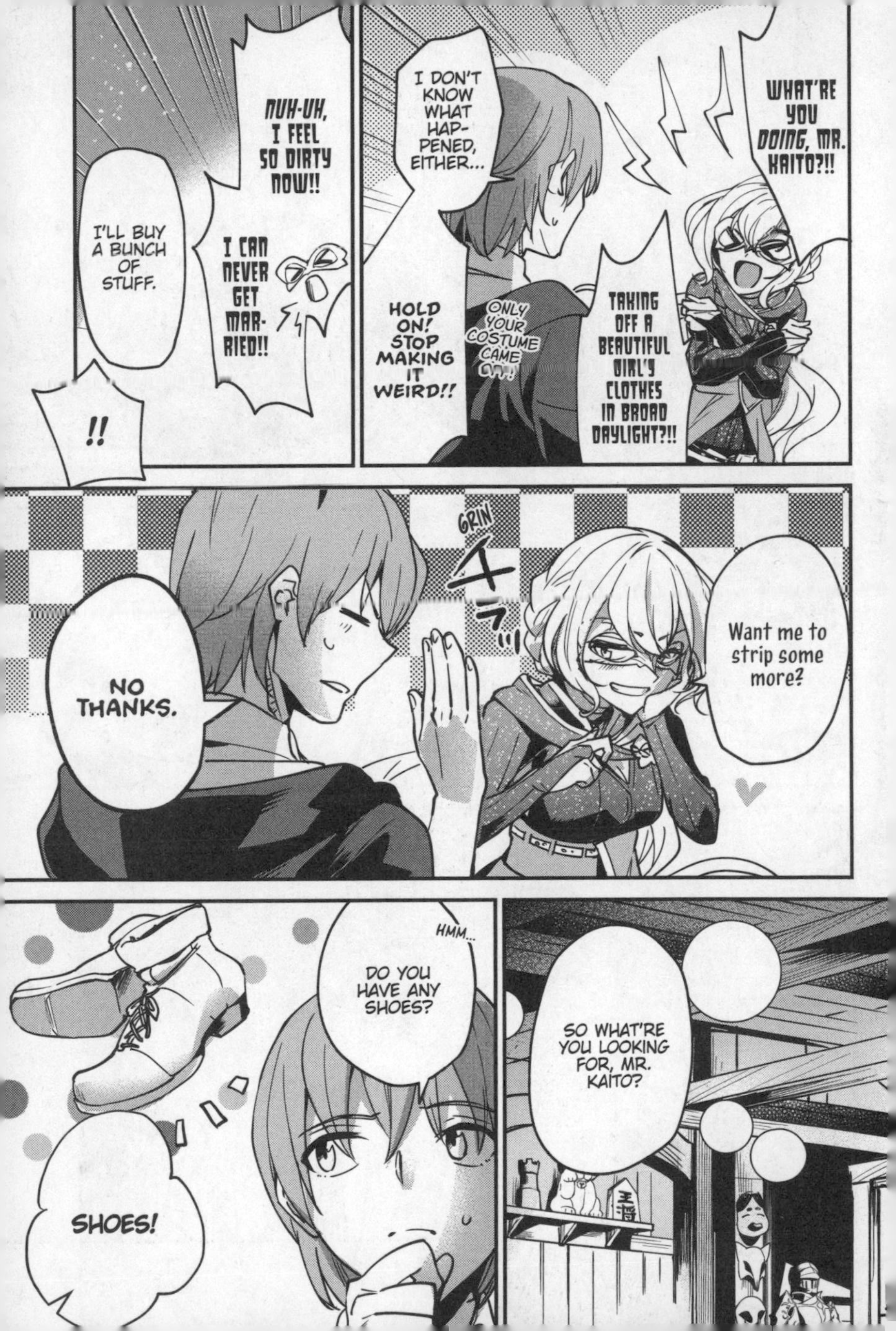

WHAT'RE YOU DOING, MR. KAITO?!!
TAKING OFF A BEAUTIFUL GIRL'S CLOTHES IN BROAD DAYLIGHT?!!
I DON'T KNOW WHAT HAP-PENED, EITHER...
ONLY YOUR COSTUME CAME
HOLD ON! STOP MAKING IT WEIRD!!
NUH-UH, I FEEL SO DIRTY NOW!!
I CAN NEVER GET MAR-RIED!!
I'LL BUY A BUNCH OF STUFF.
!!
GRIN
Want me to strip some more?
NO THANKS.
SO WHAT'RE YOU LOOKING FOR, MR. KAITO?
HMM...
DO YOU HAVE ANY SHOES?
SHOES!

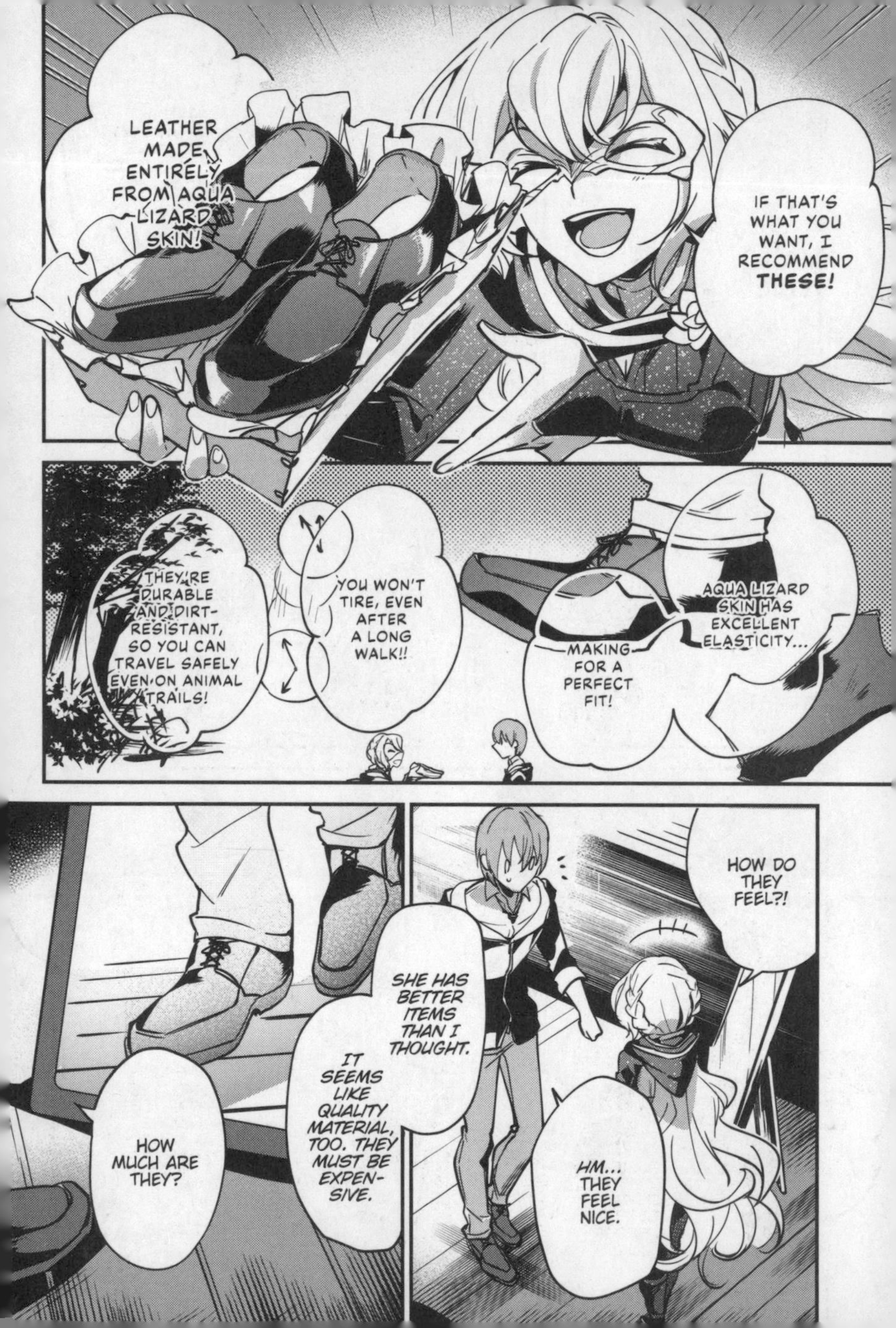
IF THAT'S WHAT YOU WANT, I RECOMMEND **THESE!**
LEATHER MADE ENTIRELY FROM AQUA LIZARD SKIN!
AQUA LIZARD SKIN HAS EXCELLENT ELASTICITY...
MAKING FOR A PERFECT FIT!
YOU WON'T TIRE, EVEN AFTER A LONG WALK!!
THEY'RE DURABLE AND DIRT-RESISTANT, SO YOU CAN TRAVEL SAFELY EVEN ON ANIMAL TRAILS!
HOW DO THEY FEEL?!
HM... THEY FEEL NICE.
SHE HAS BETTER ITEMS THAN I THOUGHT.
IT SEEMS LIKE QUALITY MATERIAL, TOO. THEY MUST BE EXPEN-SIVE.
HOW MUCH ARE THEY?

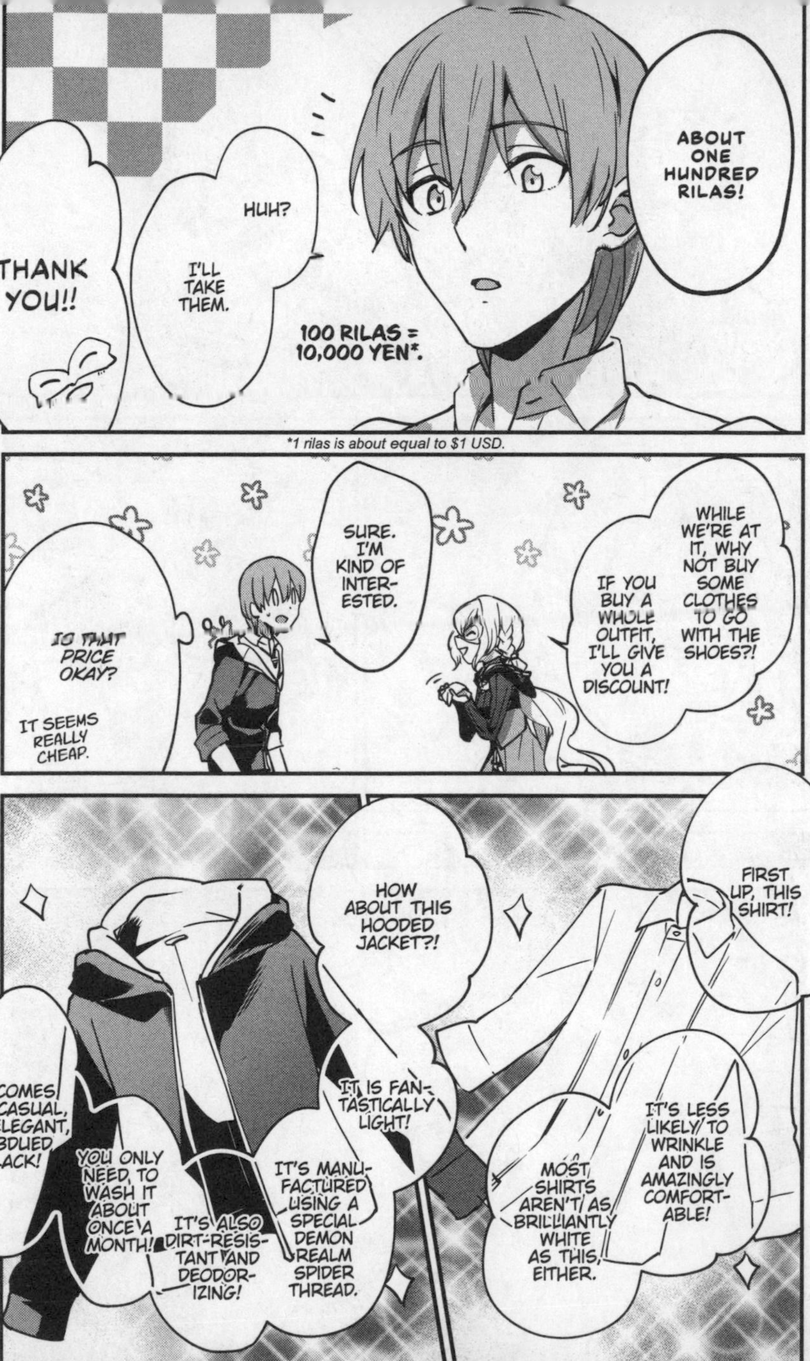
ABOUT ONE HUNDRED RILAS!
100 RILAS = 10,000 YEN*.
HUH?
I'LL TAKE THEM.
THANK YOU!!
*1 rilas is about equal to $1 USD.
WHILE WE'RE AT IT, WHY NOT BUY SOME CLOTHES TO GO WITH THE SHOES?!
IF YOU BUY A WHOLE OUTFIT, I'LL GIVE YOU A DISCOUNT!
SURE. I'M KIND OF INTER-ESTED.
IS THAT PRICE OKAY?
IT SEEMS REALLY CHEAP.
FIRST UP, THIS SHIRT!
IT'S LESS LIKELY TO WRINKLE AND IS AMAZINGLY COMFORT-ABLE!
MOST SHIRTS AREN'T AS BRILLIANTLY WHITE AS THIS, EITHER.
HOW ABOUT THIS HOODED JACKET?!
IT IS FAN-TASTICALLY LIGHT!
IT'S MANU-FACTURED USING A SPECIAL DEMON REALM SPIDER THREAD.
IT'S ALSO DIRT-RESIS-TANT AND DEODOR-IZING!
YOU ONLY NEED TO WASH IT ABOUT ONCE A MONTH!
IT COMES IN A CASUAL, YET ELEGANT, SUBDUED BLACK!

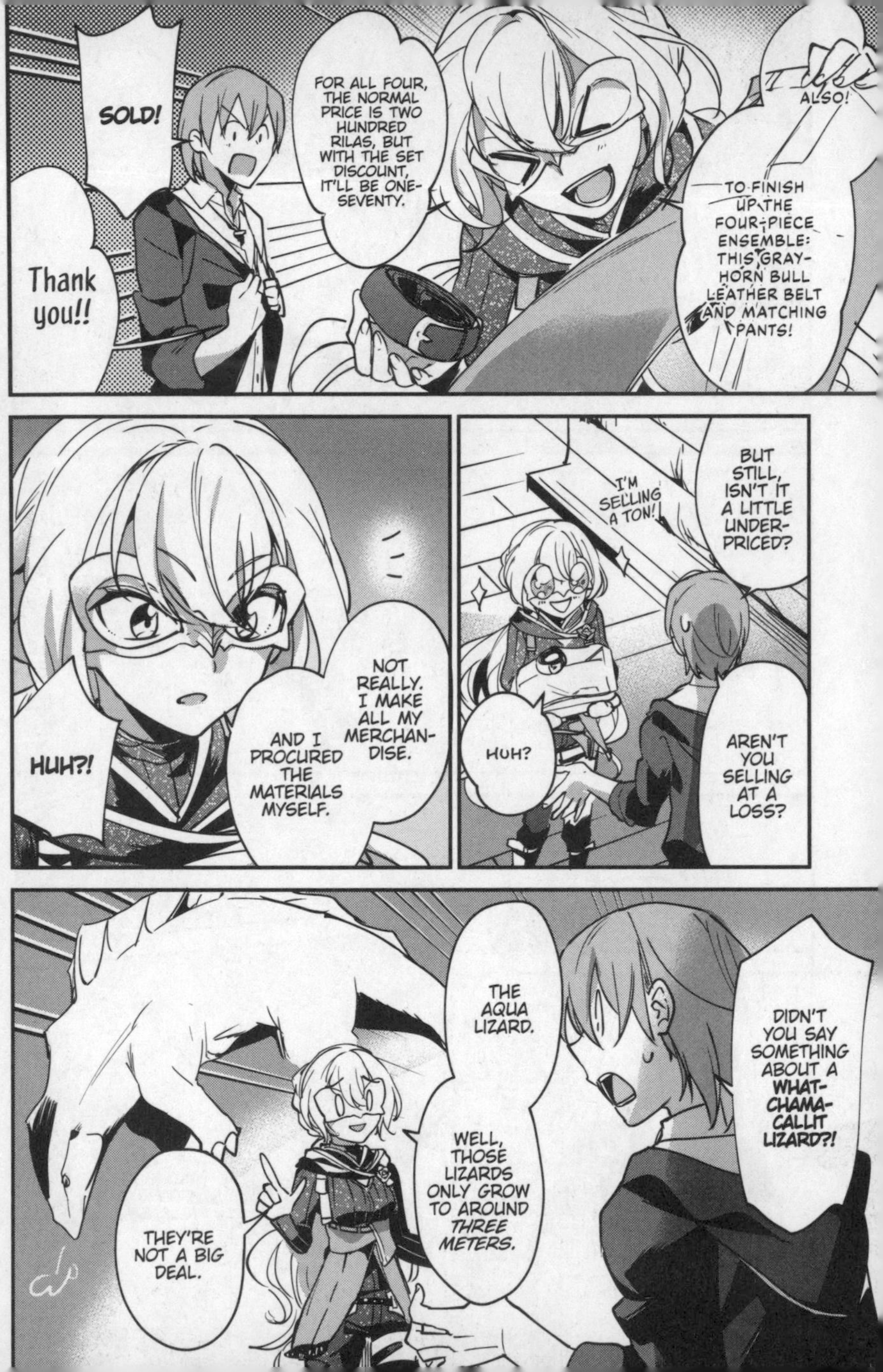
ALSO!
TO FINISH UP THE FOUR-PIECE ENSEMBLE: THIS GRAY-HORN BULL LEATHER BELT AND MATCHING PANTS!
FOR ALL FOUR, THE NORMAL PRICE IS TWO HUNDRED RILAS, BUT WITH THE SET DISCOUNT, IT'LL BE ONE-SEVENTY.
SOLD!
Thank you!!
BUT STILL, ISN'T IT A LITTLE UNDER-PRICED?
I'M SELLING A TON!
AREN'T YOU SELLING AT A LOSS?
HUH?
NOT REALLY. I MAKE ALL MY MERCHANDISE.
AND I PROCURED THE MATERIALS MYSELF.
HUH?!
DIDN'T YOU SAY SOMETHING ABOUT A WHAT-CHAMA-CALLIT LIZARD?!
THE AQUA LIZARD.
WELL, THOSE LIZARDS ONLY GROW TO AROUND THREE METERS.
THEY'RE NOT A BIG DEAL.

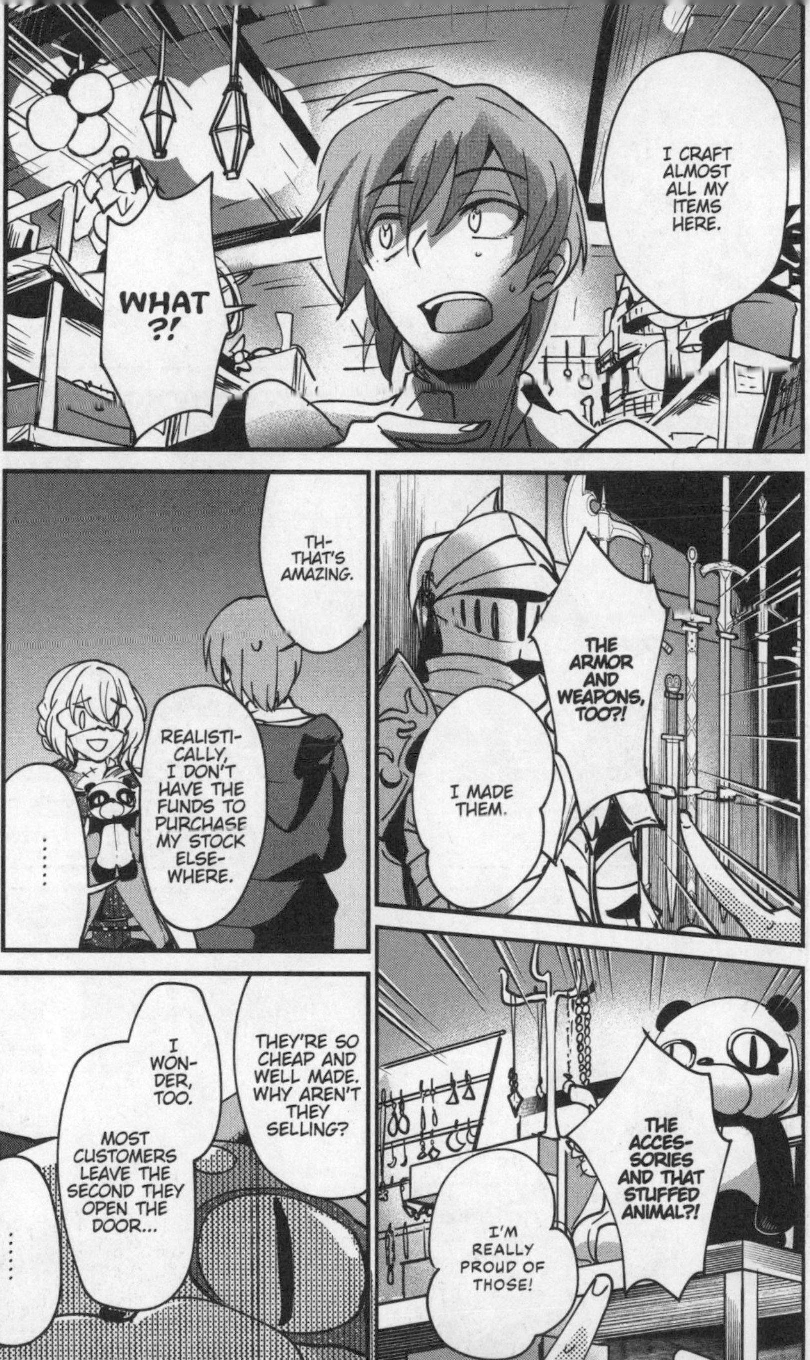
I CRAFT ALMOST ALL MY ITEMS HERE.
WHAT ?!
THE ARMOR AND WEAPONS, TOO?!
I MADE THEM.
TH- THAT'S AMAZING.
REALISTICALLY, I DON'T HAVE THE FUNDS TO PURCHASE MY STOCK ELSEWHERE.
......
THE ACCESSORIES AND THAT STUFFED ANIMAL?!
I'M REALLY PROUD OF THOSE!
THEY'RE SO CHEAP AND WELL MADE. WHY AREN'T THEY SELLING?
I WONDER, TOO.
MOST CUSTOMERS LEAVE THE SECOND THEY OPEN THE DOOR...
......

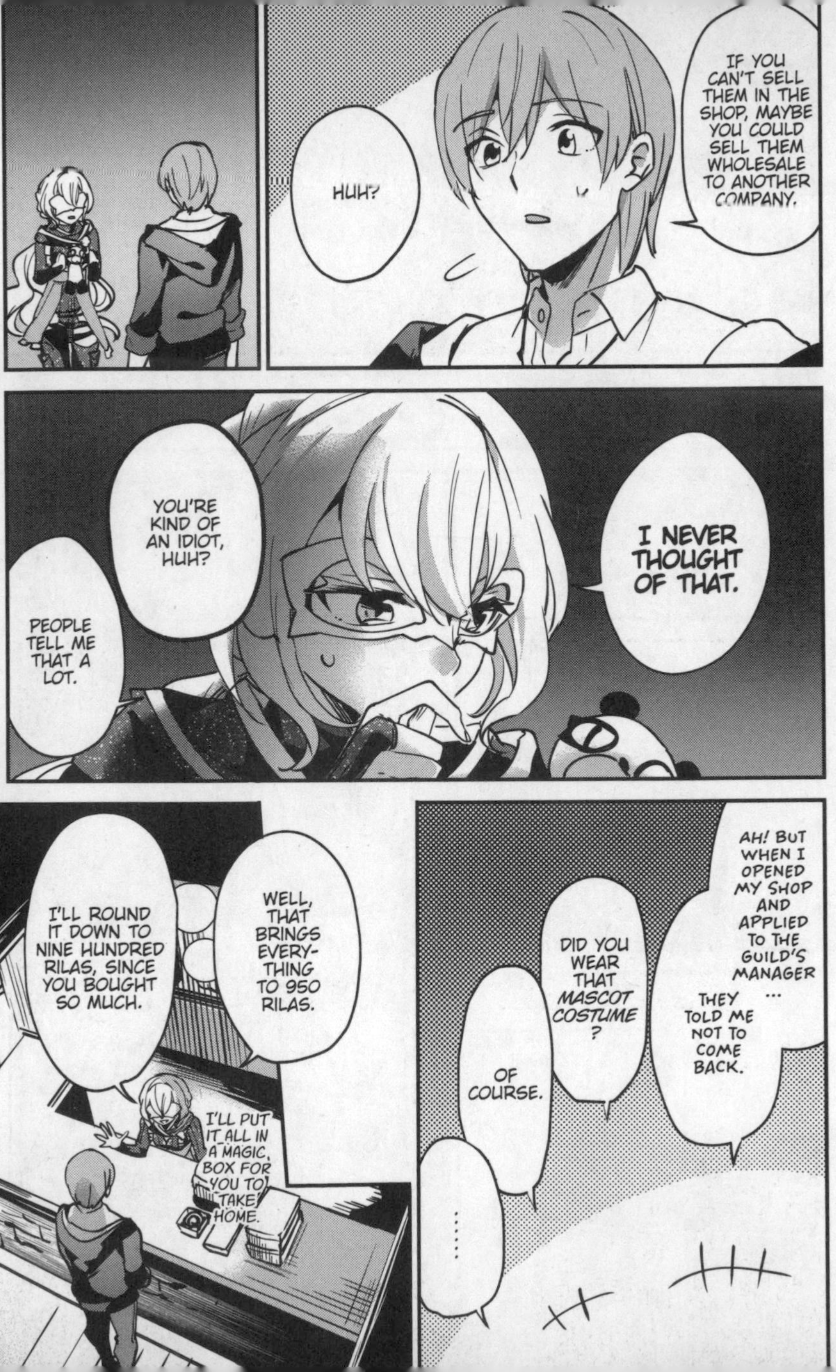
IF YOU CAN'T SELL THEM IN THE SHOP, MAYBE YOU COULD SELL THEM WHOLESALE TO ANOTHER COMPANY.
HUH?
I NEVER THOUGHT OF THAT.
YOU'RE KIND OF AN IDIOT, HUH?
PEOPLE TELL ME THAT A LOT.
AH! BUT WHEN I OPENED MY SHOP AND APPLIED TO THE GUILD'S MANAGER...
THEY TOLD ME NOT TO COME BACK.
DID YOU WEAR THAT *MASCOT COSTUME*?
OF COURSE.
......
WELL, THAT BRINGS EVERY-THING TO 950 RILAS.
I'LL ROUND IT DOWN TO NINE HUNDRED RILAS, SINCE YOU BOUGHT SO MUCH.
I'LL PUT IT ALL IN A MAGIC BOX FOR YOU TO TAKE HOME.

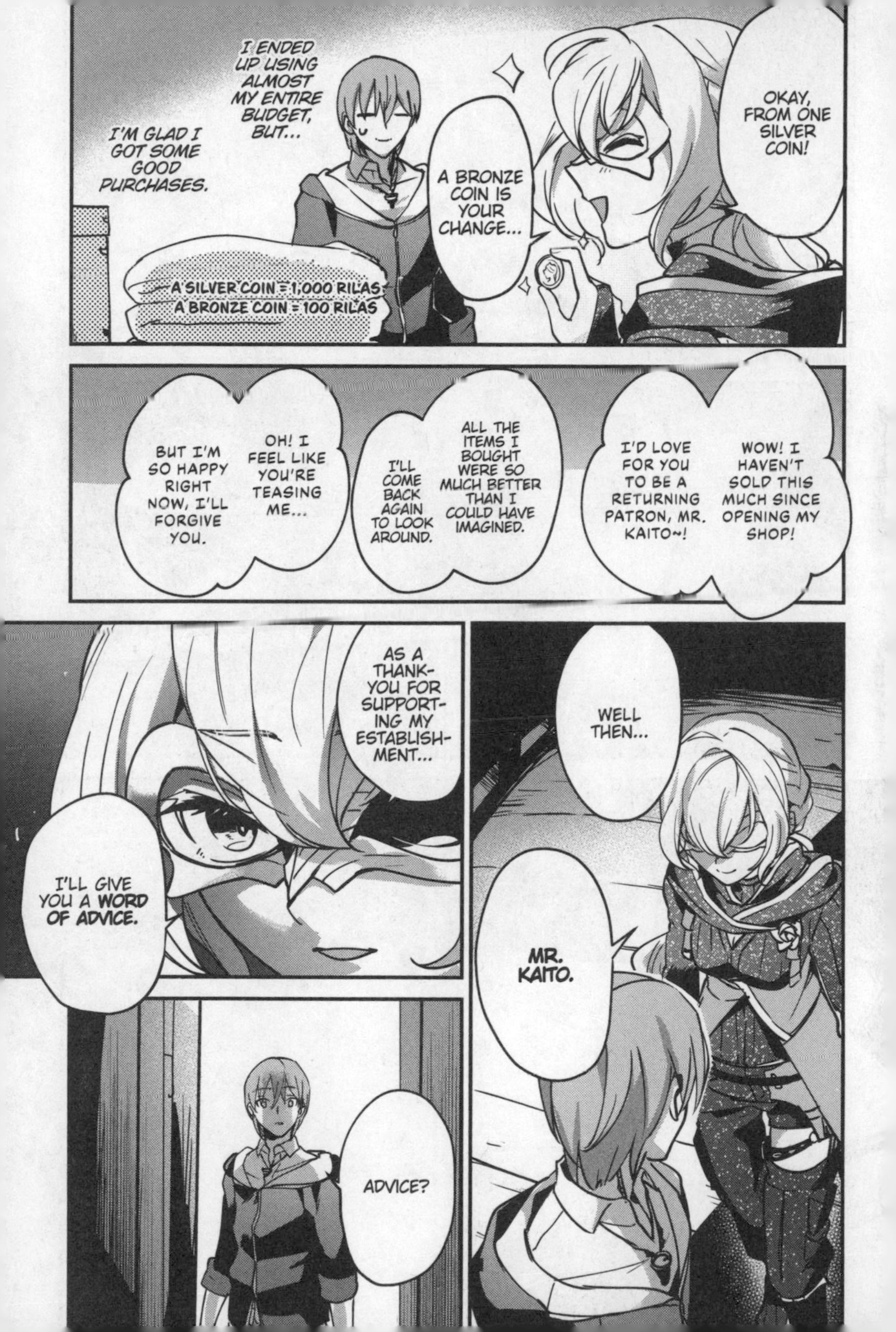
OKAY, FROM ONE SILVER COIN!
A BRONZE COIN IS YOUR CHANGE...
I ENDED UP USING ALMOST MY ENTIRE BUDGET, BUT...
I'M GLAD I GOT SOME GOOD PURCHASES.
A SILVER COIN = 1,000 RILAS
A BRONZE COIN = 100 RILAS
WOW! I HAVEN'T SOLD THIS MUCH SINCE OPENING MY SHOP!
I'D LOVE FOR YOU TO BE A RETURNING PATRON, MR. KAITO~!
ALL THE ITEMS I BOUGHT WERE SO MUCH BETTER THAN I COULD HAVE IMAGINED.
I'LL COME BACK AGAIN TO LOOK AROUND.
OH! I FEEL LIKE YOU'RE TEASING ME...
BUT I'M SO HAPPY RIGHT NOW, I'LL FORGIVE YOU.
WELL THEN...
MR. KAITO.
AS A THANK-YOU FOR SUPPORTING MY ESTABLISHMENT...
I'LL GIVE YOU A WORD OF ADVICE.
ADVICE?

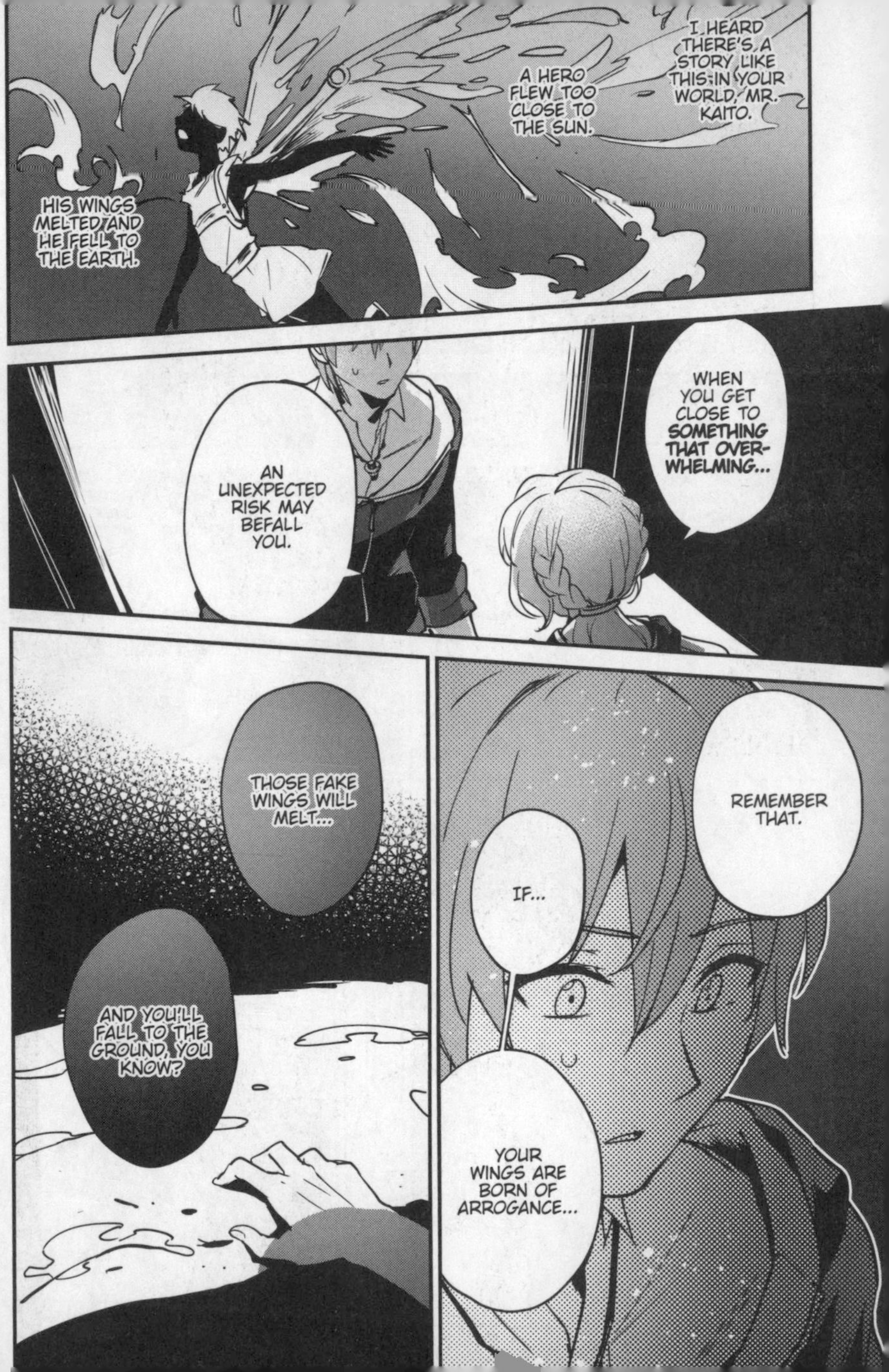
I HEARD THERE'S A STORY LIKE THIS IN YOUR WORLD, MR. KAITO.
A HERO FLEW TOO CLOSE TO THE SUN.
HIS WINGS MELTED AND HE FELL TO THE EARTH.
WHEN YOU GET CLOSE TO SOMETHING THAT OVER-WHELMING...
AN UNEXPECTED RISK MAY BEFALL YOU.
REMEMBER THAT.
IF...
YOUR WINGS ARE BORN OF ARROGANCE...
THOSE FAKE WINGS WILL MELT...
AND YOU'LL FALL TO THE GROUND, YOU KNOW?

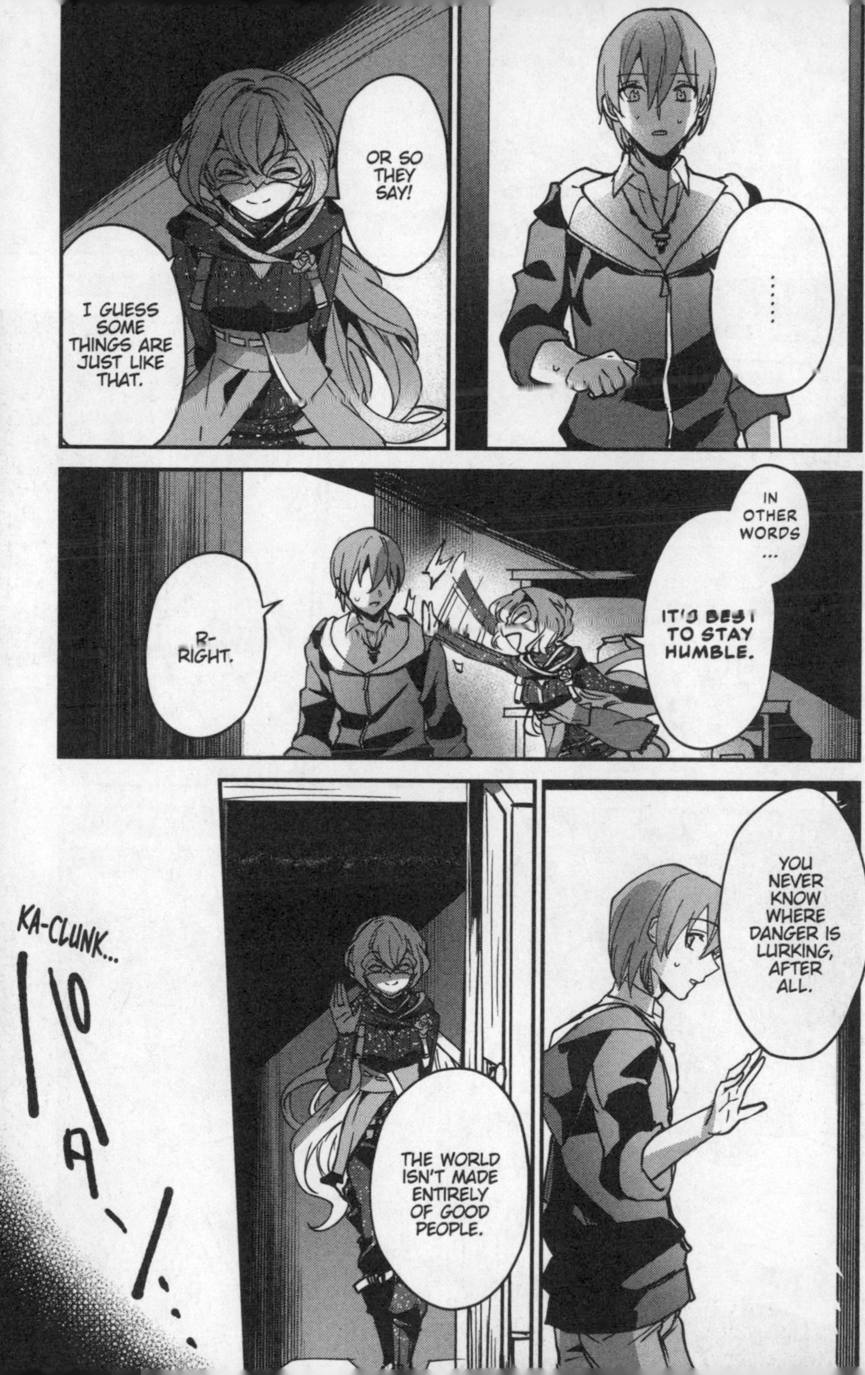
......
OR SO THEY SAY!
I GUESS SOME THINGS ARE JUST LIKE THAT.
IN OTHER WORDS...
IT'S BEST TO STAY HUMBLE.
R-RIGHT.
YOU NEVER KNOW WHERE DANGER IS LURKING, AFTER ALL.
THE WORLD ISN'T MADE ENTIRELY OF GOOD PEOPLE.
KA-CLUNK...

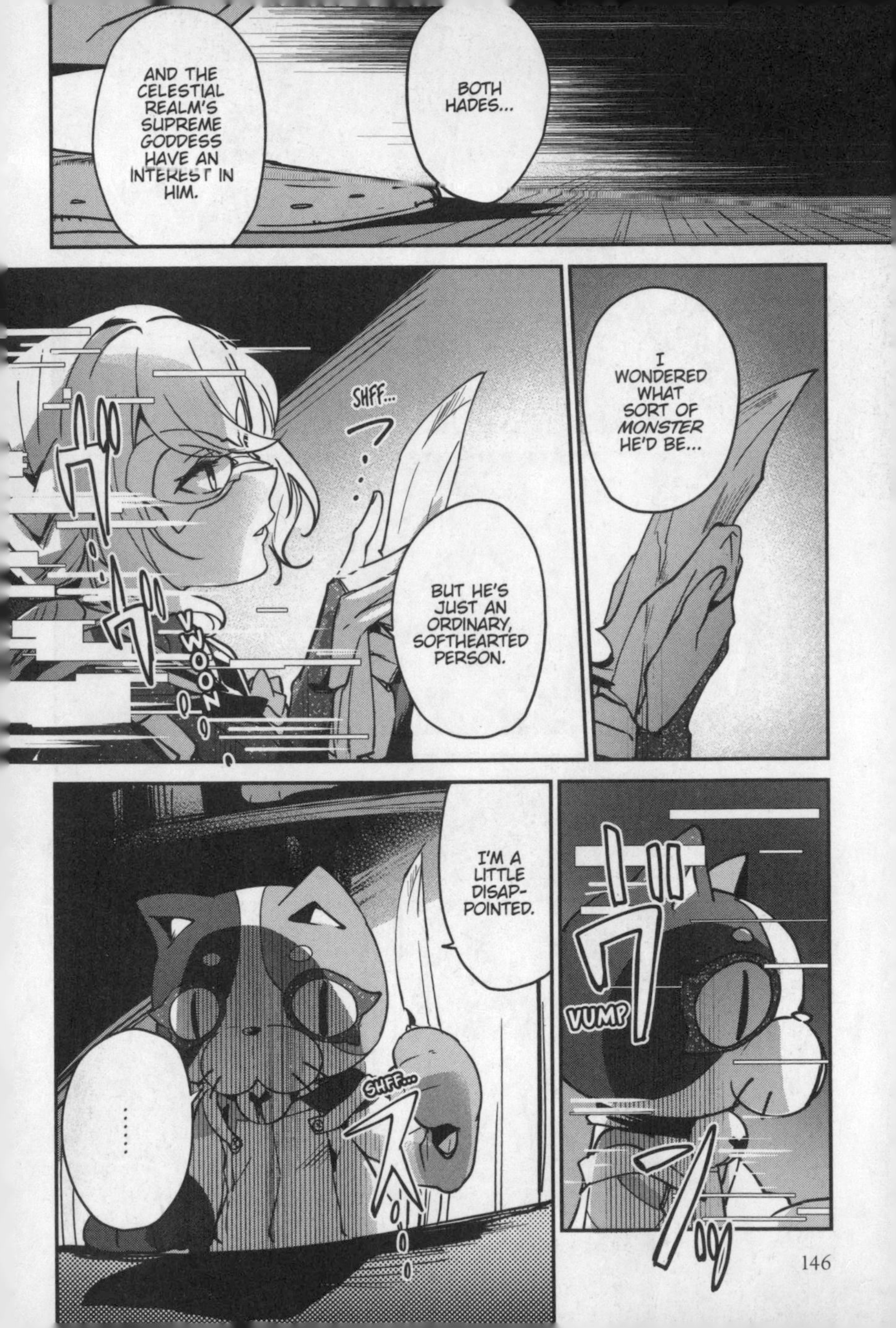
BOTH HADES...
AND THE CELESTIAL REALM'S SUPREME GODDESS HAVE AN INTEREST IN HIM.
I WONDERED WHAT SORT OF *MONSTER* HE'D BE...
SHFF...
BUT HE'S JUST AN ORDINARY, SOFTHEARTED PERSON.
VWOOOM
VUMP
I'M A LITTLE DISAP-POINTED.
......
SHFF...

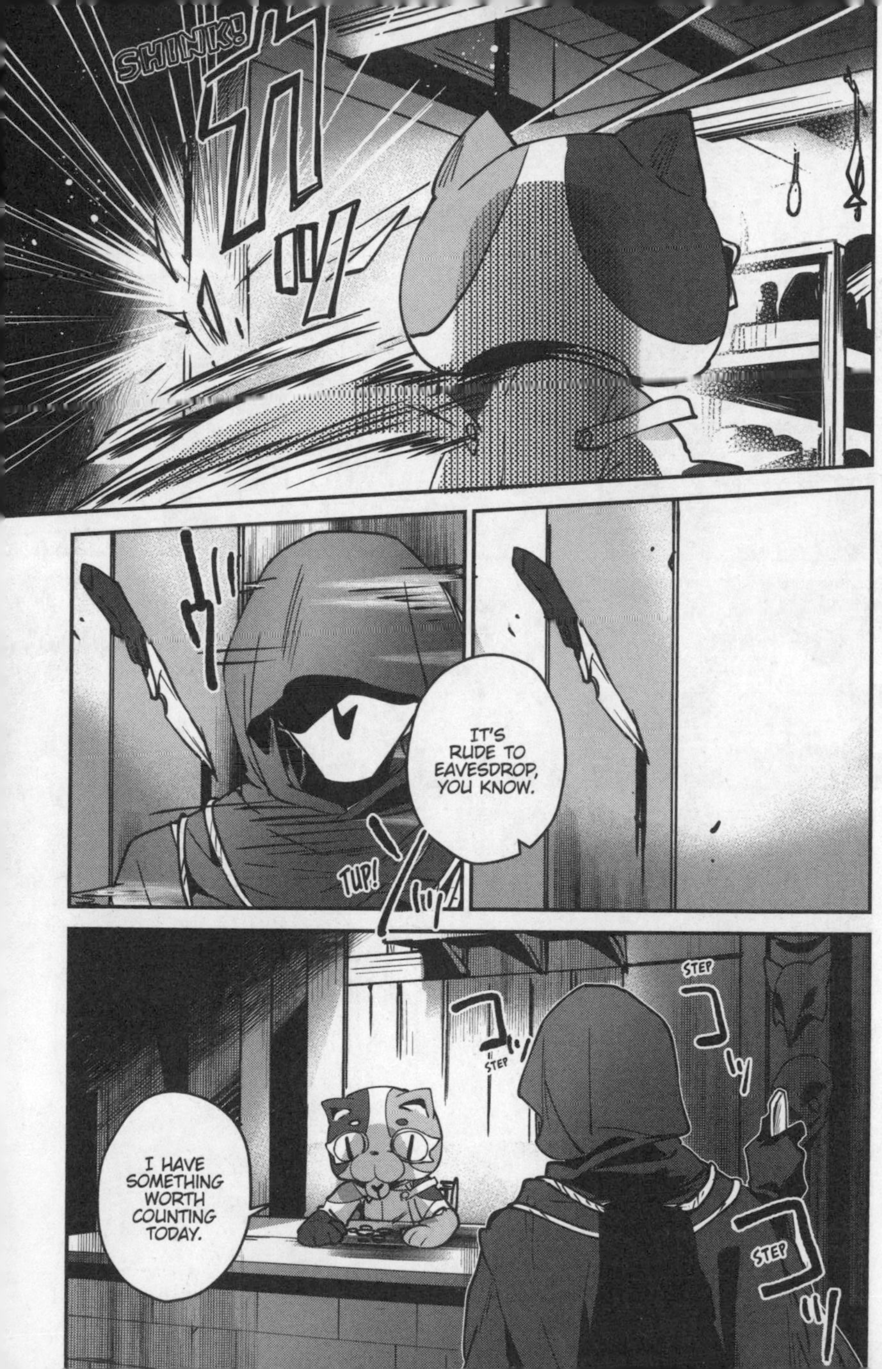
SHINK!
IT'S RUDE TO EAVESDROP, YOU KNOW.
TUP!
STEP
STEP
STEP
I HAVE SOMETHING WORTH COUNTING TODAY.

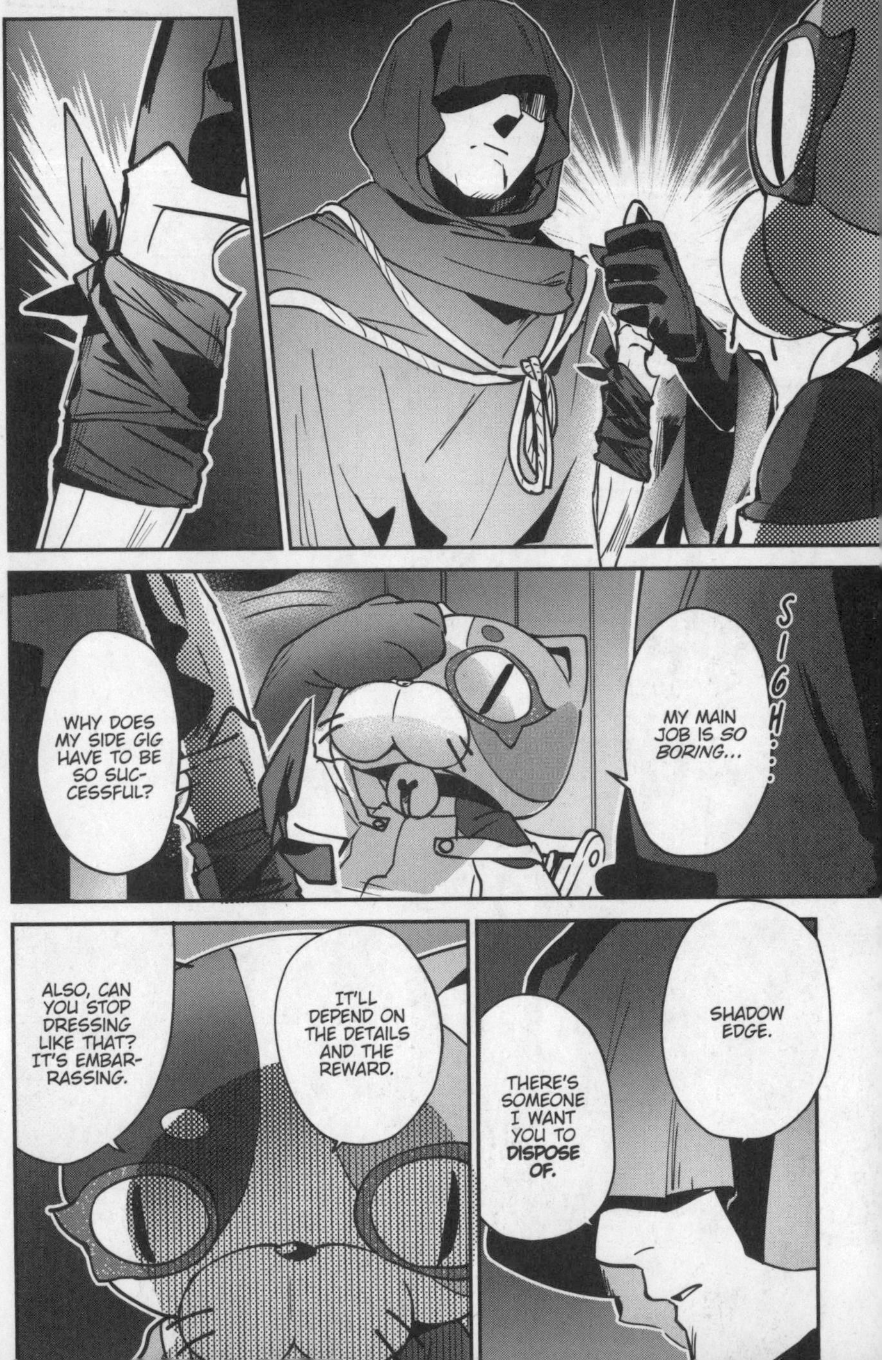
SIGH...
MY MAIN JOB IS SO BORING...
WHY DOES MY SIDE GIG HAVE TO BE SO SUC-CESSFUL?
SHADOW EDGE.
THERE'S SOMEONE I WANT YOU TO **DISPOSE OF.**
IT'LL DEPEND ON THE DETAILS AND THE REWARD.
ALSO, CAN YOU STOP DRESSING LIKE THAT? IT'S EMBAR-RASSING.

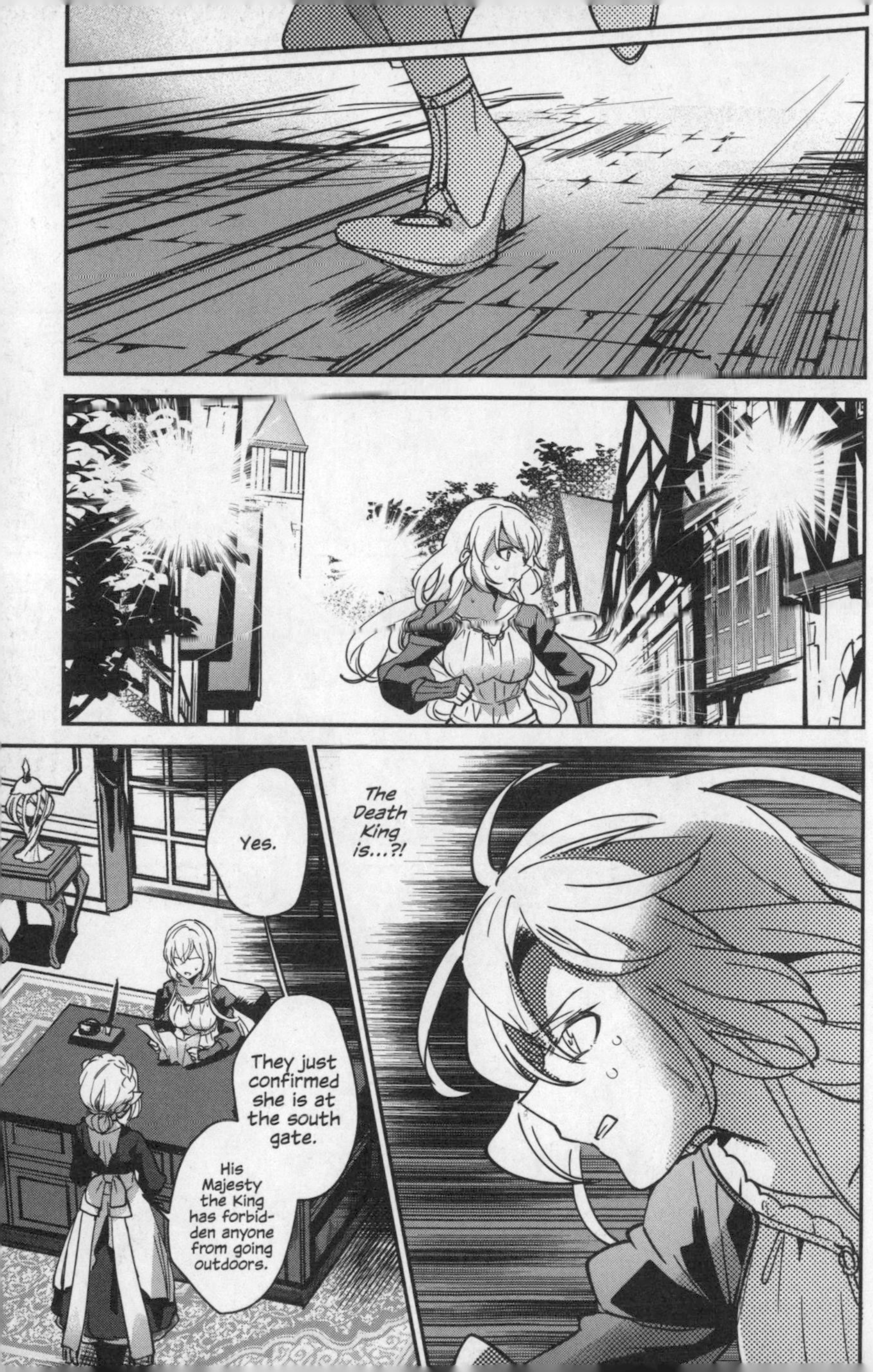
The Death King is...?!
Yes.
They just confirmed she is at the south gate.
His Majesty the King has forbidden anyone from going outdoors.

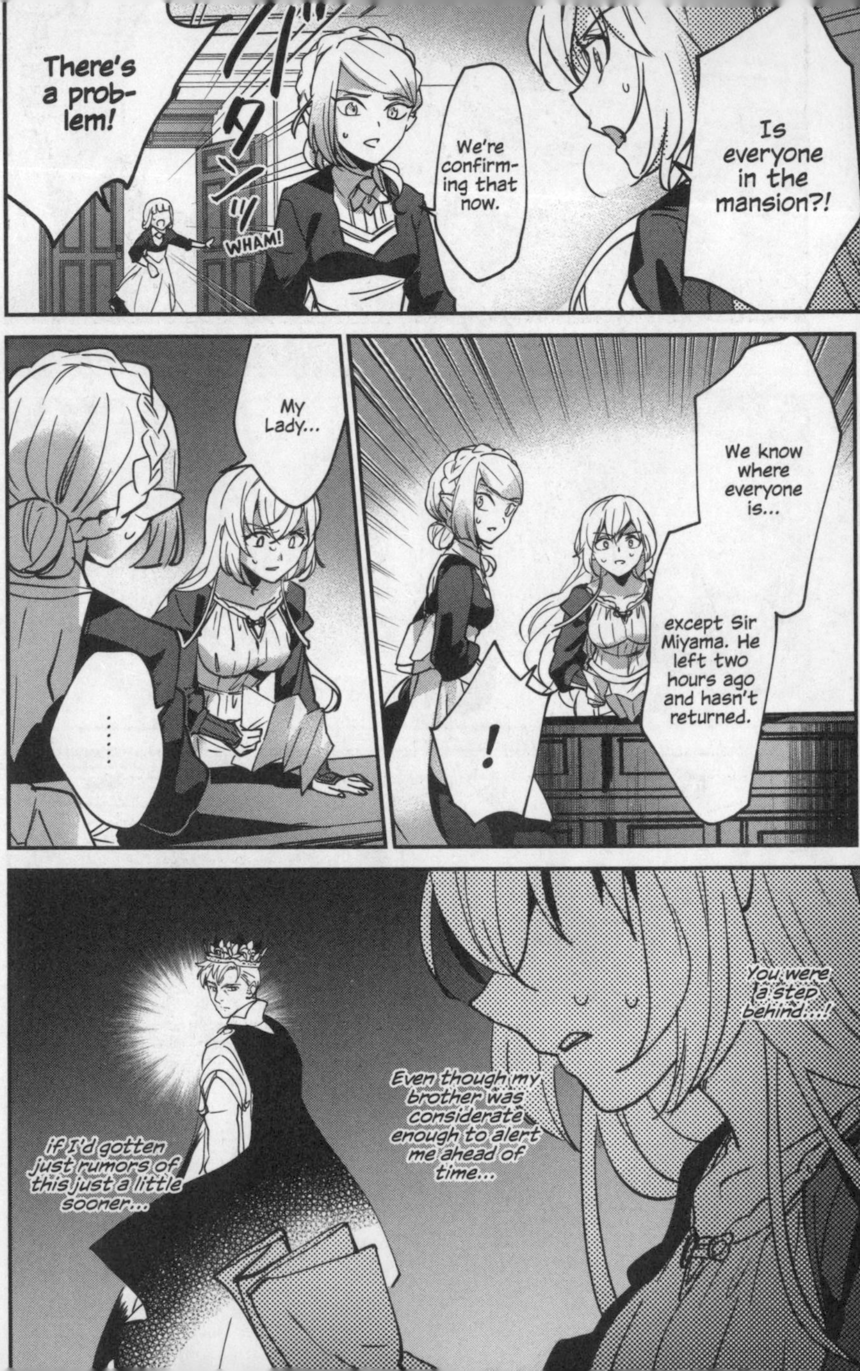
Is everyone in the mansion?!
We're confirming that now.
There's a problem!
WHAM!
We know where everyone is...
except Sir Miyama. He left two hours ago and hasn't returned.
!
My Lady...
......
You were a step behind...!
Even though my brother was considerate enough to alert me ahead of time...
if I'd gotten just rumors of this just a little sooner...

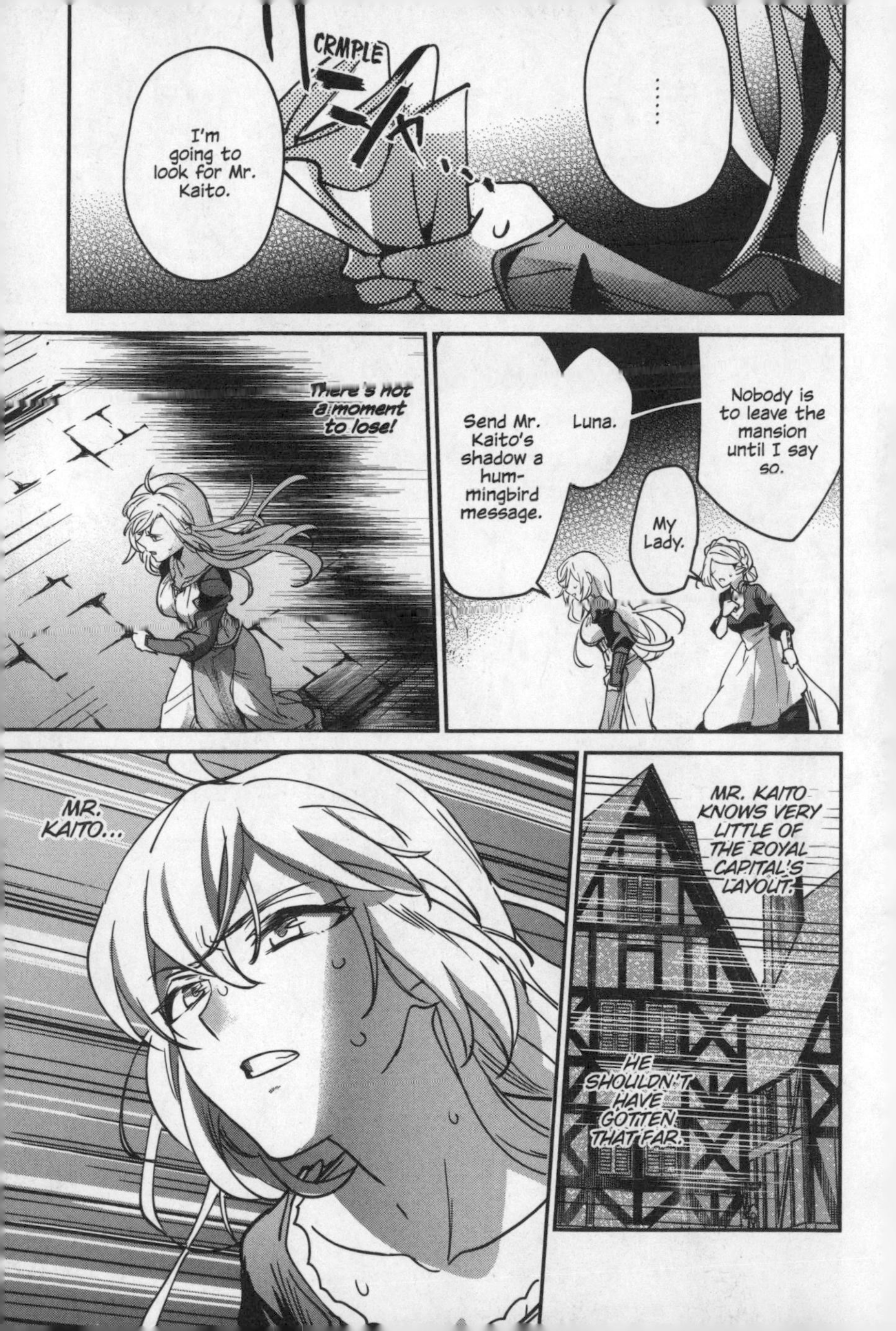
......
CRMPLE
I'm going to look for Mr. Kaito.
Nobody is to leave the mansion until I say so.
Luna.
Send Mr. Kaito's shadow a hummingbird message.
My Lady.
There's not a moment to lose!
MR. KAITO KNOWS VERY LITTLE OF THE ROYAL CAPITAL'S LAYOUT.
HE SHOULDN'T HAVE GOTTEN THAT FAR.
MR. KAITO...

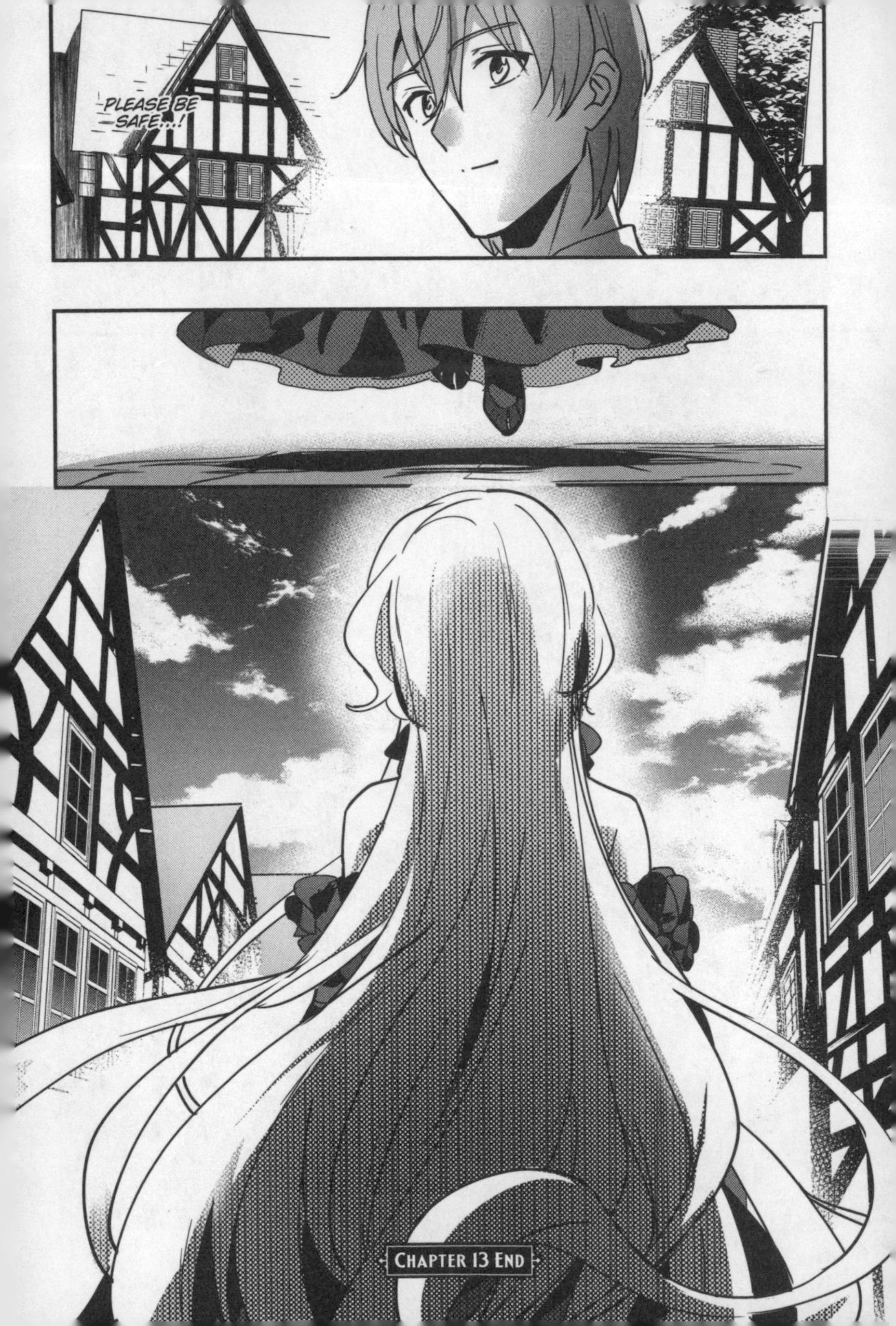
PLEASE BE SAFE...!
CHAPTER 13 END

I GOT CAUGHT UP IN A HERO SUMMONS,
BUT THE OTHER WORLD WAS AT PEACE!

I GOT CAUGHT
UP IN A HERO
SUMMONS,
BUT THE OTHER WORLD
WAS AT PEACE!

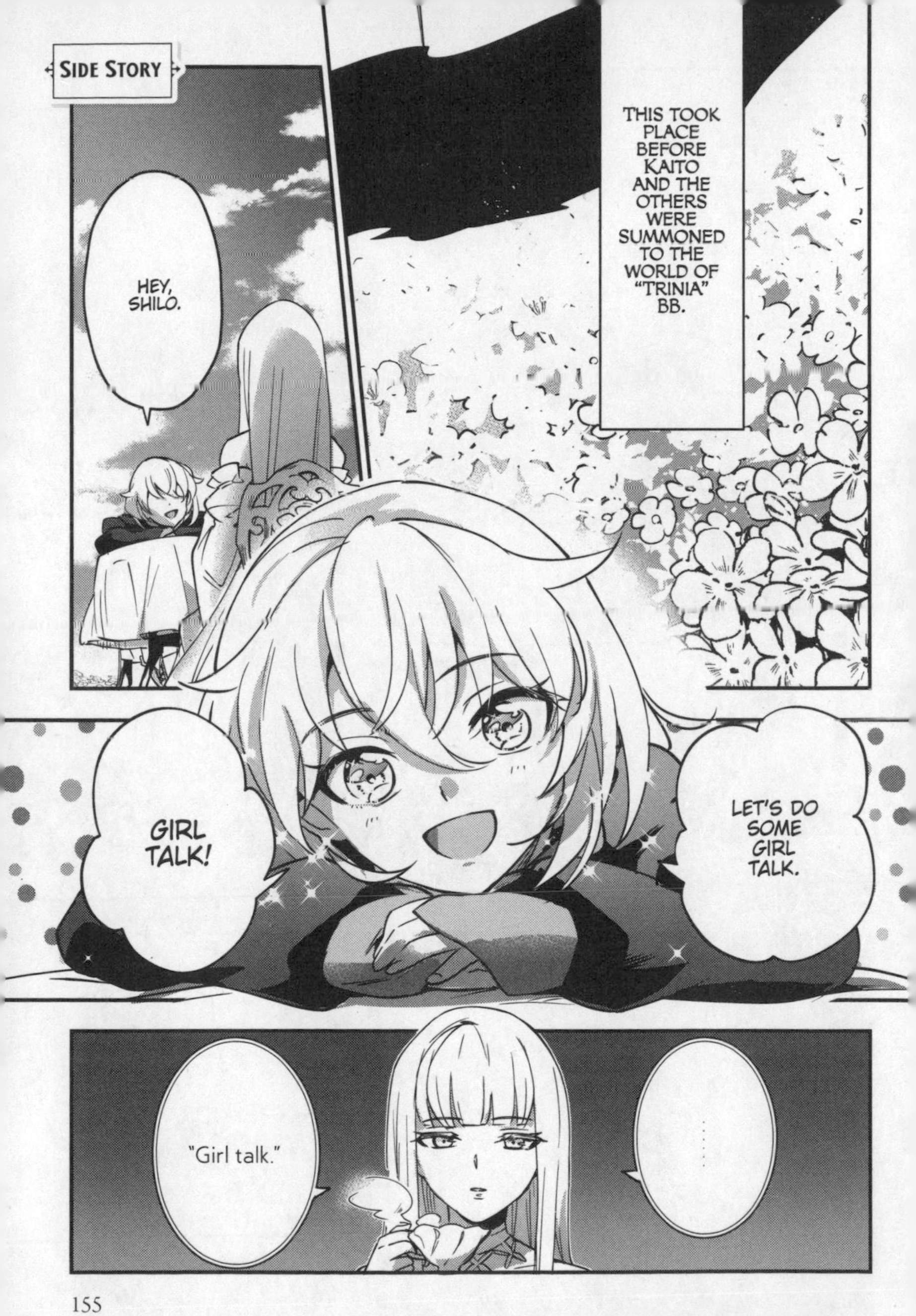
SIDE STORY
THIS TOOK PLACE BEFORE KAITO AND THE OTHERS WERE SUMMONED TO THE WORLD OF "TRINIA" BB.
HEY, SHILO.
LET'S DO SOME GIRL TALK.
GIRL TALK!
......
"Girl talk."

SIDE STORY

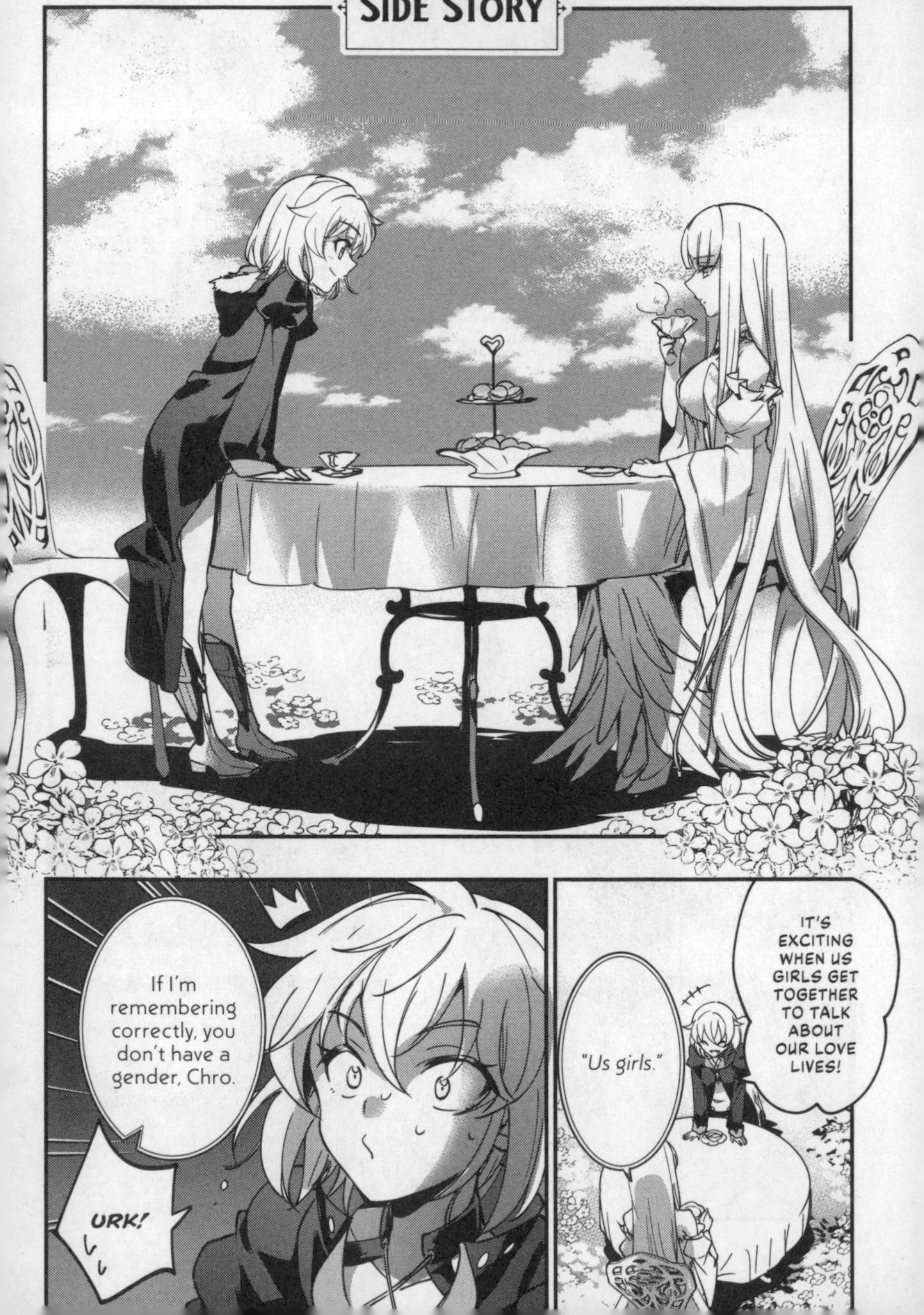
IT'S EXCITING WHEN US GIRLS GET TOGETHER TO TALK ABOUT OUR LOVE LIVES!
"Us girls."
If I'm remembering correctly, you don't have a gender, Chro.
URK!

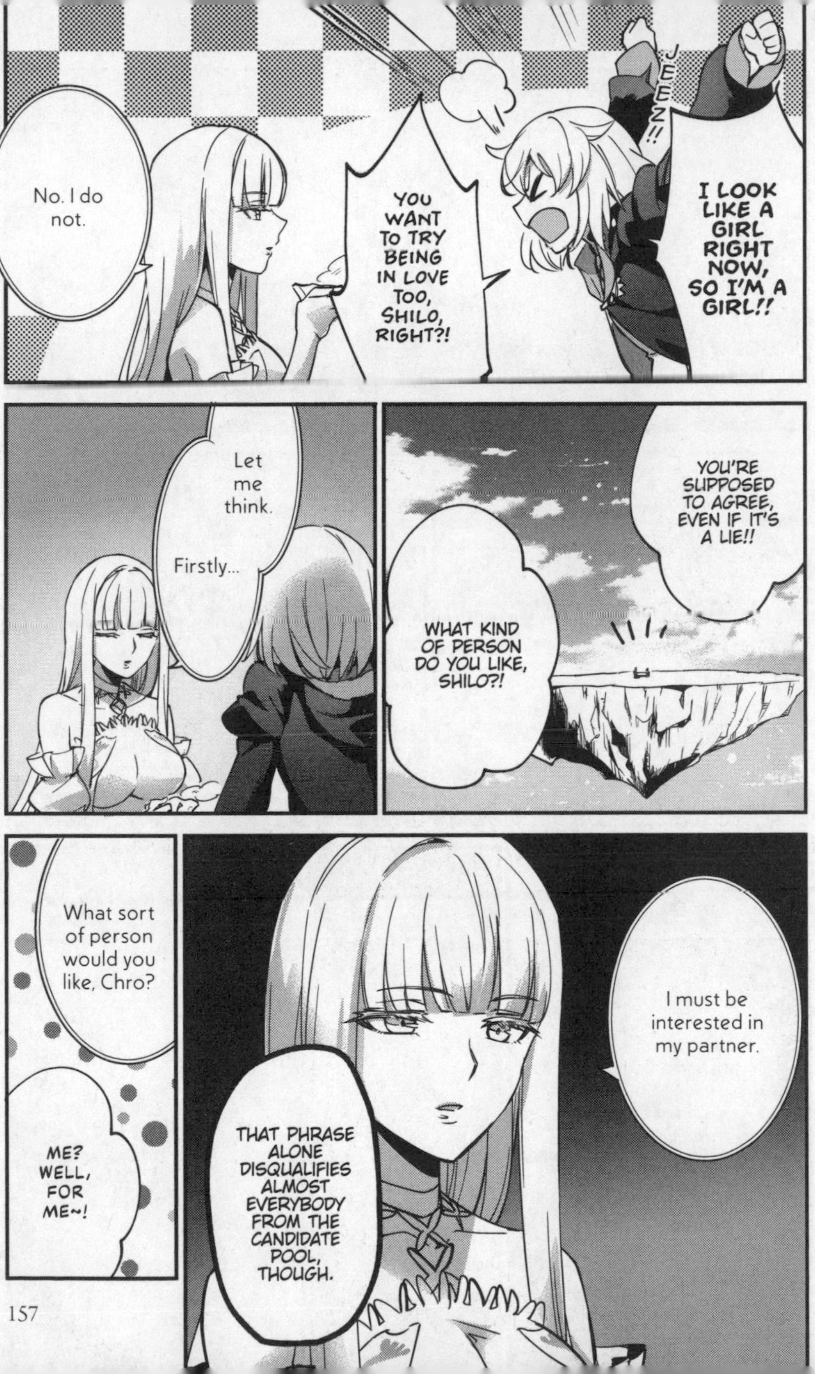
JEEZ!!
I LOOK LIKE A GIRL RIGHT NOW, SO I'M A GIRL!!
YOU WANT TO TRY BEING IN LOVE TOO, SHILO, RIGHT?!
No. I do not.
YOU'RE SUPPOSED TO AGREE, EVEN IF IT'S A LIE!!
WHAT KIND OF PERSON DO YOU LIKE, SHILO?!
Let me think.
Firstly...
I must be interested in my partner.
THAT PHRASE ALONE DISQUALIFIES ALMOST EVERYBODY FROM THE CANDIDATE POOL, THOUGH.
What sort of person would you like, Chro?
ME? WELL, FOR ME~!

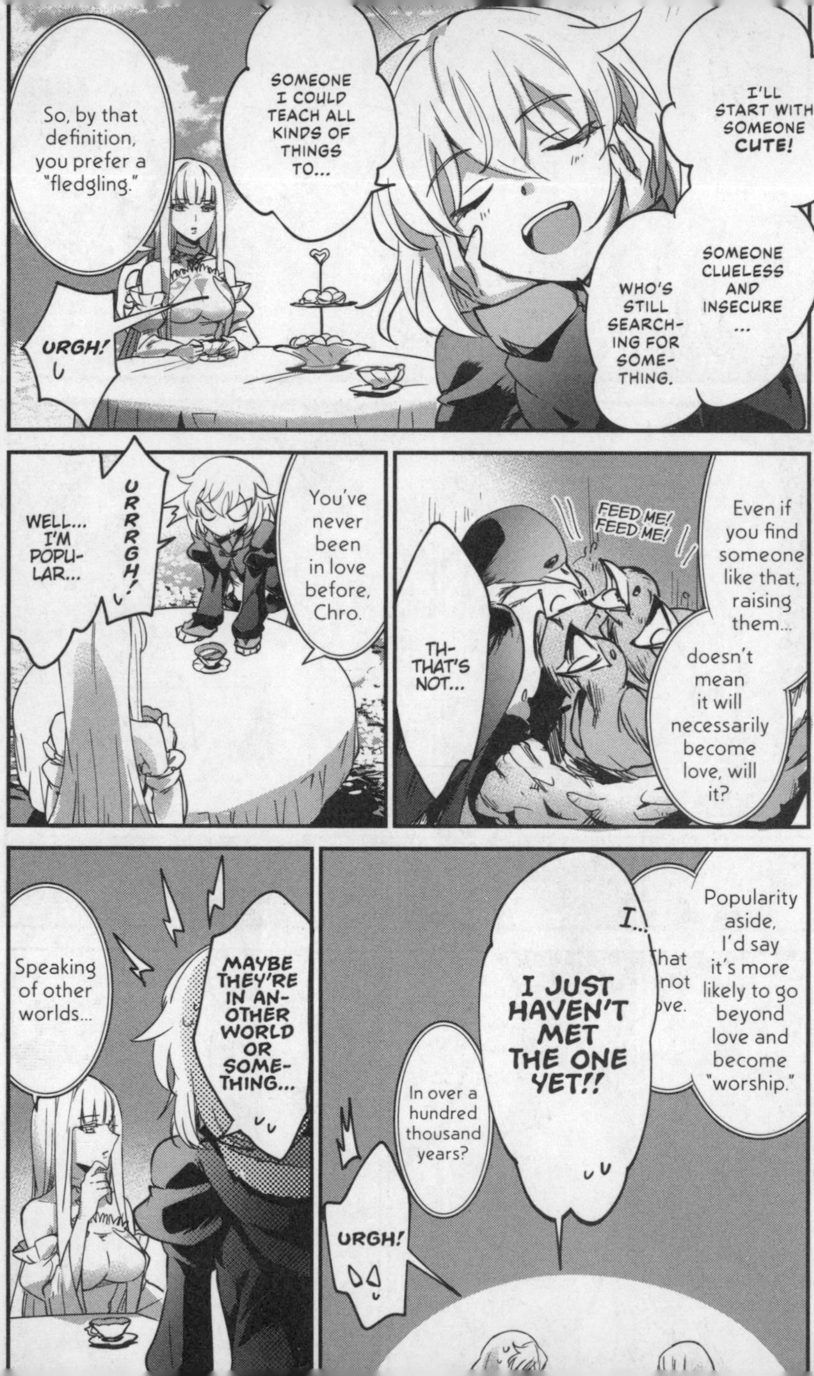
I'LL START WITH SOMEONE CUTE!
SOMEONE CLUELESS AND INSECURE...
WHO'S STILL SEARCH-ING FOR SOME-THING.
SOMEONE I COULD TEACH ALL KINDS OF THINGS TO...
So, by that definition, you prefer a "fledgling."
URGH!
Even if you find someone like that, raising them...
FEED ME! FEED ME!
doesn't mean it will necessarily become love, will it?
TH-THAT'S NOT...
You've never been in love before, Chro.
URRRGH!
WELL... I'M POPU-LAR...
Popularity aside, I'd say it's more likely to go beyond love and become "worship."
I...
I JUST HAVEN'T MET THE ONE YET!!
In over a hundred thousand years?
URGH!
MAYBE THEY'RE IN AN-OTHER WORLD OR SOME-THING...
Speaking of other worlds...

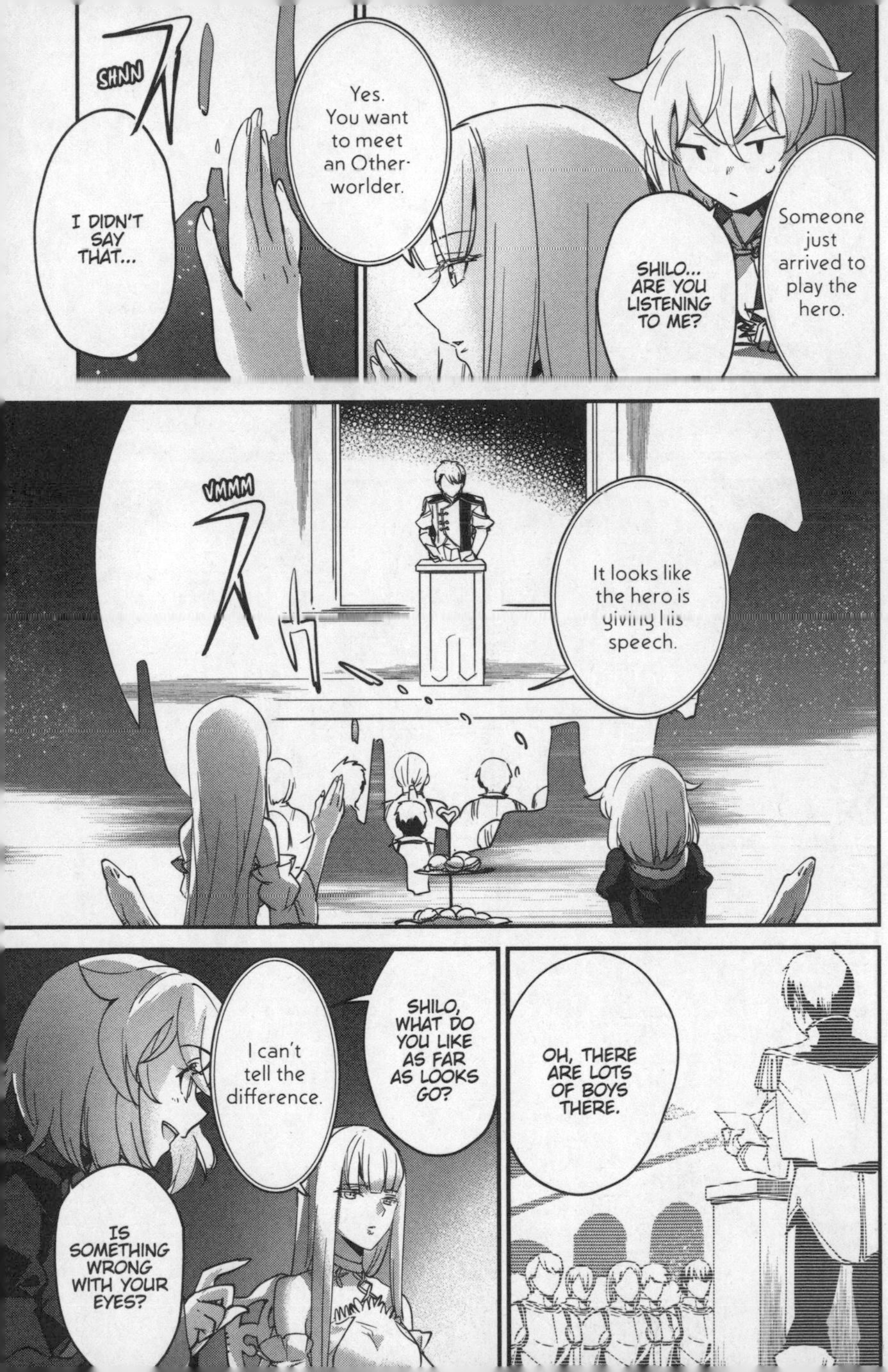

Someone just arrived to play the hero.
SHILO... ARE YOU LISTENING TO ME?
Yes. You want to meet an Otherworlder.
SHNN
I DIDN'T SAY THAT...
It looks like the hero is giving his speech.
VMMM
OH, THERE ARE LOTS OF BOYS THERE.
SHILO, WHAT DO YOU LIKE AS FAR AS LOOKS GO?
I can't tell the difference.
IS SOMETHING WRONG WITH YOUR EYES?

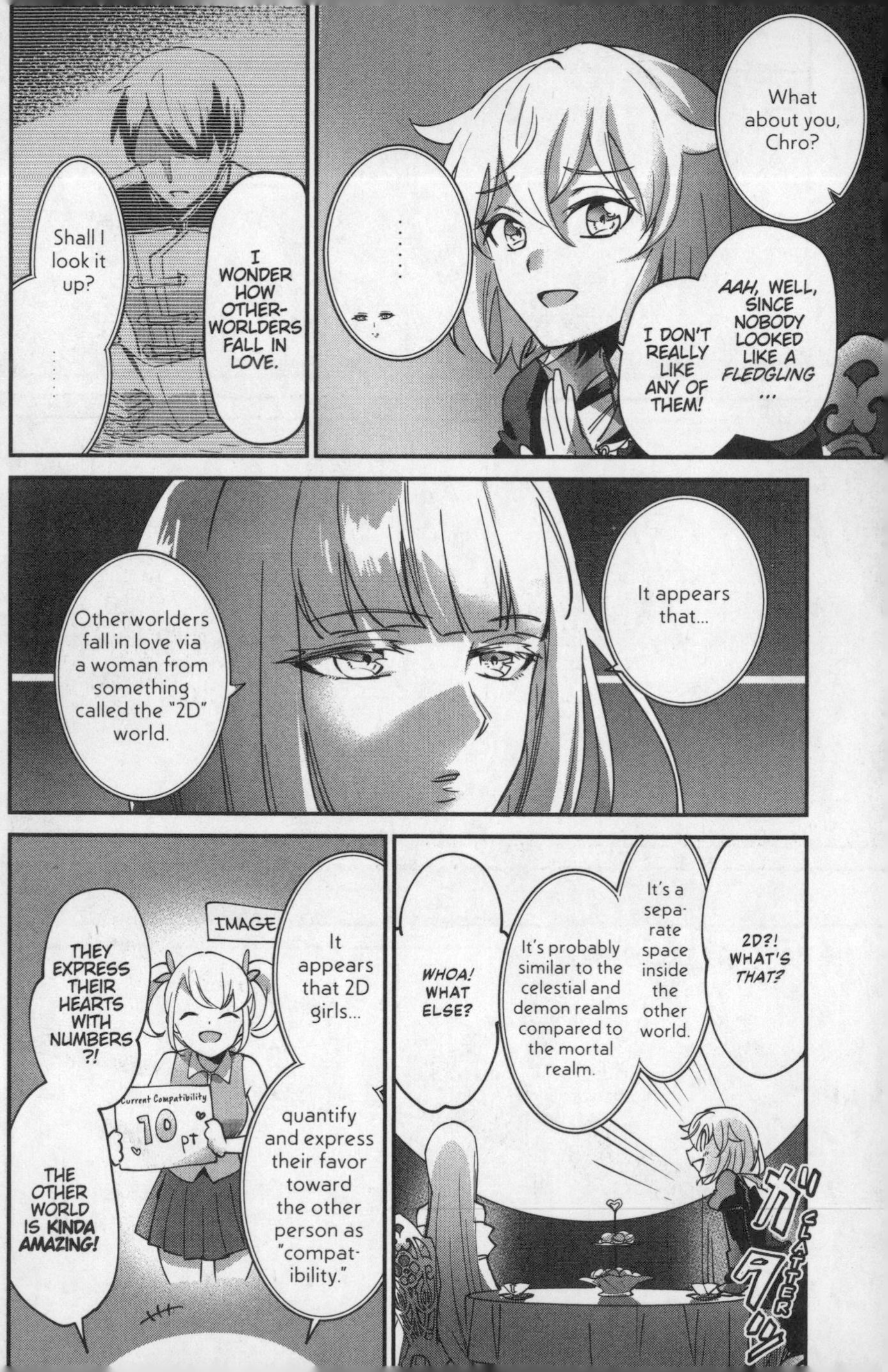
What about you, Chro?
AAH, WELL, SINCE NOBODY LOOKED LIKE A *FLEDGLING*...
I DON'T REALLY LIKE ANY OF THEM!
......
I WONDER HOW OTHER-WORLDERS FALL IN LOVE.
Shall I look it up?
......
It appears that...
Otherworlders fall in love via a woman from something called the "2D" world.
2D?! WHAT'S THAT?
It's a sepa-rate space inside the other world.
It's probably similar to the celestial and demon realms compared to the mortal realm.
WHOA! WHAT ELSE?
CLATTER
It appears that 2D girls...
quantify and express their favor toward the other person as "compat-ibility."
IMAGE
Current Compatibility
10 pt
THEY EXPRESS THEIR HEARTS WITH NUMBERS?!
THE OTHER WORLD IS KINDA AMAZING!

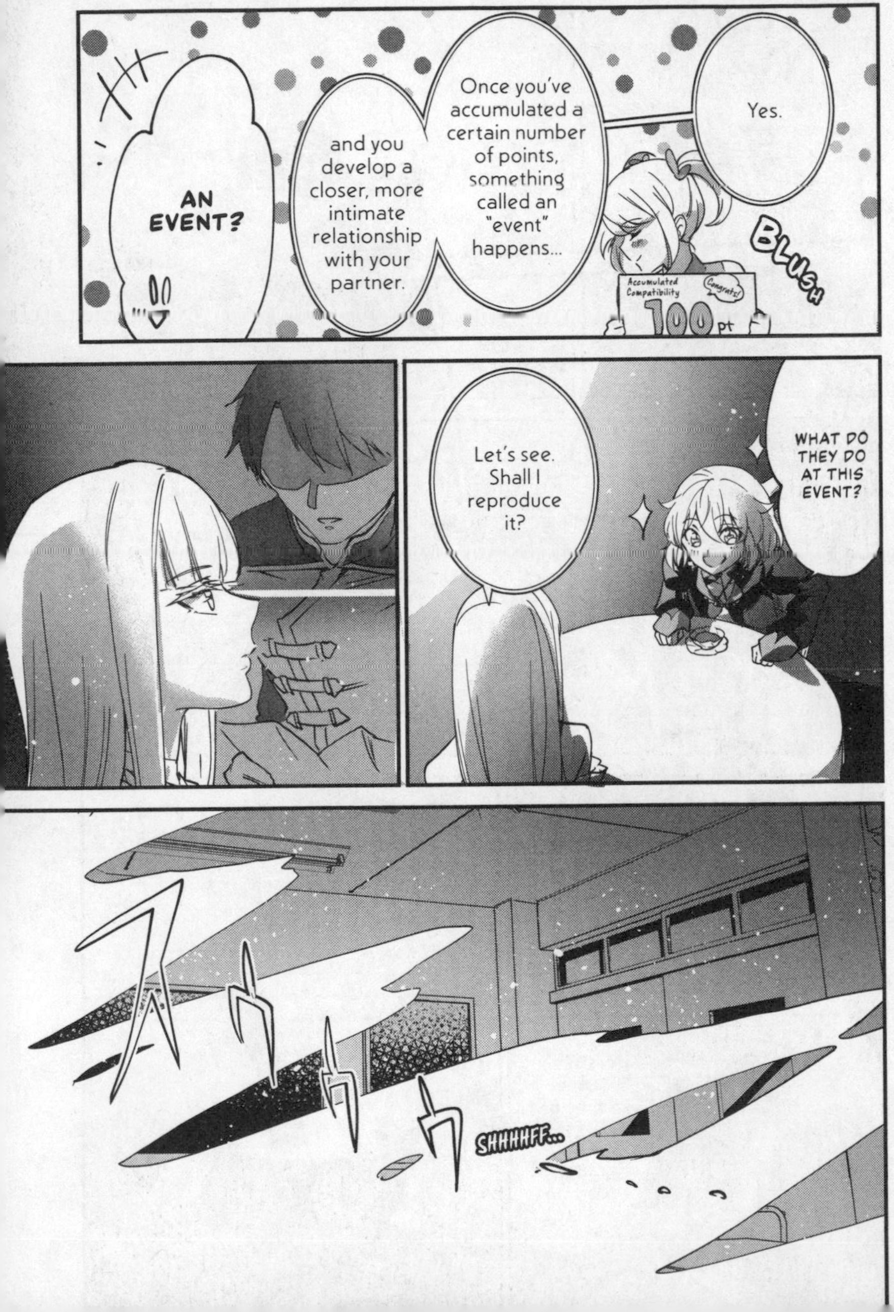
Yes.
Accumulated Compatibility
Congrats!
100 pt
BLUSH
Once you've accumulated a certain number of points, something called an "event" happens...
and you develop a closer, more intimate relationship with your partner.
AN EVENT?
WHAT DO THEY DO AT THIS EVENT?
Let's see. Shall I reproduce it?
SHHHFF...

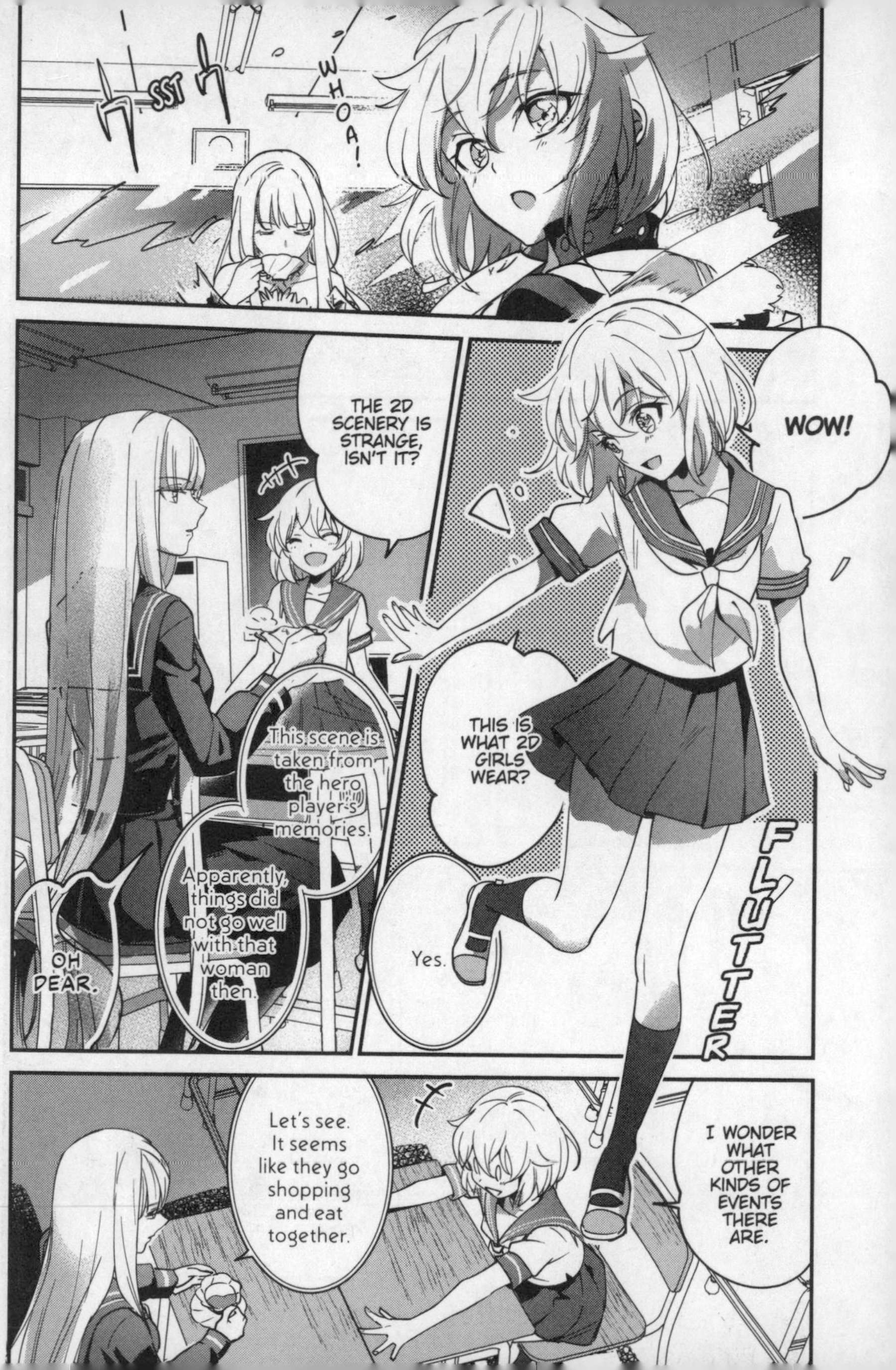
WHOA!
SST
WOW!
THIS IS WHAT 2D GIRLS WEAR?
Yes.
FLUTTER
THE 2D SCENERY IS STRANGE, ISN'T IT?
This scene is taken from the hero player's memories.
Apparently, things did not go well with that woman then.
OH DEAR.
I WONDER WHAT OTHER KINDS OF EVENTS THERE ARE.
Let's see. It seems like they go shopping and eat together.

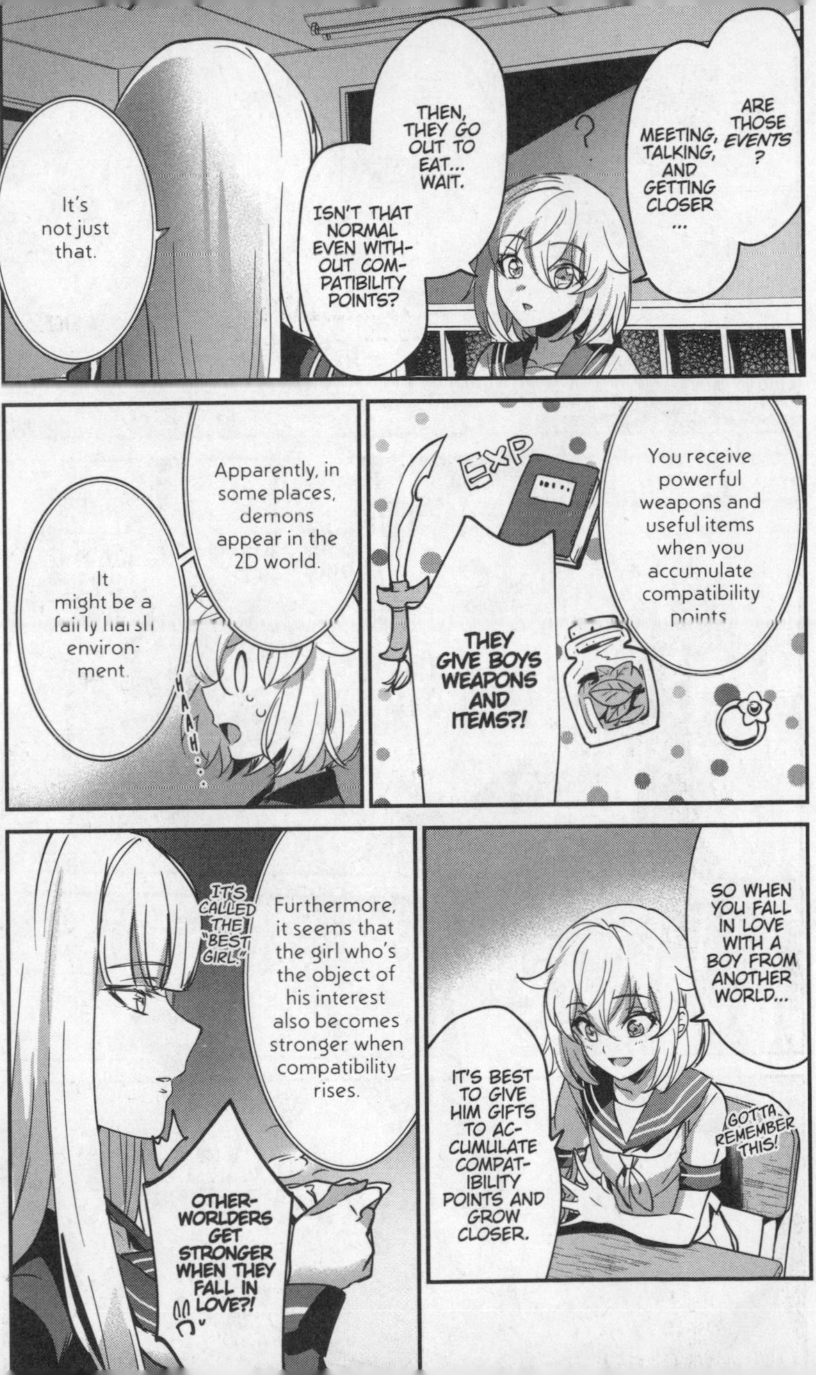
MEETING, TALKING, AND GETTING CLOSER... ARE THOSE *EVENTS*?
THEN, THEY GO OUT TO EAT... WAIT.
ISN'T THAT NORMAL EVEN WITHOUT COMPATIBILITY POINTS?
It's not just that.
You receive powerful weapons and useful items when you accumulate compatibility points.
EXP
THEY GIVE BOYS WEAPONS AND ITEMS?!
Apparently, in some places, demons appear in the 2D world.
It might be a fairly harsh environment.
HAAH...
SO WHEN YOU FALL IN LOVE WITH A BOY FROM ANOTHER WORLD...
IT'S BEST TO GIVE HIM GIFTS TO ACCUMULATE COMPATIBILITY POINTS AND GROW CLOSER.
GOTTA REMEMBER THIS!
Furthermore, it seems that the girl who's the object of his interest also becomes stronger when compatibility rises.
IT'S CALLED THE "BEST GIRL."
OTHERWORLDERS GET STRONGER WHEN THEY FALL IN LOVE?!

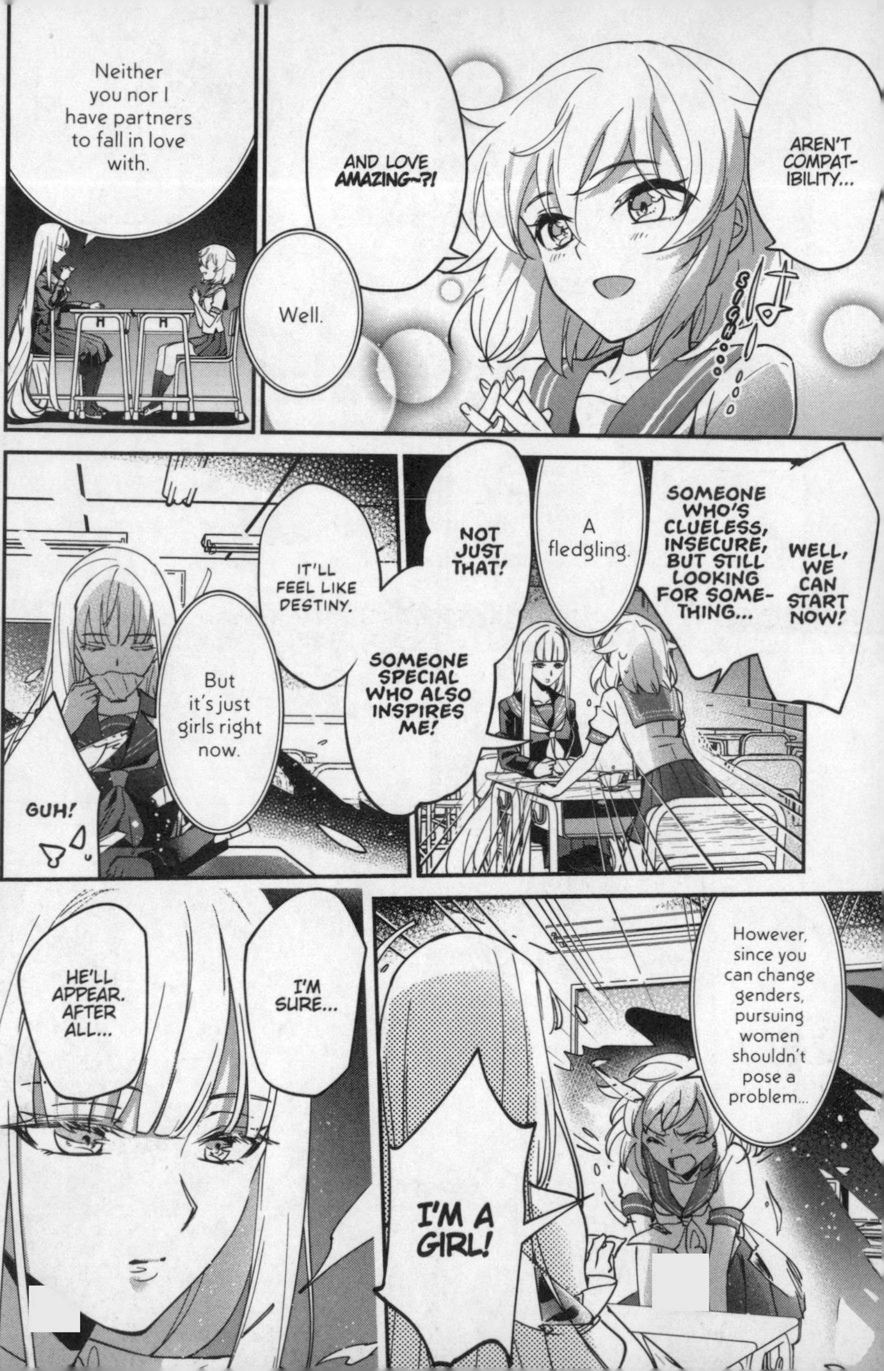
AREN'T COMPATIBILITY...
AND LOVE AMAZING~?!
Well.
Neither you nor I have partners to fall in love with.
WELL, WE CAN START NOW!
SOMEONE WHO'S CLUELESS, INSECURE, BUT STILL LOOKING FOR SOMETHING...
A fledgling.
NOT JUST THAT!
SOMEONE SPECIAL WHO ALSO INSPIRES ME!
IT'LL FEEL LIKE DESTINY.
But it's just girls right now.
GUH!
However, since you can change genders, pursuing women shouldn't pose a problem...
I'M A GIRL!
I'M SURE...
HE'LL APPEAR. AFTER ALL...

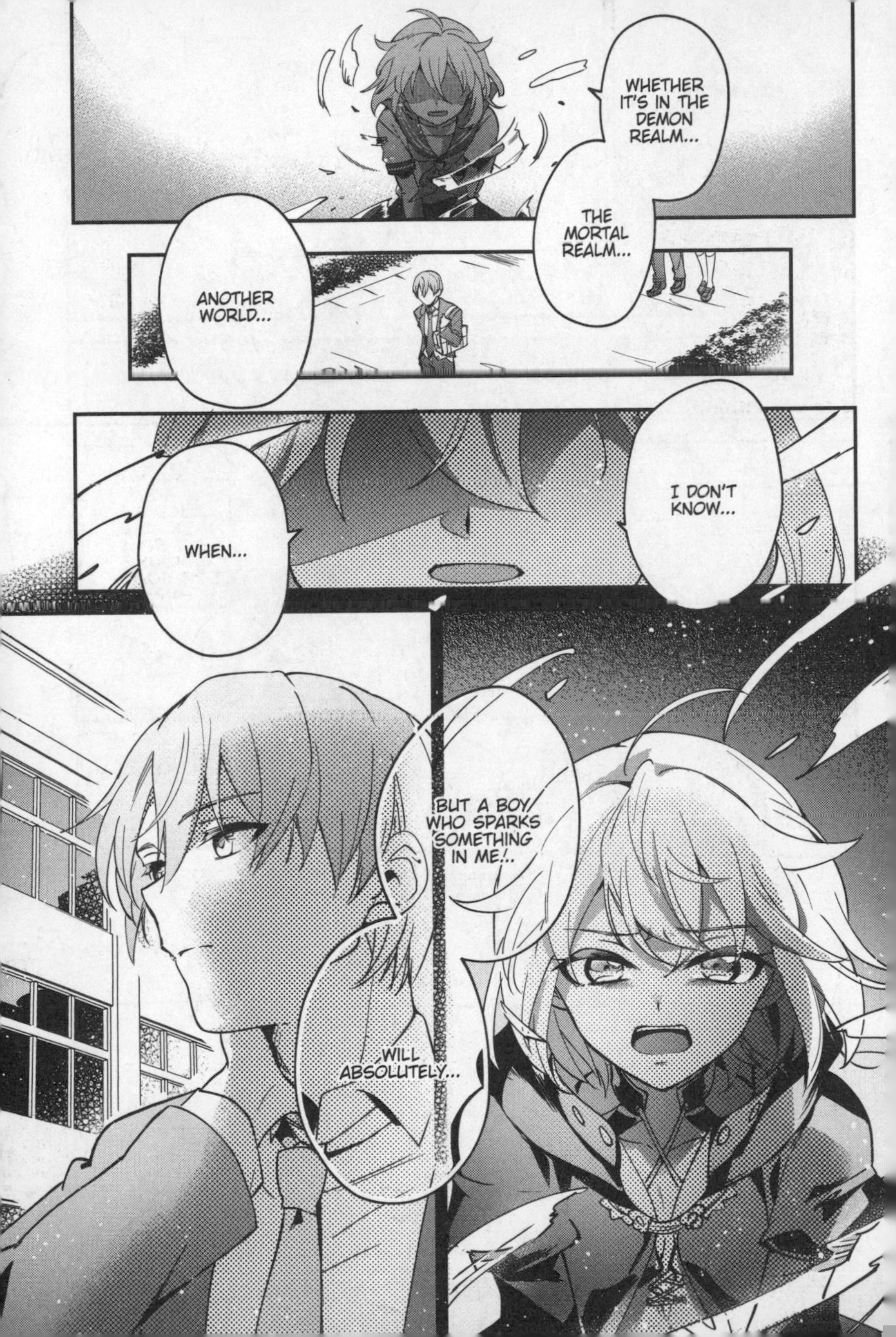
WHETHER IT'S IN THE DEMON REALM...
THE MORTAL REALM...
ANOTHER WORLD...
I DON'T KNOW...
WHEN...
BUT A BOY WHO SPARKS SOMETHING IN ME...
WILL ABSOLUTELY...

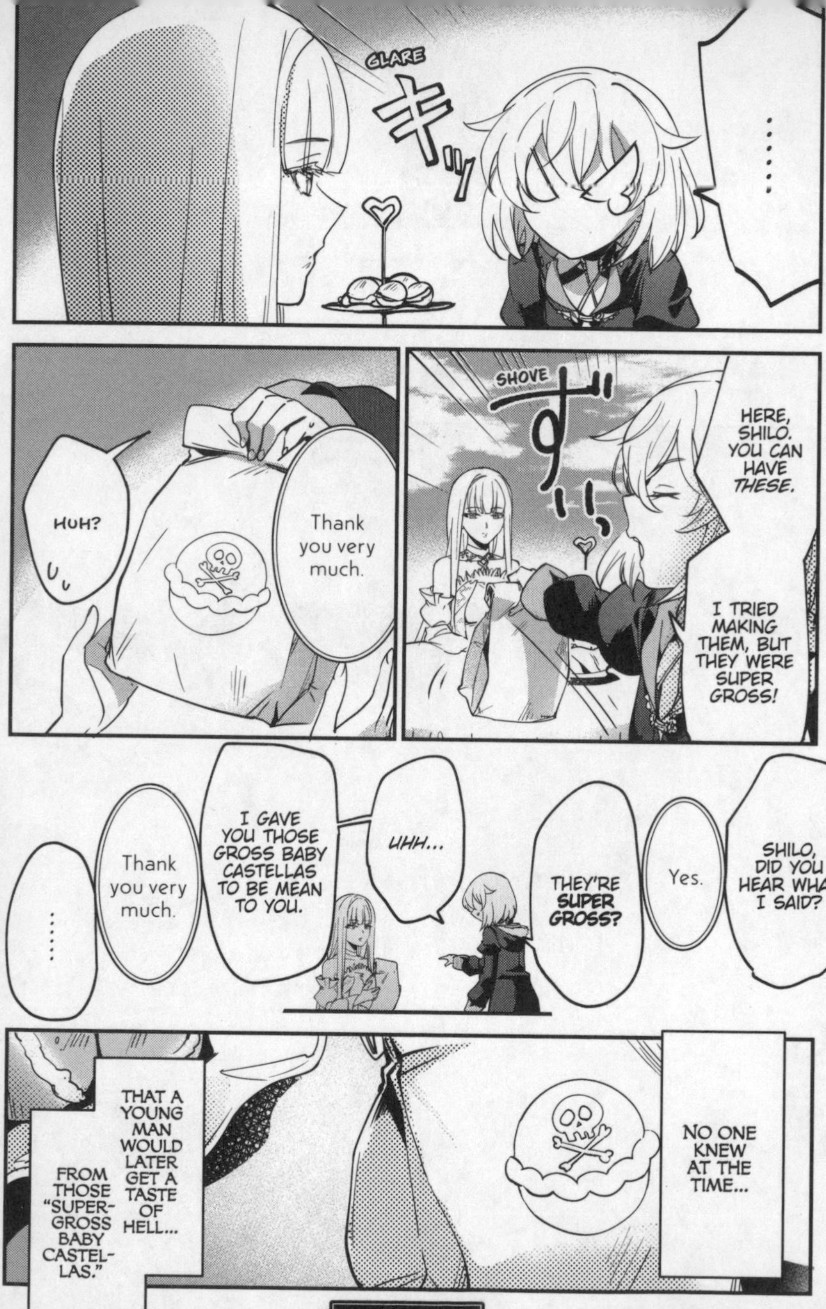
......
GLARE
キッ
HERE, SHILO. YOU CAN HAVE *THESE.*
SHOVE
ず
I TRIED MAKING THEM, BUT THEY WERE SUPER GROSS!
Thank you very much.
HUH?
SHILO, DID YOU HEAR WHAT I SAID?
Yes.
THEY'RE SUPER GROSS?
UHH...
I GAVE YOU THOSE GROSS BABY CASTELLAS TO BE MEAN TO YOU.
Thank you very much.
......
NO ONE KNEW AT THE TIME...
THAT A YOUNG MAN WOULD LATER GET A TASTE OF HELL...
FROM THOSE "SUPER-GROSS BABY CASTEL-LAS."

SIDE STORY END

I GOT CAUGHT UP IN A HERO SUMMONS, SUMMONS,

BUT THE OTHER WORLD
WAS AT PEACE!

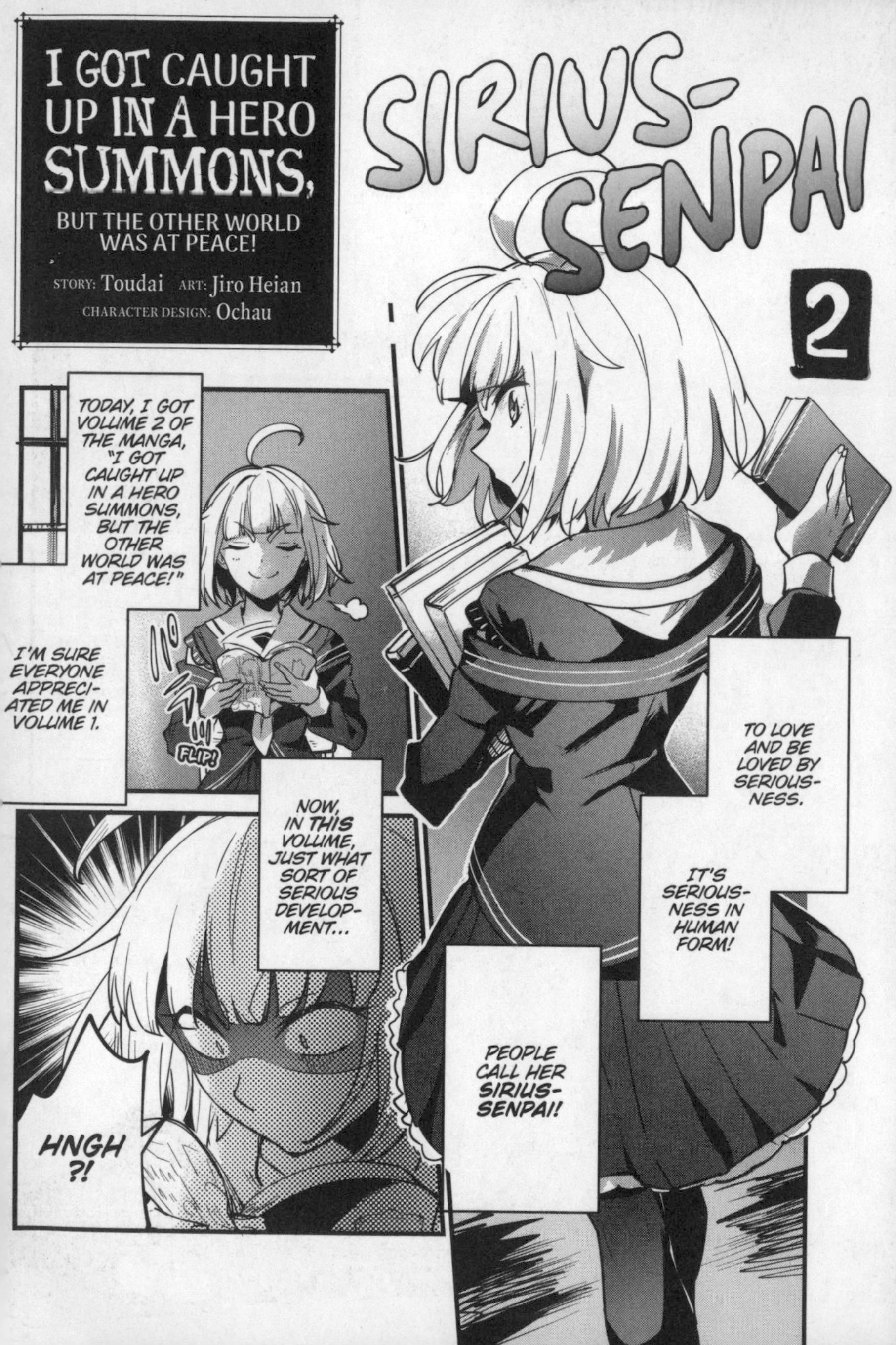
SIRIUS-SENPAI
2
I GOT CAUGHT UP IN A HERO SUMMONS, BUT THE OTHER WORLD WAS AT PEACE!
STORY: Toudai ART: Jiro Heian
CHARACTER DESIGN: Ochau
TO LOVE AND BE LOVED BY SERIOUS-NESS.
IT'S SERIOUS-NESS IN HUMAN FORM!
PEOPLE CALL HER SIRIUS-SENPAI!
TODAY, I GOT VOLUME 2 OF THE MANGA, "I GOT CAUGHT UP IN A HERO SUMMONS, BUT THE OTHER WORLD WAS AT PEACE!"
FLIP!
I'M SURE EVERYONE APPRECI-ATED ME IN VOLUME 1.
NOW, IN THIS VOLUME, JUST WHAT SORT OF SERIOUS DEVELOP-MENT...
HNGH ?!

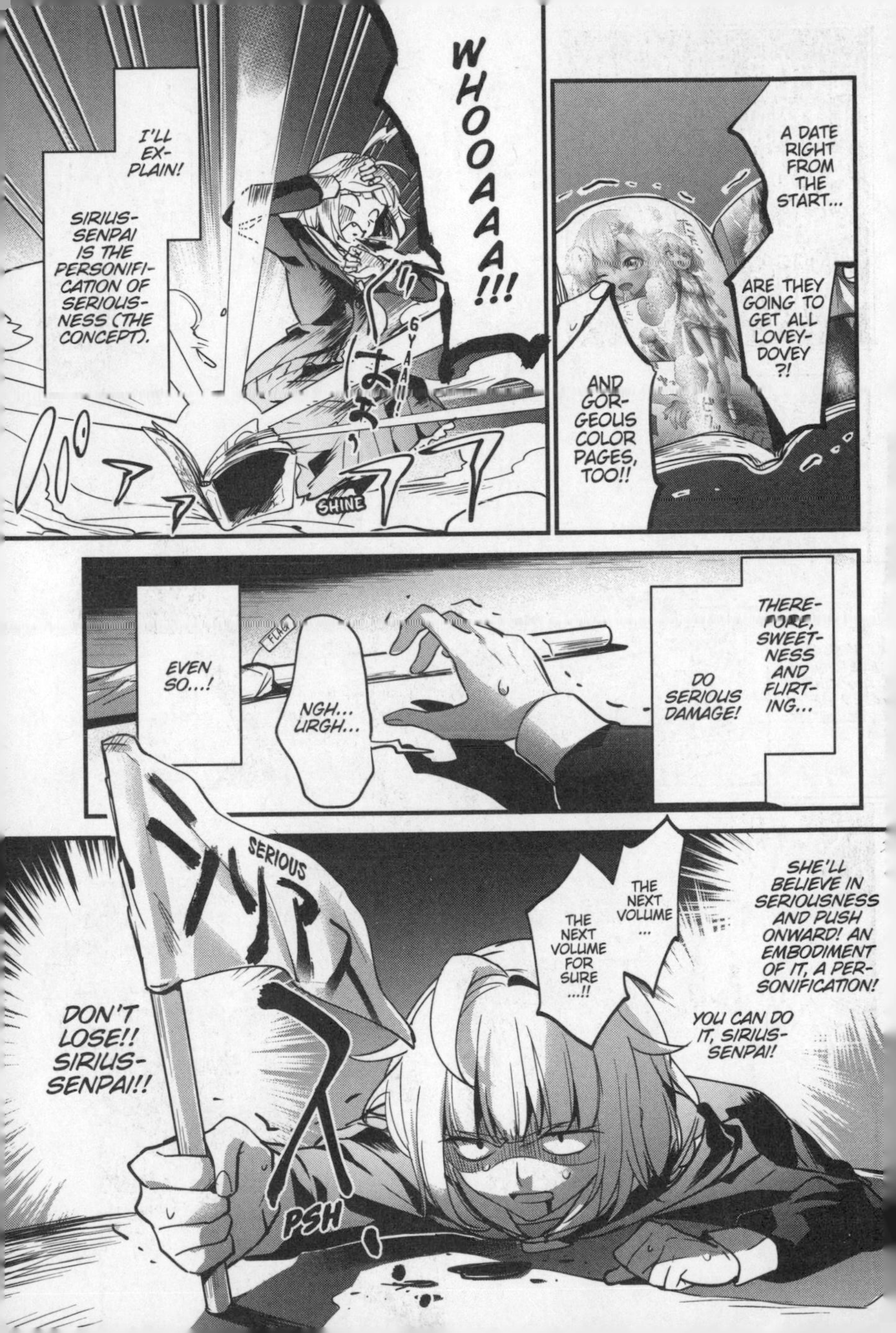
A DATE RIGHT FROM THE START...
ARE THEY GOING TO GET ALL LOVEY-DOVEY?!
AND GORGEOUS COLOR PAGES, TOO!!
WHOOAAAA!!!
I'LL EXPLAIN!
SIRIUS-SENPAI IS THE PERSONIFICATION OF SERIOUSNESS (THE CONCEPT).
SHINE
THEREFORE, SWEETNESS AND FLIRTING...
DO SERIOUS DAMAGE!
NGH... URGH...
FLAG
EVEN SO...!
SHE'LL BELIEVE IN SERIOUSNESS AND PUSH ONWARD! AN EMBODIMENT OF IT, A PERSONIFICATION!
THE NEXT VOLUME...
THE NEXT VOLUME FOR SURE...!!
YOU CAN DO IT, SIRIUS-SENPAI!
SERIOUS
DON'T LOSE!! SIRIUS-SENPAI!!
PSH

I GOT CAUGHT UP IN A HERO SUMMONS,

BUT THE OTHER WORLD WAS AT PEACE!